THE
DIVINE EYE
AND THE DIASPORA

THE

DIVINE EYE

AND THE DIASPORA

VIETNAMESE SYNCRETISM BECOMES

TRANSPACIFIC CAODAISM

Janet Alison Hoskins

University of Hawai'i Press
Honolulu

20 19 18 17 16 15   6 5 4 3 2

Library of Congress Cataloging-in-Publication Data

Hoskins, Janet Alison, author.
    The divine eye and the diaspora : Vietnamese syncretism becomes transpacific
Caodaism / Janet Alison Hoskins.
        pages cm
    Includes bibliographical references and index.
    ISBN 978-0-8248-4004-4 (hardcover : alk. paper) — ISBN 978-0-8248-5140-8
(pbk. : alk. paper)
    1. Caodaism.   2. Syncretism (Religion)—Vietnam.   I.   Title.
    BL2057.C36H67 2015
    299.5'922—dc23

                                                                            2014031902

University of Hawai'i Press books are printed on acid-free
paper and meet the guidelines for permanence and
durability of the Council on Library Resources.

Designed by Binbin Li

Printed by Sheridan Books, Inc.

This book is dedicated to Sylvana and Artemisia Valeri, my beloved daughters, who traveled several times with me to Vietnam, shared vegetarian meals with Caodai visitors in California, and have sustained me with their love and companionship for years.

CONTENTS

ACKNOWLEDGMENTS

This book is the result of over ten years of research, supported by many people and institutions. The Center for Religion and Civic Culture of the University of Southern California (USC) provided the first research funding in 2003, drawing on a grant from Pew Charitable Trusts, which allowed me to visit Vietnam in 2004. I began archival research as a Research Scholar at the Getty Research Institute in Los Angeles. I studied Vietnamese at the University of California–Los Angeles and participated in several conferences sponsored by the Center for Southeast Asian Studies there. I produced and wrote the ethnographic documentary *The Left Eye of God: Caodaism Travels from Vietnam to California* (2008, distributed by Documentary Educational Resources, www.der.org), funded by a grant from the California Council for the Humanities, directed and edited by my sister Susan Hoskins. From 2008–2010, the National Science Foundation funded research in both Vietnam and California as Grant No. 0752511, "Ethnic Resilience and Indigenous Religion: A Transnational Perspective on Vietnamese Immigrant Congregations in California." From 2011–2014, the Henry R. Luce Foundation funded additional research and program development in a grant, received with Viet Thanh Nguyen, titled "Transpacific Connections, Translocal Imaginations," under the auspices of our jointly founded Center for Transpacific Studies at USC. Additional research travel to Vietnam in 2013 was funded by USC's Center for International Studies.

I am grateful to several institutions that provided me with the opportunity to write up this research in a congenial and stimulating environment with colleagues in regional studies. I spent six months as a Visiting Researcher in Residence at the Kyoto University Center for Southeast Asian Studies, 2011–2012, and another six months at the Asia Research Institute (ARI) of the National University of Singapore in 2012–2013. A Lee Kong Chian International Fellowship supported me at Stanford's Shorenstein Institute for Asia Pacific

Research for three months in 2013. I am especially grateful to Yoko Hayami and Hiro Shimizu in Kyoto, to Prasenjit Duara and Michael Feener at ARI, and to Don Emmerson at Stanford. Participants in three different conferences helped me to rethink some of the key concepts of transpacific connection, syncretism, and diaspora: the 2010 conference at USC on "Transpacific Studies"; the April 2013 meeting of the Society for the Anthropology of Religion on "Religious Syncretisms and Synergies" in Pasadena, California; and the January 2013 workshop at the Asia Research Institute, Singapore, on "Invisible Connections between Asia and the West: Syncretism and Esotericism."

More informally, I have been sustained by the friendship and intellectual companionship of Walter Berry, Soo Young Chin, Ken Dean, Gelya Frank, Macarena Gomez-Barris, Catherine Hermann, Laurel Kendall, Dorinne Kondo, Nancy Lutkehaus, Cheryl Mattingly, Randi Mavestrand, Viet Thanh Nguyen, Oona Paredes, Joel Robbins, Judy Robinson, Jeff Samuels, Connie Stewart, and Mayfair Yang.

Students who have traveled with me to Vietnam to assist this research include Judy Cao, Việt Lê, and Thiên-Hương Ninh (who made an invaluable contribution over two years of fieldwork in both California and Vietnam). Both Việt Lê and Thiên-Hương Ninh have finished their dissertations and are now my colleagues as researchers on transnational Vietnamese culture and religion. Colleagues who studied related topics and have contributed to this research from a distance include Sergei Blagov, Louis-Jacques Dorais, Jérémy Jammes, Philip Taylor, and Jayne Werner. Lương Văn Hy served as my "elder brother" in Vietnamese studies, providing valuable advice at many different stages, and Huỳnh Ngọc Thư has been both my student and my colleague, and is now heading the Anthropology Department at Vietnam National University in Hồ Chí Minh City. I am grateful to Julius Bautista, Karen Fjelstad, Nguyễn Thị Hiền, Huệ-Tâm Hồ Tài, Paul Harrison, Susan Hoskins, and Peter Zinoman for comments on works in progress. Each of the living individuals profiled in this book—Bùi Văn Khâm, Bùi Đắc Hùm, Trần Quang Cảnh, Đỗ Vạn Lý, and Lâm Lý Hùng—has read drafts of the chapters concerning their lives and offered comments and corrections, as have Ngọc Quốc Minh, Nguyên Việt Cường, and Đặng Thị Hồng Vân. Within the Caodai community, I am also grateful to David Tùng Chế, Kim Phương Đặng, Đồng Tân, Đinh Thị Thanh Tùng, and Đinh Thị Thanh Mai, Lê Anh Dũng, Huệ Ý, and Nguyễn Văn Trạch.

CHRONOLOGY

Major events in the history of Caodaism

1921   Ngô Văn Chiêu has a vision on the island of Phú Quốc of the Left Eye of God (Thiên Nhãn) in the sky with both the rising sun and the moon present.

1925   Saigon Séances begin in July with the participation of the three founding mediums Cao Quỳnh Cư (1888–1929), Cao Hoài Sang (1901–1971), and Phạm Công Tắc (1890–1959) plus Hương Hiếu as scribe.

1925   Christmas Eve séance—Cao Đài, previously known as the spirit A Ă Â, reveals his true identity as the Jade Emperor (who is also Jehovah).

1926   Tết or Vietnamese New Year séance—the Jade Emperor founds "the Great Way of the Third Era of Redemption" (Đại Đạo Tam Kỳ Phổ Độ).

1926   On October 7, a "Declaration" signed by 28 prominent Vietnamese leaders and 245 followers is submitted to the French government. Lê Văn Trung heads the delegation and becomes the Interim Human Pope (Giáo Tông). Huge ceremony to inaugurate Caodaism is held on November 19 at Gò Kén Pagoda in Tây Ninh province.

1934   New denominations are formed, establishing their own administrative hierarchies or Holy Sees after the death of Interim Pope Lê Văn Trung, in order of size:

    a. Ban Chỉnh Đạo (The Reformed Religion) founded in 1934 in Bến Tre, Mekong Delta, by Pope Nguyễn Ngọc Tương, became the second largest denomination, using statues on its altar instead of ancestor tablets.

 b. Tiên Thiên (Primordial Heaven) founded in 1932 by Pope Nguyễn Hữu Chính, also in Bến Tre, with "meditation temples" (*thanh tịnh*) and all white robes and turbans worn during rituals.

 c. Hội Thánh Truyền Giáo (Mission to Central Vietnam) formed in 1956 by a committee with its headquarters in Đà Nẵng.

 d. Minh Chơn Đạo (Enlightened Choice) formed in 1935 in Cà Mau and led by Cao Triều Phát, a resistance leader who died in Hanoi in 1955.

 e. Chơn Lý (The True Principle) founded in 1930 by Pope Nguyễn Văn Ca at Mỹ Tho in Tiền Giang, using an image of the Left Eye inside the heart. These "Caodaists of the Sacred Heart" have a Holy See that resembles Sacré Coeur.

 f. Cầu Kho Tam Quan formed in 1931 in Cầu Kho in the third district (Tam Quan), at a temple where the Saigon Teaching Center held séances in the 1960s and 1970s.

 g. Chiếu Minh Long Châu formed in 1956 in Long Châu, Kiên Giang, by disciples of Ngô Văn Chiêu, following a demanding ascetic tradition.

 h. Bạch Y Liên Đoàn Chơn Lý (White Clothing, True Principles) established in 1935 and reorganized in 1955 in Kiên Giang, following Tiên Thiên practices.

 i. Chiếu Minh Tam Thanh Vô Vi (Esoteric Disciples of Ngô Văn Chiêu), established in Cần Thơ around the tomb where Ngô Văn Chiêu is buried.

1935 Phạm Công Tắc assumes leadership of the Tây Ninh "Vatican," but keeps his original title of Hộ Pháp (Defender of the Dharma, head spirit medium).

1941 French forces arrest Phạm Công Tắc and send him into exile at colonial prison on islands near Madagascar.

 The Japanese invade French Indochina, but leave the French administration in charge. Caodai dockworkers train as an informal militia in the port.

1945 In March, Caodai militia members from Tây Ninh assist the Japanese in overthrowing the French in Saigon.

1945 The "August revolution" is celebrated by Caodaists and Communists together.

Massacres of Caodai civilians in Quảng Ngãi and elsewhere divide nationalist forces and the informal Caodai militia becomes a "defensive army."

1946   After the end of World War II, French forces try to reconquer Indochina. Trần Quang Vinh negotiates for the return of Phạm Công Tắc, agreeing to use his troops as a "peace-keeping force" that will not attack the French.

1954   French forces surrender after their defeat at Điện Biên Phủ in the North. The Geneva Accords divide Vietnam along the seventeenth parallel, a move that is condemned by Phạm Công Tắc, who attends the accords as an advisor to the former emperor Bảo Đại.

1955   Ngô Đình Diệm becomes president of the Republic of Vietnam and appoints Đỗ Vạn Lý as the head of diplomatic missions to Indonesia and India.

1957   The Caodai Armed Forces are disbanded, and Phạm Công Tắc escapes arrest by fleeing to Cambodia.

1959   Phạm Công Tắc dies in Cambodia, asking the king to allow his body to remain there "until Vietnam is unified, peaceful, and neutral."

1963   Ngô Đình Diệm is assassinated, and a series of short-term presidents serve in the government, including Caodaist Phan Khắc Sửu (from 1964–1965).

1964   The Saigon Teaching Agency (Cơ Quan Phổ Thông Giáo Lý) is founded under the leadership of Trần Văn Quế and Đỗ Vạn Lý. Đỗ Vạn Lý leaves in 1973 to serve as the South Vietnamese Ambassador to Japan.

1971   Cao Hoài Sang, the last of the founding mediums, dies in Tây Ninh and is given an elaborate funeral. Hồ Tấn Khoa becomes the highest-ranking medium, or Bảo Đạo, until his retirement in 1983.

1975   Saigon falls and hundreds of thousands of people try to escape after the Communist victory. A large percentage of Caodaists who remain in Vietnam serve long terms in "reeducation camps," or are required to attend "reeducation training" from their homes. Caodai religious property is "nationalized," and most temples are closed down.

Formation of temple networks in the diaspora

1978   The Temple of Celestial Reason (Thiên Lý Bửu Tòa) is established in San Jose, California, by female medium Bạch Diệu Hoa and female archbishop Ngọc Tuyết Thiên.

1979   Đỗ Vạn Lý heads the first congregation in Los Angeles, which meets at his home.

1983   Caodai temples are established in Westminster (what is now "Little Saigon") and Anaheim, California.

1989   Đỗ Vạn Lý publishes *Understanding Caodaism* in California for the overseas Vietnamese community, a Vietnamese-language manifesto of diasporic faith.

1992   The Catholic Pope invites a delegation of Caodai leaders to travel to Rome to "pray for peace in Vietnam" and coordinate a strategy to keep religions alive and request the return of properties nationalized in 1975.

1998   The Caodai Overseas Mission is founded with Trần Quang Cảnh as its president and nineteen affiliated temples in the United States, France, Canada, and Australia.

2000   *Cao Dai Faith of Unity* is published in English by Hum Dac Bui (Vietnamese: Bùi Đắc Hùm) and Ngasha Beck. Bùi Đắc Hùm also spearheads plans to build a big new temple in Riverside, California, to be open to all Caodai denominations.

2007   The "California" temple in Garden Grove replicates the distinctive architecture of Tây Ninh, as do new temples in New Orleans; Dallas; Houston; Seattle; and Wichita, Kansas (constructed from 2007–2013). Forty-four Tây Ninh overseas temples and twenty-five affiliated with other denominations form international networks.

Normalization of Caodai sects in Vietnam

1995   The Reformed Religion (Ban Chỉnh Đạo), the second-largest Caodai group, and Primordial Heaven (Tiên Thiên), both of Bến Tre, are recognized by the Vietnamese government, as well as the Transcendent Enlightenment (Chiếu Minh Long Châu) sect of Long Châu.

1996   Central Vietnam's Missionary Society (Hội Thánh Truyền Giáo), with its headquarters in Đà Nẵng, is recognized, as well as the Enlightened Choice (Minh Chơn Đạo) sect of Cà Mau.

1997   The "Vatican" of Caodaism (Tòa Thánh Tây Ninh), the first and largest branch, is recognized by the government.

1998   The White Clothing, True Principles Group (Bạch Y Liên Đoan Chơn Lý) of Kiên Giang is recognized.

2000   The Saigon Teaching Agency (Cơ Quan Phổ Thông Giáo Lý) is recognized by the government, as well as the Cầu Kho Heartfelt Group (Cầu Kho Tam Quan).

2008   Minh Lý Đạo, the "Caodaists in Black," are recognized by the government and become the twelfth official religion in the nation, headed by Lâm Lý Hùng.

2011   Trần Quang Cảnh becomes the first American citizen to be admitted into the Tây Ninh administrative hierarchy.

THE
DIVINE EYE
AND THE DIASPORA

INTRODUCTION
"OUTRAGEOUS SYNCRETISM"?

It is almost noon in Tây Ninh, a steamy provincial capital sixty-five miles southwest of Hồ Chí Minh City. Dozens of tour buses pull up into a parking lot across the street from the high Gothic towers of the Great Temple of Caodaism (Tòa Thánh Tây Ninh), which loom with the outline of a cathedral above a complex of shops and restaurants. Hundreds of tourists of all nationalities— Europeans, Japanese, Americans, Australians, and increasing numbers of visitors from mainland China, Singapore, and Taiwan—pour out of the buses and stream toward the Temple, where dozens of Caodai dignitaries have put on robes of white, yellow, turquoise, and red and wait patiently to file in through the two doors at the entrance—one on the left, under the statue of the Interim Pope Lê Văn Trung, the other on the right, under the statue of the female founder, Cardinal Lâm Ngọc Thanh (see Plate 3).

A huge drum resonates from the upper floor, and gongs and other instruments chime in with a vigorous rhythm. Dignitaries enter on the ground floor and march in disciplined lines to bow in front of the divinities at the front and back of the Great Temple, then kneel on pillows arranged on the gleaming marble floor. Offerings of fruits and flowers, tea, and incense are carried to the altar by high-stepping ritualists wearing conical hats. The rigorously synchronized prostrations of the faithful involve holding their hands clasped, with the thumb touching the third finger, and bowing their foreheads to the floor. Here, the dignitaries marry propriety, austerity, and a sober regime of bodily and spiritual self-cultivation with elaborate ritual ceremonialism.

1

Tourists are directed up the stairway to the upper balcony, on either side of the orchestra and choir, where they can watch the ceremony and take dozens of photographs. Caodaism becomes a spectacle, filled with exotic chanting and incomprehensible prayers, lots of kowtowing and "Oriental bells and smells," but little that is understandable. On the buses traveling to the Caodai sacred city, tour guides (usually university students working a side job) offer a mixture of facts and misunderstandings, gleaned from a few colorful brochures issued by travel agencies, without much regard for their accuracy.

The Great Temple in Tây Ninh is now the second-most popular tourist destination in southern Vietnam (after the War Remnants Museum). Usually coupled with a trip down the winding Củ Chi tunnels used by Communist guerilla forces, it is part of a standard tourist itinerary, which balances a simulated experience of war with an only vaguely understood religion of peace. This is the public face that Caodaism offers to some two thousand tourists a day (up to three thousand in the peak months of July and August). It is exotic, enticing, and often provocative, and a great many tourists are later moved to post their videos and photographs online, supplemented with a few explanations from guidebooks.

Several guidebooks describe Caodaism with the words of the famous English novelist Graham Greene, who visited Tây Ninh in 1952:

> Of all France's allies in Indo-china, the most astonishing are the Caodaists, members of a religious sect founded around 1920. At the entrance to the fantastic, technicolour cathedral are hung the portraits of three minor saints of the Caodaist regime: Dr. Sun Yat Sen, Trạng Trình, a primitive Vietnamese poet, and Victor Hugo, attired in the uniform of a member of the Académie Francaise with a halo around his tricorn hat. In the nave of the cathedral, in the full Asiatic splendour of a Walt Disney fantasy, pastel dragons coil around the columns and pulpit; from every stained glass window a great eye of God follows one, an enormous serpent forms the papal throne and high up under the arches are the effigies of three major saints: Buddha, Confucius, and Christ displaying his Sacred Heart.... The saints, Victor Hugo in particular, still address the faithful through the medium of a pencil and a basket covered by a kind of moveable Ouija board; the religious ceremonies are intolerably long, and a vegetarian diet is rigorously imposed.... One should not therefore be surprised to learn that missionaries have been sent to Los Angeles.[1]

The "great eye of God" refers to the large naturalistic image of the Left Eye, which is the *Thiên Nhãn*, or celestial symbol of divinity, honored by all Caodaists.

The eclectic architecture of the Great Temple is often described as appropriate for a syncretistic fusion of many different religions: The Gothic towers at the entrance are, however, something of a European front, since they are the least sacred part of the structure. The mural of Sun Yat-sen, Trạng Trình (also known as Nguyễn Bỉnh Khiêm, a fifteenth-century writer sometimes called the Nostradamus of Vietnam), and Victor Hugo depicts the "prophets" who predicted the emergence of Asian nationalism, Vietnamese unity, and a new hybrid religion combining East and West (see Plates 2 and 3).

Seen from the side, the structure has nine levels, which slowly ascend to the eight-sided tower at the rear, the most sacred part, called the Bát Quái Đài, or "Eight Trigram Palace," where spirit communications are held. The Maitreya Buddha sits astride a tiger (since Caodaism was founded in 1926, the year of the tiger) on top of the central tower of the front façade. Another onion-domed tower rises over the center, showing a global map of the world topped by a mythical dragon-horse. Two pulpits, one for male speakers and one for female ones, are sculpted with the curving arabesque lines of an Islamic minbar, supported by smoke-breathing dragons coiled around pink pillars. Three rows of red and gold chairs for the highest dignitaries stand in front of an altar and twelve steps, ringed by eight golden dragons coiled on silvery blue pillars. The Left Eye of God stares out from the middle of a huge globe, painted blue and green and decorated with clouds and stars, watching over the Cung Đạo, the space where séances are held under a ceiling painted with images of divination tools (see Plates 1, 4, and 6).

My Own Encounter with Caodaism

I first saw the portraits and decorations famously described by Graham Greene not in today's Vietnam, but at a Caodai temple on Tenth Street in Pomona, California, in 2003, about ten minutes from the home where I grew up. Pomona is a working-class suburb of Los Angeles with small stucco houses, many of them now run-down, where recent Southeast Asian immigrants have settled. Aside from the colorful Left Eye painted above its doorway, the Pomona temple was just another beige bungalow on the corner of a small street, with a white picket fence surrounding it. In discovering Caodaism through a diasporic temple, I did not witness the full Asiatic splendor Greene described, but I was immediately intrigued at this unorthodox combination of Asian and European elements and curious to know more about its history and beliefs.

As a scholar of Southeast Asian religions and cultures, I had read a bit about Caodaism before. The best-known article I had seen—Bernard Fall's piece on southern Vietnamese political-religious sects—had described Caodaism as a colorful millenarian movement that attracted millions of followers in the 1930s and 1940s, but had become "a dinosaur" by the mid-1950s, when it was forcibly demilitarized, and was doomed to extinction within a few decades (Fall 1955, 253). So it was particularly surprising to find out that not only was a new Caodai temple open in Pomona, but there were already at least a dozen others in California—and the huge temple that Greene described as a cathedral in Tây Ninh had recently been renovated and was now opening its doors to thousands of tourists each day.

Greene's ironic description of the Great Temple of Caodaism in Tây Ninh has fixed its image in Western literary circles as a spectacle of exotic absurdity, what the French called *un syncrétisme à l'outrance,* an extreme form of religious mixing, an excessive, even trangressive combination, in which East and West are mixed up in a "Walt Disney fantasia of the Orient" that could only be reimagined in California. While Greene was wrong about missionaries having been sent to Los Angeles in the 1950s, by the late 1970s Caodaism was being reborn in California. Today copies of the portrait of the three saints he described can be found in Los Angeles County (Pomona), Orange County (Garden Grove, Westminster, and Anaheim), and San Jose, as well as New Orleans, Dallas, Houston, Washington, D.C., Wichita (Kansas), Montreal, Sydney, and the suburbs of Paris, where new temples have been built for this now globalized faith.

Caodaism is a new religion that emerged in the context of the struggles of decolonization, was shattered and spatially dispersed by cold war conflicts, and is now trying to reshape its goals in a globalized world. In 1925, a group of colonized intellectuals educated at French-language schools held séances in Saigon and received spirit messages from the Jade Emperor ordering them to establish a new organization. Over a million people converted in the religion's first decade, forming the largest mass movement in southern Vietnam. Its religious leaders were first imprisoned and then courted by the French, eventually being absorbed into anti-Communist factions within the Saigon Republic. From 1975 to 1995, its temples were virtually closed down, but in the last two decades they have reopened. Caodaism is now officially Vietnam's third largest religion (after Buddhism and Catholicism), practiced by at least 3.2 million people in Vietnam, and it has about 4 million followers worldwide. Estimates of the world's top ten religions by numbers of adherents have often included Caodaism.[2]

Caodaism between Syncretism and Diaspora

This book explores the question of why Caodaism was initially perceived as "outrageous" and described by many writers as "the least understood of all Vietnamese movements of the 20th century" (Popkin 1979, 193; see also Wolf 1968; Smith 1970b; Taylor 2001; Woodside 2006). One example comes from Francis Fitzgerald's *Fire in the Lake,* the most widely read book on Vietnamese culture published during the period of American military intervention, which describes Caodaism as a "traditionalist movement," that "rose out of the mystical depths of the Mekong Delta," and consisted of peasants "merely waiting for the will of Heaven to change, at which point (so they were convinced) the French would disappear and all the Vietnamese would become Cao Dai" (Fitzgerald 1972, 59).

I argue, in contrast, that Caodaism represented a conversion to a kind of modernity, an exercise of individual choice based on reason, careful deliberation, and historical consciousness. It was a movement designed to assert the right to practice Vietnamese syncretistic traditions under the label of a religion, rather than as a motley set of indigenous practices and superstitions not dignified by this label. Caodaists wanted, through their new revealed religion, to sit as equals with Catholic religious leaders, to have their own Vatican and their own high-ranking clergy, and thus have Vietnamese spirituality recognized on the same plane as the faith of their French colonial masters. To do so, they forged alliances with French Freemasons, freethinkers, and those involved in lengthy flirtations with Oriental wisdom, but their goal was to transcend the Western exterior of modernity to reveal a more encompassing Eastern spiritual doctrine.

In the early twentieth century, Caodaism emerged as a syncretic mixture of Buddhism, Taoism, and Confucianism, reimagined within the external structure of a modern, monotheistic religion. Caodaism embraces the three jewels (matter, energy, and soul) and the five elements (mineral, wood/plant, water, fire, and earth) of Taoism, the three duties (ruler and subject, father and son, husband and wife) and five virtues (love, justice, respect, wisdom, loyalty) of Confucianism, and the three refuges (the Buddha, dharma, sangha) and five prohibitions (no killing, no stealing, no drunkenness, no extravagance, no lying) of Buddhism. Through leading moral lives, engaging in social service and practicing meditation, Caodai disciples hope to eventually be released from the cycle of reincarnation and be united with a higher reality. These doctrines and practices were deeply tied to Vietnamese history and the disruptions of the French colonial conquest of Saigon in 1859. Caodaism today is a Transpacific[3] religion, which spans the world's largest ocean and operates through global networks. Based on ten years of fieldwork in California and in Vietnam, as well as interviews with Caodaists in France, Canada, Cambodia, and Australia, I look at the relation between the divine eye revealed in the French colony of Indochina and the diaspora of Caodaists now spread through many different countries. Ninety years after it was born, and almost forty years after the fall of Saigon, Caodaism has become a global syncretism, tying a new generation of Caodaists to founders in their homeland through a theology that is at once cosmopolitan and indigenous.

Religious Diversity in Today's Vietnam

In the teeming streets of Saigon, waves of motorcyclists rush across intersections like invading armies. Elegant ladies who work in offices ride their scooters in high heels and mini-skirts, their bare legs stretched out underneath layers of clothing protecting their upper bodies—their arms covered in long evening gloves to block the sun's rays, their faces hidden behind stylish sunglasses, and designer scarves tied over their noses to block out the exhaust fumes of the crowded streets. In this mysterious disguise, they slide incognito through the city, floating along like fashionable bandits, uncontaminated by the noise and confusion of the roaring traffic.

Other motorcycle passengers also mark their belonging to another world by their dress: Caodaists flock to ceremonies in the flowing white robes of the *áo dài* tunic and pants, the men wearing black turbans on their heads. Buddhist monks wear long robes of grey or brown, their heads shaven and exposed, while Minh Lý disciples wear black tunics over white pants, their heads also covered with dark turbans. The confluence of religious costumes and modern transportation appears paradoxical, but it is increasingly common in a city where the stress of modern life has led to a resurgence of religious fervor, a new search for calm and tranquility in the rush of honking horns and flashing lights.

The rainbow of religious outfits and secular ones lays out the cultural diversity of Vietnam's largest city in its many colors. In a country with a Marxist government, still resolutely atheistic in its official orientation, the reemergence of popular religion and even several once-disfavored "indigenous religions" is remarkable. And the reemergence of Caodaism is especially astonishing, given that it had been condemned just twenty-five years before as a "reactionary organization with some religious overtones" (Blagov 2001a, 158). Like the phoenix bird, a favored Caodai symbolic icon, which rises from the ashes, this once much-maligned new religion is now once again taking its place on the public stage.

Syncretism as a Problem: Coherence or Confusion?

The first adjective used to describe Caodaism in most accounts of its history and theology is "syncretistic," followed by a number of other ways of describing the mixing of religious elements as "eclectic," "a combination religion," "a Russian salad of different creeds," a "jumble of undigested cosmologies," and an "ersatz religion" born as a hybrid of French modernity and Asian tradition (Jensen 2000, 220). The label of syncretism is a problem for both anthropologists and Caodaists, since it is a notoriously slippery term, used both to describe and to evaluate diverse religious groups.

In an essay critically evaluating syncretism, Charles Stewart notes that the concept has "an objectionable but nevertheless instructive past" (1999, 40). If we can understand the ways it has been used and misused by both scholars and theologians, syncretism can be reappropriated to inform a new ethnographic study of cultural mixtures. Local versions of world religions were criticized as being "syncretic" when they absorbed indigenous content, supposedly making them impure and somehow inauthentic. In these contexts, it was usually European Christianity that was regarded as official, and deviations from this essential faith were seen as aberrations. Nativist movements might also have had an "anti-syncretism" agenda as they tried to purge hybrid traditions in order to return to an imagined timeless vision of African or Native American authenticity (Matory 2005; Johnson 2007). More recent discussions have presented syncretism as a sign of cultural survival, a mode of resisting colonial domination, and an innovative response to the transformations of modernity.[4]

The etymology of the term "syncretism" is controversial: while it actually stems from the Greek word for "mixture,"[5] it was famously used by Plutarch in his essay on brotherly love (first century AD) to refer to the unified front of the Cretan people, who suspended debates about minor differences in order to face a common enemy. Syncretism here was a *defensive tactic* to resist hostile outsiders, and it referred not only to religion, but more broadly to any number of divisive loyalties to people, states, or ideologies that had to be overcome. This highlights several of the themes I hope to develop—the placement of syncretizing forces within a particular historical context and the hierarchy that is brought into being by a syncretistic reordering of priorities.

The idea of syncretism has an interesting history in anthropology. Earlier ideas of a laboratory of human cultures, isolated and to some extent self-generating, which each presented a unique experiment in human diversity, are no longer given much credence. The search for relatively untouched peoples with an original form of culture in a system of homeostasis is gone. In the 1920s and 1930s, when disapproving missionaries spoke scornfully of "syncretic cultures," this description might have discouraged ethnographic researchers. But these ideas of impurity and degeneration, which accompanied its use by nineteenth-century historians of religion, have largely been replaced by an emphasis on tolerance, reinterpretation, and invention in contemporary ethnographic discourse (Clifford 1988, 1992, 1994; Stewart and Shaw 2004).

It can be argued that this semantic shift reflects a sea change in the ways in which we think about other cultures. Nineteenth-century European intellectuals were concerned with developing an idea of national identity and difference—even a national essence—in order to define themselves both in relation to other European cultures and to the non-Western world of colonized others. Colonized peoples picked up this notion of a national essence and used it to fuel independence struggles that eventually broke apart the great colonial empires. What emerged were new nations often characterized by a great mixture of races, languages, and religions, their boundaries shifting in bloody conflicts about the precise borders of each cultural essence.

The new discipline of comparative religion started to use the term "syncretism" in the mid twentieth century to refer to religions in Haiti and Brazil that mixed elements of African, American Indian, and Catholic ritual, as well as the hybrid cultures of South and Southeast Asia.[6] Syncretism was contrasted with conversion as an integrative, dynamic response to contact with other religions. While conversion was seen as defeating or downgrading the values of another belief system, syncretism could be based on mutual respect and a reciprocal exchange of values and beliefs. In Asia and the Americas, syncretism was portrayed in a largely positive light, but in Africa it remained haunted by the shadows of missionary condemnations (Brook 1993; Peel 1968; Shaw 1994; Stewart 1999). Kuan-Hsing Chen, a leading figure in Inter-Asian Cultural Studies, proposes "critical syncretism" (similar to my explicit syncretism) as a liberating strategy in *Asia as Method,* since it uses an active and reflective frame of reference for new cultural identities (Chen 2010, 99–101).

The Tourist's View of Caodai Syncretism

Most tourist guides to Vietnam make reference not only to Graham Greene's ironic description, but also to his predecessor Norman Lewis, another famed English travel writer who declared in 1951, "This cathedral must be the most outrageously vulgar building ever to have been erected with serious intent."[7] For both Greene and Lewis, the most disturbing aspect of Caodai architecture was its "grotesque" mixture of European and Asian elements, which showed a pretentious presumption on the part of the religion's founders. As Greene wrote: "The dragons with lion-like heads climbed the pulpit: on the roof, Christ exposed his bleeding heart. Buddha sat, as Buddha always sits, with his lap empty. Confucius' beard hung meagerly down like a waterfall in the dry season. This was playacting: the great globe above the altar was ambition; the basket with a movable lid in which the Pope worked his prophecy was trickery" (Greene (1996, 86).

Today, we might interpret Greene's disdain through the lens of postcolonial theory: he saw Caodaism as an unseemly attempt by colonial subjects to imagine that they could ever achieve ascendancy over the great minds of the Western world. His journalism from the same period confirms this, since he condemned Caodaists as unreliable allies of the French, unwilling to attack fellow nationalists. Fowler, his fictional alter ego, was able to see the folly of America's increasing military presence in Vietnam, but did not think highly of Vietnamese efforts at self-determination.

Norman Lewis was most offended by the "kidnapping" of Jesus Christ and his imprisonment within an East Asian pantheon.[8] He called the Great Temple a "palace in candy from a coloured fantasy by Disney, an example of funfair architecture in extreme form," and was especially horrified by the blue pediment with the pantheon of divinities sent by Cao Đài. Buddha sits at the apex, flanked by Lao Tzu on his right and Confucius on his left, with the Tang-dynasty poet Lý Thái Bạch (the "invisible Pope") below him, the female Bodhisattva Quan Âm to his right and the red-faced warrior Quan Công to his left. On the third level is Jesus, and below him is Khương Thượng, a figure representing the veneration of local spirits and heroes (thần). They represent the five stages of spiritual attainment: the Buddhist path of enlightenment (Đạo Phật), the way of the immortals (Đạo Tiên), the way of the saints (Đạo Thánh), the way of local spirits (Đạo Thần), and finally the way of humanity and ancestor veneration (Đạo Nhơn) (see Plate 7).

Lewis describes the pediment in these words: "Over the doorway was a grotesquely undignified piece of statuary showing Jesus Christ borne upon the shoulders of Lao Tse and in his turn carrying Confucius and Buddha. They are made to look like Japanese acrobats about to begin their act. Once inside, one expected continually to hear bellowing laughter relayed from some nearby tunnel of love" (Lewis 1951, 44). Intriguingly, while his description stresses how "undignified" it is to bring these religious leaders together, it inaccurately portrays Jesus as placed higher than Lao Tzu, but below Confucius and Buddha, when in fact the opposite is true. Jesus' way of the saints sits at the third level, below both the way of enlightenment and the way of the immortals. The full indignity must have been unimaginable for Lewis.

Informed by these sarcastic descriptions in foreign-language guidebooks, and without access to any explanations of their religion from Caodaists themselves, most tourists have an understandably vague notion of what is actually believed in this "outrageous syncretism." They can be forgiven for failing to realize that Caodaism stems from a centuries-old combination of Buddhism,

Taoism, and Confucianism as the three religions of Asia (*tam giáo*). One of the most interesting aspects of Caodai conversion, at least when studied comparatively, is that it represents a conversion to an already well-established set of beliefs. It innovated mainly by creating an elaborate institutional structure and administrative hierarchy for a set of beliefs that had earlier appeared somewhat amorphous, disorganized, and fluid.

Early converts to Caodaism did not have to change many of their customs. They followed ritual practices that were not radically different from those of devotional Buddhism, which was already infused with elements of Taoist occultism and Confucian morality. But they entered a radical new form of social organization. They became part of a mass movement that revalorized Vietnamese tradition in a more cosmopolitan context and responded to French criticisms of the "unruly, unordered" jungle of beliefs by clearly delineating different components of Vietnamese tradition and providing a framework in which they would be integrated through divine decree.

Many of the most "outrageous" elements of Caodaism, such as the inclusion of European figures like Victor Hugo and Jeanne d'Arc, were introduced only several years after the first revelations, and only in Tây Ninh, not in other denominations (as we will see in Chapter 2). The core elements of Caodai theology come from a Sino-Vietnamese heritage of "secret societies" that deployed spirit mediumship to produce a canon of texts transmitted over time. Later influences from a very wide variety of external sources (European Spiritism, The Theosophical Society, Freemasons) took their place alongside the most important lines of transmission from temples that merged the three doctrines of East Asia with a new technology for contacting the spirits.

Serious studies of Caodaism by academics began to appear during the period of the American war in Vietnam. Ralph B. Smith, in the first thorough account of Caodai history and doctrine, examined its Sino-Vietnamese roots and wondered whether Hugo's messages in Caodai scriptures were simply a sly propaganda tool to delude the French, by associating themselves with an iconic nineteenth-century literary figure (Smith 1970b, 336). Jayne Werner, based on a detailed study of French archives and fieldwork in both North and South Vietnam, looked at the political history of Caodaism, and did an invaluable sociological study of its early founders (1981). Victor Oliver did fieldwork in Saigon in the 1970s, examining the administrative structure of Caodaism and the problem of sectarian divisions (1976). Sergei Blagov used Russian archives to document the more recent travails of Caodaists, especially since the 1975 Communist victory (2001a). Christopher Hartney studied the opening of a Caodai temple in Sydney, Australia (2004).

French anthropologist Jeremy Jammes did more than fifteen years of research on Caodaists in Paris and in Vietnam and has written a fascinating analysis of the history of Caodai spirit messages or "oracles" (2006a, 2014). He describes the shifting emphases of Caodai religious practice, and especially the relationship of spirit mediumship to meditation. Because of the Communist government's ban on spirit mediumship since 1975, the importance of spirit messages had to be reevaluated. In the 1980s and 1990s, much of the mystique of spirit mediumship was shifted to secret, esoteric forms of meditation, which offer the possibility of "having conversations with divinities" and receiving new religious texts. Thus, although the official position of Caodaists in Vietnam has to be that the age of revelations has passed, in fact their theology is constantly expanding and adapting itself to new contexts, not only through extensive commentaries on earlier messages but also through new incidents of religious inspiration.

French Views of Vietnamese Religion as "Confusionism"

Even relatively sympathetic French observers described Vietnamese religion as a shapeless, anarchic jungle of elements. In 1949 the French missionary scholar Léopold Cadière described the religion of the Vietnamese especially vividly: "Vietnamese religion (if indeed one can use the singular) produces an impression like that which is inspired by a journey into the great forest of the Annamite Cordillera: on all sides are great tree trunks, their roots penetrating to unfathomable depths, supporting a vault of foliage lost in shadow; branches stoop down to the earth and take root; seemingly endless creepers run from tree to tree, their origins undiscoverable . . ." (Cadière 1989, 1). While his description is not without an appreciation for aesthetic value of Vietnamese ritual ("there are inextricable thorns, and fronds of surpassing elegance and delicacy"), it also stresses elements of decadence ("the bark of the trees is dark, gnarled, or slimy, and one cannot touch it without a shudder, there are dead branches upon a thick carpet of mold and decay"). And yet he finds within it a vitality and exuberance that is inspiring ("on all sides sap thrusts up and life abounds in overwhelming profusion") (Cadière 1989, 1).

What he does not find is coherence, or order, or a logical relation between the parts. While he argues that "religious feeling makes itself fully manifest and dominates the whole of life," he describes it as parading in the pomp of official ceremonies or "lurking furtively" at the foot of a tree or in front of a rough stone. Because of this strong religious feeling, the Vietnamese may "bow down before baleful idols" or "make a serpent into an object of worship": "Magic, with its barbaric or absurd practices, is mingled with the noblest of religious observances." While he recognizes Buddhist and Taoist elements, he concludes that "in the bulk of its beliefs and practices," Vietnamese religion is "close kin to (and almost confounding itself with) the baser religions characteristic of primitive mountain dwellers" (Cadière 1989, 1).

It was descriptions like these that inspired the rage of Vietnamese intellectuals, who responded to these French scholars by deciding that they needed their own "Jesuits"—religious scholars who would help them to claim a position within the religious field and reinvent Vietnamese traditions in a religion as centralized and imposing as the Catholic Church. They also needed their own organization—"a Vatican in Vietnam"—with a powerful administrative hierarchy and the capacity to transform worldly service to their new religion into celestial ranks after death. And they received spirit messages telling them that the Supreme Being had recognized their sufferings and their humiliations and would provide them not only with a divine mandate to organize such a religion but also a new set of revelations to guide its growth.

The Jade Emperor Reveals a "New Religion of the South"

The mandate to form a new religion came from the Jade Emperor, who contacted a group of three young Spiritists who worked in French colonial offices in Saigon. After months of refusing to reveal his identity, a very erudite and literary spirit came down in a midnight séance in 1925 to declare:

> For as long as we have seen, the southern country has not had its own religion. Its foundation must now be laid.... I, as the highest Master, have founded the Tao in this southern region to compensate a country that since the beginning of its history has regularly suffered my vicissitudes. This time, I have decided to forgive you for your sins and redeem you by returning glory to your country. Since Heaven created the earth, no other country on this 68th planet of the universe has been capable of what you will be able to do. I will give the greatest rewards to those disciples who show that they are most worthy of my favor.... From this day on, there is only one true religious pathway, the Tao, and that is my pathway, that of your Master, which I have founded for my disciples and named as the national religion of this region. Have you understood me?[9]

Inspired by these messages, Caodaists went off in a bold new direction that was significantly different from that of other "redemptive societies" in the Sino-

Vietnamese world (Duara 2003, 2015; Goossaert and Palmer 2011). They built a splendid holy city, including a Great Temple with a Gothic front, and 1,338 smaller versions of this temple throughout the countryside (as well as almost a dozen replicas of the temple overseas). This "edifice complex" buttressed a congregational and ceremonial form of ritual that in many respects resurrected the vestments and pomp of the now banned Confucian rituals.

Caodaism's "outrageous syncretism" was not as innovative as it appeared initially, but it managed to grow into a large, doctrinally complex religion whose "dogmatic grandeur" (Woodside 1976, 184) gave it more stability and resilience than other twentieth-century East Asian salvationist groups that tried to reconcile Asian religious traditions with Western belief systems.[10] Caodai founders argued in 1926 that both Eastern and Western traditions had become morally bankrupt and proposed to restore a lost social equilibrium through a new congregational discipline, which would rehabilitate the ancient Confucian virtues. The religious syncretism that existed implicitly in the Vietnamese combination of Buddhism, Taoism, and Confucianism now needed to be defined explicitly against the pressures of European culture. This was done by casting it into newly marked institutional forms, in which the red robes of Confucian and Catholic dignitaries represented the administrative branch, the turquoise robes of Taoist occultists represented spiritual purity and tolerance, and the saffron robes of Buddhist dignitaries represented compassion and charity. The revival of the pomp and pageantry of the imperial past was conducted "in an atmosphere of almost voluptuous nostalgia and strict liturgical discipline," but it was able to connect at a deep cultural level with the population, since "the eighth century Chinese poet Li Po [Lý Thái Bạch] . . . still touched the hearts of more Vietnamese peasants than did the Paris commune" (Woodside 1976, 187–188).

The Concept of the Religious Field and Clashes with Christianity

Pierre Bourdieu developed the concept of the religious field to study the history of Roman Catholicism, and Stanley Tambiah has developed a similar concept applied to Buddhism.[11] Goossaert and Palmer applied this concept to Chinese religion using this definition: "A religious field comes into being when a class of religious specialists emerge and try to centralize, systematize and control a body of knowledge. In doing so, they assert their religious authority and create a field of power in which others are disqualified as laypeople or dismissed as practicing 'superstition,' 'magic' or some lower form of popular religion" (Goossaert and Palmer 2011, 6–13).

I argue that Caodaism created a new religious field in French Indochina, and in doing so invested a number of very traditional elements with new significance and new dynamism. While it later also added a number of French influences and other references to world historical figures, these came somewhat later in its development and were not essential to its formation. In Vietnam, as in China, when a self-consciously religious field was opened up in the nineteenth and early twentieth centuries, it was as a result of a dialogue between Vietnamese heritage and both Christian missionaries and secularizing political reformers and revolutionaries.

The creation of a new religious field can be described as the modernization of religion, but it can also be the opposite of modernization. Paradoxically, this new religious field can be a *defensive weapon* used by the advocates of tradition who want to claim the same status for the beliefs and practices they already have as for the beliefs and practices of Christianity. The colonial setting in which Caodaism emerged requires a modification of Bourdieu's theories of competition in the religious field, as well as the "dispossession" of the laity, the domination of religious specialists, and the struggle for legitimation. Building on earlier engagements with Bourdieu (Hoskins 1993, 1998, 2015), I develop here an interpretation of how this framework can be used to understand both colonial syncretism and postcolonial diaspora.

Christianity sees itself as a broad and welcoming spiritual land, but those who choose to immigrate there must observe the conventions of conversion—the right papers and documents, a waiting period of learning catechisms before applying for the citizenship of the baptism, and of course an exclusive commitment to keeping Christian figures at the top of the pantheon, not messing things up with other religious teachers. Because Caodaism saw itself as a modern religion, with clear boundaries, ceremonies of initiation, and congregational activity, it soon came to compete with the Catholic Church and to clash with Christianized notions of what a religion should be. I argue that this clash was articulated in relation to ideas of borders and institutions, which complicate our notions of how syncretism works.

Implicit versus Explicit Forms of Religious Mixing

In order to move toward a more positive sense of syncretism, we must recognize it as a process, a project in itself, which moves from an implicit stage to a more explicit one and acquires a more complex, hierarchical, and deliberate character in this second stage. What I call "implicit syncretism" works through idiosyncratic adjustments—the decision to appeal to a new god here, to adopt a

Plate 1. Interior of the Great Temple, facing the entrance and the three spirit mediums

Plate 2. Mural at entrance showing Sun Yat-sen, Victor Hugo, and Trạng Trình, signing an alliance with divinity, based on "God and Humanity, Love and Justice"

Plate 3. The Gothic façade at the entrance is a "European front" to an Asian interior

Plate 4. Dignitaries dressed in red (Confucianism, Catholicism), yellow (Buddhism) and turquoise (Taoism) sit meditating with the white-robed disciples on the nine levels ascending to the globe with the Left Eye of God

Plate 5. *A side view shows the nine ascending levels from the Gothic front, through a central portion with Hindu and Muslim elements, to the highest level octagonal Bát Quái Đài*

Plate 6. *The Left Eye of God on the Celestial Globe in front of the table where spirit séances are held (the Cung Đạo)*

Plate 7. *The five levels of spiritual attainment, with Buddha at the top, followed by Lao Tzu and Confucius, then Quan Âm, Lý Thái Bạch and Quan Công, followed by Jesus Christ and then Khương Thượng (from the Garden Grove temple in California)*

Plate 8. *Phạm Công Tắc, the Hộ Pháp, is the head spirit medium, and his statue stands between his secular and sacred assistants in the Tây Ninh Great Temple*

new practice there. It involves a tacit sense of correspondences, without extensive reflection or deliberate selection. Its logic is often instrumental and moved
more by concerns with efficacy ("something that works") rather than theology.
Explicit syncretism involves the conscious selection and combination of different traditions, often led by an intellectual elite, which produces new doctrines
and a new religious field.[12]

"Syncretism" is a useful term because it helps us to focus on a particular
stage in religious mixing and development—*the explicit syncretizing moment:*
when religious mixing becomes conscious and is reflected upon. Intellectuals
and religious specialists may become explicit syncretizers as a retrospective jus-
tification of popular religious mixing. This is when the transition from implicit,
instrumental religion is made to explicit, doctrinal syncretism. The moment of
reflective awareness is a theologizing moment, a time when implicit connections
need to be made explicit.

Caodaism can be understood as an explicit form of syncretism, which
built on a much longer implicit syncretic tradition. For almost a thousand
years, Vietnamese people had practiced a symbiotic fusion of Buddhism, Taoism, and Confucianism, and scholar-officials applied for government positions
by writing essays commenting on the relationship of the three great traditions.
The implicit mixture of these three teachings—none of them explicitly recognized as a "world religion" before the end of the nineteenth century (Asad 1993;
Masuzawa 2005)—was destabilized by colonial conquest. Southern Vietnam
became the first part of East Asia to be brought under full European colonial
rule—a rule complete only in the southern third of the country (colonial Cochinchina, where the French ruled directly), and less complete in other parts of
French Indochina, which were protectorates under the indirect rule funneled
through the Nguyễn imperial dynasty. For this reason, the clash between Asian
tradition and French modernism was most intense in Saigon and its surrounding area.

The Generation of Caodai founders in 1925 sought to unite all the Vietnamese people into a single national religion, a kind of "Vietnamism" that
would provide the spiritual basis for achieving independent national sovereignty. They did so by incorporating organizational elements from the Catholic
Church and Chinese redemptive societies, as well as Spiritist texts from French
writers like Victor Hugo and Allan Kardec. Caodai doctrine formalizes and
institutionalizes the relationship of different religious traditions in Vietnam, as
well as other world religions, in the five levels of spiritual attainment. While Buddha's path to enlightenment (Đạo Phật) is at the top, and encompasses his Hindu
predecessors (since Brahma, Shiva, Vishnu, and Krishna are all "Buddhas"), this

is not necessarily the best or most appropriate pathway for many disciples. Those with interests in spirit séances will follow the way of the immortals (Đạo Tiên), directed by the Invisible Pope Lý Thái Bạch. The way of the saints (Đạo Thánh) incudes not only Jesus and Vietnamese heroes, but also Judaism and Islam. The way of local spirits (Đạo Thần) incorporates popular religious practices of propitiating village gods. The way of humanity and ancestor worship (Đạo Nhơn) provides models of citizenship and family life.

The syncretistic synthesis of these formalized levels described an already existing religious field in Vietnam, but it was to be challenged by the new context of diasporic settlements. Half a century later, the generation of Caodaists in 1975 included refugees and exiles who reworked the doctrines of this new religion to make it into a more flexible faith of unity that could develop outside of Vietnam and expand its syncretism into a new cosmopolitanism.

Syncretism as a Process of Restructuring a Religious Field

My approach is based on a concept of historically located dynamics in a religious field. It stresses the guiding narrative of this syncretism, and in particular the hierarchy of values that it embodies, rather than the assemblage of its parts. It differentiates between those religions that reach a short distance, to incorporate local practices from related religions, and those that reach a longer distance, to bring together widely disparate doctrines. The work of selection and reconciliation is, understandably, greater the wider the cultural distances concerned. But the "outrageous mixture" becomes more comprehensible (and more coherent) once one makes the effort to understand the principles by which it is organized.

Reviewing the most "outrageous" figures in the Caodai pantheon of saints— Victor Hugo, Jeanne d'Arc, Rousseau, La Fontaine, even Vladimir Lenin—one thing that is notable is that many of them were already "canonized" in the secular shrine of the French Republic—the Panthéon mausoleum in Paris. Victor Hugo was significant to colonized intellectuals because he was a proponent of human emancipation and an opponent of the death penalty who defined himself as the sworn enemy of Napoleon III, the conqueror of French Indochina. Transcripts of Spiritist séances in which Hugo participated were published in 1923 and contained messages from Jesus "reconsidering" aspects of Christianity as well as prophecies that a new global religion would emerge in the twentieth century, with Hugo as one of its prophets. Hugo virtually applied for the position of a Caodai prophet with this prophecy, which came to be fulfilled three years after these transcripts appeared in print in Saigon and were the subject of many articles by Vietnamese journalists (see Chapter 3 in this volume).

Jeanne d'Arc was canonized by the Catholic Church in 1920, and her feast day on May 11 became an official holiday in French Indochina. The celebration of the 500th anniversary of her victory at Orléans was boycotted by nationalist Vietnamese student organizations in 1930 (Lâm 2000, 65). Her status as a French national heroine centered on the story of a poor peasant girl who heard voices telling her to rise up against a foreign army occupying her homeland. In 1934, she "came down" in a Caodai séance to defend the right of oppressed people to self-determination: "When a people achieves consciousness of itself and finds its own force in this self-consciousness, this is already a weapon that no one can defeat."[13] Jeanne d'Arc also called for the emancipation of women and is identified with the sixth of the nine muses attending the Mother Goddess (Lục Nương Diêu Trì Cung).[14] Lenin spoke briefly in a séance on February 25, 1934 (ten years after his death), to concede that the revolution of the proletariat was already suggested in Buddhist ideas of equality, so the central moral lessons of Communism were already there in Asian tradition. Thus, the literary and cultural figures who spoke to Caodaists might have been drawn from the arts and letters curriculum of the colonial *lycée,* but their messages turn the tables on the French instructors who taught Vietnamese elites.

European philosophers, writers, and revolutionaries who "come down" and provide teachings in Caodai séances do so to preach against French colonial domination. Most of them speak in French, and Victor Hugo delivers elaborate verses in Alexandrine couplets—much as the Taoist poets speak in the standard seven-eight verse form of Vietnamese classical poetry. The inclusion of Western figures is, therefore, an argument for parity—for the fact that Asian literary figures are the equivalent of European ones—and not for the worship of European figures themselves. Caodaism imagines the creation of a new religion as a conversation of sages of all ages, in which the heroes of France's cultural heritage take seriously Vietnamese claims to sovereignty and autonomy.

The French predilection for naming streets, schools, and public places after the secular heroes and heroines of the French Republic reinforced the sense that these secular revolutionaries were the real teachers of a generation of younger Vietnamese educated in French. The *lycée,* or secondary school, in Saigon where many Caodai leaders were schooled was named first after the colonial conqueror Chasseloup-Laubat, then after Jean-Jacques Rousseau. Girls went to study at the Lycée Marie Curie in Saigon or the Lycée Jeanne d'Arc in Huế. It is not surprising that they found that the values of *liberté égalité et fraternité* they were taught in school were not consistent with the actions of the French colonial regime.

We need to move beyond notions of syncretism that isolate particular elements but do not look at the overall hierarchical principles involved in selecting these particular figures. Rather than cataloging the number of old and new elements, we need instead to look at the structural relationship between values. The "three great Asian traditions" (*tam giáo*) had already been fused in the syncretic doctrines of early twentieth-century "Minh" temples, redemptive societies formed by descendants of Ming Chinese refugees who had intermarried with local Vietnamese women (the "Minh Hương"). (Chapter 5 of this volume traces the linkages with this tradition in greater detail.) They had a three-stage eschatology, which led to belief in a "third era" when the world would be redeemed, after many years of suffering. Caodaism innovated in explicitly identifying this third era with the fall of European empires. It was therefore a "religion of decolonization" that fused the project of restoring Vietnamese sovereignty with the religious goals of moral and ethical revitalization.

Trespassing: Crossing the Border into the Territory of Another Religion

The German systems theorist Ulrich Berner has proposed a "heuristic model" for the interdisciplinary study of syncretism, which distinguishes between "syncretism on the level of elements" and "syncretism on the level of systems." Elements can be incorporated from different religious systems while still emphasizing the boundaries between the systems, and even condemning the other system. Syncretism on the level of systems, on the other hand, refers to "the process of abolishing the boundaries between different religious systems with the intention of reducing the tension between them" (Berner 2001, 503). I am intrigued by his argument that syncretism works by removing borders and neutralizing competition by allowing a sort of interpenetration. Syncretism, in effect, denies the privilege of a particular religion to stake out its own territory, and is therefore comparable to the work of the trespasser or the illegal alien. Porous borders allow reconciliation, mixing, and creative recombinations.

Berner's idea that borders are simply "removed," however, begs the question of *who* has removed them—whether this is an involuntary penetration (as in the familiar metaphor of "colonial rape" that has been rehearsed perhaps a bit too much in postcolonial theory) or a somewhat more mutual process of attraction and combination. Caodaists elaborated a more systematic form of syncretism since they sought to reclaim their own country by removing the borders erected by French church authorities around a set of Christian ideas that had already taken root in Vietnam. They wanted to be let into the land of Christendom without having to give up the teachings of the great Asian sages, which they saw as complementing the Bible rather than being replaced by it. Since Caodaism is a defensive reaction to the French invasion of Vietnamese religious space, it takes the form of erecting a new, more inclusive framework—but one very much policed by a new revealed scripture, a new administrative hierarchy, and a very elaborate apparatus of power that was almost a localized theocracy.

Colonized intellectuals in Saigon perceived Christianity through the lens of anticolonial struggle. While fusing Buddhism, Confucianism, and Taoism, they also embraced biblical ideas about history and popular emancipation: the notion of the Vietnamese as "God's chosen people," the idea of a prophet who would fight for the independence of his people against an empire based in Rome, and the erection of an intricate administrative hierarchy blending Confucian titles with Catholic ones (a Pope, female and male cardinals, bishops, and a Vatican in Vietnam). Berner refers to "systematic syncretism" (which corresponds to my explicit syncretism) as a "strategy for survival," since it both helps traditional elements to be infused with new meaning and can resolve the tension caused by rival religious claims on an individual (Berner 2001, 509). It is a defensive mechanism that generates a new and innovative synthesis in response to a changing cultural context.

Trespassing: Crossing the Border between Religion and Politics

Caodaism is well known for its colorful appropriation of Catholic titles of office for Vietnamese dignitaries. Looking more closely at the holder of these titles, however, we see several interesting twists in these appropriations. The "Invisible Pope" (Giáo Tông Vô Vi) of Caodaism is the spirit of the Tang-dynasty Taoist poet Li Bai (Lý Thái Bạch in Vietnamese). The first human to be called the "Interim Pope" headed the administrative division and had a Vietnamese title (Giáo Tông) closer to the term for "president" (Tổng Thống) than the term for the Catholic Pope, "Religious Emperor" (Giáo Hoàng). He was Lê Văn Trung, a once-successful businessman who had become a naturalized French citizen and the first "native" included on the Indochinese Colonial Council. Lê Văn Trung, after years of "collaborating" with the French, lost all of his wealth, went bankrupt, and became addicted to opium. In 1926, when he was visited by the three young Spiritists who received messages from the Jade Emperor, he suddenly came to see the light, rather literally: his vision was restored, and he came to see that he had to change his path, quitting opium cold turkey and assuming the temporal leadership of this new religious movement. His conversion galvanized thousands of others, and his image still appears on the front of the Great Temple, beside that of his cofounder, Madame Lâm Thị Thanh, the first female Cardinal and the first signer of the October 7, 1926, official declaration sent to the French government.[15]

That document, signed by twenty-eight prominent Vietnamese and 245 others, was a "Declaration of Religious Independence" that clearly stated that dozens of once-secret societies were to be united under one banner to reform morality and revive traditional ethics. What was not explicitly stated—but was clear for all to see—was that this ambitious unification of religious groups in Vietnam was meant to create a community strong enough to stand up to both the French Catholic Church and the secular French state. Since 1905, France has had the strongest separation of church and state of any European power, which guaranteed the neutrality of the state and the freedom of religious exercise. While the colonial state made no such guarantee of political freedoms (especially for incipient nationalists), when a community was incorporated as a religion, it would be hard to challenge its legality.

Since its birth, the agents of the Sûreté, or French secret police, have suspected that Caodaism was a "political movement masquerading as a religion." (In the colonial archives in Aix-en-Provence, Caodaism is indexed under politics, not religion.) Caodaists are nothing if not sincere in their belief in the truth of the religious revelations they received from 1925–1934. But they also recognized the strategic advantage of seeking to reform the country through a religious vision at a time when there was a severe repression of political dissent. The kinds of moral and ethical reform that they proposed were part of the nationalist project, but their own redrawing of the borders around religion (modeled on Western notions) were also motivated by a shrewd analysis of what could be prohibited by a secular state and what it should be committed to tolerate.

Many French colonial officers—including all of the governors of Indochina—were Freemasons, part of an esoteric community that was itself a product of the secularizing forces that broke off from the Catholic Church. Several Caodai leaders were also Freemasons (as was Hồ Chí Minh, who joined in Paris in 1921), and the "Loge Confucius"—the first Masonry Lodge in Indochina to accept Vietnamese members—was a virtual incubation tank where Caodaists interacted with sympathetic Frenchmen who would help them to fight for religious freedom (Nguyễn Ngọc Châu 2001, 7).

The most significant title in the Caodai hierarchy is the title of the head spirit medium, the Hộ Pháp, which can be translated as "Defender of the Dharma." *Pháp* is the word used by Buddhists for dharma, or religious law, but it also carries the sense of a method or spiritual technology. The title comes from popular Buddhism, the fierce general called the Dharmapala, who in Vietnam is one of the four Lokapalas or spatial guardians (Tư Đài Kin Cáng). He fights enemies from the East, West, and South, and, after having converted them, becomes their chief. Phạm Công Tắc came to incarnate this divine general through a process in which his perispirit, or "mental body" (*Chơn Thần*), was pushed out of his human body, and his body was filled with the spirit of Dharmapala (see Plate 8) (Đức Nguyên 2000 1: 1507; Jammes 2006b, 227).

As we shall see in Chapter 2, Phạm Công Tắc became Caodaism's most charismatic and controversial leader, receiving all the messages from European figures in the 1930s, when his struggle against the French colonial regime stressed exposing its hypocrisy. In 1940, when he and many other Vietnamese came to see Japan as a possible liberator, he was arrested and sent into exile on prison islands off the coast of Madagascar. During this time, the Japanese occupied Vietnam and trained Caodai militia to help them overthrow the French administration in March 1945. After the Japanese surrender, the Caodai military leader Trần Quang Vinh (designated as the "spiritual son of Victor Hugo") negotiated for the release and return of Caodai leaders by agreeing to serve as a "peace-keeping force" to defend Caodai communities against attacks from the Communist-led Việt Minh.

When Phạm Công Tắc returned to Vietnam in 1946, he said he was "following in the path of Gandhi" in working for a nonviolent end to French colonialism and traveling to Geneva to resist the partition of his homeland along cold war lines. He tried to use Orientalism against empire: ideas of Eastern spirituality (embodied, for him, in the image of the Left Eye—closer to the heart, but also yang—positive, dynamic, and masculine) were used to oppose Western materialism (embodied in the right eye—a rationality without ethics, also dark and destructive). By inverting the Orientalist stereotype of a passive, feminized East, he reimagined Vietnamese religion as a dynamic masculine monotheism that could encompass Western religious teachings into the culmination of religious unity.

Caodaism as a "Religion of Decolonization"

Caodai theology fuses the anticolonial struggle for national sovereignty with the personal struggle for self-perfection. The Vietnamese people as a whole are seen as having suffered from many vicissitudes but—through virtuous conduct—having earned the right to redemption. If they cultivate themselves and reform their society, the Vietnamese should be able to achieve not only self-determination but also a leadership role in showing the rest of the world how to resolve religious difference. Of course, the three traditions of Vietnam—Buddhism, Taoism, and Confucianism—were all relatively nonterritorial, so their teachings could be spread expansively over a vast region without much concern to maintain a pure, bounded area of strict adherents.

Christianity and Islam, on the other hand, have erected strict borders around their congregations, defining those inside the borders as the faithful and those outside their borders as infidels, heretics, and apostates. Particular denominations or sects within Christianity and Islam may be more or less directly concerned with these borders, enforcing them strictly or leniently, but the idea that individuals can be identified as "inside" or "outside" the fold makes these religions into units whose membership is conceptualized using a spatial metaphor. Abrahamic religions conceive of themselves as a sacred, bounded territory, with clear protocols as to how to gain entry and what one might call "permanent residence status" (or even eventual "citizenship"). Asian religions have instead been religions without borders, open to anyone who washes up on their shores or shows an interest in wandering into their temples.

Caodaism's blending of East and West reworks ideas of religious boundaries by institutionalizing a regulated, congregational mode of membership for a set of doctrines whose limits have been more porous and permeable in the past. Much of what has been considered "Caodai syncretism" is less about including particular figures in a pantheon and more about the narrative of what a religion itself consists of, how it should act within society, and how it is institutionalized and related to an administrative hierarchy.

Caodaists wanted to modernize Vietnamese tradition and defend it from European critics by using the same weapons used by their colonial masters: they wanted to create a strong institutionalized religious hierarchy, with a Vatican and a clear chain of command, in which elements of Buddhism, Confucianism, and Taoism, but also Mother Goddess worship and Catholicism, would be fused into a seamless whole and guided by enlightened intellectuals who could explain to the faithful masses how they were related.

Caodaists speak of the first twelve disciples of Caodai—designated by name in an early spirit message—as "the apostles," and there are conflicting interpretations of which one of these apostles might have ultimately betrayed the Master. They often say that prophecies from the first years indicated that Caodaism would be riven by factionalism, with many apostles breaking off to form their own denominations—"much as the Catholic Vatican saw many of its members leave to join Protestant churches." The opposition between smaller groups more focused on meditation, ascetic practice, and self-cultivation and the larger ceremonial and congregational rituals of Tây Ninh also "replicated" bits of Christian history, but it was expected they would all be reunified in the final days of the "Dragon Flower Assembly" (Hội Long Hoa).

Caodaism has in this way spun a very Christian narrative about the birth of a new religion with predominantly East Asian content. The colonial age of revelations created an obligation for each Caodai dignitary to write a syncretistic treatise, explaining his or her own interpretation of how different religions all sprang from the same origin and could be reconciled harmoniously. Spirit messages are the scriptures that guide these treatises, but individuals choose how to apply them to their own lives.

The Loss of Country at Two Crucial Moments

Caodaism was formed in response to the colonial crisis, when sovereignty was lost to the French. Vietnamese intellectuals responded to a need to create a new nation on the spiritual plane, since full nationhood was denied them in civil life. Fifty years later, it met its greatest challenge at the time of the fall of Saigon, a refugee crisis in which many thousands of Caodai disciples were sent into exile. This crisis eventually led to the globalization of the religion, and the reformulation of doctrines and practices in a new world. Both of these crises were described in Vietnamese as the "loss of country" (*mất nước*), a severing of the bonds between nation, faith, and sovereignty. The 1925 conversion to modernity was an effort to reclaim spiritual nationhood through seeking equivalence with French notions of what a religion could and should do in the public sphere. The 1975 conversion to a global faith of unity was an effort to reformulate this religion so that it could be both practiced in other countries and normalized within the Socialist Republic of Vietnam.

The anthropology of religion has shifted from seeing religion as an experience of belief to studying it as a discursive tradition (Asad 1993, 2009). Caodaists in the 1920s and 1930s were not really inventing a new religion out of whole cloth, but seeking divine guidance to establish a more coherent spirituality that could encompass the upheavals of the colonial period—described by Phạm Công Tắc as a "complete reversal" (*bouleversement total*)—and provide a newly integrated sense of Vietnamese identity. Caodai syncretism was a project with a teleological agenda, since it was inspired by a set of instructions set down by the Jade Emperor. It was also a modernist project to take the disparate parts of Vietnam's cultural heritage and fuse them into a modern religion—with a liturgy, a priesthood, an elaborate ecclesiastical hierarchy, and a set of impressive temples tied to a "Vatican in Vietnam." It was a project to reclaim Vietnamese identity from European colonial masters and to make Vietnamese marginalized intellectuals into the authors of their own history.

Talal Asad alerts us to the fact that we need to examine "the authorizing process by which 'religion' is created" (1993, 37). Caodaists in the 1920s and 1930s explicitly planned to create a new religious field, building a new sacred city and erecting an elaborate scaffolding of ecclesiastical offices. Like the medieval Church that both Asad and Bourdieu refer to, they "did not attempt to establish absolute uniformity of practice; on the contrary, its authoritative discourse was always concerned to specify differences, gradations, exceptions. What it sought was the subjection of all practice to a unified authority, to a single authentic source that could tell truth from falsehood" (Asad 1993, 38). They sought to create a sacred center for a Vietnamese fusion faith of unity.

Syncretism and Idiosyncratism

The idea of syncretism, like that of religious influence, has been criticized for falsely asserting that religions are disembodied forces that can "interact" (Walters 1995). This notion is misguided both because it displaces human agency onto unreal entities and because it supposes that religions represent mutually exclusive categories. To put it more simply, it is never Buddhism and Christianity that "interact," but particular Buddhists and Christians. A more careful usage of the term "syncretism" is possible, referring to "an activity, not of unreal entities transferring substances magically but of conscious human agents (like the ancient Cretans) recognizing and attempting to mitigate difference among themselves, for some particular reason, by bringing different things together in a shared space. It describes an attempt at reconciling or joining together opposing beliefs or practices, which presupposes human actors" (Walters 1995, 34–35).

While Caodaism is a shared project, its many founders and disciples have articulated its goals quite differently. As a religion founded by a committee, not by any one person, it provides us with a group of "syncretizers"—people who actively seek to select and reconcile elements of various religions to bring them into a single unified vision. Their "idiosyncratism"—their own special brew of religious inspirations—is a particular variation on a wider pattern of religious mixing. In order to capture the dynamic of these individual, idiosyncratic interpretations of Caodai doctrine, I trace the religious biographies of five people from the founding generation (the colonial age of revelations) and five people from today's diasporic communities.

Paired Biographies of Founders and Followers

The structure of this book is an attempt to capture the dynamic between these individual projects (the connections between specific masters and disciples, specific ancestors and descendants) and the wider cultural phenomena that is Caodaism. Caodaism is distinguished by its flexibility and diversity, so while it is in most respects highly institutionalized, with an especially elaborate administrative hierarchy, it is also filled with openings for religious inspiration and idiosyncratic interpretations. The various chapters chart a course that moves from the reclusive first disciple, through the controversial career of Caodaism's most prominent twentieth-century figure, to the founder of its army, and diasporic pioneers who established the first congregations in California.

Ten lives are profiled in these pages: five of them were lived in the early twentieth century, during what Caodaists call the Age of Revelations when the religion was founded in the 1920s and 1930s. Five others extend into the twenty-first century, in an age of globalization and transnational networks. Each chapter deals both with a member of the founding generation of Caodaists and followers or descendants in the diaspora. So it moves along a Transpacific axis, journeying from the French colony of Indochina through the Saigon Republic to communities in California, Texas, Virginia, and even France, Canada, Australia, and Cambodia. It focuses on the Vietnamese homeland as seen from overseas, so it has a diasporic perspective, but it draws on fieldwork on both sides of the Pacific, and makes the tension between these perspectives a focus of the analysis. The shifting point of view narration emphasizes the multiple perspectives that Caodaists can have, while sharing a common and rather flexible theology, which can mean different things to different people.

In each chapter, a tension is described between the leader who emerged in Vietnam and his disciples or descendants in the diaspora. The first chapter begins with Ngô Văn Chiêu (1876–1932), in some respects the "invisible" founder, since he is depicted only on the altar of the relatively few temples that practice a particularly select and demanding form of ascetic meditation. He is often described as the first disciple of the esoteric tradition (Phần Vô Vi), which emphasizes the immaterial rather than the material and is portable and personal. Bùi Văn Khâm, practicing as an individual spiritual seeker or "yogi," carries on the legacy of Ngô Văn Chiêu but also draws on his exposure to a much wider array of New Age options in California. The chapter opens with a description of a spirit séance I attended at his home near Los Angeles.

The second chapter looks at Phạm Công Tắc (1890–1957), the most famous, but also the most controversial, Caodai leader of the twentieth century.

A charismatic speaker who built the magnificent Tây Ninh Temple as a new Vatican in Vietnam and was intensely involved in nationalist politics, he has sometimes been described as "the Mahatma of Vietnam"—a Gandhian leader who fused religion and politics. He oversaw the architecture of a monument to symbolic encompassment, visualizing a new theology and presenting it as an alternative apparatus of power in an age of revolution. He was a translator and a popularizer, publishing abundantly in both French and Vietnamese, trying to heal the wounds of colonialism with a language of spiritual reconciliation.

He is paired with Bùi Đắc Hùm, the most prolific translator of Caodai scriptures into English, who has spearheaded a diasporic outreach program based on educating a new generation in Vietnamese religious and cultural traditions. Practicing an inclusive, nondenominational form of Caodaism, he seems to have renounced the possibility of returning to Vietnam, unconvinced that recent reforms will allow the religion to return to viability in its homeland. So, for him, the search for new mediums and new leadership must continue overseas and includes reaching beyond the Vietnamese community.

The third chapter deals with his rival for visibility as a leader of overseas Caodaists—Trần Quang Cảnh, the son of Caodaism's greatest military commander, Trần Quang Vinh (1901–1975), who also served as South Vietnam's Minister of Defense (1947–1952). Taking on the mantle of his father's divine appointment as Victor Hugo's "spiritual son," Cảnh believes that the Vatican in Vietnam cannot be moved elsewhere. After many years of criticizing government suppression, he is now the most prominent advocate of reconciliation with the Tây Ninh hierarchy. In 2011 he became the first American citizen to be ordained as an official member of the Tây Ninh administration. He wants to rebuild Caodaism in Vietnam by focusing on a new information center for tourists, recognition at academic conferences, and Internet connections.

The fourth chapter looks at Đỗ Vạn Lý (1910–2008), an important Caodai leader during the period of American military intervention in Saigon, whose career mixed religion and politics in ways reminiscent of Phạm Công Tắc, especially in the intensity of his commitment to Vietnamese nationalism. He was appointed to be South Vietnamese President Ngô Đình Diệm last ambassador to the United States and served as a diplomat in India, Indonesia, and Japan. After Diệm was killed, Đỗ Vạn Lý embraced Caodaism as a "modern" synthesis of the diverse religious perspectives he had experienced in other Asian countries. As the leader of the first congregation in Los Angeles, he crafted a "diasporic theology" by interpreting Caodai history from a more international perspective. His father, Đỗ Thuần Hậu, had been a famous Taoist master, who also had disciples in many different countries, but in his case the father-son dynamic was one of rupture rather than continuity. Both Chapters 3 and 4 deal with pairings of a father and a son.

The fifth chapter explores the "Caodaists in black," members of Tam Tông Miếu, an esoteric temple dedicated to the "three great Asian traditions" of Taoism, Buddhism, and Confucianism in the Sino-Vietnamese lineage. It is led by Lâm Lý Hùng, who spent three decades in California as a member of Caodai congregations. Called through a series of spirit séances to return to assume a position once held by his grandfather, Âu Kiệt Lâm, he is now a transnational religious leader (like Trần Quang Cảnh) who spends most of each year in Vietnam. The black-robed disciples of Tam Tông Miếu practice a "religion of the shadows" that counterbalances the Caodai "religion of light" by emphasizing a blend of Chinese occult sciences, spirit mediumship, and ascetic renunciation. Guided by séance messages, they have suffered many of the same sanctions as Caodaists and have formed their own pathway forward.

The sixth chapter includes a number of newer Caodai followers, many of them women. In "The Divine Eye on the Internet," I examine the influence of new technology on the creation of deterritorialized sacred communities, whose "holy land" may no longer be anchored to a specific landscape. Rival Caodai overseas groups now debate the importance of ties to their homeland on the Internet and shoot television shows to proselytize on a global scale. This allows religious communities in Vietnam and the diaspora to define each other—sometimes by reaction and exclusion—and also allows an originally "Vietnamese" set of religious images to interact extensively with many other forms of iconography that float around in cyberspace. The Internet has attracted many non-Vietnamese Americans, including several converts who have been ordained as ministers, worked as translators of Caodai scripture, and helped to broaden the appeal of a once very "Vietnamese" vision of global unity.

Vietnamese culture is immersed in ancestor worship and so both haunted and inspired by voices from the past. My study of founders and followers builds on the fact that many people I spoke to seemed to be glancing over their shoulders at their deceased teachers, parents, and grandparents whenever they had to make a decision. Meditating in front of their photographs on family altars or temple walls, they felt that they were part of a continuing conversation, going on through the generations and even crossing oceans.

Séance as a source of religious scripture is the most challenging aspect of Caodaism for Western observers, and this is a topic that I particularly wanted to explore. The first chapter immerses readers in the séance experience and includes sections of the 1925 séances, when the founding mediums explored the hybrid of French Spiritism and East Asian spirit writing (published in

English for the first time). Later chapters detail ways in which spirit messages have played a role in the lives of all my subjects. Rather than dwelling on séance as a "strange, exotic" practice that defies comprehension, I wanted to show how fundamental it is to Caodai ritual and doctrine. In doing this, I draw on the perspective of Caodai historians, including several writing from Vietnam (Đức Nguyên, Huệ Nhân, Lê Minh Sơn, Lê Anh Dũng, Nguyễn Trung Hậu) and others from Australia (Đồng Tân, Đào Công Tâm), France (Chí Tín, Quách Hiệp Long), and California (Bùi Đắc Hùm, Đỗ Vạn Lý, Trần Quang Cảnh), who also became my friends and whose lives are detailed in these pages.[16]

The final chapter examines how the syncretism of the colonial period has been transformed by the experience of exile into a diasporic formation. In 1975, Caodaism was a "religion in diaspora"—a group of refugees, "victims of an unpopular war," dispossessed—and their displacement was seen as a tragic event. In the past forty years, however, it has come to be perceived as part of a larger plan to create a "religion of diaspora," taking advantage of multiple locations around the world, using this as a spatial resource, elaborating a "global faith of unity." The story of Caodaism forces us to reconsider how anthropologists study religious mixtures in postcolonial settings, since it may reveal and challenge the "unconscious Eurocentrism" of our own notions of how religions are bounded and conceptualized.

CHAPTER 1

CONVERSATIONS WITH DIVINITIES

SÉANCE AND THE FIRST DISCIPLES

A portrait of Ngô Văn Chiêu, the first disciple of Cao Đài, hung below the large glowing left eye on the altar in the small upstairs bedroom devoted to spirit medium séances. Slipping out of my shoes and bowing respectfully in front of the altar, I caught his calm, meditative gaze through the swirls of incense that wafted upward. An oil lamp on the altar had burned a circle of ash onto the ceiling, visually suggesting the heavenly aspirations of the séance participants, who hoped to make contact with immortal spirits. Dressed in white tunics, the men tucked flowers behind their left ears, the women behind their right ears, and both groups knelt to chant in front of a beautifully sculpted wooden basket with a phoenix head.

The spirit medium sat before us, his face very pale and drained of all color, immobilized by hours of meditation the night before. He had been practicing as an independent medium in the Chiếu Minh tradition for over twenty years and had received a series of messages in complex verse. The séances he held at his home near Los Angeles were modeled on séances he had witnessed in Đà Nẵng and Saigon during his student years, when the country was torn apart by war. Like the famous esoteric medium Liên Hoa, he wore long, full sleeves and white gloves to protect his skin from direct contact with the phoenix basket.

Before we could begin, it was necessary to ask the spirits to give permission for me to attend along with Patrick Gallagher, who was helping to record it on digital video. We watched as Chinese coins, coded yin and yang, were tossed

*Figure 1.1. Bùi Văn Khâm
holding the phoenix basket
in front of his altar to Ngô
Văn Chiêu*

onto a plate in a simple divination called *xin keo:* if both times the coins fell in pairs, one head and one tails, then we could stay. If they fell as all heads or all tails, we would have to leave. We held our breath as we watched them fall. They fell as pairs, so we rejoiced that the spirits had approved our presence.

Fresh flowers, wine, and tea were arranged on the altar, which was draped with a yellow cloth. A séance protector (*Pháp Đàn*) had placed talismans around the space to protect the space from disturbances and recited incantations against evil spirits. Four smoking sticks of incense stood at attention in the incense burner, and a fifth was placed in a small hole at the top of the phoenix bird's head, so that each of its movements would leave a visible trail. The medium knelt in front of the altar and carefully lifted the basket in his gloved hands, its shiny polished wood glowing with the sheen and dimensions of a violin. This was the "precious instrument," the *ngọc cơ*, which he held gently above his head, the mediator that would allow the world of the gods and the world of humans to come closer together.

There was silence for several minutes after the chanting finished, then the basket began to move very slowly, tilting to one side and then to the other, as if the bird itself were glancing backward then lifting up its head. The medium's hands began to grip it more firmly as it started to turn more fiercely, struggling to escape from his grasp. The head swept suddenly up into the air and then crashed down, striking the glass-topped table in front of the altar with a harsh staccato rap. The bird seemed to try to take flight, thrashing and twirling with dizzying speed. It struck the table violently, again and again, and as it did so words formed in the medium's mouth and he began to speak, one syllable at a time, corresponding to the rapping on the table. The message emerged slowly, dramatically, in both the fierce rhythm of the wooden beak striking down and the whispered words that repeated those traced in the air.

The phoenix in East Asia is the magical bird of rebirth and regeneration, able to fly between the world of the living and the world of the spirits. The path that its flight takes leaves letters behind, traced into the white dust spread across the tabletop. The violent ballet of movement is achieved as the medium remains pale and barely conscious, his eyes closed and his mind attuned to other vibrations.

A tape recorder placed near the table caught his voice, and a scribe (*Điển ký*) stood to the side, noting each word as it was pronounced. At first indistinct, soon a verse pattern emerged, and the message was revealed. The medium said he felt that his hands move on their own, propelled by some other source, and the words on his lips were pronounced before he heard or understood them. The shaking and rapping went on for many minutes, with a violent forcefulness that was intimidating to the uninitiated. The spirit was not identified but he was obviously powerful, male, and commanding. He dominated the séance and would not withdraw for other spirits to come in and communicate with the participants.

As he began to speak, several of the people watching and holding their hands together in prayer trembled with excitement, their heads lifting to see the movements of the basket. The sense of discovery and power in the room was contagious. The first lines were recited in Vietnamese verse,[1] signaling the arrival of a powerful spirit, although one still nameless.

> The Original Teachings of the New Dharma set in motion in the Third Salvation
>
> To wake up all beings so they will be able to meet with the Father.
>
> From the Golden Hall the Divine Energy spreads the world over
>
> The Divine and the Human Worlds are not that far apart.
>
> The blessed wine is offered to you all,
>
> Brothers and sisters enjoy, I shall return to the Gem Palace.
>
> Please be seated.

Under the order of the Grand Master and in response to your request, I come today to bring you all a Message.

Seek not anywhere outside you for the answer to your spiritual questions.

Ask not who or what is God or Cao Đài, or who is talking.

Ask who you are. Once you know who you are, you shall know God. That is because you and God shall be one.

Seek not for miracles, because you know what had happened to the Son of Man. He showed mankind the miracles in the Power of the Father, but the message was not taken.

Therefore, the Message for today's world is turn to yourself and you shall come into contact with your Father, who is always within every one of you. Whether you are rich or poor; illiterate or intellectual, from the East or from the West; white or black; yellow or red. The Father is waiting within each of you to meet with you when you can transcend your human ordinary nature.

That is the Message I would like to deliver to any of you who would like to hear, from the Grand Master.[2]

The phoenix raised its head and turned in a slow waltz around, dipping from time to time as if listening to a hidden music that guided its movements.

The medium's body was bathed in sweat, as his movements mimicked those of a martial artist, turning sharply from one side to another, parrying blows from an invisible opponent. When he spoke about transcending human ordinary nature, the basket lifted its head again and curved down, turning its beak back to the table. Finally, the medium collapsed, exhausted but energized, and the phoenix basket came to rest once again on the table in front of him.

Then the séance ended and there were closing prayers. We sipped small servings of Manischewitz wine and returned, slowly, to our normal state of attentiveness. The medium, a normally very articulate and talkative man, slumped down and caught his breath, the color gradually returning to his cheeks. His assistants gathered to chant a prayer of farewell to the spirits, and the darkened room was opened up again to let in the warm California sunlight.

The Importance of Séance to Caodaism

This was my first experience of a Caodai séance, a ritual that I had already studied for over two years, and which I would have the opportunity to observe again, and even take part in, some time later. It was performed in accordance with the esoteric tradition (*vô vi*), sometimes called the "invisible path" or the "inner path," which focuses on the cultivation and transformation of the self rather than the changing of the world. The roots of this tradition go back many centuries, not only in Vietnam but also in China, where similar séances were a crucial part of Taoist occultism and the "three-in-one" traditions of combining Buddhism, Taoism, and Confucianism in the Ming dynasty.[3] These séances were revitalized and called upon to serve a new purpose in the early twentieth century, when the Caodai "age of revelations" began, and since 1975 they have also been practiced in exiled communities in the United States and elsewhere.

I would not have been allowed to participate in and videotape a séance like this in Vietnam. The literary séances practiced by Caodaists are still officially banned. A recent resurgence of popular religious practices, including the trance dancing of spirit mediums possessed by "the sacred mothers" of Đạo Mẫu, has softened the outlines of that ban a bit (Fjelstad and Nguyen 2011). And officials are now certainly aware that séances are held privately, for personal consultations, in a number of homes. But the time when hundreds of "demonstration séances" were held to draw new members into Caodaism and allow them to receive personalized messages from the spirits is completely past.

What desires were being enacted in the séances of the 1920s, which generated the body of Caodai teachings that have now become official doctrine? What social conditions opened the way for this "age of revelations" that coincided with the rise of Vietnamese nationalism? And how are these séances similar or different from séances held today, both in California and (privately) in Vietnam?

To answer these questions, we need to look at the intersection of French Spiritism and East Asian divination practices in the early years of the twentieth century. We need to trace the career of Ngô Văn Chiêu (1878–1933), an ascetic mystic who is sometimes described as the "founder of Caodaism." A plaque erected on his grave in Cần Thơ contains that inscription, but it seems to me that it is more accurate to call him the "first disciple of Cao Đài" (as do Caodai historians at the Saigon Teaching Agency), since he was a religious innovator but a reluctant leader. What kind of founder refuses to participate in the institutionalization of his revelations? While his name commands great respect from all Caodaists, he refused to accept the position of Pope offered to him by the Jade Emperor in a séance and retreated from the thousands of followers inspired by his vision of the Left Eye. His reclusive life of meditation, seclusion, and reflection was to continue to inspire esoteric practice within Caodaism.

His life is juxtaposed here with the life of his disciple, Bùi Văn Khâm, the California spirit medium who allowed me to attend his séance. Ngô Văn Chiêu moved in between the world of French Spiritism and ancient Chinese spirit writing. A century later, Bùi Văn Khâm came back to the same tradition after wandering through the New Age landscape of California. Called a "Caodai yogi" by his colleagues, Bùi Văn Khâm found in esoteric practice a way to connect his interests in a wide array of Asian spiritual traditions, focusing them on the experience of séance. Séances are sensual, inspirational, and visceral, and they happen in dark, dangerous, uncontrolled places, while Caodai doctrine is reflective, disciplined, and cerebral. Both modes of religiosity combined in creating this new religion and in sustaining its appeal.

The Colonial Cult of the Occult

A fascination with invisible spirit entities and a parallel world in which things were often not what they seemed was shared by both Vietnamese intellectuals and their French colonial masters. Vietnamese officials, like the Chinese mandarins who were the source of their literary heritage, evoked spirits in their homes to seek advice about proper conduct, to cultivate themselves spiritually, and as a source of poetic inspiration. The traditional education system had trained scholars for decades to pray to the spirits of two stars, in the constellation of Ursa Major, or the Big Dipper, who were grouped with the gods Wenchang and Kuixing, who were worshipped as the gods of literature (Spence 1996, 59). In the Chinese tradition, the seven stars of the northern ladle represent the Emperor's carriage [the vehicle of God's Will], rotating around the center of the universe, governing the four directions, dividing Yin from Yang, determining the four seasons, balancing the five Elements, regulating the divisions of time, the degrees of the sky, and many other things. In Vietnam they are known as Sao Bánh Lái Lớn, or Bắc Đẩu (the North Star), and Sao Bánh Lái Nhỏ, or Nam Tào (the Morning Star). According to legend, the two stars are the immortal clerks who hold the registry of birth and death, in which each person's birth date and death date is recorded on a divine ledger.

Ngô Văn Chiêu was born in an era in which the orderly regulation of the universe, symbolized by these two stars, had come apart. Today, these stars are depicted on the Great Globe on the altar in Tây Ninh, in what some might see as an effort to restore some semblance of this divine order to the present world. In 1867, eleven years before Ngô Văn Chiêu's birth, French armies took control of Saigon and the Mekong Delta, creating the new colony of Cochinchina in his homeland. During his childhood, the French expanded their empire in

Southeast Asia by moving north to take over the imperial court in Huế and then Hanoi. They also moved to annex the neighboring kingdoms of Laos and Cambodia, so that by 1906 there were four protectorates as well as one colony. In the early twentieth century, more than 30,000 French people lived in Saigon, making up about 10 percent of the urban population and living the lifestyle of residents of a French provincial city (Peycam 2012).

The French brought with them their own eclectic ideas about the spirit world. Catholic priests had been the first Frenchmen to settle in Indochina, but by the early twentieth century, French civil servants included many Freemasons, agnostics, Jews, and followers of Theosophy and Spiritism. Developed as a reaction to orthodox Christianity, Theosophy tried to find the roots of spiritual life in an experiential religion that would recapture a pantheistic theology not centered on one specific deity. Theosophists sought common ground between many world religions, without subscribing to the specific doctrines of any particular one. They were often drawn from the educated, professional classes and included many disaffected socialists. Theosophy's decentered notion of divinity was appealing to many who wanted to ground their spiritual drives in the evolution of human consciousness. Since religion was conceived as a science with its own rules and principles, it attracted people committed to a modern teleology of progress and new forms of practice that could be subject to investigation and scientific testing.

The distance established between European colonizers and their Asian subjects during the early twentieth century dovetailed with an interest in new ways of conceiving relations with unseen powers, as a number of authors have recently reminded us.[4] Occultism allowed for a cross-fertilization of language, history, and literature, since it opened up other cosmological views in which the normal distinctions between the colonizer and the colonized blurred, but it managed to do so without actual physical intimacy. French intellectuals who sought out Asian "spiritual masters" gave an ironic twist to the term "master," since they inverted the relations of domination and subordination to explore a new uncolonized space in which more transcendent values were invoked and there was a striving for universal principles.

Spiritualism emerged in the mid-nineteenth century in upstate New York, a region that had already witnessed decades of religious revivalism and social experiments. It developed amidst an atmosphere of optimism, radical ideas, and democratic principles, in which female spirit mediums were often prominent. A Spiritualist circle sometimes started lightheartedly as a form of home entertainment, in which women were encouraged to participate because its meetings were private and respectable. But when meaningful contact with the spirits developed, it became a more serious endeavor (Owen 2004). Anglo-Saxon

Spiritualism crossed the channel to France and was developed there as "Spiritism," under the charismatic leadership of Allan Kardec.

Kardec, and his colleague the French astronomer Camille Flammarion, believed that the methods of empirical science could be used to demonstrate the existence of immortal souls. They fused popular science and religion by developing a doctrine and ritual built around the possibility of communication between the living and the dead, which they claimed was "a science not a religion."[5] Influenced by social Darwinism, they described a universe in which reincarnated human souls cultivated themselves and continued their progress on other planets into an indefinite future. Kardec published manuals for spirit mediums—"The Book of the Spirits" (1857) and "The Spirit Medium" (1861)—that became best sellers in French Indochina, where spirit séances were a popular diversion for the wives and families of French colonial officers.

The interest in French Spiritism grew more intense in 1923, when the transcripts of a series of séances held by the great French writer Victor Hugo (1802–1885) were published, forty years after his death. *Chez Victor Hugo: Les Tables Tournantes de Jersey* recorded a series of conversations that Hugo and his Spiritist circle had with Rousseau, Voltaire, Shakespeare, and even the spirit of Death. Jesus Christ appeared several times and "revised his thinking" about Christianity, predicting that a new world religion would emerge to unite Eastern and Western doctrines, and Victor Hugo would be a prophet for this new vision.[6] The book was reviewed in several French-language newspapers in Saigon, including *L'Echo Annamite,* a paper edited by Vietnamese writers, several of whom eventually became Caodaists (Smith 1969; Goscha 2009).

The lively, experimental forms of table tipping that appealed to Victor Hugo and his circle in the mid nineteenth century were quite different from the literary forms of spirit writing séances that had been practiced in the Chinese tradition for centuries. This male-dominated tradition emphasized the divine selection of mediums who did not seek out the practice as a diversion but had it imposed upon them as a moral duty (Clart 2003). Spirit writing produced "wisdom texts" containing moral teachings used by participants as part of a disciplined process of self-cultivation. While its séances were also intimate (usually four to twelve participants) they were more hierarchically structured. An "altar master" supervised the procedure, one or two mediums held the basket carved out of peach wood with a phoenix or dragon head, and another person served as the scribe. The disciples saw themselves as the "students" of the gods, who taught them how to perfect themselves so that they, too, could ultimately become gods, escaping the human cycle of reincarnation to live on in heaven and perhaps even hold an office in the celestial hierarchy.

The séance that I witnessed in California was conducted within the Sino-Vietnamese tradition of spirit writing but was also infused with some of Caodaism's eclectic innovations. It included spirit messages in two languages, had references to more universal values, and embraced a wider range of spiritual options. Caodaists are proud of their "constantly expanding theology," which can embrace many new gods and deities, but even this seems to have a precedent in Chinese spirit writing. The huge and varied Chinese pantheon is constantly added to when the virtuous disciples of the spirit writing halls die, since new celestial offices must be created to reward them for having "realized the Way." The ranks of gods and saints are also swollen by the possibility of elevating the status of one's ancestors after their deaths, since praying for them can transfer merit to allow them to be released from purgatory. Donating money to build a new temple is the most common way of achieving this goal (Clart 2003). In Caodaism, as in the older Chinese spirit-writing tradition, the spirit medium must show his purity and sincerity for the gods to agree to speak through his body, and his selfish desires should not disturb their messages.

The World That Produced Ngô Văn Chiêu

Ngô Văn Chiêu's grandfather had served as a mandarin at the imperial court at Huế, but fled to the South just after the French took over. Ngô Văn Chiêu came from a family where literacy, and especially knowledge of the Confucian classics, was prized. In Huế, the rhythms of state-sponsored ceremonials, examinations, and official protocols regulated daily life, and the ideals of harmony and equanimity were valued. His father was displaced by the French conquest to live in the wilder, more unruly Mekong Delta, populated by Vietnamese pioneers moving into areas once occupied by the Khmer people. Conditions there were more rugged and dangerous. Many Chinese refugees fleeing after the fall of the Ming dynasty settled in Chợ Lớn, a trading center next to Saigon that eventually merged into a single metropolitan area. It was here, in what today is called "Saigon's Chinatown," that Ngô Văn Chiêu was born in 1878, in an ethnically diverse, urban setting, in which groups of Vietnamese and Chinese lived side by side with Cambodians, Indians, Malays, and Chinese, under the rule of Europeans clustered in the most expensive and well-maintained districts along the Saigon River.

At the age of six, Ngô Văn Chiêu was sent to live with his paternal aunt in the city of Mỹ Tho in the center of the Mekong Delta. She was married to a Chinese herbalist and their home contained an altar to the Chinese god of war,

Figure 1.2. Ngô Văn Chiêu
"spoke to the Master in Phú
Quốc," portrait in Cần Thơ

Quan Công, who was worshipped every day with an offering of incense and a recitation of a set of Taoist verses to teach moral lessons, the *Minh Thánh Kinh*.[7] While his parents worked in Hanoi, Ngô Văn Chiêu learned to recite lines from Chinese classics. He probably witnessed the practice of phoenix writing and divination in this childhood home, and certainly absorbed a hybrid Sino-Vietnamese cultural heritage that was to be characteristic of esoteric Caodaism (Huệ Khải 2008d).

He studied at the prestigious French Lycée Chasseloup Laubat, where he was one of a small minority of Indochinese students mixed in with French students following the standard French curriculum. After graduating in 1899, he received a position as a secretary at the Saigon Immigration Office. His parents returned to the city to live with him, and he married and fathered nine children, two of whom died as infants (Oliver 1976, 53). In 1909, he was moved twenty-nine miles west to Tân An, where he passed his civil service examinations and was appointed district chief.

Ngô Văn Chiêu first attended séances in Saigon in 1902, seeking medicine for his ailing mother at a Chinese temple in Thủ Dầu Một. She recovered briefly, then became more seriously ill in 1917. Seeking some way to extend her life, or least relieve her pain, he visited the Hiệp Minh Pagoda (Enlightened Union Pagoda) in Cần Thơ, a "three-in-one" temple uniting Buddhism, Taoism, and Confucianism. In the 1920s, this temple was a center for spirit séances and had already published a long séance message received from Lao Tzu.[8] People gathered around the *dàn tiên,* or "the platform of the immortals," in the Taoist tradition of literary communication with the afterworld. Particular spirits would descend to move a pen fitted into the phoenix-carved head of a hollow rattan basket.

I visited the temple in 2005 and was able to see and photograph the table and phoenix basket used by Ngô Văn Chiêu, which were still stored there. Temple records describe an immortal spirit descending on the spirit pen (*cơ bút*) to offer three prescriptions for his mother, and telling Ngô Văn Chiêu that he would be prepared to accept him as a disciple. Ngô Văn Chiêu agreed and prepared the medicine at home. The first batch was very bitter, and his mother showed no improvement. Then he remembered that he had neglected some of the instructions. After preparing the second batch, he stepped outside and raised the bowl to his forehead, praying to this spirit for his mother's recovery. The second time she drank the medicine, she said it tasted sweet, and after the third time, she recovered completely. Ngô Văn Chiêu returned to Cần Thơ to thank the divinity and to ask to be initiated as a disciple.[9]

In 1919, Ngô Văn Chiêu returned to the Hiệp Minh Pagoda when his mother once again became sick. But this time the spirit messages received from the phoenix basket gave him no prescription, only a prayer to say to guide her soul. He also returned to his birthplace in Chợ Lớn, to the Thủ Dầu Một Temple, but he was told there was nothing to do. His mother died later that year. The pathway that Ngô Văn Chiêu had followed to seek help for her had led him deeply into the practice of self-cultivation linked to the cult of immortality (*tu tiên*).

Ngô Văn Chiêu's interest in these societies was motivated by their reputation for divination and the production of spirit messages using methods such as astrology, chiromancy, and physiognomy. The spirit séances he participated in involved at least four participants—one to write down talismanic magic symbols to protect evil spirits from entering; one to hold the phoenix basket, designated as the spirit medium (*đồng tử*); and one to watch the movement of the phoenix basket and dictate the words traced in the air to a fourth person, who would write them down. As Ngô Văn Chiêu became more experienced in the practice, he came to serve as either the séance master (writing the talismans) or the reader (who had the crucial role of interpreting the movements of the basket). Ngô Văn Chiêu's presence in a séance was said to produce a high level of spirit communication, even in cases where spirit contact had previously been hard to achieve (Oliver 1976, 34; Đồng Tân 1967, 2006).

Ngô Văn Chiêu's Vision of the Left Eye in the Sky

Ngô Văn Chiêu first heard the name Đức Cao Đài (literally, The Master of the Highest Tower) in 1920 in a séance at his home in Hà Tiên, when a very erudite spirit spoke to him but refused to identify himself. The spirit told him: "I cannot reveal myself until you are ready. Try to guess who I am." He was instructed to follow a fully vegetarian diet to purify himself and prepare for an important vision.

On the first day of the lunar year (February 8, 1921), a female immortal called Ngô Kim Liên made contact with Ngô Văn Chiêu and gave him two poems. He was asked by this immortal to choose a sacred symbol for his practice. He suggested a cross, since the *Taoist Book of Changes* says "one yin and one yang are called the Tao," and this was represented with a horizontal stroke for the yin and vertical one for the yang. The immortal spirit said this symbol was in use by Christians, so he would need to find something else. This advice is the first of many times that future Caodai leaders are recorded to have wanted to use a European symbol or method and been told to seek out an Asian one instead.

Ngô Văn Chiêu was appointed as the district head of Phú Quốc, a small island off the southwest coast that is also the westernmost part of Vietnam. On April 20, 1921, he was sitting in his hammock in the town of Dương Đông looking west across the sea of Siam when he was suddenly flooded with an intense luminosity. He saw a large, lifelike left eye, surrounded by radiant beams of sunlight, hanging in the sky at the same time as the moons and stars. The light was blinding, so he hid his eyes in his hands. It remained before him, blazing brightly, and terrified him. He prayed to the immortals to make the eye disappear, promising to worship it later if the immortals responded to his request. It gradually faded away, but appeared again later a few days afterward. The second time, he also had a vision of the islands of the Buddhist western Paradise, which lay just at the edge of the horizon. In spirit séances, he had heard a prayer used to evoke spirits that began: "The spirit pen from the highest tower writes sacred words," and so he came to recognize that this prayer was linked to his vision.[10]

After he had the vision of the eye, Ngô Văn Chiêu began holding regular séances at Quang Âm Tự Pagoda.[11] A very young boy named Lê Văn Ngưng became his most important spirit medium. Ngưng had been totally vegetarian for three years and was only nine or ten when he started receiving messages, exemplifying the purity and innocence needed for the task. No records survive of these early séances with Ngưng as a medium, but what evidence we do have suggests that they followed the model of Sino-Vietnamese redemptive societies.

From 1921–1924, Ngô Văn Chiêu meditated and cultivated his own spiritual development. He lived separately from his family and seems to have taken a vow of celibacy to intensify his practice. In 1924, as he prepared to travel back to Saigon, he was told that his spiritual master was happy with his progress and offered this prophecy: "In the future you will ride a golden dragon back to the origin" (Huệ Nhân, 2005, 84).

In 1925, the immortal spirit allowed him to introduce a few others to his new practice. Four younger Spiritists received spiritual instructions to seek out Ngô Văn Chiêu, since they had heard that he had made contact with the same powerful spirit they had contacted. He was about a generation older than they were, so he was given the senior position, writing out the talismans to protect the séance space, while two younger mediums held the phoenix basket, with the wife of one of them (Hương Hiếu) writing out the messages and keeping a detailed journal of all that transpired.[12]

On December 24, 1925, a midnight séance spelled out the names of the twelve original disciples, sometimes also referred to as the "apostles,"[13] and recognized them as the first founders of a new religion. For three months, the group met weekly at Ngô Văn Chiêu's home. In April, a spirit message instructed Hương Hiếu to sew a special ceremonial robe for the "Pope" (Giáo Tông), designated as Ngô Văn Chiêu. Shocking his followers, he decided to decline this position. He did not state a reason for this decision. There has been a lot of speculation about why he did so, and later séances have asked his spirit to explain his actions. Two of the séance texts I have found (one from 1971 and one from 1980) give roughly the same response: "I was afraid that I had not yet reached a high enough stage of my own spiritual cultivation, so I dared not accept the office of the Pope yet. I did not realize how long I would have on this earth" (Đỗ Vạn Lý 1989, 119; Huệ Khải 2008c, 82). Other séances suggested that in 1920 Ngô Văn Chiêu received secret messages telling him to start a twelve-year program of ascetic meditation, and so he felt that the time was not yet right for him to take part in a mass movement.

Ngô Văn Chiêu returned to practice privately with a few select disciples. He did not even attend the official declaration of Caodaism in November 1926. He went on two pilgrimages to Mount Bokor in Cambodia, since he apparently had planned to die there. But his followers persuaded him to return to the Chiêu Minh Temple in Cần Thơ, where he lived a hermit's life in a simple thatched hut. On April 18, 1932, he began a trip to see his family in Tân An. While he was riding a ferry across the Mekong ("the river of nine dragons" in Vietnamese) he passed away, confirming the prophecy he had received in 1924 (Oliver 1976; Smith 1970a; Huệ Khải 2008c, 82). His left eye was wide open and startled his disciples. They later received a séance message confirming that an open left eye was a sign of transcendence: from that day on, those Chiếu Minh disciples who die with opened left eyes are known to have been guided directly into the blinding light by the Supreme Being, and their spirits will remain in heaven, never needing to reincarnate again on this earth.[14]

Ngô Văn Chiêu: The "Invisible" Founder

All histories of Caodaism begin with Ngô Văn Chiêu's vision, but it is paradoxically also one of the moments most charged with ambivalence and questions: Western interpreters ask how a quiet and unassuming man could become the first member of the largest mass movement in colonial Cochinchina. Where did the symbol of the Left Eye come from, and what did it mean? Why did Ngô Văn Chiêu initially suggest a cross? Is it related to the symbol of the intersection of yin and yang, or perhaps the Chinese number ten, which also appears on all altars in the Chiếu Minh tradition? Exoteric Caodaism (Phần Phổ Độ) is visually expressed through the ascending levels of the Nine Level Palace (Cửu Trùng Đài). Some people have suggested that the "ten" on the Chiếu Minh altar represents a final, highest stage, which goes further than the nine stages of exoteric Caodaism and is only accessible through the esoteric pathway.

Caodaists ask themselves why the Jade Emperor chose to reveal himself first to an ascetic mandarin who had no taste for mass movements. While he had a reputation for moral purity and mystical power, the "first disciple" was not a leader of men but a seeker of enlightenment, who would eventually turn away from the huge spiritual movement that he had initiated. His refusal to accept the office of Pope, even though God had specifically requested that he assume the office, has puzzled Caodaists for generations. His legacy is therefore both inspiring and mysterious, a leader who served as an example but not as a participant, a man reputed to have great spiritual powers who is best known for having been reluctant to wield them in public.

Ngô Văn Chiêu's legacy is often neglected in English- and French-language histories, since the French agents of the secret police wrote very disparaging accounts of his life and influence. Focused mainly on Caodaism's political ambitions, they saw him as "naïve" and "gullible," easily pushed aside by the more activist faction eventually led by Phạm Công Tắc. The 1931 report concerning "Phủ Chiêu" (referring to him by his title as district head of Phú Quốc) is an example:

> Since 1902, Chiêu devoted himself to various Taoist delusions. Soft-spoken, timid, and submissive, he moved without attracting much notice through a civil service career because of his goodwill and meritorious conduct, but his mental limitations, his weakness, and his neurosis made him prey to charlatanism. He was deeply impressed by a session of table tipping at Thủ Dầu Một [This was probably phoenix writing, not table tipping]. To be so easily in contact with spirits, whom he often addressed during sleepless evenings devoted to the supernatural, led him to ask them to provide the key to his problems and to the mysteries of life, and he became stunned and captivated. Appointed as the administrative director of Phú Quốc, he repeated the séances that he had witnessed using young boys as mediums. His progress was so quick that his spirit sailed each day more to mix the real with the imaginary, unconscious memories of his various readings joined to sensory hallucinations. We must add right away that this state of mental imbalance only got worse with time. Today, Phủ Chiêu, incapable of assuming any responsible position, is able to support his family by working in the Government's Second Bureau, where he carries out a menial job (*une besogne subalterne*) with the automatism of an inoffensive paranoiac. (Lalaurette and Vilmont 1931)

In spite of this ironic dismissal by his subordinates, the Resident governor of Cochinchina, Aristide Le Fol, seems to have taken a greater interest. He sent a message to Ngô Văn Chiêu, asking him if he could come to his home to take part in a séance, so that he could see what all the commotion was about. Ngô Văn Chiêu agreed, and (apparently under cover of secrecy) Le Fol and his wife were instructed to sit before the altar and ask the spirits whatever question they had. They asked what news would come to them from Europe and were told that there would soon be a death in the family. This news was confirmed two weeks later, when a close relative in Paris did die.[15]

Le Fol seems to have been among the many people in the French colonies who were curious about Spiritism and wanted to have their own experience of its effects. Caodai historians interpreted the results of this séance as making the French governor better disposed toward the new religion, since he answered the 1926 declaration with a polite but noncommittal response (Bùi and Beck 2000; Đỗ Văn Lý 1989). The story cannot be confirmed in French sources, but if Le Fol did attend an early séance, then he was merely the first of a great many other French men and women who were at times invited to do so.

Le Fol's curiosity provided the precedent for my attending and participating in a séance in the Los Angeles area of California in 2005. The spirit medium and reader discussed their interpretations of this event when they agreed to invite me to join them in front of the phoenix basket, and they patterned their own actions on those of the "first disciple."

Ngô Văn Chiêu models one form of religious leadership, which fits the paradigm of the Taoist master and has prevailed in the esoteric tradition of Caodaism. In the published scholarship on this era, this paradigm has been largely overshadowed by the more flamboyant and syncretistic leadership of his successor, Phạm Công Tắc, who served as the head spirit medium and chief administrator in Tây Ninh. But Ngô Văn Chiêu's influence has been important since its inception, and his legacy remains important for many today. It is notable, however, that there is no image or statue of Ngô Văn Chiêu in Tây Ninh (although there are life-size statues of the three younger spirit mediums, Tắc, Cư, and Sang). It could be argued that he is represented through the ubiquitous images of his vision—the left eye hovering in the sky with both the rising sun and the moon and stars visible. But perhaps his very invisibility is the point: Ngô Văn Chiêu practiced forms of self-purification and self-cultivation that led him away from worldly concerns and so his kingdom is not of this world.

The Socialist Republic of Vietnam's policy of "nationalizing" religious property destroyed one of the most sacred sites of Caodaism: the area outside the district office in Phú Quốc where Ngô Văn Chiêu had his first vision. In the 1950s, a group of Ngô Văn Chiêu's disciples carved a memorial stone that was erected there, with text in both English and Vietnamese, explaining that this was where the Left Eye of God first appeared to a human being. It became a site of pilgrimage and meditation for Caodaists of all denominations for the quarter century that the Saigon Republic remained in power, since it was a policy of the secular government to allow all religions to flourish. After the Communist victory, however, the memorial tablet was removed. It is now stored behind the Buddhist temple where Ngô Văn Chiêu held séances with his young boy medium Ngưng. The simple colonial office was torn down and replaced by a two-story stucco office building. The sacred site was remodeled to become a parking lot for the local office of the People's Committee. When I visited the Caodaist community on Phú Quốc, they took me to the beautiful seashore where Ngô Văn Chiêu had a vision of the "islands of the western Paradise," but noted that the place where he sat was now "defiled by the boots of Communist Party members."

"Secretaries of the Invisible": Christmas Revelations 1925

Now we will turn to another set of Spiritists who were to vastly increase the visibility of spirit mediumship on the national stage. They followed a quite different pathway to make contact with Cao Đài, one grounded in recent French fashions for "table tipping" and Allan Kardec-inspired "Spiritism" rather than ancient Chinese tradition.

On Christmas Eve 1925, four people gathered in a small apartment in Saigon where they had been holding spirit séances for some time. As the bells in the churches of the city began to sound, they darkened the lights, lit incense sticks, and bowed in front of an altar they had erected to a particularly witty, erudite, and philosophical spirit, who had instructed them to call him by the first three letters of the Romanized Vietnamese alphabet (A Ă Â). They prepared themselves for a message from this spirit, who was soon to reveal his true identity.

Vietnam has long had a cultural reverence for the written word, and a sense that literary traditions should serve as a moral guide to inspire not only individual creativity but also worldly leadership. The four people gathered in the darkened room were all educated in French-language schools, and they were experimenting with what they perceived as "new technologies for contacting the invisible ones." Inspired by reading Victor Hugo's recently published séance transcripts, as well as by Kardec and Flammarion, they set out to hold séances using the same method Hugo used on the island of Jersey. Their goals in doing so were initially to seek female muses who would help them to compose new verses, but also to divine the future of their people and see whether they would remain under French colonial rule.

The experimentation with table turning began as a game, but it was also motivated by a spiritual search: Cao Hoài Sang described their initial attraction to Spiritism this way: "Being poetic, and holding deep in our hearts a resentment of living in a conquered nation, we indulged in the pleasure of evoking spirits, using these devices to raise questions about the country's future and to compose and exchange poetry as a pastime" (Hương Hiếu 1997, 1:6).

Sang was a twenty-four-year-old clerk in the customs department, as was a friend of his from the office, Phạm Công Tắc, an intense and literary young man of thirty-two. They were joined by Sang's uncle, Cao Quỳnh Cư, then thirty-eight, who worked in the railway office in Saigon, and his wife, Hương Hiếu. Unlike Ngô Văn Chiêu, these early Saigon Spiritists had not studied Chinese methods of spirit mediumship beforehand and were not even vegetarians when they began their quest. Sang, Cư, and Hiếu followed the traditional family cult of ancestor worship, but Tắc had been baptized as a Catholic. The most literary and most skeptical of the Saigon Spiritists, Tắc had long been interested in journalism and nationalist politics.

As a student, Phạm Công Tắc had wanted to follow the advice of nationalist activist Phan Bội Châu to "travel east" and study in Japan, but his plans were discovered by the French secret police, and he was expelled from his prestigious French high school and forced to hide near his ancestral home in Tây Ninh (Trần Thu Dung 1996; Trần Mỹ-Vân 2000, 4). Because of his excellent French, he managed to get a modest position first as a waiter, then as a government clerk in Saigon, but lost that position as well when his involvement in illicit activities was discovered. For some years he was transferred to Qui Nhơn, a remote part of central Vietnam. He wrote for several newspapers published in French that were critical of the colonial government (*La Voix Libre, La Cloche Felée*) and developed an intense and forceful personality that was to have a major impact. Phạm Công Tắc was to become the most important emissary prophet of Caodaism, and also its most charismatic and controversial public figure.

In the table tipping method, the spirits would tap out numbers corresponding to letters in the alphabet, and from these raps messages were received. Hương Hiếu kept a full transcript of everything that happened. The table began to shake when they first sat down with their hands resting on its surface. Sensing that they were about to discover something unexpected, these four people soon committed themselves to pursuing this new technology of communication.

Their first contact with a spirit occurred shortly after midnight on July 25, 1925, when they received this poem:[16]

> When I left this world I was fifty years old,
> And you were only ten.
> You should remember with perseverance my counsels
> To try to promote love in your life.
> I have been teasing you sometimes during your dreams,
> But now forever, I am free in the world of the immortals.
> I am still sorry for my gentle wife, old and weak,
> These are just some words for our meeting today!

Cao Quỳnh Cư realized, with tears in his eyes, that the spirit speaking was his father, who had died twenty-five years before. Phạm Công Tắc was doubtful, since he had no faith or belief at all in spirits. He had been raised Catholic, and his many years in French schools had made him suspicious of anything that smelled of magic or sorcery. But he was willing to go along with it as a game, an amusing pastime that had engrossed many other young people in both Europe and Asia. Cao Quỳnh Cư invited the spirit to return the following night for him to show his devotion. The spirit knocked twice on the floor as a sign of agreement. A special meal was prepared for him, and his son and great nephew were grateful to have this message.

The next spirit to contact them, on July 30, 1925, was a young girl who wrote a poignant poem about her loneliness in the spirit world:

To whom may I confide my heart?

I have left this world young wasting all my talent and beauty!

I thought I would marry a noble gentleman,

But it was my fate to die early instead.

I could not repay my parents for raising me,

I could not keep my marriage promise either,

I carry the weight of these feelings on my shoulders,

To whom may I confide my heart?

Moved by her words, they questioned her about her name and her schooling. The next day, they looked in cemetery at Chợ Lớn, and found that there was a local girl named Vương Thị Lễ who had died young, as she said. Cao Quỳnh Cư wrote a poem replying to hers and expressing sympathy for her plight. They continued to exchange messages with her, eventually adopting her as a spiritual young sister.

Then, on August 25, 1925, she told them another spirit was coming, who presented them with a riddle:[17]

Hot pepper, pepper so hot, the more you think of it, the hotter it is

Salt, salt that is so strong, its flavor lasts for over three years, so long

Because I have no money to travel, I came to visit you

I don't want to have to beg for leftovers, signed A Ă Â.

Phạm Công Tắc was disturbed by the riddle, and did not want to continue. Cao Quỳnh Cư insisted this spirit was very special and asked how old he was. The spirit began knocking and knocking for so long that none of them could count how many raps had passed. Tắc wanted to drop the game, saying he could not take this answer seriously, but he asked the spirit a final question: "Where do you live?" The spirit answered:

I am poor, so poor that I have nothing but my body,

And a white lotus for my shelter.

My house is the dark blue cloud,

My form of transportation is a white crane.

I arrange humanity to establish the Tao,

And bless my disciples to build love.

When the earth rises and the sky changes

Then Buddhas, Immortals, and Saints will come to earth

This poem was their first indication that this spirit was in fact a much more evolved, philosophical spirit who would teach them many things. His first contacts with them were mysterious and frustrating. Asked to identify himself, he rapped out the first letters of the Romanized Vietnamese alphabet. Phạm Công Tắc lost his patience and thought they should stop trying to speak to such a strange spirit. A Ă Â told them: "Don't ask me any personal questions, but I can teach you the Tao." He then showed a great knowledge of Chinese literary classics and such lyrical grace that they agreed to serve him.

A few days later, the spirit of A Ă Â told them to prepare a banquet table to receive the spirits of nine female Immortals and the Mother Goddess herself. The banquet had to be vegetarian, and it had to take place on the full moon of the eighth lunar month—the time of the mid-Autumn Festival (Tết Trung Thu) in September 1925.

Under his instructions, preparations were made for an elaborate feast to receive the Mother Goddess (Diêu Trì Kim Mẫu) and the nine female Immortals of the Jaspar Pond Palace. On the fifteenth day of the eighth month of the year of the Buffalo (Ất Sửu), at Cao Quỳnh Cư's residence at 134 Bourdais, Saigon, they set up an altar with beautiful and fragrant flowers in the middle of the house. They burned incense all day long, wore the long flowing white tunics and pants of the national costume, and knelt in front of the altar to pray to the Mother Goddess and the nine female Immortals. After the prayers, Hương Hiếu served cooked foods, including a wide range of delicious cakes and pastries, on the altar and on the table. Then they held a séance to invite the Mother Goddess herself and the nine female Immortals to come and exchange poems with them.

The elaborate table was decorated with flowers, incense, and sweets and delicacies of all kinds, and the four members of the séance group gathered around it. Each member of the Spiritist group made up a gallant, eloquent poem that he would offer to one of the spirit ladies, and she would answer in kind.

This banquet established a ritual precedent, since it is repeated each year in all Caodai temples around the world (as Lễ Hội Đức Phật Mẫu, the festival of the Mother Goddess). Female dignitaries preside over these rituals, organizing them and serving as the prime ritual intermediaries, following in the footsteps of Hương Hiếu. The poems presented by each of the nine female Immortals are sung, and young female disciples attend these Immortals by serving them tea and beautifully designed cakes and pastries.

The worship of the Mother Goddess was consistent with East Asian popular religion, and this particular festival was similar to others held at the same time to honor popular Vietnamese female spirits. But the prolonged dialogue with such an articulate, learned spirit was new. Soon, a number of curious outsiders started to attend their séances to test the powers of this new spirit. One was a famous poet of the time, Nguyễn Trung Hậu, who doubted that any spirit could match his cleverness with words. Although he arrived anonymously, the first poem received from A Ă Â (on November 14, 1925) spelled out his secret pen name, Thuần Đức, and gave him a message that showed he had been recognized:

Your talent with your fine writing and kind virtue

Made you famous in the poetry society.

If you want to be known as a hero of the country

You have to wait for the right time.

Startled, the poet devised a challenge in the popular verse form of parallel sentences: he wrote one line, which had to be exactly matched, noun for noun and verb for verb, with another in the same format. The first line read

Ngồi yên ngựa đừng bỏ con nghé   Riding on the horse's saddle, don't crawl (cow) dear child (baby buffalo).

The spirit A Ă Â responded immediately, with the solution to the riddle:

Cởi lưng trâu chớ khi thằng tê   Riding on the back of buffalo, don't tease (monkey) that lad (rhinoceros).

The sense of each phrase depended on the puns hidden in words that had double meanings. The famous poet became convinced of the divinity of the spirit A Ă Â through a poetry contest, a set of word games or *jeu d'esprit* that showed that A Ă Â was in fact a supreme poet, a master wordsmith.

The playful, entertaining tenor of these evenings spent with the spirit A Ă Â in the early months was soon to change, as his messages became more serious. But it is worth noting that many of these literary exercises were similar to tests required of candidates for advanced degrees under the Confucian system of competitive examinations. The French had disbanded these examinations in their efforts to separate the Vietnamese from Chinese cultural influences and move away from the study of Chinese literature and characters to reading in the vernacular, written with the Romanized phonetic alphabet *quốc ngữ*. The use of these tests was not only a game, but a way of testing the authority of the speaker, his cultural competence, and understanding of literature and philosophical nuances.

Many of the spirit messages received from A Ă Â reflected on the troubled social relations of colonial society. A Buddhist came to ask the spirit how to tell what is true and what is false. The spirit gave him a poem:

Orchids often grow among wild flowers

To recognize them one must get close and smell their fragrance.

A kind and gentle person living among the tyrants,

Might resemble them despite his purity of heart.

A second poem on the same subject hinted at the possible divinity of A Ă Â:

When there is right, there should be wrong naturally.

It's difficult to distinguish between them.

Secular persons wanting to become an Immortal or Buddha

They have to come to Me.

From European Spiritism to Asian Phoenix Writing

Once a number of people had become convinced of his spiritual wisdom, A Ă Â advised them to use another method—the *ngọc cơ,* or phoenix-headed writing instrument, long used in Taoist séances, to make their conversations easier.

Instead of waiting for the table to rap out the number of each letter, the phoenix basket, held by two mediums and consecrated with prayers and incense, could trace the response of the spirits in the air. Responses could be received much more quickly with this method, and their accuracy checked by reading them back to the medium. A similar basket was used by European Spiritists like Allan Kardec, who called it the *corbeille à bec* ("bird-beaked basket"), often with a pencil fitted into the bird's head to trace letters in sand or write on a piece of paper. The choice of this form of spirit communication—which was to become and remains the preferred form of Caodai séances—marked the *intersection* of centuries of Asian occult practices with a modern, twentieth-century technique that was all the rage in Paris in the 1920s.

On January 6, 1926, the use of the basket was explained in this séance message:

> The spirit is your second body. It is very difficult for the spirit of a human being to transcend the physical body. The spirits of Saints, Immortals, and Buddha are very marvelous and immortal. The spirit of an enlightened person may transcend the body and even travel the universe. Only the spirit may approach Me. When the basket with a beak is used in Spiritism, if the person is unconscious, the spirit may then leave the physical body, hear My instructions, and have the body transcribe the messages. If the interpreter's reading is incorrect, the medium's spirit will not agree with the interpretation. They will be obliged to write again. In the other form of spiritual contact known as automatic writing, or inspired writing, I will come to you and make your spirit unstable for a while. During that time, your spirit will be able to listen to Me. Your hand will obey and write. In this form of spiritual contact, I cooperate with you so that you can reach Universal Truths. (*Thánh Ngôn Hiệp Tuyển* [Official selection of spirit messages])

The phoenix basket has to be carefully constructed and consecrated with a particular ritual, so the young Spiritists did not try to build their own. They turned, instead, to a famous center for divination in the Sino-Vietnamese style: the temple of Minh Lý Đạo, headed by Âu Kiệt Lâm, a half-Chinese herbalist who had already used this particular instrument to receive a series of spirit messages.

Âu Kiệt Lâm was a spirit medium who established Minh Lý Đạo just two years earlier, in 1924. He received a séance message telling him to form a strict new ascetic group, whose members would all practice full vegetarianism, follow an exacting schedule of daily meditation, and go on quarterly retreats to seek spiritual guidance through séances. Later called the "Caodaists in black" (see

Chapter 5), Minh Lý disciples remained important counterparts to the "Cao-daists in white," the two groups appearing as the yin-yang polarities of the same period of revelation, one living in the shadows and remaining small, the other stepping into the sunlight and expanding at great speed (Jammes 2010, 358; Smith 1970a).

The move from table tipping to the phoenix basket was a significant one, since it inscribed the agency of mediumship in Caodaism in a Sino-Vietnamese tradition, rather than a European one. I call the European inspired forms of communication "Spiritism," but consider the séances part of the Asian tradition of spirit mediumship.[18] Conversations with Caodai mediums today suggest that the phoenix basket is useful for a period of apprenticeship. Holding it puts the medium in contact with a long tradition of communicating with the spirits, but after a certain point it can be dispensed with.

This also suggests a hierarchy of levels of spiritual attainment that we also see in the five levels of the pantheon: at the highest level, one can have "conversations with God" through meditation, with no use of devices or intermediaries. This is the level of the highest Buddha and his Bodhisattvas (Đạo Phật). At the second-highest level, one needs to contact the immortals with certain long-respected devices that serve to focus attention and provide a corporeal expression (the shaking of the basket, its movements as it "flies" in the hands of the medium or mediums). These are Taoist techniques associated with the "way of the immortals" (Đạo Tiên). At the third-highest level, we find the more "primitive" form of European Spiritism, such as table tipping, which is very slow in producing messages. It was used by Victor Hugo, who still identified himself as a sort of renegade Christian (Đạo Thánh). Although they are all familiar with its historical role in the genesis of Caodaism, I have not heard of any contemporary Caodai mediums who still practice table tipping. At the level of local spirits (Đạo Thần), prayers and offerings are made without a specific technology for communicating with the spirits, as is also true for the level of ancestor worship and filial piety (Đạo Nhơn).

The first séance to use the phoenix basket was held on December 16, 1925, the first day of the eleventh lunar month. The séance opened with the mention of a new divinity that no one had ever heard speak:

Jade Emperor or Cao Đài Tiên Ông Đại Bồ Tát Ma Ha Tát

Teaching the Tao to the lands of the South

Heaven is striking the bell like thunder

To guide all humanity of this world to self-realization

The true Tao is now open for the benefit of a thousand generations
For the unity of all religions on this third revelation.

When the disciples asked for more explanation, A Ă Â told them that God had come to unite Confucianism, Taoism, and Buddhism together and to offer new teachings.

Finally, shortly after midnight on Christmas morning, the tantalizing but mysterious spirit A Ă Â announced to his followers that he was the Jade Emperor and Supreme God, who came to them with the name Cao Đài.

> Rejoice this day, it is the anniversary of My coming to teach the Tao in the West. Your allegiance and respect bring much satisfaction. This house will be abundantly blessed. You will see more miracles, which will lead you to further belief. For some times I have used the symbol A Ă Â to lead you to the religious life. Soon you must found a novel faith under My instruction. . . .

For ten thousand generations, I have been holding the power,

If you would please cultivate self, you will be blessed.

The miraculous Tao is spread all over the earth.

Your names will be remembered forever.

Jade Emperor Cao Đài

That same evening, another important spirit revealed his identity—the eighth-century Chinese lyrical poet Li Bái, known in Vietnam as Lý Thái Bạch, who had written of nature and the intoxicating powers of the imagination. He sent this poem:

I came to the earth in the Tang dynasty

I did not care about honors and positions, but leisure.

People remembered my love of wine and my hundreds of poems

I have remained an Immortal for thousands of generations.

With a gourd of wine, I drank for days and nights,

Filling my bag full of poems.

I dreamed of the immortal realm when I moved my pen

To describe people's sentiments toward the country.

The Supreme Being announced that he made this announcement on Christmas morning because he was coming to "the East" on the anniversary of his coming to "the West" (as Jesus). This time, he would "teach religion in the southern quarter" (*giáo đạo Nam-Phương*)—establish an Asian basis for proselytizing a modern, monotheistic religion, one that would group together the teachings of the great philosophers of the East and the West.

In later séances, Cao Đài explained that he had sent his messengers earlier under many different names. In the era of the first revelation, he sent Dipankara Buddha and the Taoist master Lão Quân as well as the Chinese Emperor Phục Hy. This was also the era of Old Testament Jehovah who addressed Moses on Mount Sinai. In the second era of revelation, he sent the historical Buddha Sakyamuni, Lao Tzu, Confucius, and Jesus, his own son, to preach to humanity. But each time their original messages had been corrupted and transformed so they were hardly recognizable. Finally, at the dawn of a new third period of revelations, he decided he had to speak more directly to humanity, without trusting the scepter to the hands of any one man.

The possibility of a new global faith, he said, emerged along with improved technology of communication and the possibility of travel from East to West:

> Formerly, people lacked transportation and therefore did not know each other. I then founded at different epochs and in different areas, five branches of the way: The way of sages, the way of local spirits, the way of saints, the way of Immortals, and the way of Buddha, each based on the customs of its respective race. In present days, transportation has been improved and people have come to know each other better but do not live in harmony because of the multiplicity of religions. That is why I have decided to unite all of the religions back into one, to return them to their primordial unity.

The spirit of the Jade Emperor directed that the five smaller pathways of the Great Way should be represented on Caodai altars as five levels of spiritual attainment. They correspond to the stages of mystical development Ngô Văn Chiêu was familiar with but are articulated in a more global language: The way of the sages (*Đạo Nhơn*), for instance, also translated as "Asian humanism," corresponds to Confucian teachings about ethics and citizenship. The way of consecrated local spirits (*Đạo Thánh*) refers to the veneration of heroes and village guardian spirits, and was translated into French as the "culte des genies."[19] The way of saints (*Đạo Thánh*) refers both to East Asian saints like the Vietnamese national hero Trần Hưng Đạo and the saints of the Catholic and Muslim traditions. The way of immortals (*Đạo Tiên*) includes the Taoist immortals but also Christian archangels. The way of Buddha (Đạo Phật) marks the transcendence of fully enlightened beings, who are finally united with God.

Listening to New Masters: Analysis of the Séance Texts

The transcribed texts of these early séance texts provide us with an intimate window onto the formation of Caodai practices. The blending of literary and spiritual aspirations, the many verbal tricks and puns, all suggest that the central question for evaluating spirit séances was determining the correct identity of the spirit source. From a Caodaist perspective, the spirit of Cao Đài was playing with these young Spiritists for months, preparing them for revelations that would have been too overwhelming at the beginning of their exchanges. From an outsider's perspective, these séance texts could be said to reveal a process of self-conversion, in which the participants came to be convinced that they were part of a much larger event, whose true meaning they would only gradually be permitted to discover.

The negotiation of this identification was a group process, and one that eventually came to include Ngô Văn Chiêu, after news of his vision of the Left Eye spread to Saigon. The texts also document the initial skepticism and secular inclinations of Phạm Công Tắc, who was to emerge as the most prominent Caodai leader of the twentieth century. They show uncertainty and the testing of both the spirits and of each other as the three active Spiritists struggled to make sense of a new and uncharted spiritual world.

The first spirits to make contact with them responded to very personal longings. Many people who have suffered the loss of a family member cannot accept the extinction of the self at death or an eternal separation from loved ones. Cao Quỳnh Cư's reconciliation with the spirit of his dead father fits that pattern. The vulnerable spirit of a young girl, dead before she could marry, reaches out to them next, and she can be integrated into their world as a "younger sister." Caodaists who have discussed these séances with me have said that the Supreme Being decided to start with nonthreatening spirits, who would appear close to the everyday lives of these young disciples, so that they could get used to them gradually. As the California-based Caodai historian Đỗ Vạn Lý told me: "They needed to be eased into the spirit world, because Asian people are taught to fear the highest spirits. By approaching them through intermediaries, he was able to slowly reveal the extent of his knowledge and importance. When he finally revealed his identity as the Supreme Being, he did not have to persuade them anymore."

The revelation that they could speak directly to the Jade Emperor was the most important one. Đỗ Vạn Lý remembered hearing about this event when he was a schoolboy in Vietnam in the 1920s: "When he revealed this, the three of them were amazed. So was everyone else who heard this news. Someone like the Jade Emperor existed only in literature. We had read about him, but he was simply a name used in stories. We could not imagine that it would be possible to have a conversation with him."[20] French teachers had taught their native students that only Christians could talk directly to God. This was not a possibility for followers of Asian religions. But talking directly to a divinity was only the first of a number of innovations that would be introduced.

The Saigon Spiritists came out of a bilingual, bicultural world in which they were taught Christian religious history in French schools but came home to families steeped in Vietnamese tradition. Scholars of East Asian religions might note that contact between monotheistic Christianity and the more polytheistic Asian pantheon has often produced a renewed emphasis on the power of the Jade Emperor.[21] The fusion that Caodaists were to make between the Christian idea of a forceful, active God and the usually distant, imperious Chinese lord of the heavens took this identification in a new direction. It made the Supreme Being the direct source of the earliest revelations. The Jade Emperor in these séances acts a lot like Jehovah in the Old Testament: he is a loving but stern father, who speaks directly to his disciples, and does not deal with them through the immense celestial bureaucracy that Chinese religious traditions had established. He speaks clearly and forcefully, but these early texts are more a series of revelations and commands than conversations. Although he appeared playful and ironic in the earliest messages, once his true identity is revealed he becomes more serious and even authoritarian.

The "age of revelation" that inaugurated Caodaism with the messages received from 1925 to 1933 is characterized by the revolutionary directness of spirit communication. There are few questions or challenges to the words of the Jade Emperor. When Phạm Công Tắc started a longer series of conversations while he was receiving the Religious Constitution, however, the tone had changed. The appointment of Lý Thái Bạch as his "Invisible Pope" and the development of a pantheon of saints, immortals, and advisors of various kinds allowed the Jade Emperor to retreat back to his celestial palace. He would rarely speak directly to his followers after these first exciting years.

Caodaism's Double Genesis: Vision versus Séance

What provides the impetus for new religious inspiration? Is it a solitary vision like Ngô Văn Chiêu's experience, prepared for by years in immersion in ascetic discipline and meditation? Or it is a complex group process like that of the Saigon Spiritists, in which the collective imagination is coaxed into a new set of beliefs through a series of negotiated exchanges? Caodai accounts of the genesis of their faith combine both elements and involve both visual and textual modalities.

This "double genesis" helped to catch the attention of a wide range of people in colonial Indochina and to catapult a handful of Spiritists and mystics into the leadership of a huge mass movement. But it also laid the way for a "two-fold" emphasis on esoteric and exoteric elements—the secret dark world of the initiated and the open brightness of a worldly campaign—which has continued to divide Caodaists even as they have all rallied to the ideal of a unified practice.

Ngô Văn Chiêu approached the mysteries of the universe from the standpoint of the private, intimate séances held in Sino-Vietnamese secret societies. The Saigon Spiritists were initially drawn to an amusing pastime popular at that time in France. Although their initiation gradually drew them more deeply into Asian tradition, it was deliberately syncretistic and cosmopolitan from the start. The spirits that early Caodaists spoke to were already moving between several different worlds, and it was therefore not surprising that their messages soon provoked extended debates about their source and authenticity.

Characteristics of Esoteric Caodaism

Ngô Văn Chiêu's legacy is an esoteric school of Caodaism, very "East Asian" in its configuration, which is practiced by an educated elite and seeks wisdom and transcendence through meditation. Meditation is not a goal in itself, however: meditation is a way to prepare the mind to receive direct communications from deities. It is these conversations with higher spiritual teachers that are the goal of both meditation and spirit medium séances. At the same time, as Bùi Văn Khâm explained to me, it is not only the message, tapped out by the phoenix basket, which is sought out, but also the experience of making contact with the unseen world: the "energy" that is summoned and then released.

The Chiếu Minh "branch" of esoteric Caodaism (as it is now described by Caodai historians like Đồng Tân and Bùi Đắc Hùm) continues rather seamlessly in the mold set by the Sino-Vietnamese redemptive societies. It incorporates popular religious traditions into a new synthesis based on intense individual practice but has none of the characteristics that would later be seen as differentiating Caodaism from the early Minh groups. It does not proselytize, its spirit writing séances do not contain messages from European spirits, and it is egalitarian rather than hierarchical, reclusive and ascetic rather than congregational and ceremonial.

The oral tradition is important in Chiếu Minh: each person must be guided in meditation by a teacher and will form a lifelong bond to the spiritual teacher who initiated him or her. Male teachers initiate men and female teachers initiate women. There may be some differences in their ritual practice, but this is hard to determine since these details cannot be revealed to noninitiates.

Ngô Văn Chiêu wrote down almost nothing. His disciples in Cần Thơ had to search through a number of government documents to find just his signature. While there have been a number of messages attributed to him by spirit mediums, it is notable that there is no body of work that can be said to be his. The collection of messages titled *Đại Thừa Chơn Giáo,* received by the medium Liên Hoa in 1936 (translated in French as the "Great Cycle of Esoteric Teachings" in 1950) serves as the unofficial guide for most esoteric practitioners of Caodaism. The spirit of Ngô Văn Chiêu is honored in these teachings but speaks only rarely.

Chiếu Minh followers say that the profundities of the secret doctrines cannot be found in any single text. They have to be experienced through a life of disciplined sacrifice, vegetarianism, and many hours of meditation. Chiếu Minh groups meet and conduct spirit medium séances that are generally closed to outsiders. Once a disciple is initiated, there are secret mantras that are given and a number of prayers that must be memorized. The key ritual practice, however, is not focused on doctrine or any generalizable principles: it is a personal practice structured and acquired through a particular tradition, but in a very real sense the individual is ultimately alone and on his or her own spiritual journey.

The Chiếu Minh Cénacle or Inner Circle

There is, however, an important group dynamic in the Chiếu Minh séance groups, described in French as *cénacles* (from the Latin term designating the "upper room" where Jesus met with his disciples for the Last Supper). The term is also used to refer to a selective, exclusive group of writers or poets who practice an elite literary tradition, so it could be translated as a "literary coterie," an elite inner circle that probes the mysteries of the universe in obscure, often metaphorical language.

I visited the rather closed, private world of the Chiếu Minh Cénacle in three places in Vietnam—in Dương Đông, the site of Ngô Văn Chiêu's original vision on the island of Phú Quốc; in Cần Thơ, at the Chiếu Minh Temple across the street from Ngô Văn Chiêu's tomb; and in Hồ Chí Minh City. In each of these centers of worship, the temple is a sort of dormitory where disciples can practice sleeping in a sitting position and meditating at intervals throughout the night. Most Chiếu Minh disciples hold jobs and remain active in society, but no longer live with their families in order to find the inner calm needed for intense concentration. Most temples will not admit members younger than thirty-five, and it is usually necessary to be initiated by the age of sixty.

In California, a Chiếu Minh Cénacle was formed under the leadership of Đào Văn Sử, the spiritual master who initiated Bùi Văn Khâm. Đào Văn Sử had settled first in Belgium, and only moved to California a decade before his death. His home in Ojai was sometimes where the group would gather, but more often they would come together in Los Angeles, since most of the members were in Los Angeles or Orange County. While I have interviewed several members of this inner circle, I have not been allowed to attend their séances. Several Chiếu Minh disciples in California (including Bùi Văn Khâm) allowed me to visit their own small home altars, erected in a room dedicated to meditation practice and séances.

Bùi Văn Khâm was initiated into Chiếu Minh in 1982 and was for many years a member of the inner circle of Chiếu Minh disciples in Los Angeles, where he served as the medium for twice-monthly sessions for a period of about a year. He later yielded this position to an older man who qualified to become a medium, and then began to practice in a more solitary fashion, with just a few other disciples. Khâm decided to "follow exactly the footsteps of Ngô Văn Chiêu," not affiliating himself with any group. He continued to practice with the phoenix basket (*Ngọc Cơ*), explaining that he sensed a kinetic reason for the use of the object: "To my opinion, the whole idea of the use of *Ngọc Cơ* is to create a kind of coordination between the hands, the brain, the mind and beyond, through the momentum of movement." From 1997 onward, he began an even more solitary practice, after he inadvertently stumbled upon a series of spirit revelations from a mysterious entity who would not initially reveal her true identity.

The World That Produced Bùi Văn Khâm: A California Medium

Caodaists who describe the spiritual quest say it often operates as a spiral: it is necessary to move away from the goal in order to achieve the momentum to spiral back toward it. Becoming a medium was for Bùi Văn Khâm not a straight line at all, but a series of curving explorations outward that finally became a "return" to the esoteric traditions he had first encountered as a child in Vietnam.

Born on September 9, 1949, in a small village in central Vietnam (Bình Phủ, Quảng Nam Province, near Đà Nẵng), Bùi Văn Khâm was supposed to start school just after the fall of French rule and the Geneva Convention accords in 1954. But there was no school in his village, only a Caodai temple. So he was sent as young boy to board at the Caodai school. His mother died when he was very young, before he started school, and he had just two sisters. His father died when he was thirteen. He was raised by his two older sisters, who sent him to middle school in Quí Sơn, a rural district in Quảng Nam Province, and then to an elite high school in Đà Nẵng, which was very competitive. He graduated in 1967, having worked as a tutor to support himself. He scored well on his final exam and wanted to continue his education in the United States. But because of wartime conditions, he was mobilized and sent to pharmacy school in Saigon. From 1974 to 1975, he served as a pharmacist in the South Vietnamese Army.

When Saigon fell, he and some friends were among "the very first boat people." They drove a military jeep to the mouth of a river, where they got in a small boat to get away from the city. After a few days, they were picked up by the American Navy, transferred to another ship, and taken to the Philippines for four days, then Guam for a month. When Khâm arrived at the Guam Refugee Center, he contacted an American missionary he had known in Vietnam, who was affiliated with the Church of Christ, where he had taken English lessons. This missionary sponsored him to come to Fort Chaffee, Arkansas, and he was placed very soon in a college dormitory at Oklahoma Christian College, where his missionary friend was a professor.

Bùi Văn Khâm was twenty-six years old when he came to the United States, and the first thing he learned about was Christianity: "We had church three times a week. Thursday was a devotional night, and there was a Christian Missionary Workshop where I went with volunteers to study the Bible. But the more I learned about Christianity, the more questions I had. My sponsor saw that I was interested in studying religion and he wanted me to become a preacher. But since my background was in science, I decided I did not want to give up my science education." In 1976 he was admitted to Oklahoma University Medical Center to study biochemistry and hoped to train to do medical research.

He felt dissatisfied with his studies and started to read about Transcendental Meditation. He was initiated into Transcendental Meditation in 1976 and practiced it faithfully. He decided to move to California and try to study neurochemistry at UCLA. While establishing residency, he went to Zazen at a Buddhist temple and met his future wife, whom he married in 1978: "I used to joke that I spent the first five years in the United States looking for God—in the Christian church in Oklahoma, in TM, in Zazen. I was also very interested in Tibetan Buddhism. If I didn't happen to get married, I might be in the Himalayas right now."

In 1980, he started working for Los Angeles County as a caseworker and hearing specialist for legal cases. Vietnamese pharmacists organized in 1983 to get the right to take licensing examinations to work as pharmacists, and there was a class in San Diego to prepare for the exam, but his plans to follow this course were interrupted by his religious interests. He was drawn back to Caodai and was initiated into the esoteric tradition in 1983, and finally decided to pursue religious training instead of pharmacy training.

For Bùi Văn Khâm, this was in many respects a way of returning home: "I had been born into a Caodai family, and was raised in a very intense Caodai tradition, praying four times a day and serving as an altar boy as child." He remembered that when he was drafted into the South Vietnamese Army, and working as a pharmacist, he had clung to a Caodai rosary that he received as a boy that remained in his pocket until April 29, 1975. When his unit was being shelled, he took the rosary out to pray. It had a number of beads (54 or 108 or 18) and you could use it to chant a mantra to calm your nerves and keep your mind from wandering. He felt that it might have been efficacious in protecting him, or at least protecting his mind from the strain of battle. But then he left it behind and it did not come with him to the United States.

Bùi Văn Khâm had been "spiritually oriented" when he was studying in Saigon and had taken meditation courses and even attended a few séances at the Caodai temples in Đà Nẵng. But he began to have doubts about all the trappings of a large organized religion. "I wondered whether the religion could accomplish that objective without its hierarchies, its special costumes, its rituals. God would not want to create a new religion to compete with other religions." Once he came to California, he explored a more diverse set of options: "Since California was the land of the New Age, I had lots of other choices. There were several Indian and Tibetan gurus I thought of seeking out. But then I went back and read the history of Caodai all over again. I read about Ngô Văn Chiêu and one thing he said seemed right to me. He said he would not find a teacher of higher spiritual forms in human form. I tried to read between the lines of the life of the first Caodai disciple. It took six years for the first Caodai temple to be founded, after his first vision of the Left Eye of God in 1920."

So Bùi Văn Khâm came to resituate himself in a Vietnamese lineage that was not the same one he was raised in as a child, although he still saw it as a way of returning to the source: "Just as Christians go back to Jesus, in a sort of fundamental return to the source, I decided to go back to Ngô Văn Chiêu. There were two sides of Caodai. The exoteric tradition was the one that I was brought up in and knew from my childhood. But the esoteric one was the one that I came to embrace. Since I was initiated in September 1982, I have not wavered in my choice."

Ten years after he was initiated, he made contact through séance with the spirit of a young woman who identified herself as a Vietnamese heroine who was killed by the French in Chí Hòa Prison in Saigon in 1941. Like the young woman Vương Thị Lễ who made contact with the first Saigon Spiritists, she died in her twenties, and her tragic early death was perceived as making her particularly responsive and empathetic. She provided a series of detailed séance texts, often in quite obscure language, describing the path of self-cultivation and guiding him to respond to its challenges.

Once it became possible to travel back to Vietnam, Bùi Văn Khâm went to visit his sister and other family members in Saigon and also traveled extensively. In the far North he had an uncomfortable experience while touring the battlefield at Điện Biên Phủ, the site of the definitive victory won by the Việt Minh against the French. While he had served in the army of the Saigon Republic and came from a family that was anti-Communist, he wondered at that time: "Is it possible that we were on the wrong side of history?" In some ways, his extended conversations with the spirit of the woman killed in prison might be seen as a gesture of reconciliation, and also a reflection on how his own history was dictated by cold war politics that he did not play a role in shaping.

He has been active in the last few decades in teaching a younger generation of California Caodaists about their religious heritage, but he does so with a strong sense that the earliest messages received might be the most important ones: "Ngô Văn Chiêu had the first vision, but he did not want to become the Pope of Caodai. It was the Interim Pope Lê Văn Trung who developed it in its exoteric forms. Ngô Văn Chiêu was like Krishnamurti, who in 1929 declined to lead the Theosophists. He told his teachers that he was not the Messiah, and no man could ever have that role. Ngô Văn Chiêu's attitude to the Caodai organization was similar."

In spite of the vast production of volumes of spirit messages, laws, and commentaries by Caodai leaders, Bùi Văn Khâm stresses the experiential and fundamentally nonverbal form of spiritual practice: "Ngô Văn Chiêu was selected to show that an ordinary human being could be transformed into a higher level. Before he died, Ngô Văn Chiêu left a letter instructing his followers not to pray for him, because he knew who he was. He reached enlightenment and was united with God. He attained self-realization."

Tradition and Innovation: The Minh Legacy and the Issue of Syncretism

The ideas that Ngô Văn Chiêu brought into Caodaism were in many respects very old ideas, going back to the Ming dynasty in China. The slogans found in many Caodai temples (*Vạn Giáo Nhứt Lý*, literally "Ten Thousand Religions, A Single Principle") echo locutions in circulation in the fourteenth to the seventeenth centuries in China about how "the three religions go back to one source" (*sangiao guiyi*) and "the three religions have one origin" (*Tam giáo quy nguyên* in Vietnamese, *sangiao tongyuan* in Chinese) (Brook 1993, 17–18). Buddhism, Confucianism, and Taoism were seen as distinct discourses or repertoires that nevertheless had the same message. There was a unitary reality that could be approached through different pathways, and the teachings themselves were to some extent simply tools or techniques to manage the self, the body, and society. Emperor Xiaozong (r. 1163–1189) famously compartmentalized their functions, saying that he would "Use Buddhism to rule the mind, Taoism to rule the body, and Confucianism to rule world" (Brook 1993, 17).

Other formulations set up the three religions sequentially in a person's development: in progressing from Confucianism to Taoism to Buddhism, one starts by dealing with the world, then forgetting the world, and finally transcending the world. This formulation, established by Hanshan Deqing (1546–1643), argues that Buddhism is the highest vehicle, but all three vehicles are moving in the same direction (Brook 1993, 21). The Chinese practice of joint worship—the veneration of deities from different religious traditions at the same ritual site—was well established in the Ming dynasty. In some ways, the main "innovation" of Caodaism was to take this practice, established for over five hundred years, and apply it not only to Eastern traditions but also to the "Abrahamic" religions of Judaism, Christianity, and Islam. In Caodaism, these three traditions belong to the "way of the saints" (*Đạo Thánh*), which includes the veneration of deified national heroes like the famous Vietnamese general Trần Hưng Đạo.[22]

Some redemptive societies denied that they were religions, proposing to offer a high form of cultivation that transcended the religions of the past.[23] I have heard this argument also made by Caodaists, who see Caodaism as a "greater way," representing the culmination of humanity's spiritual traditions and not the selection of a single way. Others, like Bùi Văn Khâm, stress it as a "new way of life," a practice not tied to particular written doctrines but more to the direct experience of meditation and the exciting energy felt during a séance. They acknowledge that most practicing Caodaists are part of large congregations, performing elaborate rituals according to strict liturgical rules, policed by an especially elaborate administrative hierarchy. However, they favor the esoteric pathway because it seems more open to tolerance, collaboration, and ecumenical interaction and has to some extent avoided the factionalism of the branches that practice in the exoteric mode.

The year that Saigon fell and millions of Vietnamese refugees fled to other countries was also the time when New Age currents were coalescing as a movement in the California religious field. New Age esoterism developed in the mirror of secular thought, in reaction to the secularization of earlier religious traditions through a dialogue with science (Hanegraaff 1998, 517). Allan Kardec's *Book of the Spirits* called for a "new science" of mystical connections but was written in the form of a catechism. In 1975, Fritjof Capra's *The Tao of Physics: An Exploration of the Parallels Between Modern Physics and Eastern Mysticism* provided a new and more detailed bridge between Caodai cosmogony (drawn from the Taoist tradition) and the scientific education of many Vietnamese intellectuals.

In 1975, southern Vietnam lost half of its medical doctors, the majority of its civil engineers, and many other highly trained professionals who had been associated with the American regime and feared imprisonment or even death. The trauma of losing the country and being displaced as refugees made this moment into a theological one, one in which many intellectuals asked themselves questions about their faith in rationality, science, and progress. Writers like Capra developed a new philosophy linking ancient religious teachings to modern science that had a great appeal. Caodaists in the diaspora found a new validation for their own traditional spiritual practices in the writers of the 1970s who celebrated the dawning of the "age of Aquarius" in which the "occult sciences" of both East and West would come together. After 1995, a number of them started making pilgrimages back to Vietnam to visit family members and do meditation workshops at the Saigon Teaching Agency.

Meditating in the Market: Seeking Calm in Today's Hồ Chí Minh City

> *There are three places that you can mediate: You can meditate in the temple, which is already calm and peaceful. You can meditate in the home, where your family may dedicate one room to this purpose. Or you can meditate in*

*the market, in the midst of a noisy throng of people going about their busi-
ness. That is the most difficult place to meditate, and if you can concentrate
there your spirit is very strong.*

Đỗ Vạn Lý, interviews in Chatsworth

The small chapel at the Saigon Teaching Agency is across the street from one of
the city's largest markets. The roar of motorcycle engines, the cries of street
hawkers selling their wares, the sounds of loads of bananas, papayas, and duri-
ans being transferred from pedal carts and bicycles into fruit stands penetrate
the flimsy stucco walls of the structure. Downstairs, immediately below the
meditation room, is a bustling vegetarian restaurant, where steaming bowls
of tofu phở sprinkled with fresh herbs are handed out to visitors, and huge
platters of sautéed vegetables, fried bananas, and chopped greens are ladled
onto plates.

Esoteric disciples who attend the meditation workshops at the Saigon Teaching Agency are often taking a few hours off from busy careers; many of them are
professionals who work in office buildings downtown. They say that they need
to seek an inner stillness because of the stress of their present lives, and because
meditation provides them with a focus useful to navigate the shifting terrain of
an expanding market economy. Years of meditation practice can move them
into the inner circle of disciples who are eventually invited to attend the secret
séances held by the highest dignitaries.

The famously restrictive Chiếu Minh Đàn, or Saigon Cénacle, in today's
Hồ Chí Minh City practices perhaps the most demanding meditation regime.
My visit there was made possible through my ties to the American-educated
Minh Lý Đạo leader Lâm Lý Hùng (see Chapter 5). It was a fascinating example of the "reveal and conceal" dynamic of esoteric practice. I came as part of
a "delegation" that also included two spirit mediums, a Caodaist student of
Minh Lý Đạo esoteric traditions, and Lâm Lý Hùng himself. The practices
of the Chiếu Minh Đàn are, by definition, shrouded in secrets and forms of
knowledge open only to the initiate. But in order to draw others in and convince them of the importance of these forms of knowledge, they also have to be
advertised in some way.

So the head of the temple received us graciously and served us tea in his
offices, then led us upstairs past a number of occult symbols and images whose
meaning he told us he could not divulge. We were ushered into the most sacred
Chiếu Minh space, the altar used by Ngô Văn Chiêu during his years in Saigon, and I was instructed that it was forbidden to take photographs within that
inner sanctum. I was encouraged, however, to take many photographs of the

external architecture of the temple, its octagonal upper tower and its meditation rooms, vegetarian kitchen, and classroom.

A stack of laminated photographs of members of this Cénacle who had died was placed before my eyes. Men and women with pale, stiffened features, most sitting in meditation position, were proudly displayed on the table, all of them with at least the glint of an opening of the left eye. A woman spirit medium shared stories from others who were at the deathbed of Liên Hoa, the famous Minh Lý medium who received the largest number of esoteric teachings through séances. They said that he had fallen asleep, with his eyes gently closed, until he stopped breathing. Then his left eye opened, suddenly, triumphantly, at the moment that his soul was released. "He spent thirty years preparing for that moment," she noted.

Later that same year, the most senior member of the Teaching Agency, called by the religious name Chí Tín, passed away at his home in Saigon. I had met him briefly, but since he was very near the end of his life, I had never managed to have a sustained conversation with him. One of his sons, Lê Quang Sơn, was in contrast very articulate and eager to share his father's teachings as well as his own experiences of esoteric practice. We talked for many hours during my 2005 visit to the Alfortville Temple near Paris and again in 2008 when I met him on the island of Phú Quốc, where he had purchased a home for his future retirement. He had returned to Hồ Chí Minh City to care for his father during his final months. When Chí Tín died, I was one of many people who received the news by e-mail from his son. The attached photo showed Chí Tín's frail frame and his left eye, wide open, its deathly gaze blazing with the achievement of transcendence.

CHAPTER 2

A SPIRIT MEDIUM AS
NATIONALIST LEADER

CHARISMA AND ANTICOLONIALISM

On November 1, 2006, an excited crowd of almost 100,000 people gathered in Tây Ninh in front of the huge central gate to their sacred city, which had not been opened for half a century. The large octagonal tomb on the way to the Great Temple had been built for Phạm Công Tắc, Caodaism's most famous and controversial twentieth-century leader, and planned as his final resting place, but it had sat empty for decades. Now, news had come that the gate would be opened on this day to receive a funeral procession coming from Cambodia, bearing his remains in a dragon-shaped carriage, where his body would be welcomed, celebrated with a full night of prayers and chanting, and finally laid to rest.

Since his death, a larger-than-life-size statue had been erected on the balcony of the large saffron-colored building that had been his office in the 1940s and 1950s, from which he had delivered sermons that still define the ideals of worship for Tây Ninh followers. Just below the statue, a colorful hologram showed an image of Jesus Christ when looked at from the front, an image of Buddha when looked at from his right, and an image of Phạm Công Tắc when looked at from his left. This summarized a key doctrine of the Tây Ninh religious hierarchy: Phạm Công Tắc is seen as a spiritual leader of the same order as Buddha and Jesus, perhaps even a reincarnation of them both. It should be noted, however, that Tắc never made this claim himself, and that it might be

Figure 2.1. Phạm Công Tắc, the Hộ Pháp, raising his sword in 1949. Archive of Trần Quang Cảnh

contested not only by followers of other religions but also by Caodaists affiliated with other denominations.

The British historian Ralph B. Smith (1970a, 336) noted accurately that Phạm Công Tắc was "the most prominent, but not necessarily the most important" Caodai leader, and his legacy is one both of extraordinary charisma and activism and also of divisive exclusions. The ambitious and articulate spirit medium remained a controversial figure half a century after his death. Within the Tây Ninh Caodai community, some eight hundred temples display his image facing the great altar and portray him as the human being who came closest to achieving divinity. About five hundred non-Tây Ninh–affiliated Caodai temples display the images of Ngô Văn Chiêu, Nguyễn Ngọc Tương, or another leader, and see Phạm Công Tắc as an important medium in the early years who later tried to monopolize access to spiritual communication.

At the very moment when hundreds of Caodai followers thronged into the incense-choked courtyard to pay their last respects to Phạm Công Tắc, debates were raging in Caodai temples around the world about whether this sudden return to the Great Temple at Tây Ninh was premature. Many Caodaists had anticipated that the day their leader's body would be returned would come to mark the return of religious freedom to Vietnam, allowing the religious leadership to follow the original constitution received in spirit séances, and the end of decades of state censure. I had visited the temporary resting place of the Hộ Pháp in Phnom Penh in 2004 and interviewed a group of dignitaries and followers there. They were aware of efforts by some in the Tây Ninh hierarchy to bring him back to the stupa-like tomb erected for him decades before, but they said the time when that would be possible was still "very far away." "Our leader would not want to return to Vietnam as it is today," they told me. "He had to leave because of conflict between one Vietnamese brother and another. He asked King Sihanouk to let him stay in Cambodia until Vietnam was peaceful, unified and neutral."

In Pomona, California, the small Caodai temple on Tenth Street, nestled among the one-story stucco houses of a working-class immigrant community, was filled with dissenting voices. Many members of the overseas community were skeptical and even openly hostile to these plans. They said that bringing Phạm Công Tắc's body home now would be putting the cart before the horse: his return was to mark the achievement of a full normalization of Caodaism in its relation to the present government. This full normalization would include the resanctification of the section of the Great Temple reserved for séance communications with the deities and the reopening of séances (forbidden since 1975) as the authorized pathway of communication between humanity and deities.[1]

But, in November 2006, when the return actually occurred, none of these concessions had yet been made. The government of Vietnam was responding to pressures from the American government to "show progress" on issues of human rights. In 2004, the U.S. State Department listed Vietnam as a "country of particular concern" for violations of religious freedom. Vietnam wanted to join the World Trade Organization. It was rumored that this might happen just before President George W. Bush visited Vietnam to attend the ASEAN meetings in Hanoi. On the day that the presidential delegation landed, there was still no approval for the WTO, but the U.S. government offered another concession: they removed Vietnam from the list of countries abusing religious freedom. One condition of this change was some immediate action to reintegrate once sanctioned religious groups. Phạm Công Tắc, after resting for forty-seven years in Cambodia, was suddenly unearthed to "return to his homeland" and take his place in the tomb that awaited him in Tây Ninh.

How would Phạm Công Tắc have reacted to the challenge of this politically charged decision? Would his famously powerful spirit consent to this transfer of his bodily remains? Many skeptics argued that, once opened in

Phnom Penh, his tomb would be revealed to be empty—perhaps because of looting by thieves looking for gold, or perhaps because this government scheme was predestined to fail. Others condemned the Tây Ninh Governance Committee (Hội Đồng Chưởng Quản) for "collaborating" with the Communist regime and playing into their strategy of masking the continued suppression of religious organizations.

This chapter explores the legacy of Phạm Công Tắc, Caodaism's most visible promoter and proselytizer in the twentieth century, by juxtaposing it with the life of Bùi Đắc Hùm, the most visible translator and English-language Caodaist of the twenty-first century. Since the 2000 publication of *Cao Dai Faith of Unity*, he has developed new websites, recruited non-Vietnamese followers, and participated in interfaith dialogues to present this new religion to a wider audience. Born in Tây Ninh, he listened to Phạm Công Tắc's famous sermons as a child, and since 1975 he has worked ceaselessly to globalize Caodai teachings in the New World.

Like Phạm Công Tắc, he emphasized the universal ambitions of Caodaism and has participated in international congresses. Tắc sent representatives to the International Spiritualistic Congress of Barcelona in 1934; the World Congress of Religions in London, 1936; the International Spiritualistic Congress of Glasgow, 1937; and the World Congress of Beliefs in Paris, 1939. Hùm, accompanied by his wife and several other delegates, traveled to meet with the Pope at the Vatican in 1992, presented a paper on Caodaism at the Parliament of the World's Religions in South Africa in 1999, in Barcelona in 2004, at the 2006 conference on World's Religions after 9/11, and at the Southern California Committee for a Parliament of the World's Religions in 2012 and 2013.

A Spirit Medium as Anticolonial Activist

The heavily polarized debates within the Caodai community that centered on his controversial return would be familiar to Phạm Công Tắc. He was the most politicized of Caodai leaders and the one most willing to be seen as a spokesman not only for the religious hierarchy but also for Vietnam's nationalist aspirations. Misrepresented in most English histories as the Caodai "Pope" (which is *not* the office he held as "Hộ Pháp" or head spirit medium), he fused religion and politics when he attended the Geneva Peace Conference in 1954 and tried in vain to prevent the partition of the country. A reading of official Vietnamese histories after 1975 presents him as the leader of a "reactionary and opportunistic organization with some religious overtones" (Blagov 2001a, 151).

I argue that Phạm Công Tắc's most important contribution lay in formulating a utopian project that supported the struggle for independence by providing a new repertoire of concepts for imagining national independence and a separate apparatus of power to try to achieve them. Rather than stressing Phạm Công Tắc's political actions, which have been well documented in earlier studies, I focus instead on a reading of his sermons, his séance transcripts and commentaries, histories published both in Vietnam and in the diaspora,[2] and conversations with Caodaists in both countries when the appropriateness of returning his body was being debated.

Phạm Công Tắc was an important religious innovator who created a new style of mediumistic séances and a new type of scripture. Breaking with a tradition of many centuries of Sino-Vietnamese phoenix writing, Phạm Công Tắc's séances resulted in receiving messages not in Chinese characters traced in sand, but written in the Romanized cursive of *quốc ngữ*. This form of literacy made it possible to receive dictation in both Vietnamese and French and was thus supremely well adapted to the bicultural and bilingual milieu of the early Spiritist circles of young colonial subjects educated in French-language schools. As a spirit medium, however, he never claimed "authorship" of these innovations, which were all attributed to divine guidance. But the model that he presented of having conversations with divinities, rather than serving as a simple vehicle (the "voice" or "hand" of the spirit dictating a message), was to have profound implications on Caodai doctrine. This doctrine developed in new directions over the almost thirty-five years that he played a pivotal role in articulating Caodai teachings, and his subtle finessing of the issue of authorship was one of his most significant leadership strategies.

Phạm Công Tắc was the figure most identified with fusing national aspirations and religious teachings in Vietnam. He fashioned a modernist millenarianism designed to develop a new kind of agency, giving the Vietnamese people the confidence that they could change the course of history and that they were, in fact, destined to do so. Drawing on the power of older prophecies that "One day, a country now in servitude will become the master teacher of all humanity" (Hương Hiếu 1968, 1: 242), Phạm Công Tắc identified the Left Eye of God (Thiên Nhãn) with dynamism, progression, and modernity (dương), upsetting Orientalist clichés and encompassing Jesus into an Asian pantheon by designating him as the son of the Jade Emperor.

Building on Phạm Công Tắc's autobiographic reflections and writings, it is possible to link his stagecraft (dramatic presentations in ritual) to statecraft (creating "Vietnam" as an autonomous religious space, "a state within a state"). Phạm Công Tắc's official title of Hộ Pháp (head spirit medium)

places him in the Weberian role of a charismatic prophet—challenging orthodoxies with new revelations—but he also later assumed the administrative duties associated with the charisma of office and the role of the Pope
(Giáo Tông).[3]

Many contemporary Caodaists express ambivalence about Phạm Công
Tắc's later political prominence, although they all acknowledge his importance
during the formation of the new religion. One of his most stringent critics,
Đồng Tân, acknowledges that "he was the main person that God used during
the early years of the Great Way," but says he became too attached to his own
power after 1934 (Đồng Tân 2006, 46). Signs of schisms began very early,
because of what critics have called Phạm Công Tắc's "strong personality," his
efforts to establish exclusive religious authority, and his efforts to use spirit
messages to mobilize the masses against colonial rule.[4] Đỗ Vạn Lý argued that
Phạm Công Tắc "wanted to be Richelieu to Emperor Bảo Đại's Louis the thirteenth, serving as a religious advisor to a secular king."[5] Others claim, even
more critically, that he came to imagine himself more like Louis the fourteenth:
"Le Caodaisme, c'est moi"—eclipsing the ideal of spreading mystical enlightenment throughout the fold and monopolizing contact with the divine to himself and his own specially trained mediums (Đồng Tân 2006, 46). At the same
time that some of his followers identify him as a reincarnation of Jesus (Chong
1999) or Buddha (Danny Pham 2006), others argue that he corrupted the
original intent of the Caodai Religious Constitution (which he himself received as a medium and published) and compromised the faith by tying it to
political and military agendas.

The World That Made Phạm Công Tắc

Phạm Công Tắc was born on June 21, 1890, in Bình Lập village, Châu Thành,
in Long An, where his father was working as a minor official for the colonial
administration. He was the eighth of nine children, and since his father was
Catholic, he was baptized as a baby, although his mother was Buddhist (Trần
Mỹ-Vân 2000, 3). Phạm Công Tắc described his father as an official in the
French colonial administration who achieved a good position but "objected
strongly to the authorities when they were unjust" (Sermon #18, January 6,
1949, 56).[6] His father was fired when Phạm Công Tắc was four years old, forc-
ing him to work as a trader in order to support the family, "a herd of children
in a very ragged nest." As the youngest son, Phạm Công Tắc described himself
as "the one who remained with the parents because the second to last must stay

with family," and the youngest child was a daughter. He remembered a childhood in which he played the peacemaker in the family, trying to persuade his older brothers and sisters not to quarrel.

He was a good student, attending Catholic schools and appearing healthy, but also prone to long, deep sleeps, sometimes accompanied by fever and strange visions. His mother was greatly disturbed by this condition and tried unsuccessfully to find a cure (Trần Mỹ-Vân 2000, 3). His father died when Phạm Công Tắc was twelve years old, and he remembered childhood fears that his mother would also die soon. At sixteen, he was accepted to study at the prestigious French Lycée Chasseloup Laubat in Saigon. There he became involved in nationalist student politics, and particularly the Travel to the East Movement (Phong Trào Đông Du) spearheaded by Phan Bội Châu. After the Japanese defeated the Russians in 1905, the Japanese independent path to modernity inspired a number of Vietnamese nationalist leaders, including the exiled Prince Cường Để and Phan Bội Châu, who wanted to send a new generation of students to Japan to have "both their minds and their vision transformed" (Phan Bội Châu 1999, 43; Trần Mỹ-Vân 2000, 4). Phạm Công Tắc was selected to go in the fourth group and received financial sponsorship to pursue studies in Japan to train him for eventual leadership in organizations seeking Vietnamese independence.

However, French Sûreté forces caught wind of the scheme and raided Travel to the East's Saigon headquarters, capturing documents in which Phạm Công Tắc's name was listed as a scholarship recipient. Fearing arrest, Phạm Công Tắc fled the city and went to live with his grandparents in An Hòa Village, Trảng Bàng District, Tây Ninh Province. He realized that his chances for study overseas were doomed. The French had signed an alliance with the Japanese, expelling Phan Bội Châu and other Vietnamese nationalists from Japan. In 1949, forty years later, Phạm Công Tắc would speak with some regret of "those children of upper-class families who are fortunate enough to be able to study overseas" (Sermon #24, February 27, 1949, 76), and that experience seems to have left a bitter taste in his mouth, which developed into a strong commitment to nationalist struggle. His sermons do not, however, include any direct reference to the educational opportunities he first enjoyed and then saw cut short because of his political activism.

Expelled from his prestigious lycée, Phạm Công Tắc completed his studies in Tây Ninh and returned to Saigon to work as a waiter at the famous Continental Restaurant. There, he met the Chief of the Customs Office when he was ordering a meal and impressed him with his fluent French. In 1910, he was hired to serve as this Chief's private secretary and began a career as a civil servant (Đồng Tân 2006, 36). He also studied traditional Vietnamese music and performed with the "Pathé" folk-singing group.

Phạm Công Tắc was married to Nguyễn Thị Nhiễu on May 30, 1911, and soon became a father. He later spoke of working from the age of seventeen to support his family, eventually choosing government service because his brother-in-law advised him that there was "no honor" in working in commerce (Sermon #18, January 1, 1949, 51). Phạm Công Tắc remembers his mother's death when he was twenty-two, while his wife was pregnant, and says his grief at that time was relieved only by the thought that she "entered into the spiritual form of the Great Divine Mother" (Sermon #20, January 16, 1949, 62). Without parents, he became attached to his brother-in-law ("I loved him more than my blood brother") and his younger sister, but both of them also died within a few years. His sorrow at the loss of family members was not assuaged until he received "a touch of enlightenment" and followed the Supreme Being who "delivered a profound love to me, a love a million times more rewarding than the love of a family" (Sermon #18, January 1, 1949, 57).

Phạm Công Tắc and his wife eventually had eight children, six of them dying in childhood (Đồng Tân 2006, 36), but these personal losses of descendants are not mentioned in his sermons. Nor does he make any explicit reference to the fact that the two children who did survive were daughters, thus depriving him of any direct descendants in the Phạm line. In the 1930s, he trained a small number of male mediums in what was called the "Phạm Môn," or "Secret Mediums' College" (the name can be interpreted as "Buddha's gateway" or as his own family name), who were very loyal to him. Some commentators have implied that this was done to ensure his spiritual legacy would live on, even though he did not produce any human sons (Đồng Tân 2006, 36).

There are also suggestions that he blamed the French for his loss of sons who could carry on his descent line. Phạm Công Tắc worked for the French Office of Customs and Monopolies, first posted to Saigon, then Qui Nhơn, and then back in Saigon. Jayne Werner notes: "After working as a clerk for 18 years, his 'penchant for spirits' (as the comment in his Sûreté file dryly put it) and involvement in Caodaism was discovered, at which point he was abruptly transferred from Saigon to Phnom Penh, and perhaps demoted. This was evidently a hard blow since he was seeking care for a sick child in Saigon who later died" (Werner 1976, 96; Lalaurette and Vilmont 1931, 62–63). Phạm Công Tắc was transferred in 1927 and finally decided to quit his job in Phnom Penh in 1928 to devote himself full time to his religious duties in Tây Ninh. His French superior described him as "intelligent but unstable" (Werner 1976, 96).

In Qui Nhơn, Phạm Công Tắc helped establish a literary journal (*Văn Dân Thị Xã*) in the period 1915–1920, publishing articles under the pen name Ái Dân ("He who loves the people"). In Saigon, he wrote for two other Vietnamese periodicals (*Nông Cơ Minh* in 1907, *Lục Tỉnh Tân Văn* in 1908) as well as the French-language *La Voix Libre* (1907) and *La Cloche Fêlée,* all of them critical of the colonial government. One article published in *La Cloche Fêlée* in 1907 was titled "Illegitimate grandeur, rebellion in the lower ranks" and appeared alongside the writings of Nguyễn Ái Quốc, the future Hồ Chí Minh (Jammes 2006a, 184). Similar critiques of colonial abuses were later found in spirit messages Phạm Công Tắc received from Victor Hugo and other French literary and historical figures.

From Intimate Séances in Saigon to a Massive Social Movement

In the previous chapter, we followed Phạm Công Tắc and his companions through their first experiments with spirit writing. One important innovation they introduced was that he and other members of his generation received their messages only in *quốc ngữ,* and—increasingly, for Tắc—in French. Employing the language of the colonial masters in order to criticize them with a technology—Spiritism—that also had its origins in Europe was to become the most distinctive characteristic of the séances that Phạm Công Tắc was soon to lead, after the death of Cao Quỳnh Cư in April 1929.

The Christmas Eve message from Lý Thái Bạch, the Tang-dynasty Chinese poet who wrote vividly about natural beauty, introduced a new dynamic to the séances, since he was designated as the "Invisible Pope" (Giáo Tông Vô Vi), who introduced others and passed on instructions from the Supreme Being. His presence was a clear "Sinicizing" of Caodai séances, which came to assume the characteristics of a younger generation of mediums, educated in French-language schools, but kneeling before the sages of Asia, and soon Europe as well, awaiting instruction and guidance. Authoritative discourse flowed down from distant centuries, along with many practical instructions about how to organize a more open, worldly, and activist version of the earlier secret societies that had suffered from French repression.

The Saigon Spiritists were instructed to visit two prominent city residents: the secular materialist Lê Văn Trung, a once-successful entrepreneur known for his fondness for wine, women, and opium, who had served as the only Vietnamese member of the Conseil Supérieur de l'Indochine, and the ascetic mystic Ngô Văn Chiêu, discussed in the previous chapter. Lê Văn Trung had benefited from a lot of favor from the French colonial regime and had been allowed to acquire French citizenship as a kind of reward for showing himself to be "more highly evolved" (*evolué*) than many of his fellow countrymen.

Phạm Công Tắc's animosity to those who supported French colonial rule was so intense that he later admitted that he disliked Lê Văn Trung and was reluctant to visit his home even after being instructed to do so in a spirit séance: "Lê Văn Trung met regularly with people in the French government, the only Vietnamese able to reach such a position. . . . I could not tolerate him. I could never be a mandarin for the French powers after our country was taken away from us. So when we brought the phoenix basket to him, we were just following orders from the Supreme Being" (Trần Văn Rạng 1971, 4). Lê Văn Trung was known for his hostility to religion. Out of curiosity, he attended a séance where he received messages from Lý Thái Bạch, encouraging him to believe that he could be cured of his failing vision. Suddenly, as the phoenix basket began to move, Lê Văn Trung found that his eyesight was restored, and the Supreme Being instructed him: "Now you can see, and you should remember why you have become able to see!" Lê Văn Trung became a Cao Dai disciple immediately and was soon divinely appointed as a Cardinal (Đầu Sư) and afterward as Interim Pope. He was also able to rid himself of his opium habit and commit to a new life of eating a vegetarian diet and practicing religious discipline.

Caodaism in its exoteric branch (*phổ độ* or *ngoại giáo công truyền*) was inaugurated on the first day of the Vietnamese New Year in 1926 with the message quoted in the Introduction from the Jade Emperor. Demonstration séances were organized to recruit thousands of new members, more relaxed rules (ten vegetarian days a month) were established for most of the disciples, and intensive proselytizing was begun to provide salvation to millions before the impending end of the present world. Lê Văn Trung's conversion galvanized hundreds of others to follow suit, and soon a very large number of civil servants, notables, and teachers had joined the new faith.

On October 7, 1926, the official declaration, signed by twenty-eight prominent Vietnamese leaders and 245 disciples—employees of the colonial administration, teachers, and businessmen, most of them educated and some wealthy—was sent to Governor Le Fol, asking that Caodaism be formally recognized as a new religion in Cochinchina. The first signature came from Madame Lâm Ngọc Thanh, who would become the first female Cardinal. The gesture made in this declaration was a revolutionary one: it brought together a coalition of hundreds of secret societies, which had practiced esoteric arts in the shadows and under the threat of French investigations, out into the public sphere, and claimed the protection of the law based on French ideas of religious freedom.[7] The new religion was presented as entirely traditional, synthesizing the lost moral values shared by Confucianism, Buddhism, and Taoism, and there was no mention of Jesus Christ or any European spirits.

While Lê Văn Trung, a respected government figure in his sixties, was the nominal head of this movement (described—wrongly—in colonial documents as its "creator"), he was upstaged in many ways by Phạm Công Tắc, whose flamboyant leadership of the spirit séances and announcement of doctrinal innovations drew increasing attention. In 1931, the French colonial officer Lalaurette identified Phạm Công Tắc as "the indomitable driving force behind Caodai occultism at the Holy See and the instinctive adversary to everything that is French," and the real behind-the-scenes force defining its political direction. Phạm Công Tắc was credited with "intelligence and generally wide knowledge" (and seen as more dynamic than the by-then ailing Lê Văn Trung), but mocked as an "ex-petty clerk" who aspired to dress in "feudal robes" (Lalaurette and Vilmont 1931, 63–64).

The first photograph that we have of the Saigon Spiritists shows a group of young men and women dressed in Western clothing. The mysterious spirit A Ă Â instructed his disciples to dress in white *áo dài* tunics for worship, but Phạm Công Tắc apparently showed up in something much more elaborate, since an early séance text has the Supreme Being chortling gently on his arrival, speaking to him in the tones that an indulgent father might well take to his rather flamboyantly dressed son: "Laughing: Perhaps he was supposed to get himself that costume as an opera performer. But he is so poor. I as his Teacher did not tell him to do so" (*Thánh Ngôn Hiệp Tuyển* 1972, 36). The chatty intimacy of the conversations these young mediums had with the Jade Emperor underscore the ways in which a distant ruler of the universe was brought closer, addressed in a personal and parental role, transforming the abstract doctrines of the "Great Teachings" into a new Asian monotheism in which the ascension of the dynamic, masculine power of the Left Eye was linked to the end of the colonial era and a New Age of self-determination for formerly subjugated peoples.

Phạm Công Tắc was divinely appointed to be the Hộ Pháp, "Defender of the Dharma," a guardian figure represented near the entrance to Buddhist pagodas. In the Caodai Constitution, the Hộ Pháp heads the Hiệp Thiên Đài, or "College of Spirit Mediums," which receives the divine laws. Wearing the warrior's costume was dictated by this title, but a French observer saw this dress as due to Phạm Công Tắc's sense of dramatic performance: "He knows perfectly well that if he is to strike the imagination of the adherents who listen to him, he must comport himself in imposing mandarinal dress, so he has chosen a costume from the tradition of Sino-Annamite theater, the costume worn by a conquering general. He even wears the sword, and there he is, primed mentally and physically to play a role in the new religion: the Hộ Pháp, Grand Master of Rites and of Justice and Chief of the Corps of Mediums!" (Lalaurette and Vilmont 1931, 63–64; Werner 1981, 29).

The costumes of each Caodai dignitary and the duties of her or his office are specified in the Caodai Religious Constitution (*Pháp Chánh Truyền*), which Phạm Công Tắc compiled, translated, and published. This document is composed of a series of séance messages received after the inauguration ceremony at the Gò Kén Pagoda in Tây Ninh. The divine text is supplemented by explanations and commentaries by Phạm Công Tắc, which record not only the instructions he received, but also—amazingly—his own reservations and occasional efforts at insubordination. From this document, it is very clear that instead of simply serving as the vehicle for spirit writing, Phạm Công Tắc became a direct interlocutor in these conversations. For this reason, his influence upon the divine charter of the faith is much greater than that of Lê Văn Trung or any other of the founding disciples.

In a section that would soon become the focus of controversy, the Hộ Pháp asks his divine interlocutor to explain the role of the Pope (Giáo Tông):

> "According to the teachings of Catholicism, the Pope has full power on the bodies and the spirits. Because of this extensive power, Catholicism has much material influence. If today, you remove part of the power on the spirits, I fear that the Pope would not have enough authority in guiding humanity to conversion."
>
> His Master answers, smiling: "That was mistake on my part. When I carried a physical body, I gave to an incarnated person the same authority on the spirits as myself. He climbed on my throne, took over the supreme powers, abused them, and rendered man slave of his own body. Moreover, I did not realize that the precious powers I gave you because I loved you represented a double-edged sword that encouraged you to generate disorder among yourselves. Today, I am not coming to take these powers back but rather to destroy their deleterious effects. . . . The best way is to divide those powers so as to prevent dictatorship. . . . Once these powers belong to the hands of one, man escapes only rarely from oppression." (*Pháp Chánh Truyền* 1972, 119)

Phạm Công Tắc, a young man baptized and raised in the Catholic Church, argues for a centralized Pope, who could provide effective leadership, but he is told that the errors made in designing the Catholic hierarchy need to be rectified by a more clearly defined separation of powers, in a complexly structured spiritual bureaucracy.

In a later section, Phạm Công Tắc challenges his interlocutor, who had decreed that Caodaism would establish equal rights for female and male dignitaries, by asking why, if this was the case, women were not able to become Censor Cardinals (Chưởng Pháp) or Pope (Giáo Tông). The Supreme Being answers: "Heaven and Earth possess two constitutive elements, yin and yang (âm-dương). If yang dominates, everything lives, if the yin rules, everything dies . . . If a day came when the yang disappeared and the yin reigned, the universe would fall into decay and be destroyed. . . . If I allow the female college to hold the power of Pope in its hands, I will be sanctioning the triumph of yin over yang, so that the holy doctrine will be brought to nothing." Even after this strict correction, the Hộ Pháp presses once again for an explanation for an apparent inconsistency in the doctrine of sexual equality, and the divine master answers angrily "The Law of heaven is thus set down," closing off discussion and leaving the séance abruptly.

Both of these passages suggest that Phạm Công Tắc wished to introduce a number of European-influenced ideas (a centralized ecclesiastical hierarchy, women's rights) into a more traditional Confucian spiritual bureaucracy headed by Lý Thái Bạch as the "Great Immortal" (Đại Tiên) administering a complex hierarchical apparatus. The young man in his thirties who wanted to train in Japan as a soldier for the revolution is told in no uncertain terms that he must learn patience and incorporate a more nuanced and gradualist perspective on changing the world. But, as events came to show, schisms and defections soon placed Phạm Công Tắc in a position to bypass the counsel he received from the ancient Chinese masters and seek further advice from French writers and heroines who would support his innovations.

Schisms and Sanctions: The Road to the Eighth Decree

The three-day festival held to inaugurate the "Great Way" on November 19, 1926, eventually stretched on, in Caodai legend, to almost three months and attracted a huge number of pilgrims, onlookers, and new converts, including thousands of Cambodians who crossed the border to kneel in front of a huge statue of Buddha-Sakyamuni on a white horse. Almost immediately, government sanctions were imposed to limit Caodaism's expansion, with French colonial officers denying permits for the construction of new temples and the Cambodian king calling back his subjects amidst rumors that a new religious leader might try to usurp his power. Some French analysts noted with concern that this kind of popular messianism had the potential to produce "another Gandhi"[8] (since M. K. Gandhi at that time had captured the leadership of the

Indian Congress Party, allying Hindus with Muslims on a platform fusing religious and nationalist ideals). Others linked Caodaism to the religious and political agitators responsible for armed insurrection, calling it "communism masquerading as a religion" (Thompson 1937, 474).

The brief, inspirational unification of a number of disparate groups began to fragment by the early 1930s, when Lê Văn Trung assumed the papacy and claimed a million disciples. Several charismatic leaders from the Mekong Delta, almost all of whom had been involved in the clandestine Minh Sư secret societies, eventually returned to their home territory rather than accepting to remain as Cardinals at the "Vatican" in Tây Ninh. The first of these was Nguyễn Văn Ca, who became the Pope of the dissident branch Minh Chơn Lý (Enlightened Truth) in Mỹ Tho.

The most serious rift involved the defection of Nguyễn Ngọc Tương, the *đốc phủ sứ* or District Chief of Cần Giuộc, and Lê Bá Trang, a Chợ Lớn official, since Nguyễn Ngọc Tương had been suggested as a possible successor to Pope Lê Văn Trung. Phạm Công Tắc accused them of being "Francophiles" and failing to stand up to colonial restrictions on the expansion of Caodaism, and Lê Bá Trang filed a complaint against Lê Văn Trung at the French tribunal. Lê Văn Trung agreed to step down momentarily, citing his failing health, and designated four others—Phạm Công Tắc, Nguyễn Ngọc Tương, Lê Bá Trang, and the female Cardinal Lâm Ngọc Thanh—as his replacements. Sanctions imposed by the French government increased, and in 1934 the "Interim Pope" himself was imprisoned by the French on charges of fiscal irregularities. He protested by furiously returning his Legion d'Honneur medal. Shortly after he was released, Lê Văn Trung fell ill and died, on the very day two others (Nguyễn Ngọc Tương and Lê Bá Trang) had convened a conference to "reform the religion." When Nguyễn Ngọc Tương and Lê Bá Trang tried to return to attend the funeral, they were not allowed to enter the sanctuary, since Lê Văn Trung told his supporters he did not want them to see his face.

Pope Lê Văn Trung declared on his deathbed that Phạm Công Tắc was the only one he trusted to become the leader of the faith, even if Phạm Công Tắc, as the divinely appointed Hộ Pháp, could not actually assume the position of Pope (Giáo Tông). The Hộ Pháp heads the College of Mediums (Hiệp Thiên Đài), receiving religious laws, while the Pope heads the executive branch (Cửu Trùng Đài). For some of his critics, Phạm Công Tắc's assuming leadership of both branches violated the Religious Constitution he had just published. The dissidents, Nguyễn Ngọc Tương and Lê Bá Trang, eventually formed the second largest branch of Caodaism, "the Reformed Religion" (Ban Chỉnh Đạo) in Bến Tre. In 1935, a council of dignitaries remaining in Tây Ninh proclaimed Phạm

Công Tắc the "Superior" of the "mother church of Caodaism." He was still called by his religious title—the Hộ Pháp—and never became the Caodai Pope.

How could a religion founded on the separation of the "executive" (Cửu Trùng Đài) and "legislative" branch (Hiệp Thiên Đài) be administered by a single person? Phạm Công Tắc answers this question in a cleverly constructed commentary to the Religious Constitution, in which exegesis of the symbolism of the Hộ Pháp's costume is used to "demonstrate" that this fusion of different branches was preordained by the divine decrees issued in 1926. At the largest religious ceremonies, the Hộ Pháp wears elaborate golden armor with a trident "Three Mountain" (Tam Sơn) headdress as he sits on his throne in front of the *khí* (breath, energy) character. His right hand grasps the "Rule over Evil" staff, intended to exorcise demons, while the left cradles the beads of compassion. The explanation for this reads: "This means that the Hộ Pháp holds the power over both spiritual and temporal affairs" (*Pháp Chánh Truyền* 1972, 190–191). Using the rhetorical strategy of explaining the arcane symbolism of his dress, Phạm Công Tắc argues against his critics within Caodaism who protest that he has "monopolized" the powers that should have been divided. His sacramental dress establishes his spiritual mandate and presents a visual confirmation of his powers to all who might challenge him.[9]

Visual statements are often more subtle and nuanced than verbal ones. In later years, the Hộ Pháp chose to make most of his public appearances in simpler yellow silk robes, without the elaborate coverings or general's insignia that he wore so often in the early years of the religion. The "spiritual warrior" who wielded a sword as well as a pen at the age of thirty-two came to present himself as a "poor monk" (Bần Đạo) in his fifties and sixties, becoming more humble and self-ironic as he ascended to a position of greater temporal power. The martial dress of his early years, redolent of stereotypes of Oriental despots, feudal lords, and medieval fiefdoms, was, however, to continue to haunt his public image, and to make it all the more difficult for him to convince a European (and later American) public that he was really a prophet of peace and nonviolence.

Other Caodai spiritual leaders have tended to dress more modestly. The second most famous Caodai medium of the 1920s and 1930s, Liên Hoa, who received the messages contained in the "Great Cycle of Esoterism" (*Đại Thừa Chơn Giáo*) followed a more conventional Sino-Vietnamese model. Liên Hoa's own voice was never heard in the messages themselves. He "ventriloquized" the words of great religious teachers, including figures like Buddha, Lao Tzu, and Confucius, who spoke only rarely in the Tây Ninh séances organized by Phạm Công Tắc.[10] Liên Hoa himself dressed either in the severe black robes of the Minh Lý Đạo, a small temple in Saigon where he often retreated to meditate, or in the pure white used by mediums in the central Vietnamese group (Truyền Giáo Trung Việt). The texts in the esoteric "Bible" received by Liên Hoa are a series of moral instructions, in the Chinese tradition of ethical teachings (Clart 2003; Jordan and Overmyer 1986; Kelley 2007) sprinkled with Taoist aphorisms (e.g., "The Cao Đài which is not Cao Đài is the real Cao Đài," like Lao Tzu's "The Way which can be expressed in words is not the real way") and doomsday prophecies.

For several years, Caodaism as a religion of unity was in a state of crisis. In 1930, the Tây Ninh Holy See issued a series of decrees to establish doctrinal conformity. Séances could not be held outside of the sanctified space of the Cung Đạo at the Holy See, and dignitaries and adepts had no right to challenge canonical scriptures. In 1935, in response to defections and new branches, Phạm Công Tắc issued the "Eighth Decree," which excommunicated schismatic groups and treated them as apostates. Cosigned in a séance by the "Invisible Pope," Lý Thái Bạch, this document has proved to be the greatest obstacle to many decades of efforts to reunify the various branches of Caodaism. Members of many smaller groups have pledged to try to achieve a new unity, but they have failed to draw Tây Ninh leaders to their meetings in any official capacity. Phạm Công Tắc's position, which cast a great shadow over his successors, has been that the "mother church awaits the return of her errant children," but the "children" cannot start reuniting themselves.

Phạm Công Tắc's sermons speak of three times in his life when he was in deep despair: when close family members died during his youth, when he was arrested and exiled by the French (1940–1946), and "when the Đạo was in a state of emergency and about to fall" (Sermon #18, 58). His focus is on how he "offered his life for this religion" and received "solace" in return, but it is no doubt significant that he refers only to internal strife and exile as causes for great distress, and so moves the emphasis away from his extensive role in national politics.

Phạm Công Tắc proved to be a very capable and careful administrator. He rebuilt the religious hierarchy in Tây Ninh at the same time that he constructed the largest and most impressive indigenous religious structure in Vietnam. Although French critics described him as very emotional ("He gets impassioned easily, his words, his bearing give the appearance of someone in a trance" [Lalaurette and Vilmont 1931, 62]), he saw himself as a modernizer and a reformer, who sought first to heal the wounds of colonialism through persuasion and compromise. While he was described in 1931 as a figure from the past ("In his daily contact with his co-religionists, he looks like the old sorcerer/magician of the secret societies of long ago and his hold on them has taken on the allure of former times" [Lalaurette and Vilmont 1931, 63]), by 1935 the new governor of Cochinchina, Pagès, conceded that Caodaism was not a relic of another era, but "the transposition onto a modern world of ancient belief systems" (Blagov 2001a, 32). For a few years, first under the new Governor-General Robin and then under the French Leftist Front Populaire government, Caodaism was allowed to flourish.

Dialogues with European Spirits: Victor Hugo and Spiritual Kinship

Caodaism's reputation for syncretism and borrowing from European tradition is almost entirely a result of the legacy of Phạm Công Tắc, as none of the other branches aspired to the same "international" profile or received as much moral and religious instruction from non-Asian figures. The French description of a *syncretisme à l'outrance* refers to a series of séances held in Cambodia and Tây Ninh in the 1930s. Victor Hugo and Jeanne d'Arc, the most famous "European saints" in Caodaism, were both spirits who initially conversed only with Phạm Công Tắc, refusing to "come down" to a séance if he were not there as a medium to "receive" them.[11]

Victor Hugo was by far the most widely read writer in colonial Indochina, popular among the Vietnamese as well as the French, and strongly identified as a defender of the oppressed and a critic of surveillance and imprisonment. Hugo's mystical poems and his practice of Spiritism inspired a sense of recognition among his young readers in Saigon, who saw him as revealing the intersection of Eastern and Western traditions. Hugo had "oceanic" visions of Asian wisdom spreading to Europe, and toyed with vegetarianism and ideas of reincarnation in his verses, without ever forming a coherent or systematic belief based on these connections.

The inclusion of Western historical and literary figures in the Caodai pantheon is far from a glorification of Occidental culture. On the contrary, it honors a few brave souls while sounding the death knell for Western imperial rule. So Victor Hugo, the great enemy of Napoleon III during his lifetime, speaks in Caodai séances to condemn the conquest of Indochina and the "tyranny of potentates." Jeanne d'Arc, a village girl who heard voices that told her to rise up against an occupying army, tells the Vietnamese to "work hard first to consolidate and fortify your consciousness [as an oppressed people] so that deliverance will be possible. Be patient, since there is a great force latent in the soul of your people. You need to know how to exploit it." Shakespeare, although praised for having inspired an empire "without limits or truces" (*sans arrêt et sans trêve*), is also informed that the glory days of British Asia are over, and after a great war the godless colonial administration will "march into an abyss" (*marche vers le gouffre*) and perish as well (Trần Quang Vinh 1962, 58, 91, 108).

Victor Hugo is controversial in Caodaism today not because of his writings, which are still widely admired by an older generation of Vietnamese intellectuals, but because of the messages attributed to him in which he supports Phạm Công Tắc's struggles with his critics: "You are blessed, in your capacity as medium. . . . Even if terrestrial spirits are unfaithful to you, the gates of Paradise will applaud your actions" (Trần Quang Vinh 1962, 85–86). Phạm Công Tắc's assumption of the leadership of Tây Ninh is also defended by the spirit of La Fontaine, the French fabulist whose story of the hardworking black ant is used to criticize the "lazy yellow ants" who want to assume hierarchical positions based on the seniority and rank they had in the French colonial administration. The "younger brothers" of the College of Spirit Mediums (Hiệp Thiên Đài) are said to prevail "from hard work and intelligence," while their elders are swollen "with pride that will soon prove fatal" (Trần Quang Vinh 1962, 75).

In Chinese traditions, mediums are often "adopted" by the spirits they converse with, who make them part of an invisible family.[12] But while Victor Hugo spoke to Phạm Công Tắc in the affectionate tones of an avuncular schoolmaster, two other adepts in Phnom Penh were designated in séances as Hugo's spiritual sons: Đặng Trung Chữ as his older son Charles and Trần Quang Vinh as his younger son François. (Their story will be told in Chapter 3.)

It is interesting to explore the ramifications of these different forms of defining spiritual kinship within Caodaism. In his sermons, Phạm Công Tắc notes the Taoist and Buddhist traditions identify spiritual teachers as "schoolmasters" (thầy), while the Christian tradition instructs its adherents to address God as "father." In Sermon #17, the Hộ Pháp asks his advisor Victor Hugo (Chưởng Đạo): "So why is it that the Supreme Being called himself Master?" His answer comes in a poem: "As a Father I look after my children with love and diligence, As a Master I welcome them into My Divinity" (Phạm Công Tắc 1947–1949, 53). The intimate, affectionate dialogues that Phạm Công Tắc (as a medium) received and reenacted for Trần Quang Vinh and Đặng Trung Chữ made them part of a spiritual family from which he himself was excluded.

Phạm Công Tắc saw his own destiny as leading in a more ethereal direction, one more on the same plane as the divinities. His vow of celibacy is not explicitly discussed in his sermons, but its necessity for purifying the body and preparing it to receive spirit messages is acknowledged, and he had no more children after he received this divine appointment. A human being, the Hộ Pháp notes in his sermons, is to "an angel riding upon an animal" (Sermon #21, February 9, 1949, 65). Spiritual aspirations toward self-cultivation reflect "the desire to leave our animal self in order to transform into a Buddha" (Sermon #21, 67), so that "the method of our spirit is to struggle to defeat the material"

(Sermon #22, 69, February 15, 1949), since "true happiness is not corporeal, it is spiritual" (Sermon #22, 69), not transitory (or physical), but enduring.

In a sermon delivered in 1949 on the anniversary of Hugo's death, Phạm Công Tắc revealed that Victor Hugo himself emerged from the spiritual lineage of the famous Vietnamese poet Nguyễn Du, author of the *Tale of Kiều*. In this way, Hugo is "indigenized" and tied to a Vietnamese literary giant, while Du becomes more "cosmopolitan" and finds his own genius plotted on a map with French coordinates. This twist came at a political moment when efforts to renew the social contract and heal the wounds of colonialism ceded to a post–World War II realization of the inevitability of decolonization. It also marked a change in the perspective of Phạm Công Tắc himself, who once sat as a student reading the works of the French humanists, but later saw their insights as dwarfed by a more encompassing Asian religious vision. Absorbing Hugo into a new position as the "younger brother," or more recent incarnation, of Nguyễn Du can be read as an attempt to disprove the civilizing role attributed to colonialism.

Using Orientalism against Empire: Theology as Political and Cultural Critique

When the American scholar Virginia Thompson visited French Indochina in the 1930s, she found Caodaism to be "the one constructive indigenous movement among the Annamites" (1937, 475) and was particularly full of praise for what the Hộ Pháp had done with Tây Ninh: building schools, printing presses, and weaver's looms with a "Gandhiesque flavor about creating a community which is self-sufficient" (Thompson 1937, 474). Both Gandhi and Phạm Công Tắc foregrounded cultural nationalism as a strategy of anticolonial resistance. The notion of a return to pure, indigenous traditions, with emphasis on certain forms of moral and ethical strength, was important in preparing people to resist an apparently overwhelming colonial power. Influenced by Social Darwinism, Gandhi argued that Indians had brought on the degeneracy of India by their own moral faults and complicity by following foreign consumer fashions (Young 2001). Phạm Công Tắc drew on an earlier tradition of prophecies that the Vietnamese brought colonialism on themselves as a punishment for their sins, but had now paid their karmic debts and would be rewarded for their suffering under the colonial yoke by becoming the "spiritual masters of mankind" (Đỗ Văn Lý 1989, 2).

The French scholar Paul Mus, in trying to explain why the "mysticism" of the Caodaists tended to detach itself from the colonial project, argued that the

French misunderstood the religious content of Vietnamese supernaturalism: "We mistook divinatory magic for instrumental magic" (Mus 1952, 292). Diviners in the East Asian tradition seek to discern cosmic patterns rather than to change them through some sort of supernatural agency. So the philosophical and religious ideas of the great teachers were used to *diagnose* the Western malaise rather than to act directly against it. Mus explains: "Human ideas, and the means and efforts that they are part of, are nothing if they do not translate an idea of cosmic harmony, celestial order which is strong enough to make them successful. Assistance must fall from the sky and come out of the land. To build a religious restoration of a mystical Vietnam, rooted in the popular beliefs of the masses still steeped in the past, it is necessary first to prove that this is efficacious" (Mus 1952, 292–293). He was critical of French efforts to "prove" their superior power with technology, efforts which were, as his students like Frances Fitzgerald have added, later repeated by American military forces (Fitzgerald 1972).

By stating that Vietnamese "patriotism, like their religion, is divinatory," Mus argued that it was linked to efforts to discern the wider elements at work in the universe (1952, 293). Defending the land of their ancestors from foreign intrusions came to appear as a spiritual mission. Since ancestor worship is "the only religion without skeptics," Mus argues that airplanes are powerless against guerilla warriors defending their native soil who believe that their own ancestors empower them by remaining within the bodies of their descendants and who visualize these ancestors at each incense offering in front of the family altar.

But Mus failed to take into account the innovations in Vietnamese patriotism introduced by Phạm Công Tắc's exoteric Caodaism. The Hộ Pháp established a more instrumental form of séance, which (in Marx's words) sought not only to understand the world but also to change it. While Phạm Công Tắc's religious teachings were rooted in tradition and he presented them as revivals, Caodai doctrine emphasized a number of Taoist principles and placed many practices once on the cultural periphery back in the center. The central doctrine of Caodaism was the millenarian claim that the end of the Age of Empire was also the end of a cosmic cycle, and it would be the formerly colonized peoples (and especially the Vietnamese) who would emerge as the new spiritual leaders of the world. Drawing on the "recessive elements of Christianity," which were also important in Gandhi's message (Nandy 2005, 74), Cadaoists argued that the meek would not only inherit the earth, but that they could use a sense of the moral supremacy of the oppressed as one of their most important weapons.

Far from being a "cargo cult" that worshipped the sources of foreign power and wealth and praised them, Caodaist doctrines preached that resistance to colonial ideology and material practices would allow the Vietnamese to detach themselves and experience a rebirth in which they could reincarnate East Asian cultural values restored to their pristine state. Gandhi had been quick to see that Theosophy, and an idealized notion of the spiritual values of the East, could have great political potential, and he used that potential both by allying himself with Annie Besant's Home Rule for India League and by focusing not only on colonialism itself, but also on the moral and cultural superiority of Indian civilization. Phạm Công Tắc also appropriated what we could anachronistically call "counterculture discourses" from "Annamophiles" in French Spiritist and Theosophy circles and mounted a concerted long-distance public relations campaign to force the French to permit the expansion of Caodaism.

Phạm Công Tắc used his facility in French and his wish to draw on the colonial arsenal to chart a pathway in which a Westernized young man full of anticolonial sentiment is gradually instructed by the spirits in Asian verities and moves from being the "hand" or the "pen" of the gods to becoming their conversation partner and even—in his later visions—an active combatant, driving out demonic forces. One sermon from April 19, 1949, culminates with a narrative of his voyages to the Upper World, traveling in a planelike "dharma vehicle" that moves from cloud to cloud, where he encounters Lucifer (Kim Quang Sứ), described as a "great Immortal" who is "almost at the level of a Buddha" but who was frustrated because his immense ambitions and striving for personal power undermined his sanctity (Sermon #33).

Phạm Công Tắc's exegesis directs us to read this passage as a comment on his own struggles to maintain control of Caodaism. At the time of the inauguration of the Great Way of the Third Age of Redemption, Lucifer was granted an "amnesty" (the possibility of redemption) and the gates of hell were formally closed. So Lucifer was present when the first Caodai temple was erected at Gò Kén, and "he attended the first séances, held the beaked phoenix basket and signed his name" (Sermon #33, April 19, 1949), but he has always been a force of divisiveness, leaving behind a poem at the time when "we had no bad intentions against each other there; there was not even a whisper of rebellion" (Sermon #33, 114), and suggesting an ultimatum:

All nine immortals fear my face

I may bow to Sakyamuni, but chaos thunders in my wake

You see how I'm received at that Palace of Jade

But will truth or heresy usher you into the Pure Land? (Sermon #33, 114)

The Supreme God allowed Lucifer to "carry out over 20 years, trick after scheming trick" (Sermon #33, 115) because human beings had to exercise their free will. They had to choose the Tao over alternatives. Lucifer's temptations provided the arena in which virtuous conduct would be a conscious choice rather than a simple reflex. At the gates to Paradise, Lê Văn Trung fights Lucifer off with a stick, but each time he strikes, the blow only divides his enemy into two. Aided by another Caodai dignitary, he leads a great battle, which the Hộ Pháp is finally forced to join. Phạm Công Tắc puts on his golden armor, takes up his golden whip and his exorcist's staff, and casts his whip like a giant net to isolate his enemy and finally drive him off, vaporizing him into an aura (Sermon #33, 117). Inscribing himself as the hero in a *Journey to the West*-like epic, Phạm Công Tắc in this passage moves out of his habitual role as the Buddhist monk Tripitaka (Tam Tạng), "This is why I pray to the Supreme Being as Tripitaka did on his journeys to India seeking Buddhist scriptures" (Sermon #28, 92), the bearer of scripture for a new faith, and acts much more like the Monkey Saint (Tề Thiên Đại Thánh), jumping into the fray.[13]

The older, more mature Phạm Công Tắc no longer received lessons from the French literary figures he studied in colonial schools. He no longer sought to reform colonialism by reconciling the ideals of the French enlightenment with the actions of narrow-minded administrators. Instead, he inserted himself into his own journey to the East, moving away from a nativist search for heritage to a more cosmopolitan vision of a syncretic, unifying faith.

Paul Mus described Caodaism as a "religion of reversal" (*religion de remplacement*) in which the colonial subjects would come to replace their masters: "In trying to revive a Vietnamese empire, these theocratic sects not only go beyond our ideas, they annihilate them" (1952, 248). He argued, on that basis, that their vision of change was in may ways more radical than that of the Communists, who "remain within the lines of our own worldview": "The more 'conservative' anti-colonial forces, and especially those with a mystical bent, may fight with us against communism, but they see our own cultural influence as similar to that of the communists, who are the ungrateful heirs of western materialism" (Mus 1952, 249).

While Phạm Công Tắc—like Gandhi—was usually seen as preaching a "counter-modernity," and spoke of restoring traditional values, it is also true that "his counter-modernity proved to be the most modern of all those of anti-colonial activists" (Young 2001, 334). In the final decade of his life, the Hộ Pháp began to operate a media war, using the society of spectacle as his secret weapon. He gave a series of press conferences, met with foreign reporters, and traveled to Geneva and to Japan, Taiwan, and Hanoi as a "spirit medium diplomat," desperately opposing partition.

The famous Franco-American journalist Bernard Fall visited Phạm Công Tắc in August 1953 to ask for his perspective on the decolonization process. The Hộ Pháp impressed him deeply, as noted in a letter to his wife not published until recently: "The man had a piercing intelligence and his approach to things is very realistic. I learned more about Indochina than I'd learned before in three and half months. To think that he was sitting there with me telling me about the need for French help after he'd spent five years in French banishment in Madagascar. The man was fascinating and I can see why two million people think he's the next thing to God himself—and that includes a lot of educated Europeans" (in Dorothy Fall 2006, 77–78). Fall famously described Phạm Công Tắc as "the shrewdest Vietnamese politician," but remained skeptical about whether he could use his religious base to reconcile the increasingly polarized forces of what became the Republic of (South) Vietnam and Democratic Republic of (North) Vietnam (Bernard Fall 1955, 249).

In 1953–1954, Phạm Công Tắc gave a series of press conferences praising both Bảo Đại and Hồ Chí Minh and calling for national union. When the French were defeated at Điện Biên Phủ in 1954, he called for a reconciliation of the southern nationalists with the northern Communists. Phạm Công Tắc believed that his religion of unity would provide the ideal setting for negotiations to bring Vietnam's different political groups together, and he hoped for French and American backing for this to proceed. He attended the Geneva Conventions and tried to work behind the scenes to convince others, but this proposal was doomed to defeat when the French and Việt Minh agreed to the "temporary measure" of a partition at the seventeenth parallel.

Phạm Công Tắc and many other Caodaists had been willing to work with Bảo Đại, but as Ngô Đình Diệm moved to consolidate his own power with U.S. backing, the nonaligned nationalists were forcibly dissolved. In October 1955, Ngô Đình Diệm ordered Caodai General Phương to invade the Tây Ninh Holy See and strip Phạm Công Tắc of all his temporal powers. Three hundred of his papal guardsmen were disarmed, and Phạm Công Tắc became a virtual prisoner of his own troops. On February 19, 1956, Phạm Công Tắc's daughters and a number of other religious leaders were arrested, but he himself managed to slip away. He made contact with his followers several weeks later from Phnom Penh and lived out the last three years of his life in exile in Cambodia.

The nonviolence that Phạm Công Tắc consistently preached in his final years, and his much-touted concept of "peaceful coexistence" (*chung sống hòa bình*) never had the purity of Gandhi's doctrine of passive resistance. Although he did not know about the formation of the Caodai Army during his over five years of exile in French colonial prisons in Madagascar and the Comoros Islands, Phạm Công Tắc's acceptance of the militarization of Caodaism was, for other Caodaists as well as for many outsiders, the most controversial aspect of his career. He called the Caodai militia "the fire inside the heart which may burn and destroy it" (*tam muội hỏa*) (Bùi and Beck 2000, 85) and immediately moved its military headquarters out of the Holy See, but he did see the political expediency of having a "defense force" to protect his followers and give him leverage in a precarious balancing act, suspended between the French and the Việt Minh.

Phạm Công Tắc insisted that Caodaism needed to remain "independent" (*độc lập*), refusing to align with either side and seeking a peaceful path through the decolonization process. Caodaists had long nourished a utopian vision of living as an autonomous community, owing deference neither to the French colonial government nor to the Việt Minh. During the period 1946–1954, they came close to realizing that dream, because the French agreed to create a "state within a state," where Caodaists had their own administration, collected their own taxes, enjoyed religious freedom, and received French weapons and funding for their troops. Caodai soldiers served under their own commanders, as a peacekeeping force, but were not sent to fight the Việt Minh in the North. This created a mini-theocracy within the province of Tây Ninh, whose dramatic performance of power could be interpreted as an effort to demonstrate the nationalist dream of autonomy, even though it was made possible by the embattled French colonial administration.

A number of other Caodaists, associated with branches like Minh Chơn Lý, Minh Chơn Đạo, Ban Chỉnh Đạo, and Tiên Thiên, joined the Việt Minh against the French. The "Franco-Caodai Pact," negotiated with the Tây Ninh Church, did not provide for the release of other Caodai leaders from prison or exile, and for this reason it served to divide rather than unite the religion. Phạm Công Tắc's efforts to play the peacemaker were ultimately unsuccessful, and his praise for the principle of "peaceful co-existence" put him out of favor with more strongly anti-Communist leaders. Although Phạm Công Tắc described himself as following "the same path as Gandhi" (Sermon #20, 1946), even those sympathetic to his political goals found his choice of a martial idiom showed "more ego and a greater search for personal power" than the Indian independence leader.

Gandhi considered the partition of India on one level a personal failure, and Phạm Công Tắc's final writings sound a similar note, suggesting that

Caodaists, and all Vietnamese, should seek expiation for their divisiveness.[14] His deathbed request to King Sihanouk was that he would not be returned to Vietnam until the country was "unified, or pursuing the policy of peace and neutrality to which I gave my life." But even as he saw many of his hopes crushed, the Hộ Pháp still knew how to use man's sense of guilt creatively. He promised his followers a moral victory by drawing on the nonmartial self of the apparent victors to instill them with doubts about their victory. On an ethical plane, his final words echoed Romain Rolland's formula, "Victory is always more catastrophic for the vanquishers than for the vanquished" (Nandy 2005). The suffering of the defeated can enhance their moral character and make them strong, while the triumphant celebrations of their opponents open the way for corruption and decadence.

A Legacy Combining Stagecraft and Statecraft

The lively debates that I witnessed about the repatriation of the Hộ Pháp's remains in November 2006 reflect several dimensions of the mimesis among religions in the colonial and postcolonial contexts and the propensities of southern Vietnamese religions to both imitate and assimilate symbolically various sources of power (Thiên Đỗ 2003). The precocious embrace of modernity that we see in Caodaism went further than normative colonial or even Communist ideologies at the time, and was part of a "spiritual restructuring" of the nation also evident in other Vietnamese religions (Taylor 2007). Understanding Phạm Công Tắc as a performer, drawing on various "repertoires" and fusing them into an efficacious enactment of a discourse of power, allows our analysis to come closer to that of contemporary scholars of East Asian religion, who have argued that Confucianism, Taoism, and Buddhism are—as Caodai scriptures teach—closer to "repertoires" than to "religions," since their doctrines are not mutually exclusive and they are more properly understood as cultural resources from which individuals have marshaled different ideas and practices at different times (Campany 2003, 2006).

Since Caodaists formed pacts with a series of allies who failed to lead them to victory, it can be argued that Caodai leaders like Phạm Công Tắc may have perfected, perhaps a bit opportunistically, a "theology of the vanquished," which privileges the moral authority of the oppressed and constantly defers the moment when the prophesied triumph will come. While that may be true, it is also a theology that has periodically—like the magical phoenix bird that is its central occult icon—managed to regenerate itself and regain its moral forcefulness at critical junctures. For many Tây Ninh Caodaists, the return of the Hộ

Pháp's body in November 2006 was one of those junctures, and whether this means that the Hộ Pháp's spirit will be "pushing the wheel of karma in a new direction" (as one of his followers recently told me) remains to be seen.

The World That Made Bùi Đắc Hùm

Bùi Đắc Hùm was among those who criticized the return of the Hộ Pháp's body to Vietnam, seeing it as premature. He thought the Vietnamese government should first apologize for how they had treated Caodaists for the past two decades: "The government has ignored the fact that the Hộ Pháp was considered a criminal in a judgment in 1978. He was considered a criminal to the country and to the Communist government. But right now, when they moved him back to the country, they did not mention anything about that. It was not the ritual that a leader of the religion deserved to have."[15] Hùm's perspective grew out of his lifelong commitment to Caodaism and his own experiences as a refugee.

Bùi Đắc Hùm was born in 1943 in Tây Ninh, to a family that was already steeped in the religion. His grandfather, Bùi Đắc Hùm Vị, had been a member of the Lão Minh Sư, one of the Sino-Vietnamese redemptive societies that practiced spirit writing in the Chinese tradition. Bùi Đắc Vị had ten children: The first five were raised in the Sino-Vietnamese tradition of literacy in characters, and the second five were sent to French-language schools. Hùm's father, born in 1904, had been among the older group. Once his skeptical younger brother had wanted to test the reality of spirit séances. He asked a question in French and placed it in an envelope presented to the spirits. He was amazed when he received an answer from the spirits that was also in French. "Perhaps then there is something to spirit séances," his father's younger brother concluded.

Hùm's father rose to become a Bishop (Giáo Sư) in Caodaism, and he required that his children go to the temple every day. On New Year's Day, the whole family also had to go to the home of the Hộ Pháp to present their greetings to him, a ritual that Hùm remembers resenting. Ironically, Phạm Công Tắc later became a relative by marriage, since one of his daughters married Hùm's father's brother Bùi Công Kỉnh. When Hùm started to learn to write, he was told to practice his penmanship by copying out spirit messages so that they could be distributed to the congregation. "In the days before photocopies, the hands of children were the main means of reproducing our doctrines," he explained. "But I got tired copying out things that I could not understand."

The first message he was taught was a famous one, the message from the Jade Emperor that said: "*Các con là Thầy, Thầy là các con,*" which could be trans-

Figure 2.2. Bùi Đắc Hùm with the author at the Caodai temple in Pomona in 2004

lated as "You my children are the Master, and I as your Master am my children." As Hùm told me: "It made no sense to me at first. How could the children also be the Master? Now only recently have I come to see that it tells us that we have God inside us all, as a potential, and we need to work on that potential." The most sacred moments of the month were the midnight services held in the Great Temple and the huge assemblies when the Hộ Pháp would also present his teachings to the people. These sermons remained inscribed into Hùm's memory for many years, even if he could not understand them fully as a child.

As the youngest son of a very large family, he was the first one who got the privilege of higher education. "I was spoiled, in a sense," he said, "since I was given opportunities none of the others had had." His father and siblings combined their funds to send him to school in Saigon to prepare for an examination to be trained as an army physician. When he passed the examination, he was given a scholarship to complete his medical studies.

The Saigon medical school was run entirely by French faculty, so he received all of his scientific training in French. He also met his future wife, Hồng ("Rose"), in medical school and benefited at the time from her superior command of French. His own literary background had been strong on Sino-Vietnamese classics, so he still read Lý Thái Bạch and Nguyễn Du for pleasure, while his wife (who had grown up in Saigon and attended the French-language high school Marie-Curie) read European writers like Victor Hugo, Lamartine, La Fontaine, and the Brontë sisters. His grandfather had specialized in Chinese traditional medicine. Her father was Dean of the Saigon Medical School and also a surgeon affiliated with the Seventh-Day Adventist Hospital.

After they married in the late 1950s, Hồng moved to Tây Ninh to practice in her husband's home for some years. There she came to see how Caodaism was such an important part of people's everyday lives. Groups of twelve families gathered for prayers at each other's houses each evening, and the religious discipline provided a unified, harmonious, and integrated community. Outside, a war raged along the highway that ran from Saigon to the Cambodia border.

Soon both Bùi Đắc Hùm and Hồng were working in military hospitals, operating on wounded soldiers from both sides, and (in Hồng's case) also dealing with wounded children and civilians. They were called back to Saigon in the years just before it fell. On April 20, 1975, they got a call from Hồng's father asking them all to show up at the airport, since the Seventh-Day Adventist Hospital was evacuating its staff and their families. They showed up with four children, allowed to bring only water and one change of clothes. They flew off the day before the airport was attacked and closed, traveling first to Guam and then to Camp Pendleton. Hồng had a brother in Loma Linda, California, who had been studying medicine, and he took in the whole family for a week. The Seventh-Day Adventist Church then sponsored them, providing free housing for a year and help with food and clothing. They expected to stay no more than that, hoping to return to Vietnam once it was safe to do so.

"We did not realize why we had to leave our country at that time," Hùm noted, forty years later. "We simply wanted to be with our families out of harm's way. Now we can see that we did bring a mission with us. Our mission was to spread the message of Caodai, of the unity of all religions and the need for peace. The exodus of people from South Vietnam, and the fact that many more left in the years that followed and settled in Australia, Canada, France, and all over the world was in fact part of a divine plan. It was a way to put the followers of Caodai in many parts of the globe so that they could then carry out their spiritual mission in a new place."

He continued, "There were spiritist messages which told us, 'You will be sent to every corner of the world. You will be dispersed to every country and have to learn every language. Then, from your new homes, you will spread the message of peace and harmony, of the unity of religious faith.'" He added, "Initially, we were very sad to realize that we had to leave our country. Now, we realize that our country is here. Not here in the U.S. specifically, but here where we are in the world. In a sense, the world is all one country on a spiritual plane, and what we are trying to do is to return to our own spiritual country in our hearts, and to help others to do so as well."

As a child, Hùm felt the all-pervasive discipline of Caodai religious practice was excessive, a burden he was forced to bear out of filial piety. The image of the Hộ Pháp was of a distant authority figure he had to respect, but not someone he chose to follow. In the 1960s and early 1970s, Hùm was a young doctor and new father too busy with work and family to give much time to the religion.

But his life took a new direction when his family escaped as refugees and had to build a new life in California. The traditions that had seemed burdensome in Vietnam suddenly became a source of support and solace in a new land. They helped to build a sense of community among refugee families struggling in isolation. By the early 1980s, he and his family were driving two hours to Los Angeles to take part in the first congregations in Los Angeles, led by Đỗ Vạn Lý (the subject of Chapter 4). Caodai doctrine articulated a structure for establishing a cosmopolitan Vietnamese identity and emerged as a "faith of unity" to build bridges to other religious groups largely unknown in Vietnam—evangelical Christians (who sponsored many refugee families), Jewish Buddhists, Bahá'ís, Hare Krishnas, Taiwanese Buddhists who built the huge Hsi Lai Temple in Hacienda Heights, and the ethnically mixed congregation of Soka Gakkai Buddhists who built a new university in southern California.

Hùm began studying Caodai spirit writings and translating them with the assistance of Ngasha Beck, an American convert. He and his wife published translations of prayers and liturgical chants. By the 1990s, they traveled to Rome with a Caodai delegation invited by the Pope, set up a Caodai website, and participated in a wide range of interfaith gatherings. They did this all while practicing as doctors, working in a psychiatric ward caring for patients with serious mental illness. They retired from active practice in 2008, but both of them still operate a clinic, the New Hope Free Clinic, in Redlands, as part of their religious service. The urge to articulate a cosmoplitan spirituality that animated Phạm Công Tắc resurfaced in the diaspora as a way of reorienting the Vietnamese community in a new context.

As a translator of Phạm Công Tắc's religious constitution, his new law code, and the spirit messages that he received, Bùi Đắc Hùm has presented his teachings to a new generation of American-born Caodaists. He has emphasized the tolerant, inclusive aspects of Caodai doctrine, trying to rise above denominational factionalism. He has been open to projects to establish a California-based organization, emphasizing the shared philosophy of the Caodai founders, and welcoming members not only from Tây Ninh but also from the other branches. This emphasis has been controversial (see Chapters 6 and 7) and Hùm has at times been accused of being unfaithful to the legacy of the Hộ Pháp because of this inclusiveness. The teachings he heard as a small boy crouching in a corner of the Great Temple during the midnight services have become, in the words of Thomas Tweed, both a cultural compass and timepiece orienting his life in the new world (2006).

CHAPTER 3

THE SPIRITUAL SONS
OF VICTOR HUGO

FROM SÉANCE TO BATTLEFIELD

In his pleasant but modest home in a trailer park off Bolsa Avenue in "Little Saigon" (Orange County, California), Trần Quang Cảnh has a photograph of his father, Trần Quang Vinh, dressed in long traditional robes and seated, rather imperiously, in a chair. It was taken at a formal reception during the time when his father served as the Minister of Defense for the Saigon government (1947–1952). Trần Quang Vinh was anointed as the spiritual son of Victor Hugo in an early séance, and went on to become the founder of the Caodai Army, an important military leader under the Bảo Đại government, and Caodaism's "ambassador" and translator to Western observers. Today, his son Trần Quang Cảnh has stepped into his shoes and is trying to forge a lasting connection between overseas Caodaists and the Tây Ninh Holy See.

Traditionally, his father should be commemorated with a "death anniversary" feast, and at that time his spirit would be "fed" along with other members of the family. Since Vinh died in a Communist reeducation camp, even the date of his demise is unknown. So Cảnh follows the practice imposed on many Vietnamese who lost loved ones in uncertain conditions: he commemorates his father's death at the full moon of the seventh lunar month, at the festival of all those lost souls whose deaths have not been carefully recorded. And he also prays to the spirit of Victor Hugo, who appears in a mural at the entry to each Tây Ninh temple.

*Figure 3.1. Trần Quang
Vinh in national dress when
he was the Defense Minister
of Vietnam. Archive of Trần
Quang Cảnh*

In March 2012, Trần Quang Cảnh visited Victor Hugo's tomb at the Panthéon mausoleum in Paris. He bowed down and paid his respects to the great
man he considers his "spiritual grandfather." Then he traveled, with a delegation of a dozen other Caodaists, to the headquarters of the Centre Spirite Allan
Kardec in Lyon. There he asked the Kardec Spiritist mediums to help him to
approach the spirit of Victor Hugo to get guidance on how to revive the Caodai
Overseas Mission established in Phnom Penh in 1932. He also asked the mediums to try to contact his father's spirit, wondering if this might be a way to find
out the truth about how he died. He returned with a new sense of his mission
in life. When I met him in September of the same year he told me "we may have
spent many years studying Caodaism, but we have so much more to learn."

This seemed to me a tremendous transformation. In 2004, when I first
contacted Trần Quang Cảnh by e-mail at his earlier home near Washington,
D.C., I asked him about his spiritual kinship with Victor Hugo. He responded
jovially but seemed dismissive: "Yes, it is true that my father was told he was the
spiritual son of Victor Hugo. I guess that makes me Hugo's grandson. Haha!"
Later, in the privacy of his home, that joking acknowledgment became more

reverent: the spirit of Victor Hugo has conferred a heavy religious mission on both father and son. Cảnh has moved from defining his mission as one of opposing Communist restrictions on religious freedom and opening up public bathrooms in Tây Ninh to one of probing the mysteries of Spiritism and the pathway traveled by the soul after death.

This chapter explores that sense of mission by tracing its beginnings in nineteenth-century France, where Victor Hugo was a literary giant of such importance that he dwarfed all others—writing copious novels, plays, and poems that defined a whole era. He participated in séances that predicted he would play a leading role in a new religion that would emerge in the twentieth century. The enthusiasm of early Caodaists may have made this a self-fulfilling prophecy, and it is one that has remained important for over a hundred years. I travel here from the years when Trần Quang Vinh was the "righthand man" of the Hộ Pháp to more recent decades when his son has sought to reestablish this line of spiritual transmission in California, and to open up a dialogue with the Communist leaders he still holds responsible for his father's death. I seek to explain why Vietnamese colonized intellectuals saw themselves as "the true heirs of Victor Hugo," and how the mechanism of reincarnation expresses a spiritual lineage in the occult imagination.

Victor Hugo's Appeal for Vietnamese Readers: Spiritism and Republican Revolution

Victor Hugo's importance for colonized intellectuals stems from the radical educational reforms introduced into French Indochina in 1918, when the Confucian examination system was disbanded and primary schools were ordered to use the Romanized Vietnamese script known as *quốc ngữ*. Suddenly, a new generation of emerging intellectuals was severed from the high cultural canon of works written in Chinese characters and forced to make their way with a new alphabetic writing system. This created a "Eurocentric cosmopolitanism" in which younger people with literary ambitions had "little choice but to immerse themselves in the literary traditions of France and its European neighbors" (Zinoman 2002, 11).

Victor Hugo was the most widely read author in French Indochina, with both his novels and his poems translated, imitated, and serialized repeatedly in Vietnamese newspapers from 1913 onward (Zinoman 2001b, 29–30). *Les Misérables* was particularly popular because of its strong humanism, criticism of the death penalty, and sympathy for the imprisoned. In France, Hugo was already a national monument by the time of his death in 1885 and was buried with great pomp and ceremony in the Paris Panthéon, a secular temple for French culture heroes. He had been a vocal critic of the French State from the late 1820s of the restoration throughout the early Third Republic and was especially opposed to Emperor Louis-Napoléon Bonaparte III, who he famously called "Napoléon-le-petit." He criticized the British burning of the Beijing Summer Palace in 1861, denouncing it as a barbarous offense to a great civilization. Because he defended Asian culture in this context, colonized intellectuals in Saigon thought Hugo would have opposed the conquest of Indochina carried out by his greatest enemy, Napoléon III, and finished only in 1890, five years after Hugo's death. They also became aware of his idiosyncratic attitudes toward religion: a lifetime enemy of the Catholic Church, Hugo believed that communications with spirits would help found a new religion that would encompass Christianity and enlarge it in the same way that Christianity incorporated paganism, reconciling the wisdom of East and West, incorporating ideas of vegetarianism and reincarnation from Asia, and revealing the fundamental unity of "human faith" worldwide (Adèle Hugo 1984 [1853]; Matlock 2000, 65).

These beliefs were influenced by his reading of Asian philosophy, which prompted him to become a vegetarian, but they were also influenced by his experiments with table tipping, a popular form of French occultism in which an unstable pedestal table was induced to move mysteriously to tap out messages in a numerical code, facilitating contact with the recently deceased (Robb 1997).

From 1852 to 1855, Hugo was forced to flee France and live in exile with his family on the British island of Jersey. Unable to speak any English and restricted to the company of a few friends and guests, he suddenly became preoccupied with the accidental drowning of his daughter Léopoldine in 1843 and worked on a set of mystical poems (*Les contemplations*) that he described as drawn from the parts of himself that had died—"my dead youth, my dead heart, my dead daughter, my dead country" (Matlock 2000, 58). One of his house guests, Delphine de Girardin, suggested that they pass the long nights by trying to conjure up spirits at a séance, and after waiting for several evenings with their hands on the table, the table did suddenly seem to "shudder," and then began to move with "feverish agitation," summoning the ghost of Léopoldine and moving both her parents to tears. While skeptical scholars have speculated that Delphine, then fatally ill with cancer, might have faked the tappings to offer some consolation to both herself and her hosts, or that Hugo's son Charles might have unconsciously moved to create the same effect, it is clear from accounts by all present that Hugo became convinced of the truth of the tappings.

To discover if these messages could also be oracles, Hugo asked the table to predict the future and was told that "the evil tyrant" Louis-Napoléon Bonaparte III would fall, and France would become a republic (Victor Hugo, 1923; Matlock 2000, 58). Hugo declared that God permitted the tables to speak and to reveal the existence of the soul to the leaders of the French Republic so that they would come to believe. Without this belief, the Republicans could not escape the ghosts of 1793 and its terror. This religious sentiment was needed to make them the party of "emancipation and the future." Hugo argued that Spiritism "gives wings to human faith," and he became fascinated by these messages showing "there are more things under the sun than human philosophy has dreamed about." "Yes, I believe in the supernatural," he affirmed in a letter to his daughter, adding "better yet, I am living in the supernatural" (Matlock 2000, 65, quoting from Adèle Hugo 1984, V.3, 184–185).

In a letter to Delphine de Girardin, Hugo explicitly linked his dreams of a revolution and a new republic to the religious revelations he received from Spiritism: "What preoccupies me . . . is the enormous continuation of revolutionary activity that God is staging in the moment behind the screen of Bonaparte. I ruin that screen with a kick, but I do not wish that God take it away before its time. . . . We are living on a mysterious horizon that changes the perspective of exile. And we are thinking of you, to whom we owe this open window" (Matlock 2000, 67).

Spiritism, he argued, revealed a way to escape the ossified doctrines of heaven and hell of the Catholic Church and develop a new belief in the people and their power to help one another to achieve liberation. Hell would eventually be "abolished" (as Caodaists later announced it was) by the opening of the "Great Way of the Third Era of Redemption" (Đại Đạo Tam Kỳ Phổ Độ). Over the next two years, Hugo would converse with Aeschylus, Shakespeare, Dante, Racine, Luther, Chateaubriand, Robespierre, and Marat, as well as the Angel of Death and the Shadow of the Tomb.

For almost all of these conversations, it was Hugo's son Charles who was the medium and placed his hands on the table while questions were asked. Victor Hugo was most often the person asking the questions, noting the answers, and then writing up the transcripts. Although the alphabetic code for each letter seemed very time-consuming (1 tap for the letter A, 26 for the letter Z), it seems reasonable to assume that many words could be guessed from the context before all the letters had been tapped out, so, in effect, the person "interpreting" or "reading" the message, and then assembling the words into a full record, could well have influenced their content. Was Victor Hugo in fact conversing only with his own unconscious imagination? Were the other participants simply the vehicles of his larger-than-life sense of his own destiny, suggestible assistants whose hands moved in accord with the subtle messages Hugo sent them about the responses he expected? These controversies have haunted Spiritists for as long as the practice has been around.

In a séance held on the island of Jersey September 29, 1854, "Death" spoke to Victor Hugo and gave him some important publishing advice: "In your Last Will and testament, space out your posthumous works, one every ten years, one every five years . . . ; Jesus Christ rose from the dead only once. You can fill your grave with resurrections. . . . You can have an extraordinary death; you can say while dying, you will awaken me in 1920, you will awaken me in 1940 . . . in 1960 . . . in 1980, you will awaken me in the year 2000."[1]

The purpose of these reawakenings was to "be able to talk to posterity and tell it unknown things which will have had time to ripen in the grave" so that Hugo's death itself "would be a formidable rendezvous arranged with the light and a formidable threat launched against the night" (Hugo 1923, 323; Hugo 1998, 178–179). Hugo followed this advice and published fifteen works posthumously, extending his publishing career from 1822 to 1951. Hugo described the spirit séances as "those works willed by me to the twentieth century," "probably the basis of a new religion," and noted that by the time they appeared "it will be discovered that my revelation has already been revealed" (Hugo 1923, 326; Hugo 1998, 180).

Hugo also apparently feared that the time was not yet right to reveal his conversations with ghosts because the publication of these transcripts "would render my political line impossible . . . instead of being welcomed with respect and faith in human nature, it would be met by an enormous burst of laughter" (Matlock 2000, 63). None of the four notebooks recording the séances in which Victor Hugo participated were delivered to the Bibliothèque Nationale in 1885, where most of his papers were archived after his death. Only in the twentieth century would humanity have advanced to a stage where these works could be appreciated, since (as the Shadow of the Tomb noted in a séance) "every great soul does two works in his life span: his work as a living being, and his work as a ghost" (Hugo 1923, 325; Josephson 1942, 413). In 1923, Gustave Simon published excerpts from all four notebooks, and they were exhibited at the Maison de Victor Hugo, then mysteriously disappeared for fifty years. Today, only two notebooks can be found in the Bibliothèque Nationale. Hugo also produced a series of ink paintings based on his visions, none of which were published until 1985, the centenary of his death. The cover image used for the Bibliothèque Nationale catalog of these paintings, titled *Soleil d'Encre,* shows a globe floating in the sky with an eye in the center of it, radiating its light out onto a dark, clouded universe. This image, suggested in some of his mystical poems inspired by séances, bears an uncanny resemblance to Caodai temple images of the Eye of God.[2]

The Spirit of Victor Hugo Adopts Trần Quang Vinh in Cambodia

The founding revelations of Caodaism, which established the purpose of the new faith as well as its administrative structure (*Pháp Chánh Truyền*) and legal and moral codes (*Tân Luật*), took place in the period 1926–1927. Victor Hugo's spirit does not speak in any of these early messages, and for this reason Caodaists in a number of dissident denominations were later able to say that his teachings were, from their point of view, superfluous. Significantly, Hugo's voice came to be heard only after it was clear that the new faith needed to defend itself against interference from the French government.

In 1927, Phạm Công Tắc's employers at the Régie des Douanes told him he would be transferred from Saigon to Phnom Penh, because they disapproved of his "politically charged" activities as a spirit medium (Werner 1981, 21). He had a sick son at the time and was desperately seeking medical treatment for him. Shortly after he was forced to move to Phnom Penh, his son seems to have died, and it was in this context that he began to receive messages from the French literary figures whose humanism he had so admired in school.

The first séances in Phnom Penh were held in Phạm Công Tắc's home, and he received the messages, assisted by another medium who held the other end of the phoenix basket.[3] A literary spirit with the Vietnamese name Đức Nguyệt Tâm Chơn Nhơn ("spiritual teacher with a moon-pure heart") came down and revealed that he was in fact Victor Hugo. On June 10, 1927, at about 9 p.m., Hugo's spirit turned to address Trần Quang Vinh, another young Vietnamese clerk who was attending the session, and dictated this poem in Vietnamese when Vinh sat in front of the basket:

> Despite his achievements, Vinh Hiển[4] has not yet fulfilled his own destiny
> He has been given a mission to maintain order at home
> Hold it in the heart, be pious and truthful, and give yourself
> Over to this wholeheartedly since it is the right path.
> In the wind the good news is blowing your way
> Your name will be known for a long time

Remain true to yourself and continue to perfect your virtue

The value of your service to the faith will last a long time. (Trần Quang
Vinh 1972, 103–104)

Since he was only thirty years old, and earned barely enough to support his
family, Vinh was surprised at this prophecy, and asked simply if it would be
possible soon for him to return to his homeland in Vietnam. He was told, in
French, "Possible, aide-toi. Le ciel t'aidera"—"It's possible. Help yourself.
Heaven will help you later."

Three years later, the Protectorate of Cambodia prepared a delegation to
the Exposition Coloniale in Vincennes, Paris, and Vinh was selected to attend.
Secretly, spirit séances before his departure revealed that his French official mission was a cover for the more important spiritual mission given to him by God,
which was to spread the new religion to metropolitan France and to lobby for
religious freedom from the colonial government. The Interim Pope Lê Văn
Trung traveled with the Hộ Pháp to Cambodia to meet with him, ordain him as
a Caodai priest (Giáo Hữu), and transfer funds to him to be used in seeking allies for the new faith in Paris. The funds did not reach him, as they were kept by
a cynical dignitary who argued Vinh would only use the money to "go dancing
in Paris." Vinh arrived in France on February 10, 1931, and spent nine months
in Paris during the exposition. He was so successful in recruiting supporters that
he was able to organize a party for his benefactors at the fancy new Art Deco
Hotel Lutetia and publish a pamphlet (*Les Martyrs de la Foi Nouvelle*) about the
persecution of Caodaists in French Indochina. Henri Guernot, General Secretary of the Ligue des Droits de l'Homme, made a speech in the National Assembly calling for religious freedom in the French colony (Trần Quang Vinh 1972,
110–111).

Vinh's memoir does not record any of his impressions of France or of the
exposition itself, but it provides a detailed portrait of the reception he received in
Saigon when he returned on December 30, 1931. He was greeted by the Interim
Pope and other religious leaders who had read his letters documenting his activi-
ties in France and invited to a home where a séance was held at midnight. Victor
Hugo's spirit was the first to descend and welcomed Vinh warmly in French verse:

Bonjour, mes grands frères	Good evening, my brothers
Et la mission étrangère?	How about the foreign mission?
Viens Hiến Trung mon enfant	Come Hiến Trung my son

Voilà ton nom est maintenant grand	Now your name has become great
Viens recevoir la bénédiction de ton père	Come to receive your father's blessing
La lignée des Hugo a le droit d'être fière	The Hugo lineage is rightfully proud
Tu as assez vu n'est-ce pas?	Have you seen enough?
La France est vraiment grand état	France is truly a great nation
Oh! Ne te plains pas de son ingratitude	Oh! Don't worry about her ungratefulness
Quoiqu'elle soit France, elle garde cette habitude	Although she is France, she still has some bad habits
Tu lui a rendu grand service	You have done so much for her
Et en religion tu n'es que novice	Although in religion you are only a novice
Pauvre garçon! Tu m'as fait tant souffrir au berceau	Poor boy! You made me suffer so much when you were in the cradle
Tu me paies maintenant d'un renom de plus beau	You repay me now with your splendid fame
Ta mère a promis de venir	Your mother promised to come
Avec moi, elle voudra te bénir	To bless you beside me. (Trân Quang Vinh 1972, 114–115)

As the mediums wrote down the message, Vinh kneeled in front of the altar and the basket turned to stroke him gently on the head, as if he were a sleeping child. A few minutes later, the spirit of Adèle Hugo, Vinh's spiritual mother, came to speak as well, complaining that her husband "persists, in spite of my tears, in sending you into a world of terror," where his spiritual sons are asked to "continue his work among those who have denied [his humanism]" (Trân Quang Vinh 1972, 114). The poignant tenderness of these messages is disarmingly intimate, defining the spiritual kinship between this famous French literary family and his Vietnamese reincarnations.[5] Only Hugo's daughter, also named Adèle, refused to appear at the séance, since for her the memory of her suffering was "too raw. . . . She does not want to return to the world of the living" (Trân Quang Vinh 1972, 118).

One other adept in Phnom Penh was designated in séances as Hugo's spiritual son: Đặng Trung Chữ was his older son Charles, while Trần Quang Vinh was his younger son François. Both of Hugo's spiritual sons eventually rose to become archbishops (Phối Sư) in the Caodai administrative hierarchy.

Victor Hugo in the Classroom: "France Needs to Learn Some Lessons"

Phạm Công Tắc was allowed to return to Tây Ninh in 1930, and from this time on many of the messages received from Victor Hugo were critical of the French colonial regime. Through spirit séances, students who had been denied full access to a French literary education were granted "direct access" to one of the masters of French literature. The conversations made possible by séances with European literary and historical figures created a space for a moral critique of colonialism. Hugo presents himself as a schoolmaster lecturing not only the Vietnamese but also the French on the ethics of their behavior. His most quoted séance poem is this one:

L'univers est donc une école pour les esprits	The universe is a school for spirits
Qui la fréquentent pour être encore plus érudits	Who attend to become more cultivated
Ceux qui font souvent l'école buissonière	Those who cut their lessons to play hooky
Doivent doubler leurs années et reprendre leurs matières.	Must repeat a grade and take each subject again.
Toutes les âmes espèrent lire ce livre éternel	All souls hope to read the book of eternity
Qui contient le secret à se faire immortel.	Which contains the secret of becoming immortal.[6]

The metaphor of life as a great school, even—as Trần Quang Vinh argued in a famous speech in 1935—a graduate school of the highest spiritual wisdom—is particularly poignant when we recall that it was used to address a generation of Vietnamese students taught exclusively by French professors, who offered lessons to their native charges by drawing on the great works of French literature. In effect, spirit mediumship is used to cut out these professors as the middlemen and to show that great literary figures can speak for themselves—

and would, in fact, speak out against the inequities of colonialism if they could be summoned directly. This is the students quite literally turning the tables on their professors and applying the "lessons" of French literature to the daily life of French Indochina.

The critical message is even clearer in a message received December 11, 1931:

Nous sommes en Indochine sous le pouvoir des potentats	We in Indochina are under the power of potentates
Méfions-nous qu'au regard des lois	Watch out that in the eyes of the law
L'on ne nous traite de forçats	We may be treated as convicts
Je ne parle pas de la foi	I do not speak of faith
Le gouvernement colonial s'abaisse	The colonial government is crushed under
Sous la férule catholique	The iron rule of the Catholic Church
Notre nouvelle religion se laisse	Our new religion is becoming
Corrompre par des procès souvent publics	Corrupted by the often public trials
Des droits de liberté, de conscience	Of the rights to freedom of conscience
Tant de fois announcés	So often proclaimed
Par la France humanitaire	By a Humanitarian France
De par le monde qu'elle prétend assez chers.	Throughout the world, pretending to hold dear.
Fils d'une telle nation, que j'aime	As a son of that nation, which I love,
Quoique je n'y compte que pour une vie.	Although I only incarnated for one life there.
J'ai pu connaître vraiment à fond	I have been able to know deeply
Comme est son idéal trahi	How her ideals have been betrayed
Ses représentations, indignes d'elle,	Her colonial officers, unworthy of her

La déshonorent par leurs concussions intellectuelles,	Do her dishonor with their intellectual fraudulence
Persécutent nos frères moins spirituels.	Persecuting our less spiritual brothers.
Demandons comment nous devons nous défendre	We ask how we can defend ourselves
Quand iis emploient des moyens malhonnêtes	When they use dishonest means
Nous conduire même devant l'opinion qui se prête	Bringing us before public opinion which supports
A ceux qui ont la main la plus tendre.	Those who have the softest hands.
Dieu leur avait donné l'heur	God gave them the good fortune
De posséder un pays religieux;	Of possessing a religious country;
Ils ne savent profiter du bonheur	But they did not know how to benefit
Qui leur vient du haut des cieux.	From this blessing of the highest heavens.
Il nous reste qu'un moyen efficace	We have only one effective means left
Pour abaisser leur instinct rapace:	To counter their predatory instincts:
C'est leur tendre enfin l'ardent amour	It is to offer them our ardent love
Et les réléguer dans l'infâme tour	And relegate them to the infamous
Des athées. . . . au revoir.	Tower of atheists. . . . good-bye.[7]

Thus, ironically, Hugo was "indigenized" as a schoolmaster and father figure, taking the paternalistic stereotypes of colonial rhetoric and giving them a new twist, in which the Vietnamese sons of the great French literary figure emerge as the true champions of his prophetic ideas of humanism and emancipation, while his European descendants are criticized for their hypocrisy.

In Paris, Trần Quang Vinh converted the French philosopher and novelist Gabriel Gobron and his wife Marguerite. Gabriel later published *History and Philosophy of Caodaism* (1948), a rapturous mystical account of the

doctrines of the new faith, based, it seems, mainly on documentation provided by Vinh, conversations with Caodaist students in Paris, and séance
messages, since he never visited Vietnam. Gobron was later given the rank
of Archbishop (Tiếp Dẫn Đạo Nhơn) in the College of Spirit Mediums
(Hiệp Thiên Đài). After his death, Marguerite Gobron published a collection of photographs of Caodai festivals, costumes, and wartime propaganda
(M. Gobron 1949). In early séances, one Frenchman, M. Latapie, was appointed to the position of bishop in the overseas mission, and another, the
prominent critic of colonial exploitation Paul Monet, was appointed to be a
delegate representing Caodaism to the Parliament of the World Religions
in 1928.[8]

Although Governor Le Fol was invited to attend a séance (see Chapter 1),
relations with the French colonial governors who followed him were more
strained. Caodai historians provide a narrative of these events, in which un-
sympathetic administrators were divinely punished for their persecution of the
new religion, and came to regret it in posthumous séance messages. Governor
Pierre Pasquier (1928–1934) suspected that nationalist politics lay hiding under Caodaist doctrines of religious tolerance and increased both surveillance
and restrictions on the new faith. After the Yên Bái rebellion in early 1930, he
restricted the number of Indochinese students allowed to study in France and
tried to discourage parents from exposing their children to the grave moral
dangers of the metropole (where many students demonstrated in sympathy
with the rebels).[9] He collected a number of documents about Caodaism, perhaps including the original declaration in 1926 and even forgeries that misrepresented the religion, intending to bring them back to France. His flight ended
dramatically on January 15, 1934, when Pasquier was killed in a spectacular
plane crash described in lurid detail in newspapers in France and Indochina.
His spirit made contact with Caodaist mediums in August 18, 1936, to express
his regret that he had persecuted the religion, and thus cut short his own life.
With the retrospective wisdom granted those who speak from the afterworld,
he wished he had been more sympathetic to the new faith and did not have to
carry the karmic burden of persecuting its practitioners.[10]

A similar message was also received from the spirit of Paul Doumer, governor of Indochina from 1897 to 1902, who treated Caodaists harshly when he
was elected president of France in 1931 and was assassinated in Paris in 1932.
The spirit of Doumer notes that he was punished for failing to grant religious
freedom to Caodaists, concluding "This lapse in my sacred duty toward eternity
cost me twelve years of life."[11] Doumer's rival for the presidency, Aristide Briand,
in contrast, is part of the Tây Ninh pantheon, and his spirit was appointed to

oversee the Caodai mission in Africa because of his campaign for colonial reform (Trần Quang Vinh 1962, 102). The idea that a head of government might express posthumous regret for his policies toward Caodaism has been echoed in controversial (and unofficial) twenty-first-century messages along the same lines from Hồ Chí Minh (see Chapter 6).

Spiritual Kinship: Hugo as a Father and Teacher

Hugo's spiritual sons are considered to be reincarnations of his French sons, and like Hugo's French sons they grew up to be writers and revolutionaries, people who penned poetry and manned the ramparts of anti-imperial resistance. Like Hugo's French son François, who transcribed his father's séances and later translated Shakespeare, Hugo's Vietnamese son Trần Quang Vinh transcribed spirit séances, edited Hugo's posthumous verses in a collection published in 1962, and translated them into Vietnamese from the original French. On May 22, 1937, he consecrated a magnificent new temple in Phnom Penh containing a portrait of his spiritual father.[12] Trần Quang Vinh made the opening speech:

> We have chosen to inaugurate our first Cambodian temple on the 52nd anniversary of the disincarnation of this great Frenchman, Victor Hugo, who has been since 1927 the beloved and respected spiritual head of the overseas mission. We also mark our gratitude to France, the birthplace of this great poet we learned to love on French school benches, this chivalrous, generous and humanitarian France.... It has been long since at Phú Quốc ... the spirit breathed as he had already breathed on the island of Jersey, facing the infinite mystery of the human conscience and destiny, by those immortal tables of Mme de Girardin and Victor Hugo.[13]

This was the impetus for "a powerful doctrinal synthesis linking the gods of Asia and the gods of Europe," based on "that fraternity of men, that friendship of races" that brought Caodaists "closer to that French soul with which we believe ourselves to have many secret and mysterious affinities" (Gobron 1949, 95).

Trần Quang Vinh's praise of the "French soul" and the many French "friends of Caodaism" who had defended religious freedom in the colony (including such luminaries as Prime Minister Albert Sarrault, French residents in Vietnam and Cambodia, and nine deputies in Paris) was to be severely challenged just four years later, when the Hộ Pháp and three dignitaries were arrested by the French police for predicting a Japanese victory in World War II.

Figure 3.2. Trần Quang Vinh in his religious robes as a bishop (Phối Sư). Archive of Trần Quang Cảnh

Figure 3.3. Trần Quang Vinh in uniform as the founder of the Caodai Army. Archive of Trần Quang Cảnh

From Séance to Battlefield: The Spiritual Sons and the Revolution

In 1940, the French ordered mandarins and notables to recruit a quota of "volunteers" for the French army in Europe. Forcible recruitment was the only way district chiefs could fulfill their quotas. In Biên Hòa, the people were on the verge of revolt on this matter. The situation was finally eased when Phạm Công Tắc, as head of the Tây Ninh church, supplied Caodaist volunteers to fulfill the quotas.

This effort to win the goodwill of the French by supporting the war effort seems to have ultimately backfired: Tắc was accused by French secret agents of "having incited Caodaists to volunteer for French forces for the duration of the war with the intention, expressed many times in private conversations, of being able later to require that the French government grant independence to Indochina." He was also said to have established the Phạm Môn (spirit medium collective) and Phước Thiên (charity organization) for his own benefit and to be spreading "une propagande insidieuse contre la France."[14] The French arrested

Tắc in 1940, along with five other dignitaries suspected of sympathizing with the Japanese, and sent them into exile on Madagascar and the Comoros Islands.[15]

During his absence, Trần Quang Vinh and other Caodai leaders moved their base across the Cambodian border, where they were allowed to carry on religious activities during the Japanese occupation. When the French seized the temple in Phnom Penh, they destroyed Caodai religious relics and pushed Caodaists into the hands of the Japanese. Guided by a spirit séance that told him it was time to fight "for the religion and the country" (*cứu Đạo cứu Đời*), Trần Quang Vinh agreed to meet the Japanese secret police (Kempeitai) in Saigon, offering them information in return for promises to protect the religion and bring back Vietnamese Prince Cường Để (exiled in Japan) (Trần Quang Vinh 1972, 187).

Caodai workers volunteered to work at the shipyards around Saigon, and these workers were then organized into a militia with a Caodai uniform of white khaki and white hats. When Trần Quang Vinh asked the Japanese to give guns to his forces, they refused. Caodai forces, armed only with bamboo sticks, served as guards for the Japanese coup on March 9, 1945, that captured French soldiers and police and declared an end to French colonialism. Caodai leaders organized a massive rally on March 18 to celebrate the end of French rule. Vinh gave a speech calling for unity behind the "national religion" (*quốc giáo*) in which he said the Caodai forces would be the basis for a new "national army" to safeguard independence (Trần Mỹ-Vân 2006, 7). But then the Japanese refused to bring Prince Cường Để out of exile to lead a new independent Vietnam. Vinh and others protested and were promised that their prince and savior would come in July. A welcoming committee was formed, with banners, arches, and flags ready to welcome the exiled leader (Trần Mỹ-Vân 2006, 9). But many days and nights passed and he did not come. The Americans bombed Hiroshima, and Japan surrendered unconditionally in August. The trust that Caodaists had had in Japan seemed blind and illusory, a trust that had been betrayed.

In Vinh's autobiography, he documents not only his political actions during this period, but also the spirit messages that guided him. The spirit of the deceased interim Pope Lê Văn Trung often spoke to him, as did the "invisible Pope," Lý Thái Bạch, the spirit of the famous Tang-dynasty poet who became the primary intermediary between Caodai disciples and the world of the spirits. Trần Hưng Đạo, a famous national hero who defeated Mongol armies in the thirteenth century, came to tell Vinh: "After I fought, for many centuries there were no new heroes, until God established Caodaism. I have come to lend my support to efforts to spread the religion, since without faith there can be no victory, and even great heroes will fail to reach their goals. . . . The children must pay the karmic debts of their ancestors, but now it has all been paid back. Soon the day will come when the land of Vietnam will once again belong to the Vietnamese" (Trần Quang Vinh 1972, 162).

Looking back on these events in 1972, Trần Quang Vinh wrote that although prophecies that Cường Để would be returned and that the Japanese would free Vietnam seemed to have been inaccurate, going deeper into the "true mysteries" of history tells a different story. Cường Để died in exile in Japan, but in 1954 Phạm Công Tắc himself traveled to Tokyo to retrieve his ashes and bring them back for a commemorative ceremony in Tây Ninh. Atom bombs may have interfered with the "divine laws that were written in the heavens," but Japan and the pan-Asian movement for national self-determination ultimately won a "moral or spiritual victory," because "if Japan had not been brave enough to confront England and America, then it is unlikely that the smaller countries of Southeast Asia could have obtained a release from their servitude to the super powers" (Trần Quang Vinh 1972, 192).

After the Japanese defeat, Hồ Chí Minh issued his own declaration of independence in Hanoi in September, and most Caodaists rejoiced. The Caodai militia, allied with the separate militia of the Hòa Hảo Buddhist reformists, controlled more of southern Vietnam than any other force, including the Việt Minh, and seemed posed to share power in a new government of national unity (Fall 1955, 239). But since the religious leaders were still in exile, there was no consensus. When Việt Minh political prisoners were released from French prisons, some of them formed roaming bands determined to destroy all perceived reactionaries and traitors, including nationalist leaders who had contemplated cooperation with the Japanese (Marr 1981, 223). In Quảng Ngãi Province, former prisoners from the Ba Tơ detention camp attacked Caodai communities, killing many Caodaists who—like them—had just been released from French prisons. These killings, which began in August 1945, eventually claimed 2,791 victims—dignitaries and disciples, women and children—and the site where many of these killings occurred was commemorated in 1956 as the "graveyard of Caodai martyrs."[16] Caodaists and Hòa Hảo Buddhists were demonized in Việt Minh propaganda as terrorists and cannibals (McHale 2009).

Alienated from their former comrades-in-arms by these attacks, the Caodaists in Tây Ninh were then courted by the French, who realized that if they were to return to reconquer Indochina, they would need at least some indigenous collaborators. On June 6, 1946, Trần Quang Vinh was captured by French forces, tortured, and forced to agree to a truce. In return for his promise not to attack the French army, he was able to negotiate for the return of Phạm Công Tắc and the other exiled leaders from Madagascar. The French General Latour announced dramatically that the Caodaists had "rallied to the national cause," and a military convention was signed with the French High Command in which Caodaists promised "loyal collaboration" with the French. The French benefited immensely from this agreement, since it gave them "control over wide areas of south Vietnam which they could never have hoped to conquer militarily" (Fall 1955, 297), while the Việt Minh suffered a setback because of their brutality in attacking Caodaists and other nationalist groups who had been their allies.

When Phạm Công Tắc returned from exile, he accepted the political conditions that had made this possible and stated that a continued French presence might be "necessary" for a few more years. Some leaders of dissident denominations in Mỹ Tho and Bến Tre remained in French prisons, but the mother church in Tây Ninh functioned openly, and the Holy See was reopened as well as thousands of temples in Vietnam and Cambodia (Blagov 2001a, 94). Caodai soldiers saw themselves as a defensive force and showed some reluctance to attack Vietnamese who had not targeted Caodaists, but they served as a home guard throughout the Mekong Delta, allowing the French to concentrate on waging war against Hồ Chí Minh's armies in the north.[17]

In a sermon delivered on May 22, 1949, the sixty-fourth anniversary of Hugo's death, Tắc revealed that Victor Hugo himself emerged from the spiritual lineage of the great Vietnamese poet Nguyễn Du (1765–1820) and was in fact the reincarnation of this famous author of the *Tale of Kiều*. By "indigenizing" Hugo and tying him to a Vietnamese literary giant, Du also became more "cosmopolitan" and found his own genius plotted on a map with French coordinates. This twist came at a political moment when efforts to renew the social contract and heal the wounds of colonialism ceded to a post–World War II realization of the inevitability of decolonization. Trần Quang Vinh followed Tắc's lead in embracing a more encompassing Asian religious vision, in which Hugo was the "earlier incarnation" of Nguyễn Du and a French literary giant came to be encompassed within the legacy of a Vietnamese bard.[18]

Leadership of the Caodai Armed Forces and Greene's *Quiet American*

Trần Quang Vinh was made the commander of the Caodai Armed Forces. Both he and Phạm Công Tắc resisted pressures from the French to attack Việt Minh forces directly and in 1949 proposed that the Holy See should become a neutral zone, where nationalists from both sides could come and seek refuge. They would not agree, however, to lay down their own arms, so the Việt Minh refused to recognize this neutrality (Blagov 2001a, 96; Werner 1981, 51). When the Caodai Army reached 65,000 soldiers in 1954, they were the largest

Vietnamese armed forces in the South. They assumed many other governmental functions unrelated to their military training, such as collecting taxes in Tây Ninh, running a sawmill and brick and tile factory, and rebuilding the market at Long Hoa. The areas under their control were safe, untroubled by crime or prostitution, and drew many others who came to seek refuge under the shelter of the Holy See and its army (Blagov 2001, 98; Werner 1981, 47). About half of the rural population of the South was "protected" by Caodai forces during the First Indochina War (Werner 1980, 108).

In 1947, Trần Quang Vinh left active command of the army and was appointed Minister of Defense in the Bảo Đại government. He had already been sent by Phạm Công Tắc to meet with the former emperor when he was exiled in Hong Kong and had helped persuade him to return to head a "transition government" under French sponsorship (Werner 1976, 378). The first government was led by Nguyễn Phan Long, a famous journalist who had tried to unify different Caodai branches in Saigon, and his goal was to "negotiate independence" for a unified Vietnam in the form of a constitutional monarchy. Vinh continued to serve in three other provisional governments until 1951, when he stepped down to return to Tây Ninh, where he held the religious rank of archbishop.[19]

Succession struggles about who should take over command of Caodai troops occurred in the volatile years from 1949–1954. Trần Quang Vinh was kidnapped in 1953–1954 by the renegade General Trình Minh Thế, well known to American readers as the villain of Graham Greene's 1954 novel *The Quiet American*. Vinh was held hostage at Black Lady Mountain for six months while General Thế tried to recruit Caodai soldiers for his own private army, committed to fighting against both the French and the Communists. Thế claimed credit for blowing up a car in front of the Saigon Opera House in 1952, and this incident inspired a similar scene in Greene's novel.

While *The Quiet American* has attained quasi-legendary status as a "prophetic" novel about the dangers of U.S. military intervention, it appears that Greene was wrong about Americans supplying General Thế with weapons in 1952. Two years later, however, in 1954–1955, at the time that Greene's novel was published, American CIA operative Edward Lansdale did make contact with General Thế and came to see him as a "freedom fighter" who had the potential to be a national leader.[20] So Greene was—as in his statement about "missionaries sent to Los Angeles"—wrong in his facts but right in his gazing into the crystal ball of the future.

Two big-budget films re-created this scene but proposed different interpretations of the events. Both portray General Thế as a ferociously violent military leader, but in Greene's original novel he is represented as having been armed by a (fictional) American CIA agent named Alden Pyle. The 1958 film, made in Hollywood by Joseph Mankiewicz, appeared as American military involvement intervention was escalating, so the plot was changed to blame "the Reds" for killing Pyle. The young CIA agent is portrayed as dangerously naive in Greene's novel but becomes a heroic figure in the 1958 film, sacrificing his life for the fight against Communism and betrayed by the Greene surrogate, British journalist Fowler, out of sexual jealousy.

In 1957, the Hollywood film crew came to shoot some "exotic footage" of the Festival of the Mother Goddess in Tây Ninh, to accompany Michael Redgrave's sonorous voice entoning Graham Greene's famous description of Caodaism as a "Walt Disney fantasia of the Orient." They were able to witness a parade of soldiers, white-robed dignitaries, and lion dancers, but they were also very surprised to find themselves in the middle of a political demonstration. In addition to the many banners bearing quotes from spirit messages, there were huge signs calling for the government to "Return our Hộ Pháp" and "Restore Religious Freedom" to the Holy See. The filmmakers were not able to read the signs, so although they were eventually forced to stop shooting, they included footage of this demonstration in the final cut of the 1958 film.[21]

The prominence given to the story of General Thế (who is the only historical character in *The Quiet American* identified by his real name) has cast a pall over the public image of Caodaism, which is remembered by journalists and many members of the American public as "the religion with an army that was involved in terrorist attacks." While General Thế was born into a Caodai family and came up through the ranks of the Caodai Army, he had no particular commitment to the religion, and his actions were not endorsed or supported by Caodai religious leaders like Phạm Công Tắc.

Greene was furious at how his antiwar novel was turned into "American propaganda" for the very forces he criticized. General Thế did not live long enough to benefit from this twisting of the story. One of his many enemies managed to shoot him in Saigon in May 1955, bringing his bloody career to an abrupt end, but opening up speculation about who had ordered his killing. Trần Quang Vinh was freed and, exhausted by his ordeal, chose to go into exile in France. He spent the next decade writing his memoirs and editing collections of spirit messages in French (Trần Quang Vinh 1972, 52–63; Blagov 2001a, 100–106).

Almost fifty years later, Phillip Noyce announced his intention to return to Vietnam to film a new version of *The Quiet American* that would be more true to Greene's novel. He requested permission to film in Tây Ninh, but the government—probably remembering the demonstrations in 1957, and aware of tensions with the Caodai community in 2000—refused to allow this. So General Thế's camp at Black Lady Mountain was filmed at a "more scenic" location in the far north of the country, and misleading dialogue even suggested that his troops had been involved in the slaughter of Catholic villagers in Phát Diệm, northern Vietnam. The script changes pleased the current government, and the 2001 film was very successful in Vietnam—but it was hardly faithful to Greene's original intentions, or to the complexity of political alliances at the time.[22] Defending Caodaism against the "fictional history" first penned by Greene has unfortunately become an important part of the work of the Caodai Overseas Mission in the twenty-first century.

Hugo's Sons and Their Descendants

Caodaism remained a vital and expanding religion during the years of U.S. military intervention, but Victor Hugo's spirit was not heard from again in Saigon or Tây Ninh. Tắc's move in 1949 to "Vietnamize" the pantheon continued with increased attention being given to the spirit of Lê Văn Duyệt, the southern general who ended a civil war in 1802 by leading southern forces to victory and establishing the Nguyễn dynasty.

In 1975, the imminent fall of Saigon inspired many Caodaists to escape overseas, and over the next few decades diasporic temples were established in California, France, Australia, and Canada. But Trần Quang Vinh did not escape: He was arrested, at the age of seventy-eight, and sent to do forced labor at a "re-education" camp. As his son Trần Quang Cảnh later told me:

> After the fall of Saigon, it was a different story for Caodai. The Communist regime considered us Caodaists as purely political enemies to be eliminated because of the past: we collaborated with the Japanese, then with the French, where both forces were enemies of the Communists. So the first order of business under the Communist government was to arrest all Caodai leaders. My father was one of the many dignitaries who were arrested and jailed incommunicado. Up to now, our family still does not know when, where, or how he died. The official story from the government was that he died of cardiac arrest in a prison. The unofficial story came from a French friend of my father who worked for the French government informing us in late 1975 that my father was executed.

The controversy about how Trần Quang Vinh died should ideally be resolved by calling on his spiritual father, Victor Hugo. As Cảnh explained:

Victor Hugo is the one who taught my father and his companions when they were sent to live in a foreign country, and he is the spirit who moves between all of the former French colonies and inspires them with his message of freedom and humanity. He could tell us how my father really died and why it was a necessary part of the divine plan. Victor Hugo should determine if the various translations of Caodai doctrine into English are correct, and he should advise us on how to connect the overseas congregations to the Holy See in Tây Ninh.

The problem, as he acknowledged, is that in spite of "normalized relations" with the Tây Ninh hierarchy, spirit séances and spirit mediumship are still illegal in Vietnam.[23] Victor Hugo's spirit can only be called to speak with authority from the Cung Đạo in the Great Temple in Tây Ninh, the inner sanctum in front of the globe with the Left Eye of God gazing outward.

Although he did not use this language, I would describe Victor Hugo's status within Caodaism as a "transcolony" saint and spiritual advisor. Victor Hugo's spirit first "made contact" with Caodai leaders in exile, forced to leave their homeland in southern Vietnam (then the French colony of Cochinchina) to live in Cambodia. Both were then parts of French Indochina, but it was a sign of the already strong power of "Vietnamese" nationalism that a posting to Cambodia was considered an "exile," while a posting to Hanoi or Đà Nẵng (capital cities of the protectorates of Tonkin and Annam) would not be. Victor Hugo was, therefore, a paradoxically "familiar" figure from French literature who came to console young civil servants forced to live in an unfamiliar cultural setting. Hugo considered himself both a "poet and a prophet," and wrote that he produced his most important poetic works during the period of mystical contemplation on the islands of Jersey and Guernsey.[24] In a Caodai séance in 1932, Hugo was divinely appointed to lead the "foreign mission" (Hội Thánh Hải Ngoại, literally overseas mission), although of course it was the Mekong River, not the ocean, that was crossed to travel to Phnom Penh. This appointment established a precedent for calling on Hugo to provide advice for the expansion of Caodaism outside Vietnam, and thus later for his involvement in diasporic congregations in Europe, North America, and Australia.

How should we interpret Hugo's place in Caodaism? While he is not "deified" or credited with any supernatural powers, his opinion was considered important in the 1930s, when the struggle against French colonialism was taking shape, and in the 1940s, when his spiritual sons were called to take up arms against their former colonial masters. Is his voice in séances a sign of "the colonization of consciousness" or resistance to colonial rule?

Some might argue that because Hugo was the best-selling author of French Indochina, many imaginative Vietnamese students had the impression of growing up under his tutelage. To young colonized intellectuals, Hugo appeared as a spiritual teacher and *maître de cours* who, they were sure, would have been more sympathetic than their French professors, flesh and blood presences but often distant and disdainful. The revelation that Hugo had himself held séances reinforced this identification. As a francophone literary scholar based in Paris has argued, Hugo's works provided a "magic mirror in which Oriental readers encountered the political and religious thoughts of Buddhism and Taoism" (Trần Thu Dung 1996, 190). It was the shock of recognition—seeing notions of reincarnation and communication between the living and the dead being embraced by a great French intellectual—that proved exciting and inspiring.

In Caodai belief, Hugo was not "selected" or "chosen" by his interlocutors, but chose to make contact with them from the White Cloud Lodge (Bạch Vân Động, *la loge blanche*) where he and his spiritual companions looked down at human activity. A more skeptical observer might see his words as having been internalized by a generation of young Vietnamese often described as *de culture française* (educated in the French language) who were drawn to the sweeping oceanic vision of French romanticism. The humanitarian and republican ideals that they were taught in school were not put into practice by the colonial administration, but they provided a language of freedom with tremendous appeal. Not only Vietnamese, but also disaffected colonial intellectuals in the protectorates of Laos and Cambodia, were moved by his words, as were colonized populations in Africa and the Arab world.

The "spiritual sons of Victor Hugo" could be understood to refer to a generation of people educated in French but frustrated that the ideals of liberty, equality, and fraternity that they studied in school were not accessible to colonial subjects. The voice of Victor Hugo, heard by some in spirit séances, expressed an inner tension that was much broader than Caodaism. Vinh's fourteen children almost all settled overseas, and some became active in Caodai communities in France and the United States. From 1998 to 2006, Trần Quang Cảnh was president of the Caodai Overseas Mission, an organization that has carried the religious message of Tây Ninh to many corners of the world and has developed a series of Internet sites to disseminate information.

The World That Made Trần Quang Cảnh

Trần Quang Cảnh was born in 1943 in Saigon when his father was the commander in chief of the newly created Caodai Army. Two years after his birth,

Trần Quang Vinh's forces would take part in the Japanese-led coup against the French and proclaim the independence of Vietnam (five months before the Communist-led August revolution or Hồ Chí Minh's September proclamation in Hanoi). As the oldest son of Vinh's second wife, he was one of fourteen children (seven with the first wife and seven with the second) who grew up in religious and military circles. He was ten when his father finished serving as minister of defense under the government headed by the former Emperor Bảo Đại and Premier Trần Văn Hữu. Although he only served until June 1952, the prestige of that position was to remain with the family.

Private séances were held in the family home with an alphabetic planchette (the *tiểu ngọc cơ*, or "smaller instrument"). His father would bring it out and invite a couple of mediums to come to summon spirits to give their advice. Victor Hugo was among them (especially for religious administrative decisions, since Vinh was an archbishop in the Tây Ninh hierarchy), but so was the twelfth-century military hero Trần Hưng Đạo and the Interim Pope Lê Văn Trung. Vinh's memoir (1972) provides the texts of some of those messages. The phoenix basket was brought out for larger, more official séances in the Cung Đạo in Tây Ninh, with the bird's beak tracing letters in wine or spirits poured onto glass. Cảnh remembers the hushed, solemn atmosphere of these sessions but was too young to make much sense of the messages received.

Educated at the French-language school Lycée Jean-Jacques Rousseau in Saigon, and the College of Political Science and Business Administration in Dalat, Cảnh was drafted into the South Vietnamese Army in 1968. His father had friends in high places and did not want his son to be sent into combat, so he was able to arrange to have him work for the Ministry of Information. He eventually rose to become director of personnel, with close to 20,000 employees working under him. His wife, a software engineer, was recruited to work for IBM, and it was the IBM connection that helped both of them to escape from Saigon in April 1975, just a few days before the city fell. His father, retired and living in Tây Ninh, was left behind, and the fact that none of his many children was able to save him weighed heavily on their hearts.

In their first years in the United States, Trần Quang Cảnh and his wife struggled to adapt to a new context, and both trained for new positions at IBM in the Washington, D.C., area. They raised two children and were members of Caodai congregations that began worshipping in their home, eventually building a small temple in the 1980s. Cảnh spearheaded the formation of the Cao Dai Overseas Mission in the late 1990s, working with Caodaists in Montreal (Madame Nguyễn Ngọc Lan) and Sydney, Australia (Nguyễn Chánh Giáo). He followed in his father's footsteps in targeting international conferences, where he wanted Caodaism to be represented. He spoke at the Center for Studies of the New Religions in 1998 in Philadelphia, presenting a paper titled "Religious Persecution of the Cao Dai Religion: Policy and Measures Aimed at the Abolition of the Cao Dai Religion by the Government of the Socialist Republic of Vietnam." He also spoke at the International Association for Religious Freedom's thirty-first World Congress in Budapest, Hungary, in 2002.

The United Nations and the U.S. State Department both paid attention to these presentations, and Trần Quang Cảnh became—in the early 2000s—a sort of "ambassador" of Caodaism to foreigners, much as his father had been in Paris in the 1930s. Abdelfattah Amor, the United Nations Rapporteur for religious freedom, submitted a very critical report about the Vietnamese situation in 1999. In 2003, the European Parliament issued a resolution expressing concern about the treatment of religious groups in Vietnam. These efforts, as well as those of Catholic, Protestant, Hòa Hảo Buddhist, and other religious leaders, prompted the decision of the U.S. State Department to cite Vietnam as "a country of particular concern" for issues of violating religious freedom in the years 2004 and 2005 (Taylor 2007, 53, note 2).

When Cảnh met with Abdelfattah Amor to document the situation of Caodaists since 1975, Amor persuaded him to reverse his tactics. Amor told him it was quixotic to think that the current regime could be overthrown or that the "Communists could be kicked out." Instead of plotting an armed resistance (as some young Caodaists did with smuggled weapons in 1984),[25] the Caodaists should negotiate with the state. Amor said, "You will never get anywhere unless you start talking to the government. It is the only pathway to an improved situation. Not confrontation, but dialogue."

Many Caodaists had vowed never to return to "Communist Vietnam," but Trần Quang Cảnh started traveling there in 2001. "I knew they had secret police following me all the time, but I simply allowed them to see that I was not doing anything wrong," he told me. He met with people at the Department of Religion and asked them what he could do to improve the situation of Caodaists: Could the vast amount of property that was "nationalized" in 1975 be restored to the Holy See? Could a tourist center be opened at the great temple in Tây Ninh, which currently received hundreds of tourists every day but provided no context for what they were seeing? Would Caodai religious leaders be allowed to leave Vietnam to travel to international conferences?

At first, the answers to all questions were negative. But Cảnh persisted and tried to convince Cardinal Nguyễn Thành Tám—the leader of the "progovernment" faction appointed to run the Tây Ninh Governance Council—to allow him to establish relations between the Caodai administrative hierarchy

and overseas communities. Religious leaders in Vietnam appreciated the gener-
ous contributions that overseas Caodaists made toward renovating temples and
reopening those that had been closed for years. Cảnh's efforts were widely criticized by the most "anti-Communist" of the overseas groups (see Chapters 5
and 6), but, on June 6, 2011, he was formally invested as a Lễ Sanh, the entry-
level rank of dignitaries or ritual specialists, usually translated as "deacon," and
was delegated to represent the Caodai Sacerdoce overseas.

Cảnh was the first American citizen to hold any office within the Tây
Ninh hierarchy. He showed me with great pride the high conical hat with an eye
in the front and the red robe. He posed with all of the highest-ranking Caodai
dignitaries in front of the Holy See, beaming with delight. "This is enormously
important for me. I am now officially linked to the organization in Vietnam
that my father helped to build. His name always goes before me when I travel in
Vietnam. In some ways, I am in his shadow—but I feel he is leading me on to a
better future."

The red robes, associated with Confucianism, or the "way of humanity,"
were given to him provisionally. In the past, each time a person was appointed to
any rank, there had to be a séance. His or her name was proposed and could be
either accepted or rejected. The Invisible Pope, Lý Thái Bạch, could agree to accept
the candidate, and would then bestow a special ritual name and provide a poem
in the seven-eight verse form advising him or her on how to serve the religion.

Today, with public séances forbidden, it is not possible to have these "divine appointments" (*thiên phong*), only secular ones. Cảnh was initially given
the ritual name Ngọc Cảnh Thanh (Confucian Purity), provisionally affiliating him with the administrative wing (Phài Ngọc) of governance. At a later
ceremony on December 12, 2012, he took part in another divination to place
him more permanently. His father had been a member of the Taoist branch,
whose members dress in turquoise robes and regulate spiritual communication. Privately, many people told him they hoped and expected that he would
also qualify to wear the turquoise robes.

A huge gong with colored balls was placed high on the altar in the Cung
Đạo. All the male candidates for office were asked to take a ball out of the gong,
but they were unable to see as they made this selection. They had to trust the
spirits to select wisely for them. Cảnh had another reason to hope that he would
get a turquoise ball: He came back from the Centre Spirite at Lyon convinced
that it was his mission to revive the College of Spirit Mediums in Tây Ninh.
He reached into the gong, and as he lifted his fist he could hear a sigh of approval
from the audience. The turquoise ball he held affirmed for him and for his audience the sacred power of a divination in the Cung Đạo. The Invisible Pope,

Figure 3.4. Trần Quang Cảnh at the Centre Spirite Lyonnais Allan Kardec, presenting them with a certificate from the Cao Dai Overseas Missionary. Archive of Trần Quang Cảnh

Lý Thái Bạch, gave him an official position in the Blue (Taoist/spiritual) division and the new religious name Thượng Cảnh Thanh (Spiritual Purity).[26]

Nine months later, Trần Quang Cảnh made his pilgrimage to the Kardec Spiritist Center in Lyon. They train spirit mediums from among people who showed some talent and inclination to practice in the Kardecian style and regularly perform public séances. Cảnh was given a form titled "Request for News of a Disincarnated Person," along with this explanation:

> With the assistance of the spiritual world, psychographic mediums can allow you to get news of those who have left their physical envelop and whom we call the dead. To do this you need to fill out this form. The guides at our center serve as intermediaries between the medium and the spirit you have requested to hear from. If the spirit is able to come, he is directed toward the medium to deliver a message. If that is not the case, then the information is transmitted either by the spirit guide or by the guides at our center. We do not pretend to control the truth and consider these responses at best about 70 percent right.

Cảnh filled out the form on March 28, 2012, with his own name, and the Vietnamese name given to Victor Hugo's spirit—Đức Nguyệt Chơn Nhơn (Spiritual Teacher as Pure as the Moon), listing him as his "grandfather." He did not fill out the date of Hugo's death and handed the slip to a woman medium of about thirty.

He received this message:

> My child, it will be difficult to pass through this medium. She does not speak our language and her youth and inexperience do not allow her to detach enough for me to fully take her place. I wish I knew you better but life is set up so that when one arrives, another leaves. It is the rule for all of us without exception. I pray for you each day and watch over your troubled sleep. Do you like to eat a lot still? You were such a hungry child it made me laugh. I wait for you with no haste since you still have so much to do there. Look after your family. That is the largest task. Raise yourself as much as possible in purifying your soul and being good to others. I love you with all my heart, grandson, and I am doing well, better than you right now. I am slowly coming closer to God, and in several millennia my progress will be notable.

The message finished with an effort to write Vietnamese—*chin tao,* for *xin chào,* or "good-bye." The medium noted: "It was a spirit full of humor, calm, dignified, very sweet and full of wisdom." Cảnh was mystified by much of the message. He did not feel that he had to "look after his family," since his children were all grown, married, and independent. He thought that this must be a reference to his "religious family"—the community of Caodaists. The reference to "troubled sleep" was, in his view, also a way of referring to the complex politics of getting people in Vietnam to work with those in the diaspora and in the government. His "hunger" as a child was probably also a way of talking about his desire to get so much done. He interpreted this rather conventional expression of grandfatherly affection as providing guidance and encouragement in his struggle to revive the religion.

He had also filled out a form for his father, Trần Quang Vinh, but the message was very short and unspecific. It finished "I hold you in my arms and wish you peace in your heart." But there was no reference to his death or the mission that they shared to work for the religion. When we talked about both messages together, Cảnh concluded that these messages were "just the beginning of a conversation" that he needed to have with both Victor Hugo and his father.

But Cảnh was tremendously impressed that the Kardec Spiritist Center ran a three-year course in Spiritism to train new mediums. People came to the Spiritist Center with some earlier experiences that suggested to them that they could become mediums, but they were still unformed and did not know the proper techniques and methods to develop this talent.[27] The books of Allan Kardec outline this process in some detail, and Cảnh was reading all of Kardec's works—books he had seen on his father's bookshelf, but never bothered to investigate on his own.

In 2004, he had visited another Spiritist Center in Tampa, Florida, where a shorter training course for mediums has been developed. The spirit message they sent him seemed disappointing when he first received it, but in 2012 he came to understand one of the lines differently: "Your group can develop some who would be mediums to guide and receive directly from us, your guides and spiritual mentors, which can lead to a fruitful and very protective center" (November 6, 2004). Looking back at this message, he now saw that it referred to the need for a new training program for Caodai mediums.

In the first decades of Caodaism, there was such a program: Phạm Công Tắc headed the Hiệp Thiên Đài (literally, Palace to Unite with Heaven), and translated its mission into French as the "College des Médiums." Twelve Zodiacal dignitaries (each born in a different year of the Chinese Zodiac) trained together with the Hộ Pháp to be able to receive spirit messages. Cảnh now says: "I see now that it is not only a gift from God, but something that needs to be developed and disciplined. These Kardec centers can help us to develop these techniques, since we can see what they do."

There are currently about a hundred dignitaries in the Hiệp Thiên Đài in Tây Ninh, most of them relatively low ranking. Some of the oldest members had participated in séances before 1975, but even those who were part of séances then say they are not sure they can still do it, since the practice has been forbidden for almost forty years. Mediums do lead clandestine séances at the Saigon Teaching Agency and in many of the smaller branches (*chi phái*), but Tây Ninh has always shunned those mediums as "unofficial." Training a new generation of Tây Ninh Caodaists to receive spirit messages could be a daunting project. Since he has retired from his professional career in the United States and returned to Vietnam, it is that project that now absorbs Victor Hugo's spiritual grandson and to which he is devoting his life.

CHAPTER 4

THE FALL OF SAIGON AND
THE RISE OF THE DIASPORA

A hundred years ago, Phan Bội Châu told us, "For a human being, the greatest suffering comes from losing his country." He was talking then about the French, who took our country from us when we were still living in it. His words gave voice to the nationalist movement, and in 1954 we got the country back from the French. Caodaism was a part of that struggle. But we only had it for a quarter century. I had given most of my life to fighting for the freedom of Vietnam. In 1975 I saw all my dreams trampled in front of me, kicked into dust by the boots of the invading Communist army.

Đỗ Vạn Lý told me this story as we sat in his living room in Chatsworth,[1] a suburb north of Los Angeles. At ninety-four, he was a slender man with delicate features and longish white hair that made him look like a combination of an ostrich and a sage. Still a dramatic, even intimidating speaker, his dark eyes moved quickly as he spoke, his gestures retaining a slightly Gallic inflection, but his spoken English full of charming colloquialisms: "the real McCoy Caodai," "Vietnamese liberation from the grass roots," "bless your heart," "the cream of the crop." The most international of twentieth-century Caodai leaders, Lý studied in Paris, Shanghai, Tokyo, and New York and served as a diplomat in India, Indonesia, Japan, and the United States. He was a key figure in establishing an idea of diaspora as a religious doctrine, as well as the founding leader of Caodaists in southern California.

Đỗ Vạn Lý lived his first five decades as a secular revolutionary, rebelling against what he called the "obscure mysticism" of his father, Đỗ Thuần Hậu (1887–1966), a famous "Taoist master from the mountains" (Thiên Đỗ 2003,

126

*Figure 4.1. Đỗ Vạn Lý sitting
in front of the altar at his
temple in Perris, California*

174–175). He converted to Caodaism in his fifties, cofounded the Saigon
Teaching Agency in 1965, and helped to revitalize urban Caodaism during the
period of the "American war." Pairing Đỗ Vạn Lý and his father biographically
allows us to see how Caodaism was perceived as a modern alternative to Vietnamese esoteric traditions and also how religion and politics were fused in new
ways after the fall of Saigon.

As one of the first Vietnamese "boat people," Đỗ Vạn Lý told me how completely his life was changed by the Communist victory in April 1975. "Because
I had been a diplomat, people had told me that the Americans were about to
leave, abandoning the country, but I did not believe them. It seemed inconceiv-
able, and when it happened I was crushed." A car came to bring him and his
family to safety, and he allowed his wife and children to leave by plane. Convinced that he needed to "see his country fall, and go down with it like the
captain of a ship," he stayed alone in his Saigon villa when the North Vietnamese Army marched in to take the city: "My villa was about a block from the
Presidential Palace, and I watched the North Vietnamese troops parade in the
streets. I saw the red flags and the red scarves waving, and I was all alone in my

house. . . . I felt I had to see it myself. I was frozen in front of the window, unable to believe my own eyes."

Lý's commitment to Caodaism had always been a part of his nationalism, so that the two seemed almost indivisible. Seeing his country lost for the second time in his life, at first he was unable to see any path forward.

> I sat in despair in my living room. At that time, if soldiers had broken into my house to kill me, I would have welcomed death. I tried to calm my mind with meditation, with prayer, but we seemed to have lost everything.
>
> About a week after my family left, God spoke to me in the evening. He said "You have to go. You shouldn't die needlessly. There is still much you can do for the faith."
>
> So I asked "When?" He said "Tomorrow." But all the ports were closed. There was no way to get out. God reprimanded me: "I said you should go, and you didn't." I said, "Please forgive me. All the ports were closed." But I packed my bags and got ready to go. Then a young Catholic priest came to my house. He said some boats were still leaving from Vũng Tàu, and many religious leaders were getting on them. I went to the port with him, and there was one boat that was there. About fifty people were on it, all of them religious leaders—Buddhist monks, Catholic priests. I was the only Caodaist, but they asked me to lead the prayers.

Đỗ Vạn Lý was among the first refugees to flee in an "exodus" that would soon number over a million. The days he spent drifting across the water, dressed in yellowing white robes and praying to be rescued, would remain etched on his memory forever. Buddhist priests chanted sutras to protect their boat from pirate attacks, while nuns held up pictures of Quan Âm, the goddess of mercy, dressing in long white robes and standing on top of a dragon in the churning waves. Catholic priests put their lives in the hands of the Virgin Mary. Since Đỗ Vạn Lý had been called to Caodaism by the Taoist Queen of the Heavens, Diêu Trì Kim Mẫu, she was the benevolent goddess he addressed in prayer. But, as he told me, "Caodaism teaches that they are all really one: The Blessed Mothers come to us in many costumes, from many traditions, but they all offer comfort and solace in our time of trouble."[2]

After seven days at sea, with very little food or water left, they drifted to the coast of Malaysia. A cargo ship spotted them and took the starving and bedraggled passengers on board, bringing them to the closest port. They were given small cups of orange juice and a bit of rice porridge. Đỗ Vạn Lý acted as the spokesman for the group, since he was both the most senior person and the one most fluent in English.

A few days after he gave them his name, the former Malay high commissioner in India came to identify him. While the others were processed at a refugee center, he was allowed to fly to Tokyo to meet his children, then to Guam to meet his wife, and finally to Los Angeles, where his oldest daughter Merdeka[3] was living close to the University of California campus where her husband taught.

Đỗ Vạn Lý and the others on his boat were among the lucky ones. Their escape by boat came immediately after the fall of Saigon, when humanitarian interest in the refugees was high and many passengers were rescued from boats. Over the next ten years, hundreds of thousands of Vietnamese fled illegally into the seas. Perhaps half of them (about two hundred thousand people) never reached safe land again (Desbarats 1990, 193). Most of them used fishing or riverboats that were never intended to sail the high seas, and many of the passengers could not swim. The masters of international commercial vessels were supposedly bound by maritime law to help boats in distress, but they soon learned that if they stopped to save refugees they could be prevented or delayed from docking at the next port. Neighboring governments did not welcome the red tape involved in resettling refugees and often had no resources to spare. Since humanitarian rescues were not part of a commercially viable trajectory, many larger vessels learned to refuse help and keep sailing.

For boat passengers, the large white ships looming on the horizon shimmered like the white robes of Quan Âm, seeming to promise a rescue from the sea of suffering. Surviving the ordeal of a boat escape could itself be interpreted as a sign that God had chosen someone for a special mission. People sometimes switched religions, or became newly committed to a faith they had earlier neglected, when prayers to a particular goddess proved efficacious. For Đỗ Vạn Lý—as for many others—the experience of drifting helplessly across the water was profoundly disturbing. "After crossing the seas in a small boat, I realized that life is very real. It is tangible, but also very fragile . . . a ripple on the surface of the ocean. We were so tiny and so easy to miss. Our lives hung in the balance, and it is only because I still had important things to do that Cao Đài decided to bring me to safety."

This new sense of mission was nourished by survivor's guilt, since so many others had fallen victim to hunger, thirst, attacks by Thai pirates, or a simple sense of despair. One woman had a premonition that she had to sacrifice her life in order for their boat to reach safety. While others tried to persuade her to stay with her young child, she slipped away at night and leaped to her death (Hartney 2004, 159). The trauma of fleeing under such conditions was to cast a long shadow over the following decades as Caodaists began to rebuild their faith in a new land. Đỗ Vạn Lý was also affected: "When I first fled Vietnam and came to this country I was in a state of despair. I decided that I would withdraw from the world into meditation, cultivating my own spirituality. I wanted to commune with God alone and have nothing to do with other people. We left without our books, without our sacred scriptures, without our religious objects. All we had were the clothes on our backs."

The fall of Saigon in 1975 proved a challenge to the future of Caodaism as deep and transformative as the colonial crisis of 1925 that had given birth to the first revelations. Described as "the exodus," and "a holocaust" like what had happened to the Jews in World War II, it was to mark the new religion in countless ways as it forced a reorientation of Caodai theology and marked the sacralization of the diaspora.

The World That Made Đỗ Vạn Lý

While Đỗ Vạn Lý became one of the most influential and important Caodaists of the twentieth century, he did not convert until his life was half over. Born in Sa Đéc in 1910, to a family headed by a scholar-official who had access, through his wife, to substantial lands, Đỗ Vạn Lý was an adolescent when Caodaism began to sweep across the Mekong Delta in 1926–1934. He remembered hearing the early prophecies and being excited by them, but his father sent him to continue his education in France in 1930, and he did not return to Vietnam until 1954. On our first meeting he presented a relatively generic version of his calling to Caodaism:

> When I was young, I was on a quest to find the right faith. My family was Buddhist and worshipped ancestors, but they did not have much to say about the modern world. I went to a Catholic boarding school, and my French teachers wanted me to convert. But they taught me that our ancestors were really evil spirits. I could not accept that, I wanted something more inclusive. The Christians say they have a universal faith, but it seemed to exclude Asian traditions and to teach feudal values. Buddhism has idealistic values, but it did not help people in the time of French colonialism. When I found Caodaism, it was like coming home. The rituals and altars were familiar, but the message was more universal. It was a way to worship one God, but to see him as the father of all of us.... Kipling said "East is East and West is West and never the twain shall meet." In Caodaism, we are proving that he was wrong.

In later conversations, he provided me with more details, saying that even as a young boy he became passionately committed to the cause of Vietnam's independence. His father wanted him to become a government official, and because it was becoming increasingly hard to get an advanced education inside Vietnam, he was sent to board with a French family near Paris, where he was "pampered and spoiled," but "never felt comfortable."

After completing his Baccalauréat, he was admitted to the Sorbonne School of Law. He received a fellowship to travel with French students to study Chinese language and law and was placed in the paradoxical position of being the only Asian member of the "French Social Club" in Shanghai. He became drawn into emigré networks of Vietnamese nationalists in Hong Kong and southern China and was soon spending more time on clandestine political activity than on his studies. During six years in China (1937–1943), he worked in a variety of different jobs and was active in the League for the Restoration of Vietnam (Việt Nam Phục Quốc Đồng Minh Hội), identifying himself as a follower of Phan Bội Châu.

In 1943, he traveled to Japan to join the Revolutionary Army headed by the exiled Vietnamese Prince Cường Để and managed by people trained at China's Wampoa Academy and the Japanese military. He took classes in chemical engineering, Japanese, and electronics, as well as helping Japanese forces by subtitling propaganda films for them. He headed a Society for the Independence of South and Southeast Asian People and secretly even supported Korean groups seeking independence from Japan. He and several others had already discovered that Japan was itself a colonial power, so they welcomed the Japanese surrender in 1945 and worked for the United States, setting up electrical systems on American bases. In 1946, Đỗ Vạn Lý stowed away on an American ship bound for New York.

> I came as a stowaway from Japan. I had hidden on a boat, and the boat was very big, so they did not find me until I arrived in New York. I was discovered and they sent me to Ellis Island. They called me "Frenchy" when I came to the U.S. because I spoke French and came from a former French colony. They threatened to send me back to France, but I said that the French would kill me, since I came to the U.S. to fight for the freedom of Vietnam. They told me "We have no quota for immigrants from Vietnam." I pleaded with them that I had risked death by stowing away on a U.S. ship. So finally they took my side, and they put me down to get in as part of the Chinese quota. They whispered to me that I should not tell anyone.

Armed with diplomas from Paris and Tokyo, he was accepted to study political science at Columbia University and finished a master's degree, advancing to doctoral candidacy in 1950. He explained, "When I taught in U.S. universities,

I was so interested in political issues that I did not teach much about Vietnamese culture. Then we realized that so many problems that happened during the war era were cultural problems, because Americans did not know about Vietnamese culture. Since I was the first Vietnamese to get an American graduate education, I felt a little responsible."

During his years in New York, he established the Vietnamese-American Friendship Association and worked with anticolonial activists from other parts of Asia and Africa. In 1947, the *New York Post* published an article about this association, whose members included Pearl Buck and the Socialist leader Norman Thomas. They identified "Anthony Vangly" [an Americanized version of his name] as "an apostle of Vietnamese nationalism" who came to the United States to work for the independence of Vietnam.

In 1950, Ngô Đình Diệm came to Đỗ Vạn Lý's apartment in New York, and for three days they talked long into the night about the kind of government that Vietnam needed. From that time, Đỗ Vạn Lý came to see Ngô Đình Diệm as his patron and mentor, almost a surrogate father, and he agreed to return to work as a diplomat under South Vietnamese President Ngô Đình Diệm's leadership after independence in 1954. He married a younger woman journalist who came from another prominent family in the Mekong Delta with many Caodai connections. Employed in public relations by the Ministry of Foreign Affairs, he represented his country as a UNESCO delegate, attended the 1955 Bandung Conference of nonaligned nations, and served as Consul General in Jakarta (1955–1956) and New Delhi (1957–1963). His five children were born during his postings in Indonesia and India. On September 30, 1963, he was appointed as Ngô Đình Diệm's last ambassador to the United States. Although he was not feeling well, he traveled to Saigon for a briefing and then to Washington, D.C., and waited to present his credentials. He explained, "What I was sent by Diệm to tell them was that American forces could withdraw if they were not happy. We could hold out for another three years or so. We might have to tighten our belts, cut back a bit, but we could hold on. I knew Diệm very well, and I wanted to show the Americans how to work with him. Diệm was the only one who could stand up to both the Americans and the Communists."[4]

He was watching from Washington, D.C., when television sets displayed the mutilated corpses of Ngô Đình Diệm and his brother Ngô Đình Nhu, shot as they lay with their arms bound behind their backs after a U.S.-sponsored coup. He described his reaction: "The day Diệm was assassinated I knew that Vietnam could not be saved politically. I knew that this was the only way that I could help. I felt that the people who did this coup were so stupid, so self-destructive, that it was hard for me to love my country. I thought Diệm was our last chance. So I did not join Caodaism for political reasons, but to find another way to save my people."

When Kennedy himself was assassinated three weeks later, Đỗ Vạn Lý witnessed massive national mourning as he gathered his own things to return home. "They saw him as a handsome hero, when he was really the most inept. His death was a form of karmic retribution, but it could not bring back the leader that Vietnam had lost."

Đỗ Vạn Lý's Conversion

Arriving in Saigon in late 1963, Đỗ Vạn Lý visited temples for the first time in decades, seeking some form of solace after his political hopes were crushed. He slipped in to Huỳnh Quang Sắc temple[5] and experienced a divine calling:

> I came in when they were having a séance and I sat in the back of the room. I had been away from Vietnam for so long that no one could recognize me. But then I heard my name called, once, twice. . . . The lights dimmed, and others sensed that something supernatural was happening. I heard my name again and came up. The priest told me to kneel. I said "Why should I kneel?" I had been in the U.S. and was no longer used to this. But others whispered at me to kneel, so I did. And then I heard God the Mother calling me. She said, "I sent you out for many years to learn about life, about the world, about organizations. Now you have learned enough. I brought you home, to serve the faith."
>
> Several days later, I went to a different temple at a different place. And right away, I was called again by God the Mother who said, "You must devote yourself to the religion. You must become completely vegetarian, so that you can climb to the highest level."
>
> A week later, I was called by God the Father, who asked for "Minh Lý." It was a private name, a name my father had used for me that others did not know . . . even my mother did not know this name. But now it is the name that I have in the religion, the name that I use as a Caodai leader. God the Father [the Jade Emperor, Cao Đài] said:

Mấy mươi năm học trường thế sự	For several decades you have learned the affairs of the world
Đúng cơ duyên gìn-giữ sơ đồ	Now the time has come for you to remember those blueprints
Nguyên nhơn chánh giác tìm vô	The reason for this can be revealed at this time

> *Chung tay xây đắp qui mô*   Together we can build a more
> *Đạo Trời*   extensive temple for God

The first thing Đỗ Vạn Lý did was to work with Trần Văn Quế to found the Saigon Teaching Agency by writing its bylaws. He wrote them in a state of religious inspiration, lighting a stick of incense beside his desk and feeling his hands shake with the power that was coursing through them: "I would wake at 2 in the morning, and the air was filled with the smell of a yellow flower, so I knew that God was encouraging me." It is significant, in the light of Caodai precedent, that this moment of inspiration came to him, not in the context of a séance, but when he was alone, and it can be seen as a sign of the more individualistic and rationalized path that the Saigon Teaching Agency was to follow.

In 1965, Đỗ Vạn Lý held the bylaws of the organization on his head in a great ceremony to inaugurate the Saigon Teaching Agency. The ceremony was held in the Temple of the Three Religions (Tam Tông Miếu, discussed in Chapter 5), with hundreds of disciples watching. Unlike other Caodai groups, this Agency has no affiliation with any of the dozen Holy Sees or denominations (*chi phái*), it has no dignitaries wearing red, gold, or turquoise robes, and it does not recruit converts or bestow hierarchical offices. Instead, it offers classes in meditation, religious doctrine, and esoteric philosophy, and all members address each other as "brother and sister." Public séances were held quarterly, and private ones even more often, producing a sense of new revelations, as Đỗ Vạn Lý describes them:

> The new set of messages received by the Teaching Agency were very numerous, and at a very high intellectual level. Most of the séances were public, and they drew large crowds. Intellectuals came back into the faith, because the mediumistic sessions were conducted by people who themselves had a high literary culture. The main medium was an eleven-year-old girl, Hoàng Mai, who would receive most of the messages by automatic writing, but also some of them were spoken. When she received a spoken message, her voice was quite different from her normal one, the tones were distinct and more grown-up sounding. She was from a "sanctified" family, third-generation Cao Đài.[6]
>
> We published several volumes of our messages, just like the Bible. They included not only messages from Cao Đài but also from Maitreya, the Buddha of the future, Lao Tzu, and many other important spirits. The séances were what made me feel excited about the faith. They made everyone feel excited. This was the thrill of being in conversation with God.

Meditation was taught in a series of workshops or training sessions in which disciples were taught to represent their good and bad deeds on a graph, which would show them their own progress toward inner purity (Oliver 1976, 109).

The political situation in Saigon, as U.S. military involvement grew more intense, also seems to have been reflected in some of the séance messages. In 1965, Lê Văn Duyệt, the southern military hero who fought to unite Vietnam in 1802 under the Nguyễn dynasty, was the spirit who officially sanctioned the opening of the Saigon Teaching Agency on his territory of Gia Định. In the same year, his mausoleum was renovated by the South Vietnamese government, his image appeared on South Vietnamese currency (the 100 *đồng* bill), and he was "promoted" in a public séance to the position of Đài Tiên (Great Immortal), from the one of Thánh (Saint) that he had previously occupied. Lê Văn Duyệt's ascension was part of a "Vietnamization" of the pantheon, emphasizing indigenous elements and local heroes instead of older figures from Chinese tradition. His tomb became a pilgrimage site for those wounded, displaced, or traumatized by the war, where they could seek healing and new confidence.

Đỗ Vạn Lý's father, Đỗ Thuần Hậu, was one of a number of other important religious leaders incorporated into the pantheon. When Đỗ Thuần Hậu was on his deathbed, a séance message came from Diêu Trì Kim Mẫu (the Taoist Queen of the Heavens, addressed by Đỗ Vạn Lý as "God the Mother"), prescribing a "medicine" of blessed holy water, which Đỗ Vạn Lý was told to bring to his father. Although some observers thought his father was already gone, he opened his eyes when he sipped the holy water, and recognized his son. He revived and lived for one more week, then finally succumbed at the age of eighty-six. This was interpreted as showing that his "soul had been saved" and he could be part of Caodaism's Third Universal Redemption. A posthumous séance message revealed that he had received the title of "Talismanic Monk" (Huyền Pháp Đạo Nhơn), entitling him to receive prayers and offer benedictions from the other world. The deathbed reconciliation between father and son seemed to confirm a line of transmission from esoteric Taoist mysteries to the rationalized practices of the Saigon Teaching Agency.

Caodai followers did not try to convert American soldiers or invite American advisors to attend their séances and temples, as they had once done with French colonial officials who had an interest in Taoism or Freemasonry. The messages from French luminaries (Victor Hugo, Jeanne d'Arc) that had received so much attention in the 1930s were no longer emphasized, and no more communications were received from non-Asian figures. Đỗ Vạn Lý said most of his American friends had no idea what he was doing visiting villages throughout the Mekong Delta to spread the faith and assumed that he had hidden political motivations:

> After I was called by God, I spent all my time working for the Teaching Agency. I renounced all my work in politics and diplomacy. My American friends could not understand it.[7] They said, "The Caodaists must be paying you a lot every month for you to work so hard." But of course there was no pay. And I had to remain a complete vegetarian even when attending diplomatic dinners. The American journalists and diplomats I knew could not believe that after being a career diplomat I would turn to religion. But I really found solace in Caodai teachings. I never talked to them as I have been talking to you.

Journalists covering the Vietnam War mentioned Caodaism most often through the lens of Graham Greene's 1955 novel *The Quiet American*. *The Green Berets,* the only film made about the war while it was being fought, features a scene in which Special Forces troops describe Caodai followers as "spook-sheeted dickheads," and end up blowing up one of their temples—in direct violation of Saigon government policies—because they suspect that Communists have infiltrated it. American news writers at the time showed little interest in the religion, even though it was estimated to have been followed by one of five people in South Vietnam (Popkin 1979; Oliver 1976; Werner 1981).

The most heavily concentrated Caodai area, Tây Ninh Province, was considered solidly anti-Communist, but Caodai followers in many other parts of the South, especially the Mekong Delta, included supporters of the National Liberation Front. The urban elites who frequented the Saigon Teaching Agency were perceived as supportive of the Republic, although in the mid-1970s the influence of school associations (*Liên Trường*) caused many young people to turn left, as did the expectation of an eventual Communist victory. In 1968, a sense of panic spread in the Saigon Teaching Agency:

> After the Tết offensive, people started to feel that Saigon really could collapse. At the Agency, we held a séance where many of the leaders of the faith came back. Phạm Công Tắc said he had kneeled down and asked God to allow him to come back from the dead to be able to lead his people at this crucial time. But it is not possible to bring people back from the dead. Ngô Văn Chiêu said that he had wanted to help Vietnam, but he had to reach the highest supernatural rank before he could be of use.

Political tensions and a sense that a Communist victory might be imminent led the Teaching Agency leaders to ask Đỗ Vạn Lý to leave. He had written a preface for a 1973 "nationalist" (i.e., anti-Communist) student publication that the governance committee considered "too political." The head of the Center, Trần Văn Quế, had supported him the past but agreed in 1973 that he should step down. He consented to do so, but was embittered by the experience.

> Later there were spirit messages from Phạm Công Tắc and others asking me return to the faith: "Please come back. All of this will soon dematerialize. The faith needs you to return." But I refused, since I felt I could not return to work with people who had once asked me to leave. In the last few years before 1975, many Caodaists were starting to become more leftist because of the *Liên Trường*. These young people were very taken with the legend of Hồ Chí Minh. They knew nothing about Marx or Engels, but they saw Hồ Chí Minh as a great leader. . . . I left at that time and decided not to come back because I no longer felt comfortable there. I thought I did not have that much more to offer, because I could not trust those who held power over me. But I remained a Caodaist. I stayed in the faith. I went back to the Foreign Ministry and accepted a posting as Ambassador to Japan. During the day, I would wear business suits when working as the Ambassador, but I remained a vegetarian, and in the evenings I would dress in the white robes of Caodaism.

His family moved to Tokyo and his five children went to international schools there from 1973 until after the end of the war. When Saigon was about to fall, many people advised him to stay overseas, but Đỗ Vạn Lý insisted on returning to see the end of the government he had helped establish. After his dangerous boat escape, he spent the first two years in California in meditative seclusion.

Rebuilding Caodaism in California

A group of Caodai families who had settled in southern California approached Đỗ Vạn Lý in 1979 to ask him to lead an interdenominational congregation. He was the most senior member of the Caodai community overseas, and his Teaching Agency title, Tham Lý Minh Đạo (Vice-Conservator of Religious Enlightenment), qualified him to lead services and stage séances. He decided that it was his religious duty to do so, although he said he had to tear up a job offer from an international bank.[8] To apply for U.S. government recognition of Caodaism, he wrote a ten-page summary of Caodai doctrine in English, enclosing copies of French translations of the Religious Constitution and Code of Conduct, and applied for nonprofit status. He visited Thiên Lý Bửu Tòa, the first Caodai temple founded outside Vietnam in 1977, in San Jose (discussed in

Chapter 5), and helped to raise funds for another temple, founded in 1983, in the Paris suburb of Alfortville. Transnational Caodaism was born.

Đỗ Vạn Lý was personally close to two of the most important spirit mediums active in California, Bùi Văn Khâm (see Chapter 1) and Cao Lương Thiện (see Chapter 5). Both of them receive messages that concentrate on "wisdom teachings" and spiritual guidance (rather than politics), but their practices are still very controversial, and neither of them has received public endorsement from Đỗ Vạn Lý or larger Caodai organizations. He assessed the situation in these terms:

> Spiritism is a double-edged razor for Caodaists. The faith was founded through Spiritism, it grew greatly through Spiritism, but it also got in trouble because of Spiritism. There was an inflation of Spiritism—everyone was getting into the act, holding séances at their own houses, talking directly to God. So God had to restrict it, to keep it under control, to put a stop to rampant supernaturalism without responsibility. God wanted to test the thirst for enlightenment, and he found that people really wanted it, but it was easy for it to get out of control.
>
> You have to be on the lookout for false messages. So some of these people who say they receive spirit messages may actually be fooling themselves. The séances may not be sanctioned by God. In our faith, if there is one medium who is really trusted, then he has tremendous power. He can be more powerful than the Pope or the leaders at the Holy See.

Two Styles of Spiritual Biography: Esoteric/Exemplary and Exoteric/Ethical

My interviews with Đỗ Vạn Lý can be used to examine the ways in which religious authority and charisma have been constructed within Caodaism, using models outlined by Weber and Bourdieu. A contrast emerges between the "esoteric" (*vô vi*) style of leadership, modeled by Ngô Minh Chiêu, which stresses detachment from the world and a disciplined pursuit of personal purity and self-cultivation (which fits Weber's idea of an "exemplary prophet"), and an "exoteric" (*phổ độ*) style, modeled by Phạm Công Tắc, which is much more activist, politically engaged, and focused on expanding the number of disciples through proselytizing to a wide audience (Weber's "ethical prophet") (Weber 1963). Both styles draw on visions and spirit séances, but Ngô Minh Chiêu is notable for having written almost nothing, so he offers mainly a model of ascetic virtue. Phạm Công Tắc, in contrast, was a prolific publisher of religious texts, including the Religious Constitution (*Pháp Chánh Truyền*), the New

Code (*Tân Luật*), and his selection of official spirit messages (*Thánh Ngôn Hiệp Tuyển*). Đỗ Vạn Lý summarized the different styles of leadership in this way:

> Phạm Công Tắc had the strongest spirit of the early mediums. He had a strong character, a strong will, and he was a brilliant poet and spirit medium. This is why he became a great leader, but it is also perhaps why later he wanted too much power. He confused his own spirit with communications from the divinities.
>
> To have conversations with God, often the best medium is someone who knows very little, like the eleven-year-old girl we had at the Agency. She heard only what the spirits put in her head, she was just a vehicle for their messages. She had no personal ambition or interest in power struggles as Phạm Công Tắc did. I think Ngô Văn Chiêu declined the offer to be Pope because he feared being involved in the power struggles that could emerge in leading a mass movement. He was an ascetic, a mystic who wanted to follow his own path to enlightenment, not tangle with others. Phạm Công Tắc wanted to be a power behind the throne, perhaps even the kingmaker for Prince Cường Để or Emperor Bảo Đại.

The life of Đỗ Vạn Lý, and his own assessments of its significance, moves between these two models: At times, like Phạm Công Tắc, he tried to galvanize a large number of followers, recruiting them into a unified movement (in Saigon from 1963–1973, and in California from 1979–2000). At other times, like Ngô Văn Chiêu, he wanted to retreat from the world and stressed that he had renounced politics for religion. We can see the tension and transition between the two models in the dialogue that Đỗ Vạn Lý had with the spirit of his own father.

Two Styles of Spiritual Leadership: Father and Son

Đỗ Vạn Lý describes himself as having been "completely secular" as a young man, devoted to political action and "believing only in the independence of Vietnam." His childhood spent in Sa Đéc, a provincial city in the Mekong Delta, was, however, filled with contacts with supernatural powers, since his father led and participated in spirit séances at home. Đỗ Vạn Lý told me he first encountered the spirit of Lê Văn Duyệt, the southern military hero, in the family home in 1920 and asked him, with the rudeness and passion of a rebellious son, "So why haven't you kicked the French out of our country?" Later, when people asked him why he did not follow the esoteric school established by his father (Pháp Môn Thiền Vô Vi Khoa Học Huyền Bí, "Contemplative Method of the Science of Mysterious Forces"), he answered: "In Asia, ideally, the son is supposed to follow in his father's footsteps. Taoism deals with the realm beyond mortality, so I said 'I want to work with immortals to attain immortality, not with mortals who want to teach me about immortality. For immortality, no one is better than Lao Tzu.' So I tried to start at the top." The lesson in meditation techniques "received directly" from the spirit of Lao Tzu (Đông Phương Lão Tử) was received at a séance in 1964 where only the three highest dignitaries were present. It cannot be taught to ordinary adepts, but the instruction these dignitaries provide to their "younger brothers" can be "influenced" by the knowledge they have acquired at these higher-level séances.

Đỗ Thuần Hậu published a number of books, including guides to meditation, traditional morality, and séance communication, many of them still in print in the Vietnamese diaspora.[9] Reading them, I found many themes familiar to me from conversations with Đỗ Vạn Lý, especially the idea of learning to "make the soul visible" or transparent, which is reflected in the notion of *soi hồn* (glimpsing the soul), in which the soul is held up against the light (as one would hold an egg to check that it is still good, *soi trứng*) to glimpse its inner contents. The idea of an extended contemplation of the self is also reflected (to use this metaphor rather literally) in the mirror on the altar at the Tam Tông Miếu meditation center in Long Hải. To *soi đèn* is to shed light with a lamp, to illuminate, so a person who has reached a certain level of practice is called a *người soi* or a "illuminated person."

The ties between esoteric traditions of self-cultivation and disciplined self-knowledge and Western traditions of self-reflection and autobiographical writing are intriguing. While Taoist "masters" like Đỗ Thuần Hậu would explain key religious concepts like "the way," "self-cultivation," and "contemplative meditation" (*đạo, tu hành, công phu*) through an explanation of the radicals of the Chinese characters, a Caodai theologian would be more likely to present the same explanation through a comparison of Buddhism and Christianity, or a reference to Aristotle's use of the image of an all-seeing eye. Caodai religious commentaries are often concerned with issues of translation and similarity, focusing not just on original meanings but on ways in which these meanings may be shared across religious boundaries.

Đỗ Thuần Hậu taught both a method of "mystical" meditation and a more practical method, focused on health promotion and longevity. Đỗ Vạn Lý told me that he himself used both of these, including a technique you need beyond the age of seventy to keep up your strength. He also incorporated "magical" techniques to protect himself during periods of deep concentration: "There are certain talismanic words, which you use to call on a certain guardian spirit immortal or angel (*tiên*) to watch over you, since when you reach a deep meditative state you are vulnerable to evil spirits who can disturb your consciousness."

Đỗ Vạn Lý considered that his father had a natural gift for meditation, "a knack for the mystical," which he did not inherit. Đỗ Thuần Hậu was able to sense things without seeing them, simply by concentrating:

> People from North Vietnam would come, and ask my father to tell them what had happened to their house or to their grandfather's tomb. My father would close his eyes, and concentrate, and after about three minutes, he would open them. Then he would begin describing the house or the tomb just as if he could see it directly. He had visions of places that were very far away. He knew special Oriental ways of treating people, a potion for birth control, and another for smallpox.

Healing with the hands and visions of distant places were a characteristic of the early years of Caodai expansion, and particularly associated with Phạm Công Tắc, who used blessed "holy water" to cure the malarial fevers that were common in that swampy region when the Holy See was being constructed. One spirit message in French refers to these healings and predicts that "Indochina will become the new Lourdes" (Trần Quang Vinh 1962, 70).

However, these practices are quite alien from the more "rationalized" style of the Saigon Teaching Agency, particularly since this Agency prides itself on the number of doctors, engineers, and scientists among its ranks (including its current president, Nguyễn Văn Trạch, a medical doctor). Đỗ Vạn Lý reflected on this generational difference:

> My father had his own way of doing things, which I admire but I cannot fully understand it. I am a man of science, who went to Western schools, but he was a man who could do certain things that seem to defy science. I am different from my father. He was very confident of his meditation technique. I am more modest. I have been trying for many years and I have not had the same results. Retrospectively, I can see that he did have some innate talents.

The "new method" (*tân pháp*) of meditation taught at the Saigon Teaching Agency opens a pathway for the acquisition of spiritual knowledge and for receiving communication from divine beings, but is not advertised as bringing about "miraculous" cures. Claims that this method grants access to secret knowledge play on the same "dynamic of display and concealment" that Campany has documented in his study of the quest for transcendence in early China (Campany 2006, 336). Meditation is developed as a "mystery," in which only those willing to observe strict prohibitions (on eating meat and other "unclean" foods, and on sexual relations[10]) can hope to reach the highest levels of spiritual attainment. Preparation for meditation includes memorizing certain revealed texts and following a series of oral instructions that both guide the bodily postures of the person meditating and allow him or her to understand the deliberately arcane terminology. Formal rules of transmission require adepts to swear not to reveal these instructions to the uninitiated, so that the intimacy of the spirit séance (with only six participants) is also observed in the meditation room.

Not everyone can gain access to esoteric techniques of meditation, even if they strive for many years to do so. Three levels are defined by an increasing number of restrictions. All initiates seeking to enter the exclusive Chiếu Minh meditation cell must perform a divination ritual, *xin keo,* in which Chinese coins are tossed to see if the spirits accept the candidate. (A successful toss produces a yin/yang pattern of paired heads and tails, achieved at least twice over three coin tosses.) Those who are not successful on a first try are advised to spend more time on moral improvement and social work in order to do better the next time, after six months have passed.

There is also attention to what Campany calls "a carefully controlled textual scarcity: the text is not to be transmitted so frequently as to dilute its power, but not so infrequently as to risk letting the text disappear" (2006, 302). The archives of the Saigon Teaching Agency contain hundreds of thousands of messages, 90 percent of which are open to the scrutiny of interested visitors, but 10 percent of which are restricted to those "at the highest levels" of spiritual attainment. Participation in meditation workshops can allow disciples to be "promoted to a higher level," and so many overseas Caodai followers now take part in one of these workshops while visiting family members in Vietnam. The Tây Ninh Holy See has its own archives and has similar restrictions on a certain number of messages that are considered particularly sensitive and have not been released by the ranking dignitaries for publication. (Some of these messages, it is implied, might be politically sensitive, but the emphasis is more on their "high esoteric content," which would make them unintelligible to less accomplished readers.) In California, the Thiên Lý Bửu Tòa Temple, which archives hundreds of messages and presents them on the Internet, also has a group of "secret" communications that its governance has decided to withdraw from general circulation.

Caodaists say that the Third Era of Revelation opened up secret esoteric techniques and spread them to a much wider audience. As Đỗ Vạn Lý told me: "Before Caodaism, the teaching of meditation was very secret, only from teacher to disciple ("from heart to heart, soul to soul"). After the inception of Caodaism, God made it more public, more open, so that through meditation he could save more of his children, through either the esoteric or the exoteric path. But there are still many stages you need to master." The "secret knowledge" contained in these messages is displayed at the same time that it is concealed through demonstrations of its wondrous effects. The first of these "effects," one evident over many centuries of East Asian culture, is an extension of the human life span—well evidenced by Đỗ Thuần Hậu, who died at eighty-six, and surpassed by his son, Đỗ Vạn Lý, who lived to be ninety-eight (1910–2008).

Đỗ Vạn Lý's Assessment of the Trajectory of His Own Life

Scholars have long noted that the stories we tell ourselves about our lives are structured by a search for coherence, a wish to settle "unfinished business" by discovering connections and finding a narrative line that makes sense of our experiences. In Đỗ Vạn Lý's case, the story of his life was analyzed through a series of specifically religious notions of the self and the process of spiritual perfection ("self-cultivation"), and these were contrasted to his erstwhile "worldly ambitions" (which he acknowledged emerged in the vacuum of leadership left by the death of Phạm Công Tắc). Even though he presented Phạm Công Tắc as power hungry and self-absorbed, and perhaps a bit too close to French influences in the 1930s, he recognized a certain kinship with him, which he saw as "weighing him down" and "needing to be cast off":

> At this point, I have been vegetarian for forty-two years, totally vegetarian, with no meat or alcohol, since I answered the calling of God the Mother and God the Father in Saigon. This prepares my spirit to go up to a higher level of heaven, because it becomes lighter. Meditation also helps the spirit to become lighter, as we contemplate our karmic burdens and transcend them. Caodaism has its own theory of "Anthropology," of the origins of the world and of mankind. There are several levels from the point of origin down to the earth. The earth is heavy, and its air is heavy, so we come down to earth by getting heavier and heavier. When your soul descends down all those levels they are like layers of clothing that you can eventually shed to become lighter. Meditation teaches you to go back to God by shedding the clothing that makes you heavy. If we shed the outer layer, then we can raise higher on the cosmic ladder. There are levels of enlightenment. In Caodai meditation, you say the sutras to invoke God to supervise you. So if you make mistakes, you are corrected through séances or through dreams.

Đỗ Vạn Lý admitted that it was difficult for him to submit to religious authority, and perhaps especially the religious authority represented by his own father. The crucial transformative moment came in the temple in Saigon when he decided, after thirty years of not bowing down to anything, to kneel and submit his soul to the guidance of a higher power. This corporeal expression of submission, practiced during a period of personal and spiritual crisis, was one that he would stress in a number of our conversations.

> Americans do not like to bow down. They do not want to bow all the way down, as we do, to honor the angels, immortals, bodhisattvas, and deities that we pray to. I have told people here "You should not be ashamed to bow down." This is a part of Vietnamese culture, a tradition that has been remembered through the generations and gives Asian philosophy its ethical orientation. One man saw me in my white robes and said, "You must be a very good man to dress in those robes." I told him, "I am not a good man at all. I am often carried away by my passions, so I need to look down and see the white sleeves of my robe and that reminds me that I need to learn self-control, that I should not do as I please." The white robes of Caodaism remind us of our goal of purity, and the bowing reminds us that we should seek guidance from above.

Đỗ Vạn Lý narrated his life by focusing on a series of heroes he tried to follow: As a young man, he left France to "go East," following in the footsteps of Phan Bội Châu, and eventually sitting at the feet of Prince Cường Để—feet that he found, if not exactly made of clay, at least only of flesh and blood.[11] After Franklin Roosevelt indicated that he might support Vietnamese independence, Đỗ Vạn Lý traveled to New York and became a self-appointed lobbyist for the DRV (Democratic Republic of Vietnam) and Hồ Chí Minh. The American Socialist leader Norman Thomas, the writer Pearl Buck, and Ngô Đình Diệm were people he respected who influenced his political reorientation, but it was the death of Ngô Đình Diệm that left him, briefly, without a sense of direction. His confused homecoming was reinterpreted as a divinely mandated mission once he received his calling in 1963.

But there were no more human heroes after that point. Because of the direct contact that Caodai séances provide to spiritual beings, Đỗ Vạn Lý believed he had found a more efficacious way to train himself spiritually than the pathway followed by his father. He provided the organizational skills to establish the Saigon Teaching Agency and set up protocols for visits of delegations from the Agency to the temples of different denominations. He worked with the Agency's founder, Trần Văn Quế, to provide a new context for the systematic study of Caodai teachings, guided by quarterly séances to consult spiritual authorities. Although this mission was "interrupted" by the fall of Saigon in 1975, it is reiterated in a 2003 publication that I received:

The Teaching Agency is not a temple, nor a meditation center, does not have dignitaries, and does not register the numbers of its own disciples officially. Here the main goal is to do research on the teachings of the Great Way of the Third Redemption, gathering together many intellectuals, who do not have the divisive mentality of the different denominations, since the aim is to unify the different branches into one, finding common points and a philosophical consensus to rise above petty ambitions for rank or control of a particular group. Parallel to this research, the Agency also has a lot of experience in practicing meditation (*tâm pháp,* the "method of the heart" or introspection) using both the Zen (*thiền*) and the tranquil mind practice (*tinh luyện*). Although the organization is stable, and the pathway of practicing is clear and visible, still the Teaching Agency has not yet attained the hoped for result, which was to systematize all of the Caodai teachings. This was the original goal or mission that it was given when the Teaching Agency came into being in 1965. Certain unforeseen circumstances, and events after 1975, made that task almost impossible. Only now is it possible to return to it as the religion is getting back on its feet and reestablishing ties to all the different denominations that it should be in contact with on a regular basis. (Ngô Bái Thiên 2003)

This agenda of religious rationalization was brought from Saigon to the United States and reestablished in California. Đỗ Vạn Lý was able to organize the first congregation in Los Angeles very much as he pleased, but by the 1980s an Orange County-based congregation that followed Tây Ninh procedures split off. In 1994, he established a new temple in Perris, California, on land purchased in rural Riverside County. Until his final year, he traveled the two hours from Chatsworth to Perris each Sunday to lead services and preach to his congregation.

Tying Self-Cultivation to Movements for Social Change

Thiên Đỗ's *Vietnamese Supernaturalism* outlines the linkages between a narrative of the self, the development of new modes of action, and a critique of the state in southern Vietnam:

The decision to embark on self-cultivation, considered as part of a healing process, initiates the development stages of a social engagement, or means of affecting the person's immediate social environment. Daoists (*đạo sĩ* or *ông đạo*) embodied the path of self-cultivation which began with a cathartic personal event. Their prestige was aided by popular belief in powers evinced by sacred mountains. The Daoists' innovative approaches to healing and magic also partook of the promotion of millenarian thought. Their mythic gestures concerning individual well-being overlap or intertwine with local and national aspirations. From a solitary and self-defined identity, to a leadership role which implicitly challenges existing authorities, the Daoists' contribution to southern history demands proper recognition. (Thiên Đỗ 2003, 208–209)

Đỗ Thuần Hậu is primary among the "Taoists from the mountain" that Thiên Đỗ describes (2003, 174–175, 181, 266, 270), and Đỗ Vạn Lý also figures importantly in his treatment of Cao Đài (2003, 152–154, 265, 279), although Thiên Đỗ was unaware of their family connection. The cultural connections that he documents—between what the French called "the cult of immortality" (*tu tiên*), the collective rites of the *đinh,* the "three religions" (*tam giáo*) of the pagoda, and forms of trance possession and spirit writing—show how both father and son were drawing on similar cultural resources to deploy them to effect social change.

The idea of the self as perfectible, unique, continuous, and obsessively self-evaluating, a "project" that has to finished properly, features in the work of some literary critics as "part of the story of modernity" (see Endres 2008; Waterson 2007, 8), but it has deep roots in the literary traditions of East Asian religious practice as well (Marr 2000). It is also an important component of notions of a "new socialist man" and linked by many to the origins of nationalism. Benedict Anderson argues that although nationalism is imagined in many of the same ways as religion, it could only emerge in "the dusk of religious modes of thought" (1991, 10). In nationalist thinking, the sacred community becomes territorialized, and it is endowed with a particular mission, an idea that is often expressed as a doctrine of "national exceptionalism." "American exceptionalism" is an idea that originated with Alexis de Tocqueville (1835), but more recent writers have noted critically that it cuts both ways, being associated with abuses of American power as much as with the idea of an inspiring example. In Caodaism, "Vietnamese exceptionalism" is explicitly linked to prophecies about a "chosen people" (*dân tộc chơn* or *race bénite*), selected because they were virtuous but suffered tremendously under the yoke of colonial domination (Hoskins 2012c).

In its softer form, this idea is reflected in the unique perspective of Vietnamese colonized intellectuals to heal the wounds of colonialism by reconciling the philosophies of East and West. In its stronger form (as Đỗ Vạn Lý explained to me), it becomes a mandate for revolutionary change, consistent with Jesus' call for the meek to inherit the earth. And Jesus, himself the "Oriental" subject of a colonial empire based in Rome, is seen as an anticolonial resistance leader who was persecuted for demanding self-determination for his people. Here, Christian millenarianism is used to destabilize Confucian respect for authority and combined with Buddhist millenarianism to create a syncretistic liberation theology for a postcolonial age.

Reformulations of Millenarian Messages from the Diaspora

The universalizing power of Caodaism was that it claimed to restore earlier Asian teachings to their original, pristine form, no longer corrupted by historical distortions and local practices, as well as to absorb Christianity into the more encompassing vision of the three great religious and philosophical traditions of East Asia. But at the same time a more specific spiritual mission was given to the Vietnamese people, whose destiny was tied to the fulfillment of an ancient prophecy. Đỗ Vạn Lý begins his 1989 book *Understanding Caodaism* with a message sent on September 27, 1926, from the Supreme Being:

> *Ngày kia, có một nước trong vòng nô-lệ vì ta mà làm chủ nhơn loại.*

> One day, a country now in servitude will arise, through My words, to become the master teacher of all humanity.[12]

The Vietnamese were chosen, it was detailed in other messages, because they had been able to absorb many other religions, with a spirit of tolerance and an appreciation for their value. While they had, in the past, suffered greatly under the colonial yoke, they would now be "rewarded with a compensation greater than that of any other nation" (Đỗ Vạn Lý 1989, 357; also in Hương Hiếu 1968, 1: 115). As Đỗ Vạn Lý explained, Vietnam was given at this time the potential to become the first nation to become "founded by heaven, organized by heaven, guided by heaven and managed by heaven," as long as its people agreed to embrace this universal faith and follow its precepts (1989, 490).

Huệ-Tâm Hồ Tài has interpreted this aspect of Caodaism as an effort to blend nationalist aspirations with the familiar apocalyptic rhetoric of Vietnamese millenarianism: "The Social Darwinian vision of perpetual struggle for survival had by then percolated into popular culture and was incorporated into the millenarian rhetoric of the Cao Dai sect, but with a twist. It was presented, not as an eternal law, but as a world historical stage: in the new millennium, competition over limited resources would be rendered unnecessary by unbounded prosperity" (Hồ Tài 1983, 190). Caodaists note, however, that the prophecy of a new world order was contingent on the response that the Vietnamese people would make to this new offer of salvation.

Đỗ Vạn Lý quotes a famous message from the Supreme Being in 1926: "From this day on, in Vietnam, there is only one religion which is genuine, and that is the religion of the Great Master who came to give it to his children, calling it the religion of the nation, do you understand?" (Đỗ Vạn Lý 1989, 41; *Thánh Ngôn Hiệp Tuyển* 1972, 32]). But he also said "If you, my children, do not respond to this message and take it into your hearts, then a great calamity will come, and there is nothing that even I with all my supernatural power can do to prevent it" (Đỗ Vạn Lý 1989, 38; *Thánh Ngôn Hiệp Tuyển* 1972, 77).

For many overseas Caodaists, this "great calamity" was the fall of Saigon in 1975, which was also supposedly prophesied in a famous message received October 26, 1926, and translated by Đỗ Vạn Lý in this way:

Từ nay nòi giống chẳng chia ba	From now on, the race will no longer be divided in three
Thầy hiệp các con lại một nhà	As your father I bring all of you under one roof
Nam, Bắc, cùng rồi ra ngoại quốc	Whether from the South or North, you both have to go overseas ultimately
Chủ quyền Chơn Đạo một mình Ta	I am the only true master of the faith.[13]

The words he translated as "race" (*nòi giống*) have been translated by others as "people," "country," or "descent line,"[14] and reflect a sense of collective lineage, traced back to the mythical dragon and fairy who gave birth to all of the Vietnamese. When Cochinchina, Annam, and Tonkin were in fact united in 1975, there was a huge exodus of people in boats, escaping to save their lives but also, later, founding new congregations of Caodaists all over the globe. The "True Way" (*Chơn Đạo*) according to one interpretation of this prophecy, would only be found after an experience of exile, which was itself predestined. The British Caodaist Khánh Phan argues that "Caodaism now depends on Caodaists living overseas to make it survive" (1991, 135), and a similar sentiment is echoed in studies of Caodai communities in Canada, Australia, and California (Hartney, 2004, 154–175; Dorais 2007, 57–68; Hoskins 2006, 191–209). For Đỗ Vạn Lý and several other commentators, it is because of divisions among the Vietnamese themselves ("God's children," united under one roof but only by the threat of violence) that this millenarian vision had to be postponed until after the end of the cold war.

The Teleology of Exile and Diasporic Theology

Timothy Smith argued that migration itself is a "theological experience," since it produces such a profound dislocation in space, time, and culture that it requires a dramatic reassessment of belief and practice (Smith 1978, 1115). Scholars have addressed the impact of exile on Vietnamese communities in a number of ways, often referring to notions of a "temporality," or even a "teleology" of exile. In religious discourse, a teleological argument is an argument for God's existence based on the existence of order and design in the universe. Confucian ideology is in this sense deeply teleological, since it established the mandate of heaven that justified the hierarchical order of a just ruler and the harmonious community over which he ruled.

Caodai followers have argued since the early days of revelations that their religion would eventually triumph, but only after a period of many trials, much suffering, and catastrophe appropriate to the end of one cosmological era (which one might call the Age of Empire) and the dawning of a New Age, the Third Universal Redemption of mankind. This contrasts with Ashley Carruthers' interpretations that the key trauma of the "theologizing experience" that Vietnamese refugees had was the loss of a social future, and the reconfiguration of Vietnam as "the social past." Vietnam, he was often told, is a "place without a future," a "dead end," and the primary reason for leaving Vietnam was to "give their children a future." As survivors of incarceration, torture, and flight, they had experienced the sense of powerlessness that comes from having one's social future arbitrarily taken away. Carruthers concludes that this "teleology of exile that locates Vietnam firmly in the past" is perhaps a key characteristic of overseas Vietnamese communities and notes that it is now in contradiction with a new celebratory view of Vietnam as a tiger cub, with consistent GDP rates of around 8 percent since 2000, second only to China (Carruthers 2002, 2008, 88). But I think the question of the "teleology of exile" is more complex than he acknowledges.

Đỗ Vạn Lý's explanation of Caodai teachings in *Understanding Caodaism* situates it as a millenarian tradition (including Hòa Hảo Buddhists and a number of earlier anticolonial organizations), with its own teleology of history, in some respects almost a Vietnamese form of Zionism. Caodai followers explicitly see the Vietnamese as a chosen people with a particular spiritual mission that should be fulfilled in their homeland. Today, some people argue that this millenarian goal can only be fulfilled "after the end of Communist rule," while others argue that the resurgence of popular religion in the reformation period is already a sign that "God's plan for Vietnam is being realized."

Benedict Anderson argued that "the date at the top of a newspaper" is the single most important marker of the "steady, onward clocking of homogeneous, empty time," which he opposed to the "messianic" or "millenarian" time of earlier religious worldviews (1991, 33–36). But since the specific dating of séance messages is a key characteristic of Caodai scriptures, it offers a "historicized theology" that defies this opposition. Is the conversion from secular revolutionary to religious leader necessarily a shift also in notions of time and the significance of history?

The temporality associated with a diasporic group does nourish ideas of "long-distance nationalism," but it is explicitly oriented toward future possibilities as well as past suffering. A major inspiration for any movement is to make a case that its triumph is inevitable, predestined, written in the stars, and mandated by heaven (or, if not heaven, at least a master dialectical process that has achieved an almost transcendental status). It is certainly clear, as Carruthers argues, that overseas Vietnamese temporal identifications are not limited to a "political refugee" narrative of flight from the dystopic or aberrant modernity of socialism to a utopic modernity of freedom and democracy in the West. But there are many other ways to narrate the story of exile and return. The Caodai argument that the "exodus" of 1975 was simply part of God's plan to globalize the religion and send his disciples all over the world to acquire new languages and technological expertise is based on a religious teleology that expects that these exiles will eventually return to new positions of leadership in Vietnam. And, through quite a different series of rhetorical moves, this is a conclusion that a new group of Hanoi-based publications have also begun to advance. Now that the Vietnamese government welcomes overseas Vietnamese to return to "rebuild the country" through investment and the development of global markets, Vietnam's "indigenous religions" have returned to a position of much greater official favor (as we will see in Chapter 5).

Đỗ Vạn Lý's book notes that specific references to "Vietnamese teachings" (*Cao Đài Giáo Việt Nam*) occur in spirit messages most frequently in the 1960s, when the new nation was struggling to defend itself from both internal threats and external ones, insidious American influence and Communist infiltration. In conversation, he stressed the fact that "Vietnam was divinely selected" to be the home of the new religion because the country had remained moral in spite of a long history of oppression. He says it was just the first instance of what would become a global progression: "Vietnam served as an experiment for a form of esoteric knowledge that needs to be made visible and concrete in one country, to serve as a model which can be followed in other contexts, to promote the spread of the Great Path in other countries" (1989, 449).

It is here that many of Đỗ Vạn Lý's arguments make up what I would call a specifically diasporic theology, in the sense outlined by James Clifford:

> Diasporic discourses reflect the sense of being part of an ongoing transnational network that includes the homeland, not as something simply left behind, but as a place of attachment in a contrapuntal modernity. Diasporic consciousness is thus constituted both negatively and positively. It is constituted negatively by experiences of discrimination and exclusion.... Diasporic consciousness is produced positively through identification with world historical cultural/political forces.... It is also about feeling global.... a sense of attachment elsewhere, to a different temporality and vision, a discrepant modernity.... Diaspora consciousness lives loss and hope as a defining tension. (1994, 312)

While on the one hand diasporic thinking "makes the best of a bad situation," the transcendent value that is placed on recovering the homeland is linked to a utopian vision that stretches beyond a specific territory or homeland.

Compared to other Caodai followers, Đỗ Vạn Lý's life is unusual because so much of it was lived outside of Vietnam before 1975. In this sense, he is untypical, since most early Caodai leaders came from people with a cosmopolitan education who were not able to pursue their studies overseas. However, he defined a perspective that was to become the diasporic perspective of a much larger Vietnamese community after 1975. His life thus combines the views of the "original disciples" (those born before the advent of Caodaism) and the new generation that has grown up overseas (and embraces Caodaism as a way of "returning to the homeland" through a spiritual pilgrimage, infusing their imaginary journeys with elements of long-distance nationalism).

Đỗ Vạn Lý juxtaposed Vietnamese and American perspectives most explicitly in interpreting Caodaism's key symbol, the Left Eye of God:

> Professor Hoskins, The Vietnamese and the Americans are the two peoples who worship under the sign of the eye. We have it on our temples, you have it on a sacred object in your society—the dollar bill. Yours is the right eye. Ours is the left eye. Therefore they complement each other. The left eye is closer to the heart, it is connected to morality, tradition, and ethics. The right eye is closer to the brain, it is connected to technology, industry, and development. America has given the idea of democracy to the world, but they have lost the ethical dimension. One day there will be a people that will develop that ideal of democracy and bring it back to the world with its original ethics. These people will be the Vietnamese.[15]

By articulating the left as the side of Asia/Vietnam, and also of all that is progressive, positive, and forward looking (*dương*), Đỗ Vạn Lý both inverts the usual Orientalist binary and provides a logic to justify the mission he believes will be fulfilled by Western-educated Vietnamese. This vision is part of a diasporic narrative because the remaking of the world is given meaning by ideas of a transcendent connection to "home," making the longed-for land of origin into a "holy land" (*thánh địa*) of universal importance.

Diaspora as Doctrine in Vietnam and Overseas

Đỗ Vạn Lý had a significant impact on Caodai thinking in both Vietnam and the United States in three ways. First, by cofounding the Saigon Teaching Agency, he shaped a new direction for the religion in Vietnam after the death of Phạm Công Tắc. This new direction was less rigidly hierarchical, less avowedly "political," but very much concerned with uniting the Vietnamese people across the dividing lines of both religion and cold war politics. His conversion in 1963 can be understood as motivated both by his disenchantment with politics after the fall of Ngô Đình Diệm (brought on partially by Buddhist against Catholic conflict) and by his memories as an adolescent of the tremendous appeal of Caodaism in the late 1920s and early 1930s, when it swept across the Mekong Delta as he prepared to study in France.

Second, he was the first Vietnamese religious leader to draw on his knowledge of American culture and American values and to work out an alternative vision of the unity of Vietnamese culture in reaction to the American model. (Another religious leader, the Buddhist monk Thích Nhất Hạnh, who studied in the United States in the 1960s, was to follow a different, more universalist model in his own career in exile.) While those who remained in Saigon after 1975 saw him as the most "pro-American" of the Agency leadership (based on fieldwork interviews 2005–2009), after the overthrow of Ngô Đình Diệm in 1963 he was deeply disenchanted with America and articulated a religious vision that would create a separate space for Vietnamese national aspirations, refusing collaboration with the Saigon regime and its American advisors. In the years 1965–1975, this vision had some success in recruiting new supporters among intellectuals and professionals, but larger political forces doomed its immediate future. In the millenarian framework Đỗ Vạn Lý came to embrace, the end of the colonial era was a cosmic rupture that would "test" the Vietnamese people, and cost many of them their homeland, but eventually give birth to a new global order of peace and Asian spirituality.

Third, Caodaism's relevance has reemerged with the post-1995 resurgence of popular religion and increased contacts with diasporic communities. Ideas of returning to indigenous foundations and infusing the nation with a spiritual dimension are now current and resonate with the concepts developed by Caodaism during the colonial era and the southern Republic (Taylor 2007; Salemink 2008; Phạm Quỳnh Phương and Eipper 2009). Rather than seeing leaders of this period as the victims of American foreign policy or unwitting collaborators, it is important to recognize their agency and their significance for articulating alternative models of Vietnamese modernity.

CHAPTER 5

A "CAODAIST IN BLACK" RETURNS TO LIVE IN VIETNAM

A dignified white-haired man in his sixties, dressed in long black robes, walks across the arrival lounge of the Saigon airport with a batch of lotus flowers, coming to meet me as I stumble out from my seventeen-hour flight across the Pacific. Behind him, half a dozen female disciples of "The Way of Enlightened Reason" (Minh Lý Đạo) wait in somber robes, beside a chartered minibus. Although this group may appear out of place in this modern, crowded airport, their leader, Lâm Lý Hùng, is a transnational figure now, one of an increasingly large number of religious figures who cross the Pacific several times a year and are connected to congregations in several different countries. Few have sacrificed as much as Lâm Lý Hùng, who lived in California for over thirty years as an engineer and raised his family there as part of a Caodai congregation. Called through spirit séances to return to assume a position once held by his grandfather, Âu Kiệt Lâm, he now spends eleven months a year in contemplative seclusion, reading, teaching, and meditating on esoteric wisdom. His story allows us to explore what happened in Vietnam after the fall of Saigon and how Caodaists have collaborated with other syncretistic temples in the long process of "normalizing" their religion in socialist Vietnam.

This chapter examines the different pathways followed by Tây Ninh, the largest Caodai organization, and a number of smaller groups, including the

Figure 5.1. Lâm Lý Hùng in front of his temple Tam Tông Miếu

dark-robed disciples who live with Lâm Lý Hùng in the "Temple of the Three Philosophies" (Tam Tông Miếu). Some people describe the members of this esoteric order as "pre-Caodaists," "the Caodaists in black," or the "prophets of Caodaism's emergence," since their temple was the source of the first phoenix basket used to contact divinities. In the twenty-first century, the Temple of the Three Philosophies has provided a pivot point to coordinate collaborations among twenty different organizations comprising about a million people, linking the Saigon Teaching Agency to a number of non-Tây Ninh Caodai branches and other groups who are part of the "Great Way of the Third Era of Redemption."[1] In 2008, the Vietnamese government officially recognized it as a legal organization, and in 2010 it was given its place as the "twelfth official religion," an especially auspicious number since it expresses the unity of the twelve-year cycle of Asian Zodiac calendars. This chapter tells a story of how these smaller temples came out of the shadows to emerge on the public scene and how Caodaists in Tây Ninh and at the Saigon Teaching Agency have strategized to give themselves a new twenty-first-century identity as an "indigenous religion."

The World That Made Lâm Lý Hùng

I first met Lâm Lý Hùng at the Caodai temple in Pomona, California, in 2002. I was impressed by his patient, detailed explanations of religious doctrine and his interest in how Taoist occultism could be reconciled with modern science and medial research. He was working at Edwards Life Science Corporation as an electrical engineer developing new medical technology. He told me then that he was really part of another tradition, "The Way of Enlightened Reason" (Minh Lý Đạo) that cooperated with Caodai groups in Saigon and had their own spirit mediums. He had taken classes at the Saigon Teaching Agency and was familiar with their quarterly séances, which drew members of the Minh Lý Đạo as well as others associated with Sino-Vietnamese occult traditions.

Lâm Lý Hùng was the grandson of the half-Chinese spirit medium Âu Kiệt Lâm, who provided the phoenix basket used for the first Caodai séances (described in Chapter 1). He was born just a few hundred yards from the Temple of the Three Philosophies, where he would later serve as a religious leader. Minh Lý Đạo members were instrumental in the genesis of Caodaism not only because they provided this sacred instrument, but also because their early séances produced texts that became part of Caodai scripture, including the prayers used for the offerings of incense, fruit, and flowers at each ceremony, and the long "Canon of Repentance" (*Sám Hối Tịnh Nghiệp Văng*) affirming moral values and their sanctions, sometimes described as the Jade Code (Spence 1996). These texts were revealed through spirit writing sessions with the phoenix basket, but their content stemmed from Chinese manuscripts brought to Vietnam by Ming-dynasty refugees in 1863 as part of the Minh Sư (Enlightened Master) redemptive society (Jammes 2006a, 2010; Jammes and Palmer 2013).

Minh Sư was a Sino-Vietnamese group described in French colonial archives as a "secret society," practicing in the tradition of the Chinese Heaven and Earth Association (Thiên Địa Hội) and the Primordial Heaven group (Xiantiandao in Chinese, Tiên Thiên Đạo in Vietnamese). The word Minh has a double meaning: In ordinary Vietnamese, it means "light," but it is also associated with the Chinese Ming dynasty, and the thousands of Chinese refugees who settled in what is now southern Vietnam after the Ming dynasty fell in 1644. In the late seventeenth century, the Minh associations were united under the slogan "expel the Qing dynasty and restore the Ming" (*Bài Mãn Phục Minh*). In the twentieth century, after Sun Yat-Sen's proclamation of a Chinese Republic, their slogan was adapted to the colonial context and became "expel the French and restore the Vietnamese" (*bài Pháp, phục Nam*). They identified the Vietnamese as the "original rulers of the southern domain," and so came to be identified with embryonic Vietnamese nationalism (Jammes 2010; Smith 1970a). By the 1920s, four other Minh groups were founded with primarily Vietnamese members: Minh Đường (The Palace of Light), Minh Thiện (Enlightened Generosity), Minh Tân (The New Light), and Minh Lý (Enlightened Reason).

The Minh groups shared a millenarian cosmology common to many other Chinese popular sects, with three ages ordered in a progression and a new faith needed to rescue humanity from a time of moral degeneration and natural disasters.[2] Lâm Lý Hùng's grandfather, Âu Kiệt Lâm, was an herbalist who practiced Oriental medicine and acupuncture. Literate in Chinese characters and the Vietnamese vernacular Nôm characters, he was interested in fusing traditional methods of divination, including astrology, geomancy, and chiromancy, with modern ideas of electrical magnetism and techniques used by French Spiritists like Allan Kardec. He prepared for séances by studying older Chinese texts, and then he would receive messages from spirits who "gave him the words" to translate the concepts in these ancient texts into Vietnamese verse, which was the preferred form for poems presented by divinities.[3] The messages Âu Kiệt Lâm received are in relatively simple Vietnamese, but as they became incorporated into the Caodai corpus, they often became somewhat more arcane and obscure. Lâm Lý Hùng speculated that since Caodaists liked to be identified as "educated" and part of an intellectual elite, they may have wanted to use a more complex vocabulary to impress others with their erudition. Although the Chinese organizations were all secret brotherhoods, Minh Lý Đạo included women as disciples and spirit mediums from the start, and in recent years female mediums have become more numerous than male ones.

The French governor-general of Cochinchina estimated that these "secret societies" had more than 200,000 disciples in 1916 (Coulet 1926, 117). They were illegal and always suspected of subversive activities, so they gathered secretly and operated in the shadows. In 1926, Caodaism brought together the leaders of many of these societies, and three of the Minh redemptive societies turned their temples into Caodai temples. Lê Văn Trung, the interim Pope, was ordained in the former Minh Đường Temple of Vĩnh Nguyên Tự, which still looks much more like a Buddhist pagoda than the Gothic-inspired Caodai "cathedrals." By binding together in one large organization, they were able to achieve a measure of security and establish a larger and more enduring administrative structure. Many early Caodai leaders, including Ngô Văn Chiêu and Nguyễn Ngọc Tương, the provincial governor who became the Pope of the second-largest denomination, Ban Chỉnh Đạo, participated in séances at Minh temples.

Caodaism was born among urban educated elites: more than 60 percent of the original disciples worked for the French civil service (Werner 1976,

95–96). Their social goals were to restore Confucian ideals of education and service to an administrative structure that had been dismantled by the French and to restore pride in Vietnamese culture and traditions. They also established a system of reciprocal obligations between the educated elite and the peasantry that was to the benefit of both. In the words of Phạm Công Tắc, these colonial intellectuals would "no longer accept the spiritual humiliations of before" and wanted to reassert the value of Asian religious and philosophical traditions (Werner 1976, 296).

The English historian Ralph Smith argued that the doctrines and rituals that would later become Caodaism were "already familiar" to these leaders because of their participation in Minh redemptive societies, so these groups can give us "a clue to the real roots of Caodaism" (1970a, 347). Later researchers have confirmed his insights, but nevertheless, formal relations between groups like Minh Lý Đạo and Tây Ninh Caodaism have been distant. In 1947, Phạm Công Tắc disavowed this connection, asserting in 1947 that "Minh Lyism is separated from us by a mystical and philosophical point of view" (Gobron 1949, 108). Ralph Smith speculated: "His vagueness on the actual doctrinal differences suggests that he had some political reason for making the distinction, but we have no way of knowing what it was" (1970a, 349). It seems likely that the increasing separation between Tây Ninh and the "dissident branches" was motivated both by personal animosities between rival leaders and by more emphasis on self-cultivation and spirit séances in the other branches. This emphasis brought the dissident branches closer to Minh Lý.

The emerging alliance between Minh Lý and the Caodai groups that formed around the spirit medium Liên Hoa (initially established in 1936 at Cầu Kho Temple in Saigon) later fueled the expansion of Caodaism into central Vietnam, and especially the Đà Nẵng area. Liên Hoa came out of Chiếu Minh séance tradition, and it was he who received the key scriptures of this group, "The Great Vehicle of Esoterism" (*Đại Thừa Chơn Giáo*), regarded by more reclusive, inward-looking Caodaists as the supreme teaching.[4] Persecution by the Việt Minh and especially the massacres of thousands of Caodaists of all branches in Quảng Ngãi in 1945 required the formation of a single delegation that could send representatives to Hanoi to stop the killings.

Tensions with the Hanoi government intensified when the spirit medium Liên Hoa was imprisoned by the Việt Minh from 1949–1951, then again in 1952, when he was placed in solitary confinement and tortured, remaining in solitary confinement until the signing of the Geneva Accords in 1954 (Nguyễn Trung Hậu 1956, 147–148). After his release, and the release of many other prisoners, a special reception was held on October 27, 1954, to honor those religious leaders who had suffered from prolonged imprisonment. The new Sacerdotal Council of Caodaists in central Vietnam (Hội Thánh Truyền Giáo) was established at the "Basilica" of Trung Hưng Bửu Tòa in Đà Nẵng. In 1955, this Sacerdotal Council formally recognized the five Minh redemptive societies as "religious sects that have collaborated with Caodaists since the birth of the faith."[5]

Lâm Lý Hùng grew up in the shadow of Âu Kiệt Lâm's temple, but since he had a scientific education, he had little interest in his grandfather's esoteric pursuits until 1966. As a young professor at the mathematics faculty, he started a series of experiments with divination techniques with some of his colleagues and was amazed at their accuracy. He had observed séances at Tam Tông Miếu since he was a boy, but did not find them relevant to his own life. Once his interest was awakened, he asked his father, a Minh Lý dignitary, to show him some of the spirit messages, so he could learn more about the idea of self-cultivation and hidden knowledge. His father shared some of the messages received by Âu Kiệt Lâm, and told him some stories about the grandfather he had hardly known, since Âu Kiệt Lâm died when Lâm Lý Hùng was just three years old.

Lâm Lý Hùng was formally initiated into Minh Lý Đạo at the age of twenty-six, through a "gateway ceremony" (nhập môn) in Tam Tông Miếu. He began to attend other séances at the Saigon Teaching Agency, observing both Liên Hoa and the female medium Hoàng Mai. He told me: "The Taoist tradition tells us that a spirit medium is like a musical instrument: The spirits must have a good instrument in order to produce beautiful music. So a man like Liên Hoa, who had a vast knowledge of Asian literary traditions, was able to receive elaborate spirit messages that impressed us all. Hoàng Mai, as a younger woman who had been raised in a Caodai family, received messages that were helpful but not as eloquent. I was very happy that the spirits called Liên Hoa to come to stay at Tam Tông Miếu, since we thought that he was the most accomplished spirit medium of his generation." His words have been echoed by several others (including Bùi Văn Khâm of Chapter 1) who also attended séances at both places.

When Saigon was about to fall in 1975, Lâm Lý Hùng was a thirty-five-year-old teacher of applied mathematics who hoped to continue his education overseas. He managed to sneak onto one of the boats leaving the collapsing city and escaped with his wife and young family. After some time in refugee centers and a bit more English study, he enrolled in a graduate program in electrical engineering at California State Polytechnic University in Pomona. He eventually completed his doctoral degree, worked in biological technology, and he, his wife and their four children settled in Norco, California.

In the early 1980s Caodaists contacted them and asked them to help rebuild a community in California. His wife was a Caodaist, and he and their children also joined the fledgling congregation, dressing in the long white robes and taking part in services. He participated in efforts to train three young girls as spirit mediums at the Los Angeles Caodai temple headed by Đỗ Vạn Lý. Inspired by the example of Hoàng Mai and Hồng Mai, two teenage sisters named after yellow and pink ochna flowers, who received a series of important messages at the Saigon Teaching Agency, they chose three girls who took a vow to become lifelong vegetarians and began to train them in divination using the phoenix-headed basket. The girls were told to kneel and listen to prayers chanted by the whole group that named a series of divinities that the community would like to summon to speak to them. Each of the girls would hold the phoenix basket in turn, and others would watch its movements and try to discern messages in the ways it turned and rapped on the table. The messages were garbled and inconclusive, however, and these experiments were eventually stopped.[6]

When he received news that his mother was very sick, Lâm Lý Hùng made plans to return to Vietnam for her funeral in 1994. He arrived just days after she died and went to the memorial service at Tam Tông Miếu. After the funeral, his oldest daughter was initiated into Minh Lý Đạo in a solemn ceremony, in which prayers aimed at instructing new disciples were chanted for several hours. Lâm Lý Hùng was reminded of his own vocation and the excitement he felt at being admitted into this inner circle of esoteric disciples. He participated in a religious retreat at the meditation temple in Long Hải, where he received a message from the Taoist spirit Thái Thượng Lão Quân (an earlier incarnation of Lao Tzu) giving him the religious name Đại Bác, which means "great intuitive wisdom," referring to the forms of knowledge that can come from *prana,* or the divine breath. The bestowal of that religious name was a clue that he might later be called to serve Minh Lý Đạo.

Lâm Lý Hùng was particularly interested in these efforts at training mediums in California, because he wanted to know if he had more obligations to his own spiritual lineage. He started visiting the Caodai temple near San Jose (Thiên Lý Bửu Tòa) in the early 1980s, where he met Bạch Diệu Hoa (White Precious Flower), the first medium to receive and publish spirit messages in California. She was soon to receive a message that would change his life.

Spirit Séances in San Jose

Bạch Diệu Hoa was a controversial and innovative medium who defied certain Caodai traditions and established her own path in the new world. She came to the United States in 1975, at the age of fifty-two, on an evacuation flight arranged for the family of her son-in-law, who was a member of the House of

Representatives in the Saigon government. Born with the name Nguyễn Thị Minh Châu in 1923, she was the granddaughter of a high-ranking dignitary who taught her a special intensive form of meditation. Her family lived in the Mekong Delta, and she studied meditation at the Chiếu Minh Temple in Cần Thơ. Her husband was killed in the war when she was thirty-one, and she was left pregnant, with two children to care for and another on the way. She responded to this personal crisis by deciding to *di tu*—to devote herself more intensively to the religious path of self-cultivation. She began meditating for long periods of time, and she reached very high levels that allow direct communications from divinities.

As soon as her family arrived in San Jose, she began to receive spirit messages telling her to found a new temple in California. The Jade Emperor told her on May 15, 1978, that she should follow the "golden way guided by heaven" (*huỳnh đạo thiên khai*). The term could also be translated as "the Asian way," marking the first racialization of Caodaism in North America, since it was a universal faith revealed to those with "yellow skin." On December 4, 1979, Cao Đài spoke in a spirit séance to bestow the name Thiên Lý Bửu Tòa on the new temple to be built in San Jose. The name also has a double meaning: It can be translated "Court of Heavenly Reason," but it can also be translated as "Court that is a thousand miles away," the first outpost of a religion in exile.

She took in a newly arrived refugee of nineteen, Ngọc Quang Minh, who was initiated as a disciple at the age of twenty. Separated from both his parents when he was thirteen, he had attached himself to the "Caodaists in black" temple of Tam Tông Miếu from 1975 to 1982. The temple provided him with food and spiritual guidance for the seven years that his father was incarcerated in a reeducation camp. Nurtured by the dark-robed disciples, he sought out other similar temples when he came to San Jose and studied information science. He became the webmaster of an elaborate website that went live in 2000, archiving all the spirit messages and chronicling the history of Thiên Lý Bửu Tòa. Ngọc Tuyết Tiên, a part-Chinese woman who moved to California in 1982 and ran an herbal medicine shop, headed the temple administration. She said she had been an archbishop in the Bạch Y branch of Caodaism in Rạch Giá in the western Mekong Delta, so she was committed to developing Caodaism in her new home.

Ngọc Quang Minh described séances that he watched in which Bạch Diệu Hoa received her messages, holding the phoenix basket (*ngọc cơ*) and feeling it move as she spoke, assisted by two scribes (one male, one female) and a tape recorder. Each séance was transcribed and archived. Some early séances were done with a spirit medium holding the phoenix basket, but not speaking. A skilled reader was needed to interpret the movements of the basket as they traced out letters in the air. For an ordinary observer, the messages are not always clear, but a skilled reader was said to be able to see the words "as if they were in neon lights." The first volume of spirit messages published was received in séances (*đàn cơ*), but several later volumes were received with the less public, more contemplative method of the "spirit pen" (*chấp bút*), where the medium feels moved to write as she sits alone. Most of the communications she received were from the great spiritual teachers of the past: In the "first Bible" of spirit messages received at the Thiên Lý Bửu Tòa temple (*Đại Giác Thánh Kinh* and *Kinh Thánh Giáo Pháp*), there were fifty-four messages, including twelve from the Jade Emperor, six from Jesus Christ, two from Buddha, two from the red-faced war god Quan Công (Quan Thánh Đế Quân), one from the Virgin Mary (Đức Mẹ Maria), four from the first disciple Ngô Minh Chiêu, two from Lý Thái Bạch (the "invisible" Pope in heaven), one from the Mother Goddess (Diêu Trì Kim Mẫu), one from Noah of the Old Testament, and one from the first American spirit to be heard from in the new world, Joseph Smith, the founder of Mormonism.[7]

She has also received more personal messages from former disciples who had died. One woman was a jewelry dealer from southern California who was killed by thieves at her home. The temple provided a funeral for her and many prayers to assist her soul. The woman came back as a spirit and spoke through Bạch Diệu Hoa to console her grieving son. The spirit medium is usually simply the vessel of divine messages and is not supposed to create them herself. But on this occasion Bạch Diệu Hoa herself cried as she spoke with a different woman's voice in a rare display of emotion at a spirit séance.

In the late 1970s and 1980s, spirit séances were held in San Jose on Hellyer Avenue, in front of the main altar, which displayed a photograph of Ngô Văn Chiêu on the left, Buddha in the center, then Jesus on the right. Only those initiated into Caodai could attend, sometimes with only four or five people, other times with more than fifty. If there were too many people attending, it was feared that their thoughts could disturb the stillness of the medium. As Ngọc Quang Minh explained to me: "The frequency of their own thinking would interfere with the frequency of the spirit communications." It is necessary for all participants at a séance to be peaceful and not distracted. The spirits dictate who can attend and when the séance will happen. Séances are usually held at "the hour of the rat" (around midnight), since that is believed to be the most auspicious time to contact the spirits.

Bạch Diệu Hoa dressed in a special costume for those occasions, which was closer to the costume of the Hộ Pháp than to the simple white robes of most mediums in Vietnam. She wore a white tunic with an octagon of red and yellow and a sash of turquoise, yellow, and red. The octagon (*Bát Quái*) represents the resolution of dualities, and it is considered a powerful form of protection for people who practice Chinese forms of spirit mediumship. It demonstrates the principle of multiplicity: "From one comes two, and two times two makes four, and four times two makes eight, and then there are 10,000 more." The costume was designed to show that "spiritual forces develop and multiply from the inter-action of opposites, the dialectic of cause and effect" (from a spirit message re-ceived at Thiên Lý Bửu Tòa). Later, at a ceremony to "stabilize the earth" and prevent earthquakes in 1997, Bạch Diệu Hoa dressed in gold, and her two fe-male assistants dressed in turquoise and cardinal red, colors that in Tây Ninh are reserved for male dignitaries.[8] She received two volumes of messages with Buddhist themes, one from the Maitreya Buddha (Đức Phật Di Lặc) and an-other from the "Goddess of Mercy," Quan Âm. A spirit message received at Thiên Lý Bửu Tòa explained that American Caodaism needed to emphasize the "Buddhist elements" in its practice, since Tây Ninh was following a primar-ily Confucian path, and Chiếu Minh and other denominations emphasized Taoist forms.

In 1998, Lâm Lý Hùng traveled to Thiên Lý Bửu Tòa and attended a sé-ance where Bạch Diệu Hoa received a spirit message directly addressed to him. "Since it is now possible to travel to Vietnam," the spirit said, "you should go back to Saigon to visit Tam Tông Miếu. There is an empty chair there that might need to be filled." He and others in the séance circle interpreted this phrase as a suggestion that the temple might need him to come back and take up a leadership position. But since Bạch Diệu Hoa's health was declining rap-idly, this charismatic female medium also told him that she might not be able to give him more messages in the future.

Conference at the Court of Heavenly Reason (Thiên Lý Bửu Tòa)

California Caodaists decided to bring representatives of temples from all over the United States, Canada, Australia, Belgium, and Germany to a conference in June 2003 to establish a new overseas organization that could appoint younger deacons (Lễ Sanh) and assure that there would be a continuity of leadership in the new world. These efforts were led by Cao Lương Thiện, a handsome and dynamic North Carolina–based Caodaist who had been the head of the Saigon Teaching Agency's youth organization in Saigon in the early 1970s. Cao Lương Thiện was the son of a famous spirit medium, the Bảo Đạo, or "protector of the way," of the Thiên Tiên (Primordial Heaven) denomination in the Mekong

Delta. He was raising funds to rebuild the Tam Quan Cầu Kho Temple in central Vietnam, where he would later receive a new religious title as "Respected Master" (Thừa Sử). He collaborated with Bùi Đắc Hùm (Chapter 2) and an older priest from San Bernardino named Lê Quang Sách, who was the highest-ranking non-Tây Ninh Caodaist in California. They organized the conference to sanctify a new generation of Caodai leaders. They needed to appoint them through a séance ceremony, in which their names would be proposed to the Supreme Being and receive divine approval.

The séance to do this was held in the Thiên Lý Bửu Tòa Temple at midnight. Bạch Diệu Hoa was ailing and had decided to retire. Cao Lương Thiện had come to take her place, invited to do so by the temple administrative council. He stood at the back of the temple, in the place where the statue of Phạm Công Tắc stands in Tây Ninh, in front of the *Khí* character lit up with neon lights. He was dressed in the costume worn by mediums in his father and grandfather's branch—a white head cloth as well as white tunic, pants, and gloves. The colored robes had been prepared to distribute to those Caodaists who would be appointed as dignitaries in the Taoist (blue robes), Buddhist (saffron yellow robes), and Confucian (red robes) lineages.

Lê Quang Sách, dressed in the red robes of administrative authority, presided along with the female archbishop Ngọc Tuyết Tiên, dressed in the white robes of her branch (Bạch Y, white clothing). The high-ranking dignitary prepared questions for the séance and the list of people to be appointed to high office. Cao Lương Thiện listened, seated in front of the altar with eyes closed, as messages were chanted and placed in front of the altar to be verified. He received the assent of the spirits through messages written with a red pen on yellow paper (*chấp bút*). Once the proclamations had been presented to the spirits and verified by them, they could be burned, allowing their essence to literally go up in smoke, traveling toward the heavens in disembodied form.

It was at this séance in 2003 that Lâm Lý Hùng received another California spirit message, this time from a new spirit medium. His name was called, and he heard Cao Lương Thiện speak to remind him again of his origins and his "duty to return." The specific verses were:

Tam Tông trước đó, rồi đây	Tam Tông Miếu was your home before, and now
Mở đường thánh đức nhờ tay	You should again open up the spiritual way,
con hiền	lending your hand, my child

This made a total of three spirit messages—one received in Saigon, and two others in California, each from a different medium—that called him to take a leadership role at Tam Tông Miếu. He was not the only one to receive a message. Several others at the séance also heard their names called and received personalized instructions, presented in verse, in an oblique language so that their real significance might be only discernible to the person who received the message.

A few months later, on November 9, 2003, another spirit message was received at the Court of Heavenly Reason, stating that since after 1975 the sacred centers in Vietnam could not communicate with Caodaists overseas, they should now listen to the direct spiritual guidance of Lý Thái Bạch, the Spiritual Pope. In this spirit message, seven of Caodaism's most important twentieth-century leaders (including Phạm Công Tắc and the first disciple, Ngô Văn Chiêu) stated:

> We immortals are happy to see you going overseas and carrying the Caodai messages to new people. God created the religion to save the Vietnamese and also all of humanity. His blessings will go to the good and penalties will go to those who oppose God's will. Look at the example of the past and learn from it in order to spread the teachings in the future. When we immortals were alive, we were sometimes separated by divisions, so you should not follow that example but learn to work together more effectively.... You need to unify to become the lighthouse of the Western world (*ngọn hải đăng sáng chói ở Tây phương*) so that people can find true peace, salvation and happiness. (Hoskins 2006, 207)[9]

Another conference was planned for 2005, to train student priests and to consider how to move forward with ambitious plans to establish a special California-based organization. Cao Lương Thiện spoke to me at the 2005 conference about his ambitious plans to establish a Sacerdotal Council in California. Using his religious name Huệ Tánh (Natural Wisdom), he was planning to train a new generation of mediums. Some Caodaists criticized his audacity in doing so ("Does he think he can become the Phạm Công Tắc of California?" one asked me). Trained as an engineer and skilled at public speaking in both English and Vietnamese, he seemed to be capable of great things. After a few years he separated from Thiên Lý Bửu Tòa, setting up his own Đại Đạo Monastery in San Jose. While he attracted many younger followers through his charisma and forceful personality, he alienated others. In 2009, he discovered that he had a fatal cancer and was "called back to God," dying before reaching the age of sixty.

The 2005 conference drew together people from a wide range of different branches, but Lâm Lý Hùng himself did not attend. He had returned to Vietnam and was living at Tam Tông Miếu, moving slowly toward a decision. Should he renounce his family and devote himself to a more intense form of spiritual training, or remain a layman, practicing in his own home and connected to worldly concerns? He needed to calm his mind through meditation in the silence of the temple to decide.

Tam Tông Miếu as the "Temple of Shadows"

The image of Tam Tông Miếu Temple is one of the best known in the Vietnamese diaspora, since it appears on a best-selling calendar used to trace auspicious days. The calendar also refers obliquely to a divinatory tradition that is centuries old and goes back to the famous Taoist Book of Changes (Viet. *Kinh Dịch*) and the occult sciences of East Asian literati. This famous temple no longer prints the calendars (since they could not be distributed after 1975), so today its distribution in the diaspora is a purely commercial enterprise. Inside the dark-

Figure 5.2. A spirit medium holding the "dragon basket" (the larger counterpart to the phoenix basket) at Tam Tông Miếu Temple in Hồ Chí Minh City, under a picture of Confucius

paneled rooms of this temple, however, black-robed dignitaries still study texts in many languages in an esoteric library, and teach classes and workshops dealing with divination, Chinese medicine, and Eastern philosophy.

Caodai temples are filled with light and color, but Tam Tông Miếu is full of darkness and shadows. Its main hall of worship has a series of paintings of the life of Buddha rendered in muted gold, greens, and blues, and its altar is dark wood, with its disciples silhouetted against a single golden lamp that represents the Thái Cực (eternal flame), the spark that brought the universe into existence. While Caodaists worship an active, masculine God—the Jade Emperor who is also identified as Jehovah—the followers of the Minh Lý Đạo focus their attention on the Mother Goddess, Diêu Trì Kim Mẫu, who holds down the yin pole of existence and represents darkness, mystery, and female nurturance. She is sometimes called the "Unborn Mother," since she came before all other things, and is identified with the primeval void (Vô Cực). The Jade Emperor is the Thái Cực (first principle), and the third element of the Divine Triad is the Taoist spirit Lão Tổ, the "Old Ancestor of the Heavens" (identified with Hoàng Cực, the principle of empire). Lower altars are devoted to the great religious teachers Buddha, Confucius, and Lao Tzu; Quan Âm and other famous Bodhisattvas; and celestial officers of the five directions—north, south, east, west, and center. Spirits of the drum, the earth, the ancestors, and the divine law are also venerated, and a guardian statue stands at the back of the temple where the principle of breath and vitality is located. Shuffling around in the gloomy corners of this sacred space, the women and men who devote their lives to Minh Lý worship renounce meat, alcohol, and sensual earthly pleasures for a life of disciplined contemplation.

A cheerful woman medium in her fifties called Nghiệp was one of my guides when I visited. Her name can be translated as "karma," evoking her destiny to carry out the "spiritual enterprise" (*thánh nghiệp*) of serving as a conduit between the human world and the divine one. Her name recalls the famous Sĩ Nhiếp, a Chinese administrator who worked in what is now Vietnam in the third century AD and is recognized as having introduced writing and Confucian teachings to the region (Kelley 2012, 26). Nghiệp was able to read both Chinese characters and Nôm, and so had access to divinely revealed texts like the Orthodox Scripture of the Great King who Manifests the Divine (*Hiển Thánh Đại Vương Chính Kinh*), which was revealed by the spirit of Trần Hưng Đạo in a spirit writing session in the 1890s. Liam Kelley suggests that this text was "perhaps the first such text in Vietnam," although he traces a much longer history of spirit writing in China (2012, 26). In the text, Trần Hưng Đạo urges his disciples to follow the "proper human way" (*nhân đạo*) by showing loyalty and filial piety, holding off the dark souls and engaging in "hidden virtue" (*âm chất*). The elite encouraged commoners to carry out virtuous acts without calculation, since they would receive a positive consequence as a reward. This consequence could include the birth of a son, a harmonious marriage, or even wealth and fame (which, however, were not supposed to be the goals of this behavior).

Many people would describe the Minh Lý pantheon as primarily Taoist. Confucianism is generally represented as an ethical path, but it deals primarily with relations between persons and has little to say about their relation with the natural world. Nature—which includes the human body—reveals the principle of dynamic creativity. So humans need to evaluate their own behavior to bring it into harmony with the ceaseless flow of nature. From a Taoist perspective, the Confucian preoccupation with morality and the civilized virtues is artificial and can encourage dreams of personal power. The form of personal virtue that comes from the Tao is greater than any human society, and it is the Tao that points to the beyond (Verellen 1995, 322). The Way of the Celestial Masters, a famous covenant between the spirit of Lao Tzu and his followers in mid-second century Sichuan, established the precedent of reforming the existing order, and many Taoist groups later became associated with utopianism, messianism, and periodic insurgency (Hồ Tài 1983; Goossaert and Palmer 2011).

Each time that human virtue begins to decline, new messages of revelation must be sent to establish a new era of greater wisdom. The messages received from Lao Tzu in 1924 by the founders of the Minh Lý Đạo laid the basis for a early collaboration with Caodaism, which was renewed in 2008 as Minh Lý Đạo itself achieved state recognition and continued to work in conjuction with Caodai groups like the Saigon Teaching Agency and the Đà Nẵng-based Caodai Mission (Truyền Giáo). Members of the Minh Lý Đạo invited these other groups to gather with them in the calm seclusion of the quarterly retreat center on the coast of southern Vietnam.

The Meditation and Retreat Center at Long Hải

Long Hải is a beautiful seaside community named after the "ocean dragon" who is said to visit its famous temple to the goddess of the southern seas. White sands stretch out alongside palm trees and beach resorts, and its sense of quiet and tranquility is a dramatic change from the traffic and noise of downtown Saigon. This meditation center houses disciples who come to seasonal retreats at the winter and summer solstice and at the spring and autumn equinoxes, where they can calm their minds and meditate to prepare to receive communications from divinities.

The serene and contemplative tenor of the meditation temple has not, however, been without its exposure to the horrors of war, and it is also not without its ghosts. After buying the temple in the early 1970s, Minh Lý disciples were horrified to hear that the building had been used during the previous decade as a site where dissidents were imprisoned and tortured by the Ngô Đình Diệm government. The disciple who had arranged the purchase felt particularly guilty at having led his brothers and sisters into a place of violence. According to the other temple members, he decided that he would need to give up his own life to appease these ghosts. He went into meditation and expressed this wish to sacrifice himself, and it was accepted. Just a few days later, he grew increasingly weak and died. His spirit is now venerated as the temple guardian and protector, and since his death there have been no more ghostly visitations.

When I visited Long Hải in 2007 with French researcher Jérémy Jammes, it was a small, sunbathed temple that caught the sea breezes through its windows and featured meditation rooms where dozens of disciples sat together in silent communion. The main altar to the Mother Goddess had a large mirror at the top of the altar, a common image of the Mother Goddess shared with followers of the Đạo Mẫu tradition of serving the goddesses of the four palaces (Hoskins 2013, 2014b). Several phoenix baskets were stored in the back to assist spirit mediums in contacting divinities, and there were parallel sentence poems inscribed on the pillars surrounding the sanctuary. The atmosphere of calm detachment from the worries of the world was conducive to the quarterly retreats at which the veil between the world of the mortals and the immortals could be lifted.

Institutional Ties between Minh Lý Đạo and Caodaism

Minh Lý Đạo was founded two years before Caodaism, but the two have been linked in many ways for the past century. As we saw in Chapter 1, Caodaism was born as the result of a vision that Ngô Văn Chiêu had in 1921 on Phú Quốc island as he looked at the sun rising. Minh Lý Đạo was born at midnight ("the hour of the rat"), in the year of the rat (1924), the month of the fire rat (Bính Tý), on the day of the rat (twenty-seventh day of that lunar month)—that is to say, the winter solstice, the darkest day of the year, but also the beginning of a period of enlightenment. Minh Lý represents yin (âm)—the wisdom of the shadows, the mother goddess of darkness, and inaction, while Caodaism represents

yang (dương)—the dynamism of the sun, the Supreme Being, and forceful prop-
agation. Minh Lý demands an intensive commitment from all its members, who
must devote themselves to self-cultivation and the study of erudite texts, while
Caodaism is a mass movement that reaches a much wider public, but usually at a
shallower level and without the same occult prestige (Jammes 2010). The two
have been counterparts and mirror images for eighty years.

Caodaists share scriptures with Minh Lý Đạo disciples. The most important of these is a set of spririt messages received in the 1930s to 1940s by Liên
Hoa (1920–1999), collected as the "The Great Cycle of Esoterism" (*Đại Thừa
Chơn Giáo*), the "Bible" of the Chiếu Minh branch. The revelation of these
teachings is described poetically as divinities "cutting into the bamboo stalk to
reveal a precious book" (*trước tiết tàng thơ*), opening up a world of mysteries
hidden in the natural world. They are the main teachings of the Central Vietnam group headquartered in Đà Nẵng and have been used to train spirit mediums. In 2012, a new spirit message revealed that Liên Hoa had been given the
posthumous title of Hộ Pháp, the "defender of the dharma," a title held by only
two earlier Caodaists (Phạm Công Tắc in Tây Ninh and Huệ Đức in Tiên
Thiên). During his lifetime, Liên Hoa was a simple medium, but after his death
the teachings that he received earned him a higher position in the celestial hierarchy of Minh Lý Đạo.

Liên Hoa worked closely with another very important Caodai leader, Trần
Văn Quế (1902–1984), to unite Caodaists during the 1930s. Quế was a professor of mathematics at Saigon University who became a Caodaist in 1929. He
was called by a vision in which he saw the Left Eye of God two times and was
personally told to join the "Great Way" (Đại Đạo) (Đồng Tân 2006, 164).
Trần Văn Quế took part in a number of efforts to reunify the movement after
the schisms of 1934, starting with the "Lotus Flower Coalition" (Liên Hoa
Tổng Hội), which held a series of twelve meetings to begin dialogue in the
1930s, and received this warning at their final séance in 1940:

> If Liên Hoa fails to reunite different sects, the religion faces disintegration
>
> The leaders (of the religion) may bear a tragic fate (Đồng Tân 2006, 165)

This message was interpreted as a comment on the French crackdown on Caodaism that occurred after Hitler's invasion of Paris, when French colonial authorities accused Caodaists of sending financial support to the exiled Prince
Cường Để's "Revolutionary Army to Retake the Country" (Phục Quốc) in
Tokyo. Several hundred Caodai dignitaries were arrested in 1940 and thrown
into colonial prisons.

Trần Văn Quế was sentenced to twenty years on the famous prison island of Poulo Condor. He later published a memoir of his prison years in which he noted how separation from his family forced him to develop an inner spiritual discipline.[10] Released after the Japanese coup in March 1945, he returned home to find that his property had been seized, and his wife and several of his children had died of starvation and exhaustion (Đồng Tân 2006,168). Retreating to the sanctuary of the Holy See in Tây Ninh, he taught Caodai doctrine and revitalized the bilingual journal *La Revue Caodaiste (Cao Đài Giáo Lý)*, hoping to live a life of seclusion and meditation. At this time, he also took the religious name Huệ Lương (enlightened conscience), which he used as a pen name for his religious publications (Đồng Tân 2006, 168).

A Vietnamese proverb Trần Văn Quế often cited runs "Even if the tree wants to stay still, the wind will not stop blowing" (*Cây muốn lặng mà gió chẳng dừng*). The tumultuous political situation did not allow him to retreat to a contemplative life. Because of his many advanced degrees, Trần Văn Quế was called to serve as Minister of National Planning (1949–1950), then Minister of Research and Innovation, in the government of the Caodaist Prime Minister Nguyễn Văn Tâm (1952–1953). He was charged with renaming the streets of Hanoi, replacing French names with those of Vietnamese national heroes (Đồng Tân 2006, 169). During his three years in Hanoi, he also worked to expand Caodaism in northern Vietnam, and in 1956 he became president of the new Missionary Agency of Central Vietnam.[11] Trần Văn Quế received a spirit message to found the Saigon Teaching Agency in 1964. His work with Đỗ Vạn Lý in that organization is described in Chapter 4.

After the fall of Saigon, Trần Văn Quế retreated into a more meditative mode and often stayed at the Minh Lý meditation retreat. He became ill and died in 1984, surrounded by his disciples. The séance held after his death revealed a new procedure for prophesying the spiritual rank that religious leaders could hold. During a long retreat at the coastal meditation center in Long Hải, Liên Hoa had prepared a series of envelopes filled with paper notes and bearing the names of a dozen of the most devoted and highest-ranking disciples of Minh Lý. He wrote in each one the spiritual rank that the disciples would attain in the afterworld and the religious name under which they would be known. When a disciple came close to death, a special ceremony was performed in which the envelope was taken down and opened. No one would do this until the disciple was ready to surrender his or her spirit and unite with God. When Liên Hoa himself died in 1999, his envelope was taken down and opened, revealing that he would later get a higher posthumous title. Those present at his bedside saw his eyes close for a second, then he stirred again, and his left eye pulsed open, showing that he had achieved transcendence in the Chiếu Minh tradition.

Lâm Lý Hùng witnessed this same ceremony at the deathbed of a female disciple a few years later. As the verses announcing her spirit destiny were read aloud three times, she wakened and received the news, then as the last words were read, she died. This ritual was interpreted as revealing both that the medium had known her predestined fate, and that she had accepted it. It was a prophecy of death that was also a formal introduction into the hierarchy of the afterlife.

In 2004, Lâm Lý Hùng was part of a delegation of Vietnamese religious leaders (including Bùi Đắc Hùm and his wife Hồng) who attended the Parliament of World Religions in Barcelona to present papers about their largely unknown religious organizations, in the hope that international recognition might help them in seeking government approval to register as officially recognized religions. He presented a paper titled "A Scientific Approach to the Harmonization of Religious Traditions," which described the similarities between Taoist theories of the origin of the universe and modern physics. Returning from Barcelona, he visited Vietnam again. This time, he wanted to assess what had happened to Caodaists and other syncretistic religious groups since 1975 and what the prospects were for the future.

Tây Ninh Caodaism in Vietnam after the Fall of Saigon

The Communist victory in April 1975 had devastating consequences for millions of Caodaists. The years of war had been fiercely fought in the province of Tây Ninh, but the Caodai Holy See was considered off limits. To a certain extent its neutrality as a sacred space was respected by both sides. White tunic-clad sentries guarded the twelve gates of the Holy See twenty-four hours a day, and the walled city within contained not only the Great Temple and the adjoining Mother Goddess Temple, but also several administrative buildings in colonial-style villas. There were two religiously run high schools, a fledgling university, a hospital and nursery with seventy-five beds, an orphanage, a meditation center for senior citizens, a practice hall for ritual music, a funeral parlor, and public work garages. Local businesses affiliated with the temple included dressmaking and weaving shops, a bakery, a gas station, a carpentry shop, a blacksmith's forge, and even a factory to print religious calendars. Special lodging houses had been constructed for the thousands of workers who were employed by the Holy See (Chong 1999, 119).

The Republic of South Vietnam allowed young men who worked at the Holy See to be exempt from military service, so it served as a sanctuary for those who wanted to escape the war. The "religious youth" were also not actively recruited by the National Liberation Front or Việt Cộng, which depended on the goodwill of many Caodaists, since their secret headquarters was in a remote part of Tây Ninh Province.[12] The city of Tây Ninh was attacked directly only twice during the American war: once during the Tết offensive in 1968, and once in 1969 when undercover guerillas occupied a section of the town for a couple of days (Chong 1999, 166). Communist forces built an extensive network of tunnels throughout the province to allow their cadres to travel to meetings.

Caodaists in neighboring communities were subject to heavy bombardment. On June 8, 1972, a South Vietnamese Skyraider plane dropped napalm on the heavily Caodai town of Trảng Bàng, about twenty-five miles from the Holy See. A nine-year-old girl named Phan Thị Kim Phúc had taken refuge in the Caodai temple, which her grandfather had helped to build. The Việt Cộng had started building tunnels under her family's house, causing the cement floor to crack, and they also asked her family to give them the wooden doors from their house to close off the tunnels. Rockets and shells were exploding in the business district of Trảng Bàng, and government soldiers told people to leave their homes because they were not safe there (Chong 1999, 52).

Her family left the bomb shelter made of sandbags and slipped through the gate behind the temple, heading for a rear outbuilding used for social functions and to house visiting dignitaries from the Holy See. Government soldiers popped violet and mustard smoke grenades on the temple grounds, when a smaller observation plane approached. It dipped down and fired two phosphorus rockets that spewed white smoke upon impact. They ignited the area in front of the Caodai temple with explosions of saffron, white, and red. The twin spires of the temple were barely visible above the swirling smoke (Chong 1999, 64).

Government soldiers had popped the colored smoke markers to indicate their own position and that of the people seeking refuge inside, but the villagers thought the smoke markers inside the temple grounds were a bombing target. Kim Phúc's father told her and her brothers and sisters to run toward the highway. This was a tragic decision: Americans had established an unwritten rule of engagement that no fire was to be directed at unarmed Vietnamese *unless they were running*. People running were assumed to be fleeing Việt Cộng, and therefore fair game (Chong 1999, 61).

Kim Phúc was hit by a wave of fire, which burned her back down to the bone and caused her to tear off her clothes and run toward the lens of an Associated

Figure 5.3. The famous 1972 photograph of Kim Phúc running out from the Caodai temple and being burned by napalm

Press photographer. Her naked, trembling body was also videotaped, and the images were soon plastered across the front pages of American newspapers and played on television news. The photographer, Nick Ut, saved her life by taking her and her aunt in his jeep to a hospital in Củ Chi, a site now famous as a tourist destination for foreigners who want to be able to crawl through Việt Cộng tunnels and have a simulated "war experience." She was in critical condition until transferred to an elite American-funded burn treatment center, where she stayed for six months. She would need extensive skin grafts and operations to loosen stiffened scar tissue and suffered debilitating weakness, pain, perennial headaches and nightmares and later complications like asthma and diabetes. Her story of healing from devastating wounds is paralleled by the story of efforts to heal her community after the trauma of war (Chong 1999, 96).

Kim Phúc believed that it was Phật Mẫu, the Mother Goddess, who called her back to life after weeks of hovering at the edge of death. She was able to return home after a year of treatments. On April 25, 1975, when Communist troops were marching toward Saigon, she and her family once again took refuge in the Caodai temple in Trảng Bàng. Although damaged by napalm, bombs, mortar, and gunfire, the huge saffron-colored temple still stood, bearing scars of every weapon of war. Her own family home, like most of the others in the town, was reduced to a mound of rubble, its roof collapsed and its walls in ruins (Chong 1999, 145).

A truck flying the Caodai flag, with a white tunic (*áo dài*) tied to its front, offered to transport people to the Holy See in Tây Ninh. South Vietnamese military trucks and tanks stopped them halfway there, saying that heavy fighting was going on. After waiting four days at a relative's house, Kim Phúc's family was allowed to proceed:

The landscape on the way to Tây Ninh was stained with blood. In the vicinity of the bridge, dozens of bodies of soldiers from both the south and north lay askew in death. In the middle of the junction of Route 1 with the fork that branched north into the town of Tây Ninh sat an abandoned truck of the South Vietnamese military, stacked with bodies of government soldiers. The road there was strewn with southern military gear; uniforms, helmets, leather boots, M-16 rifles, canteens and unit badges, even cigarette lighters and watches. The image conjured up was of government troops shedding any and all military identification in an effort to melt back into the civilian population. (Chong 1999, 141)

Kim Phúc's family was able to move into housing used by her brother, who had been a member of the religious youth. Tây Ninh itself was a war-free zone, with buildings and electricity still intact.

The new Communist government immediately nationalized all of the buildings except for the Great Temple itself. Over a thousand Caodai dignitaries were arrested and thirty-nine were killed in clashes with Communist forces (Chapman 2013, 194). Mass "reeducation classes" in Marxist doctrine were organized in what had been the offices of the religious dignitaries. Huge portraits of Hồ Chí Minh were hung up, and Communist Party cadres lectured for up to five hours at a time about the inspiring leadership of the party and its great patriotic victory over American imperialism. Most people had to attend three sessions each week, but twenty-five high-ranking dignitaries were detained and ordered to produce detailed reports about all of their political and religious activities. Thirteen of them were cleared after two months of detention, but twelve others remained in detention for more extensive ideological reeducation (Blagov 2001a, 152).

The most important Caodai leaders at that time—Hồ Tấn Khoa, who had succeeded Phạm Công Tắc and Cao Hoài Sang as the head spirit medium, or Bảo Đạo,[13] and two of his associates—were instructed to halt all spirit medium séances. They were forced to sign a document saying that Spiritism was a form of "superstition," and was harmful, since "messages originated from men, not deities." Caodaism itself was described as "a reactionary organization with some religious overtones" that had been duped by "French, American and Japanese spies," and was "profoundly opportunist" in character (Blagov 2001a, 151–153).

Two hundred thousand Caodaists in Tây Ninh were called together for a series of meetings from December 1978 to May 1979. They supposedly agreed at these meetings to surrender forty out of forty-six buildings inside the Holy See (retaining the Great Temple, the Mother Goddess Temple, and four offices). A new government-controlled entity was established, called the "Governance

Committee" (Hội Đồng Chưởng Quản), with a mission to stop all political and social activities and "to transform Caodaism into a true religion" (Blagov 2001a, 154–155). Most Caodaists at the time saw these measures as shutting down all religious activities and dismantling the social presence of the Holy See. The 7,500 workers who had been employed by the Holy See lost their jobs and were told to return to the villages and join revolutionary organizations to help rebuild the country after the war.

All former soldiers of the Army of the Republic of South Vietnam were ordered to report for reeducation, with lower-ranking officers told to bring food for one month and higher-ranking ones told to bring food for three months. But after thirty days, no one returned. Anyone who worked for the Saigon regime was also reeducated, as well as businessmen, doctors, and nurses and any others with real or suspected connections to the former regime or to American interests. The period of "reeducation" was never specified, and while some lower-ranking individuals were released after six months, others served for up to twelve years. The absence of so many husbands, fathers, and brothers meant that the people left to take care of Caodai temples were almost only older women.

Kim Phượng Đặng, another Caodai girl who was about the same age as Kim Phúc, told me about her father's experiences at the "reeducation" camp at Long Khánh:

> When they arrived at the camp, they discovered the rice they were alloted was old and full of worms—what was left of rice stored during the war. They were hungry and ordered to do harsh manual labor, so they wanted to find out how long they would be confined. They formed a secret small circle to hold spirit séances. The female immortal Hà Tiên Cô (the youngest and only woman of the eight immortals of ancient Chinese lore) came down to give them a poem, which spelled out her name in its initial letters:
>
> > As a young woman, I want to wash off all secular dirt
> > To be able to return to the Nothingness,
> > To enjoy the breeze of the immortal land
> > And realize my spiritual power.
>
> She provided them with a poem containing the names of her "twelve apostles" [like the poem designating the founding Caodaists in Chapter 1]. She then continued to teach them as her disciples over the next six months, sometimes introducing lessons from another one of the immortals. Through listening to these poems, my father realized that his imprisonment was a way of calling

him back to a religion he had not taken seriously before. He realized that he was being saved for a purpose, especially after mines exploded near the camp and many others were killed. The séances offered consolation and gave him a new sense of mission. (Kim Phượng Đặng 2013, 13)

The female immortal who contacted Kim Phượng Đặng's father in the reeducation camp later also came to comfort him during his dangerous boat escape. Kim Phương Đang remembered hearing her father repeat some of those verses received in the séances as their lives lay in the balance, waiting on uncertain seas to be rescued. Her own commitment to Caodaism was deepened by seeing how these messages had given courage to her father.

The dissolution of most public Caodai activities caused the head spirit medium, Hồ Tấn Khoa, to recommend a turn inward, focusing on the esoteric disciplines of meditation, prayer, and self-cultivation. Kim Phúc, grateful for her miraculous recovery, decided to become a full vegetarian, as did many others in the community. Avoiding meat was made easier because of the widespread poverty in the region, but it was also a way of expressing a passive form of political resistance. Tây Ninh was hardly a favored region in the government's plan to restore the national economy, and it soon became one of the poorest provinces in southern Vietnam (Chong 1999, 159).

In 1978, the region began to suffer even more, since it found itself at the center of a new war—Vietnam's invasion of Cambodia to oust the Khmer Rouge. For the first time, bomb shelters were built in the town. Men, women, and children dug trenches, filled and hefted out bags of earth, lay timbers as a ceiling, and repacked earth over the top. Vietnamese refugees surged over the border, fleeing the terrifying killing fields of the Khmer Rouge, and camps were built to house them.

Kim Phúc responded by recommitting herself more fully to religious activities: She came to head the local women's group, sang in the choir at evening and midnight services, and put on her white tunic four times a day on weekends, so she could attend all the daily rituals. When she turned eighteen, she formally dedicated herself to Caodaism and took the oath of allegiance to the religion. But the Great Temple was no longer as full of worshippers as it had once been, and it was allowed to deteriorate:

The interior of the temple mirrored the sad state of their religion: police had early on smashed the standing gong, along with other decorative accoutrements: vases, figurines, cranes, phoenixes and dragons. Vandalism and theft were constant problems. There was no money for upkeep; the tiles in the marble floor defining each of the nine ascending levels to the altar were badly

chipped, as were the eight plaster columns entwined with dragons supporting the dome at the far end. Ever since the Communists had dismantled the
Caodai administration, each temple relied solely on volunteers to fill all positions, from priests to caretakers. (Chong 1999, 181–182)

Kim Phúc moved away from her home in Tây Ninh after she finished high
school and went to Tiến Giang with the hope of eventually going to medical
school. The picture taken of her in 1972, however, came back to haunt her, as she
became the poster child for newspaper stories about war atrocities. Dozens of
journalists came to interview her, and she had to abandon her studies. She was
used as a propaganda symbol from 1984 onward, until she finally begged to be
released from this duty. Separated from her family in Tây Ninh, she converted
to Christianity. In 1986, she was allowed to travel to Cuba to study, where she
married another Vietnamese student. In 1992, they flew to Moscow for their
honeymoon, but left their plane at a refueling stop in Newfoundland to ask for
political asylum in Canada. She was granted Canadian citizenship in 1996, and
she and her husband became Canadian residents (Chung 1999, 367).

Her personal story has attracted attention because she became a media ce-
lebrity and is now the head of a foundation to provide medical assistance to
child victims of war. Most other Caodaists languished in the shadows in the
years from 1975 to 1995, when over a million men were detained, doing hard
labor in reeducation camps (Desbarats 1990). Hundreds of temples in the Mekong Delta were boarded up, closed down, and virtually unused for decades,
while others were open, but people feared the political repercussions of being
identified as active worshippers. Evidence of religous activity during a background check for government jobs was usually grounds for disqualification.
Younger people who hoped for higher education were told that they could not
be admitted, since spaces were saved for "patriotic families" who supported the
revolution.

When I visited the Saigon Teaching Agency in 2004 and asked to interview members about their own personal religious experiences, I was told that
no one could answer questions about the period from 1975 to 2000. "It was a
dark period in our history," they explained, "and we have moved on now." Informally, one of my guides whispered to me that up to 80 percent of the members of the Agency had been sent to reeducation camps, some of them for over a
decade, since anyone with a college degree or who held officer rank or higher
was penalized especially heavily.

The many thousands of people who tried to escape by boat, risking death,
pirate attacks, and prison if they were caught, included many religous men and

women who felt they had lost their chance for a future. In 1980, the United Nations High Commision for Refugees worked out the Humanitarian Operation to allow people who had spent at least three years in reeducation camps to come to the United States with their families. Civilians could also apply to the Orderly Departure Program to reunite with family members who had escaped earlier by plane or boat. Nearly 500,000 refugees were admitted to the United States under this program from 1980 to 1994. Once diplomatic relations were reestablished, most people coming from Vietnam entered as immigrants rather than refugees. However, a 2012 Pew survey of Asian-American communities indicates that 38 percent of all Vietnamese immigrants still say that escaping persecution and political conflict was the main motivation for their depature (Pew 2012, 118). In addition, 87 percent of all Vietnamese Americans say that freedom to practice their religion is better in the United States than in Vietnam (Pew 2012, 59).

Esoteric versus Exoteric Groups and Their Relation to the State

In a 1976 study of Caodaism in Saigon, Victor Oliver focused on the formation of the Saigon Teaching Agency and its goal of reunifying all the different denominations. He noted that the divisions between branches at times have resulted in "injections of new visions and new methods," which have presented people with an expanded range of spiritual alternatives and have also often updated elements of ritual practice and their philosophical justifications to suit new circumstances. He predicted accurately that reunification would not happen soon, but noted that it was a constant preoccupation (Oliver 1976, 115–117).

Looking back at this history more than thirty years later, Oliver's remarks remain relevant, and they were put in particularly sharp focus by a conversation that I had with Lâm Lý Hùng in the summer of 2007. He had just told me the good news that the collaboration between the Saigon Teaching Agency, the Đà Nẵng-based Sacerdotal Council of Central Vietnam, a meditation group called Thánh Tịnh Minh Quan, and Tam Tông Miếu had been reestablished, renewing bonds first established by important leaders like Trần Văn Quế and Liên Hoa, who had been involved with the three other groups. The Taoist spirit once incarnated as Lao Tzu had also recently provided his benediction to this new joint endeavor, and a mood of optimism about the future of each of the organizations involved was clearly evident.

But, at the same time, Lâm Lý Hùng noted that, in his experience, each time that people had tried to innovate, especially in the diasporic organizations in California, "Innovation had simply led to new divisions." Returning to the earliest texts and establishing a consensus around the earlier "period of revelations" (1925–1934) rather than trying to "improve" on it with more up-to-date mixtures seemed to be a surer way of building consensus over the long term. Each innovator, in effect, ended up proposing new prayers or rituals that were not acceptable to the others, so innovation and charismatic leaders seemed unfortunately almost always to lead to divisiveness, if also to new visions and some new adherents. Like many others, he repeated a proverb about Vietnamese tendencies to factionalism, noting "for every nine Vietnamese people, there are ten opinions" (*chín người, mười ý*).

Oliver had been skeptical of the claims of Caodaists that the sectarian divisions were either "predestined" (because of any early message that the "the house of God would be first divided into twelve parts before it was reunited") or "necessary" to escape the surveillance of French colonial agents. He noted, as is widely documented, that there were personality clashes and doctrinal differences that played an important role in early schisms, and most of those have not healed over the past eighty-five years (Oliver 1976, 102–103). However, institutions like the Saigon Teaching Agency have established a series of conversations to build Caodai cooperation and collaboration. Recent history seems to bear out the essence, if perhaps not the letter, of these earlier claims. In 2013, Lâm Lý Hùng told me: "We have learned not to seek organizational unity, but instead to form a looser confederation, like the European community, in which each small organization runs itself with some autonomy, but we come together for spiritual collaborations."

After the fall of Saigon, all religious organizations suffered, and many more or less disappeared from the public scene. Over this period of time, the largest, most hierarchical organizations, such as the Holy See at Tây Ninh, were most vulnerable to governmental control, and thus can best be said to have "stagnated" or been "paralyzed" by government restrictions (to use terms that appear often on Caodai overseas websites). In contrast, the Saigon Teaching Agency was able to work out a better relationship with the government, partly by "laying low" and purposefully avoiding any political activities. From 1980–2005, the Agency's College of Mediums was headed by Đinh Văn Đệ, a former opposition Parliamentarian of the Republic who had undercover contacts with Communist forces (Jammes 2006a, 2014). Chiếu Minh and Minh Lý Đạo have managed to keep going by turning inward, emphasizing self-cultivation rather than large congregations or proselytizing, and they have assured a continuity of spiritual involvement, which is admirable under trying circumstances.

So, while it would seem that exoteric outreach recruited many new members in periods when government regulation was relatively lax (in South Vietnam, this would be the 1960s and early 1970s), when it became more severe (the early French colonial period, 1926–1940, and the period after 1975), then the inward turning esoteric groups were able to keep going, and perhaps also to offer spiritual solace and guidance, in ways that the exoteric groups were no longer able to achieve. It is also part of the religious logic of esotericism that a retreat for meditative seclusion and reflection can also strengthen one's character and one's resolve to follow a religion even under difficult circumstances, so the esoteric retreat can also be seen as a kind of spiritual advance on another plane.

The benefits of the exoteric (Phổ Độ) approach were mass recruitment, prominence in the public eye, and large building projects, which made Caodai temples a distinctive part of the religious landscape of southern and central Vietnam since the 1930s. While the roughly 1,300 Caodai temples were not destroyed, many of them were boarded up for several decades. Since 1995, they have been reopened, repainted, and many are now the focus of tourism. The benefits of the esoteric path (Vô Vi) have included a small but deeply committed body of disciples, who could be discreet, and met privately for group reflection and meditation. While they did not build such impressive temples, they have maintained libraries, archives, and resources, which have preserved the history of these movements and their ties to similar groups in China, Taiwan, and overseas Chinese communities throughout Southeast Asia. Responding to outside turmoil by withdrawing into the self and seeking inner tranquility in meditation and self-cultivation has allowed the smaller groups like Minh Lý to remain open, somewhat "under the radar" of state surveillance, and also to maintain the training and cultivation of new spirit mediums.

Putting a New Face on Caodaism in the Twenty-first Century

While Lâm Lý Hùng was in Saigon, he went to the Saigon Teaching Agency, where he had taken courses in meditation and participated in séances as a young man. In 2000, the Vietnamese government officially recognized the Agency as a legitimate religious organization. The Vietnamese government recognized eleven other Caodai organizations in the period 1995–2000 (see the Chronology). Several of the Agency's leaders had developed good relations with highly placed Communist leaders from South Vietnam, especially Võ Văn Kiệt, the reform-minded prime minister. They decided to try to write "another history" of certain Caodai leaders, who could be seen as "revolutionary," and who would counterbalance the general perception that Caodaists were opposed to the current regime. The foremost "Caodai revolutionary hero" was Cao Triều Phát (1889–1956), a famous poet who had fought as a soldier for France during World War I and returned to lead the Việt Minh resistance forces in his home province of Bạc Liêu. He was a founding leader of the Indochinese Labor Party in 1926, and an important figure in the Minh Chơn Đạo branch based in the southwest. In 1954, he was among those followers of Hồ Chí Minh who traveled up to Hanoi as partition became likely, joining Hồ Chí Minh's Fatherland Front (Smith 2009, 103, 109).

A couple of journalists researched and wrote an admiring portrait of Cao Triều Phát as the "legend of the south," describing him as a man born to the landlord class who voluntarily redistributed his own lands and led resistance forces to many victories in the Mekong Delta (Lê Thanh Chơn 2002). Another book focused on the family of Nguyễn Ngọc Tương, the Pope of the Bến Tre branch (Ban Chỉnh Đạo), who had two sons who fought for the resistance. Titled "The Sleepless Nights of the Pope," it presented the events as an interior monologue in the mind of Nguyễn Ngọc Tương, torn between his wish to free his sons from French prisons and his duty to his country and his religion (Tram Thị Hương 2004). Both of his sons had studied engineering in Paris, one at the extremely prestigious École Polytechnique, and the other at the somewhat less renowned École des Ponts et Chaussés. His oldest son, Nguyễn Ngọc Bích, was arrested and tortured, but eventually his French schoolmates negotiated a deal for him to be exiled to France. His younger son, Nguyễn Ngọc Nhứt, who was married to a French woman, died as a result of his treatment in the French prisons. Prime Minister Võ Văn Kiệt endorsed both books on the back cover himself, and the tragic story of Nguyễn Ngọc Nhứt was adapted into a folk opera (*cải lương*) that toured the Mekong Delta and was broadcast on television (Nguyễn Ngọc Châu [grandson of Nguyễn Ngọc Tương], personal communication).

Lâm Lý Hùng saw all of these developments as signs that the Vietnamese government was no longer trying to wipe out Caodaism completely and had decided to normalize relations with religious leaders willing to work with them. He took heart from the fact that Tam Tông Miếu had never been directly involved in politics, since its leadership had always tried to transcend worldly divisions by practicing self-cultivation and working on individual consciousness, rather than trying to reform the world. He decided that it might be possible to work quietly to bring these organizations gently out onto the public arena again. The trickiest question would be the legality of séances.

Controversies about the Legality of Spirit Mediumship and Séances

Article 5 of the 2004 Decree on Beliefs and Religions from the central Vietnamese government does not allow what are called "superstitious activities." Ideas of what is "superstitious" have changed in recent years. The *xin xâm* or *xin keo* (divination practices using sticks tossed on the ground to designate numbered fortunes, or using Chinese coins tossed to find a yin-yang formation) at the shrine and tomb of the Imperial Viceroy Lê Văn Duyệt were considered superstitious and forbidden after 1975, but were allowed again in the 1990s and are very popular today.

In 2001, there was a general assembly of representatives from the Sacerdotal Council of Central Vietnam (Hội Thánh Truyền Giáo) in Đà Nẵng at a ceremony to celebrate the recognition of its religious constitution by the government. Government officials did not allow the word *cơ bút* (the "spirit pen," used as an instrument of spirit mediums) to be included in the constitution. Then, the senior spirit medium stood up and said: "Caodaism was founded by *cơ bút,* so if you do not allow it, we will cancel the ceremony and we will continue to practice our religion as usual." In order to avoid a protest from the assembly, the officials finally agreed to include a sentence that designated the sacred space usually occupied by mediums as a space "for the work of communicating with the Supreme Being and other spirit entities."[14] This was somewhat less explicit, since it did not identify the ways in which these spirits would send and receive messages. A Committee for Communication with the Spirits was formed (Ban Thông Công), indicating that new scriptures could now be received if they were submitted to this committee and approved by them for dissemination. The Caodaists thought that they had achieved a victory. The term used for spirit communication (*thông công*) also occurs in the religious constitution of the Protestant Church (Hội Thánh Tin Lành), referring to Communion.

Some religious leaders had private meetings with some high-ranking government officials in 2008. They asked for permission to hold spirit séances in various temples that had not been involved in any political activity during the period of the American war in Vietnam. They received verbal approval to hold séances discreetly, with only a few people present, as long as the messages were reviewed by the administrative committee and did not involve politics or "disturb public order." It is now an open secret that séances are held privately by some organizations I study in Vietnam, but I have agreed not to provide the names or locations of these séances in print.

Becoming "Indigenous": A New View from the Vietnamese State

In an introduction to the edited volume *Modernity and Re-enchantment: Religion in Post-revolutionary Vietnam,* Philip Taylor outlines several ways in which contemporary religions can be understood in Vietnam (2007, 10–15). While acknowledging the many conflicts between religious leaders and the current government, he concludes that it is wrong to overemphasize the role of the state, even if its control over publications means it can keep the "court transcript": "From time to time the official record is tactfully re-edited to find aspects of formerly censored or unnoticed popular practice to be in conformity with state policy" (Taylor 2007, 14).

In 2007, the official Religious Press of Hanoi published a book by Phạm Bích Hợp titled *The People of the Southern Region and Indigenous Religions,* with a combination of interviews, surveys, and ethnographic research concerning the southern millenarian religious movements known as Bửu Sơn Kỳ Hương ("Strange Fragrance from the Precious Mountain"), Hòa Hảo Buddhism, and Caodaism.[15] This new study expressed a more conciliatory government attitude toward groups once designated as practicing "superstition" and "reactionary politics," sanctioning them under the new and increasingly common description of these groups as "indigenous religions" (*tôn giáo bản địa*). But the nature of this new sanction and its history raises a series of questions about what exactly could be meant by "indigenous" and how it is being used in today's Vietnam.

The term "indigenous" has the general meaning of "native," originating in and characterized by a particular region or country, and the Vietnamese term (*bản địa*) means quite literally "emerging from the land." A second sense given to the English term is innate, inherent, or natural, which is rendered by another Vietnamese term often used in the book—*bản sắc,* which could be translated literally as the "true original colors" and has taken on the modern meaning of "identity." This characterization is often used to designate the religious practices of ethnic minorities who once inhabited the region but have now been displaced by larger groups who have migrated to the area.

Ethnic Vietnamese (Kinh) migrated to the region now known as southern Vietnam in the past three hundred years, and they make up almost all the followers of these "southern religions." They are not, therefore, the people who have the earliest historical connection to the land. The region had been a part of the kingdom of Kampuchia, inhabited by Khmer-speaking people and various highland groups, many of them speakers of Austronesian languages (Taylor 2014). The term "tribal" could perhaps be applied to the highlanders, many of whom lived primarily from hunting and swidden gardening, but it would be hard to use this label for the followers of "indigenous religions," who are primarily agriculturalists, and include many traders, city residents, intellectuals, and members of the professional class. Caodaism in particular originated among colonial civil servants, many of them of high rank, and was led by a number of wealthy landowners, businessmen, and journalists. The Caodai pantheon is both syncretistic and cosmopolitan, involving as it does the veneration of historical personages not only from Vietnam, China, and India, but also from Palestine, France, and Russia. So how could these belief systems come to be described as "indigenous"?

I think the labeling of these practices as "indigenous" religions is primarily a strategic one, which combines a recognition of regional traditions and a perception that the 1975 "reunification" of Vietnam also had elements of an annexation and even subjugation of the peoples of the South, who were supposedly "liberated." As part of an effort to normalize relations between religions and the state, this term revises earlier policies that had condemned Caodaism and Hòa Hảo as "superstitious" or "heterodox" practices (*mê tín*) and allows their adherents to be seen as "mainstream" (*chánh tín*) religious believers. Scholars now speak of "folk beliefs" (*tín ngưỡng dân gian*) that were never fully absorbed into elite or official culture, what Philip Taylor calls "an unofficial counterculture that reflects the priorities of groups who have been excluded from state power" (2007, 10).

The intriguing thing about these newer definitions of "indigenous" is that they suggest that the relation between the Hanoi government and the "indigenous people of the South" might have aspects of a colonization or annexation, and that the people of the South might in some way be considered subjugated by the dominant culture of the nation-state. These are claims sometimes made by southern leaders, even those who were themselves active in the National Liberation Front (Việt Cộng), who felt that reunification in 1975 did not in fact place the two formerly separated halves of Vietnam on an equal footing but resulted in a period during which all southerners, whatever their political convictions, were viewed as unreliable and were not allowed to share evenly in their own new government.

Tam Tông Miếu and Neo-Confucianism

The relationship between Lâm Lý Hùng's temple and larger Caodaist groups today is based mainly on the idea that Minh Lý dignitaries are scholars and ritual specialists who can teach their esoteric knowledge to a new generation.

Dressed in the dark robes favored by Confucian officials, they appear today as "the professors" of the almost vanished occult sciences—forms of knowledge which are, however, enjoying a certain renaissance in contemporary Vietnam.

Hồ Chí Minh City's largest bookstore, Fahasa, had two long shelves of books in a special aisle dealing with divination, meditation, yoga, Taoist mysteries, and other such subjects when I visited in 2010, but there was a sign up strictly forbidding the taking of any photographs in that aisle. Why should this be prohibited, when any of the other aisles could be photographed? Perhaps the owners of the bookstore did not want the number of titles that they carried in these subjects to be documented. The even vaster resources of the Internet supplement these printed books, and Vietnamese websites devoted to these topics are increasingly popular.

Lâm Lý Hùng teaches classes of young Caodaists associated with the Saigon Teaching Agency who are trained by him in how to read the classics alongside modern scientific discoveries. He has offered this course in English since 2004, to improve the language skills of a new generation with a more cosmopolitan outlook. One of his younger colleagues, a professor of information science who spent two years studying at Tam Tông Miếu, runs an international Vietnamese-language LISTSERV named *Kinh Dịch,* after the Taoist Book of Changes. As a long term "lurker" on that LISTSERV, I can confirm that it addresses a very wide range of topics, including parapsychology, Freemasonry, the exegesis of esoteric symbols in a number of other traditions, and scientific research dealing with lobes of the brain.

By taking a "pedagogical" approach to religion, and not seeking to proselytize as actively as the Caodaists do, the leaders of Tam Tông Miếu have managed to make a niche for themselves in contemporary Vietnam. Governmental regulations will not formally recognize a group with fewer than four hundred members. By adding a hundred "sympathizers" to their three hundred official members, Lâm Lý Hùng and his associates were able to formally apply for official recognition in 2008.

On October 17, 2008, the Minh Lý Đạo Temple was finally granted government recognition, when the Religious Affairs Office (Ban Tôn Giáo Chính Phủ) agreed to list them as an officially authorized religious pathway. The temple's black-robed dignitaries traveled to Hanoi to receive the official papers of certification in a solemn celebration. After the ceremony, many of them made pilgrimages to religious and historical sites in northern Vietnam—a part of their country that none of them had visited before. They made a pilgrimage to the shrine in Kiếp Bạc, Hải Dương province, where the great Vietnamese hero

Trần Hưng Đạo was incarnated by dozens of spirit mediums each day. They were deeply impressed by the lively activity of trance dances at the shrine, performed in the Đạo Mẫu tradition of popular spirit possession (*lên đồng*).[16] This form of largely nonverbal, visually dramatic spirit mediumship has swept across the country with great success since the early years of the twenty-first century and has been the subject of many excellent ethnographic studies.[17] The tolerance of this exuberant form of worshipping spirits from imperial times may indicate a future openness to literary spirit mediumship.

The quiet, consistent, and controlled efforts that members of Tam Tông Miếu made over the past decades had finally proved successful. Their voyage to Hanoi to receive official status confirmed the wisdom of accepting a relationship with the state in order to assure both their continuity as a group and their transnational scope. A year after this recognition, the head of the Religious Institute published a history of Minh Lý theology, and it assumed the status of an independent faith (Nguyễn Hồng Dương 2009).

Lâm Lý Hùng is among the most prominent of a number of overseas Vietnamese who have chosen to return to their homeland for religious as well as personal reasons. Retiring from his professional commitments in 2005, he responded to a "higher calling" that reconnected him to an ancestral lineage in Sino-Vietnamese occultism. Over the course of the next few years, Lâm Lý Hùng stopped being a Vietnamese-American who returned to attend rituals at the Saigon temple and became a foreign resident of Vietnam who visited his family in California to celebrate Tết, the Vietnamese New Year.

CHAPTER 6

THE DIVINE EYE ON
THE INTERNET

VISIONS AND VIRTUAL REALITIES
IN THE SHADOW OF DISNEYLAND

On December 11, 2011, I received an e-mail about the continuing search for a new spirit medium in California. At a newly opened Caodai Teaching Center on Vermont Avenue in Anaheim, local Caodaists had been contacted by a woman whose bloodlines seemed to destine her to be spiritually receptive. Jessica Dung Nguyễn was the niece of Lê Thiên Phước, the Bảo Thế, or ranking spirit medium, who had replaced Cao Hoài Sang as the head of the College of Spirit Mediums (Hiệp Thiên Đài) in Tây Ninh after his death in 1973. She had already had a series of visions, including one of the Mother Goddess (Phật Mẫu), but she was uncertain about her vocation. She had had a series of dreams that indicated she might be able to receive spirit messages. And she wanted to meet Caodai leaders who could give her guidance on this issue.

When I drove down to visit the Teaching Center, I discovered that it was across the street from one of the many entrances to Disneyland. Signs featuring Mickey Mouse pointed cars in one direction, and I turned sharply to go off just behind a tall wall cutting us off from the fantasy kingdom that claimed to be "the happiest place in the world." I was reminded not only of Graham Greene's 1952 evocation of "the full Asiatic splendor of a Walt Disney fantasy," but also of Jean Baudrillard's 1995 argument that Disneyland's main function is to make us believe that the rest of America is real and not merely of the order of

Figure 6.1. David Tùng Chế in the television studio of the Caodai Center in Anaheim, California

simulation.[1] It seemed an appropriate place to ask how modern media has re-configured "the real," and circulated new religious imagery, in an age of virtual realities.

Overseas Vietnamese in California have long sought to establish a teaching center and a place where scholars and intellectuals could come together in the New World, modeling their aspirations on both the "traditional model" provided by Tam Tông Miếu and the more "modernist model" provided by the Saigon Teaching Agency. In 2010, a group of Caodaists purchased an older office building in Anaheim. The office building is two stories high and has a large number of meeting rooms, several kitchens, an area used as a television studio, and another that is used as a meditation center. It is not a temple and has none of the external markers that are associated with the "exotic face" of Caodaism: There is no emblem of the divine Left Eye, there is no flag flying the crimson, saffron, and turquoise colors, and there are no colorfully decorated pillars with pastel dragons and lotus blossoms. There is however, a copy of the mural that stands at the entrance to the Tây Ninh Great Temple, showing Victor Hugo, Sun Yat-sen, and Trạng Trình signing the divine accord. I was told the mural was included because it represents the divine mandate to teach the doctrine and to spread it overseas, since Victor Hugo is the spiritual head of the overseas mission.

Jessica Dung Nguyễn was an attractive woman in her thirties, dressed in a short jacket, jeans, and boots, who worked as a mortgage broker. She told us that she had received visions since she was five years old and living in Vietnam.

> The first time I saw a spirit it was near a river where we lived in the country-side. She was a beautiful young girl, maybe sixteen or seventeen, wearing a white dress, and her skin glowed like neon. She called me to come to her, as her foot played with the water. But when I looked more closely, she had no face. It was just a blur, out of focus. It freaked me out. It was as if I had seen a ghost. Finally I had the courage to close my eyes and run away.

This first religious experience, described with metaphors of electric lighting and filmed images, identified her as someone who might be sensitive to invisible presences. People came to ask her to read fortune-telling cards for them, offering her candy if she would do so. At the age of eight, she wrote a letter to her sister in the United States, saying that she was afraid her sister-in-law would die. She then threw away the letter, since it seemed to make no sense. Two months later, her brother's wife, who was in her twenties and in good health, committed suicide. Jessica then felt responsible for not having been able to warn people, perhaps even to save a life.

Jessica was the last of twenty children in her family, and her birth itself was a miracle, since her mother was forty-nine at the time. The family went through many hardships, and nine of her siblings died, with eleven still alive. Her father and grandmother were both active Caodaists, so she heard about the religion from them. Her mother also sometimes had visions and suffered from poor health. She explained, "Later I had more dreams, this time about my mother. My dreams start and stop like a video. I can leave the dream and then go back to it, to the same place where it stopped. I saw my mother in the hospital, pregnant with me, and that was fine. But then in the next dream they moved her to the second floor, the floor where people go to die."

Two years later her mother died of intestinal cancer, and Jessica visited her on the second floor, knowing then that she would not survive. She had other premonitions of things she later saw on the television news—a black car in a dark tunnel, suddenly surrounded by photographers (Princess Diana's death), waves rising up and sweeping houses away (the tsunami in Japan). "My dreams are always in color, and full of sounds, like at a megaplex, but I am not sure what story they are part of."

Jessica moved to California with her family when she was ten years old. Since she started to make contact with spirits in Vietnam, she thinks her power would have been stronger if she had stayed there. She now recognizes the vision she had at age five as Quan Âm, who usually appears as a lady in white. Sometimes, Jessica is not sure whether the glowing white woman she has seen is the Buddhist Quan Âm or the Catholic Our Lady of La Vang, since both of them are represented in similar clothing. Quan Âm is represented standing on a lotus flower, and she can also be shown holding a child.

Our Lady of La Vang is omnipresent in the homes of many Vietnamese Catholics. Jessica's first husband was Catholic, so she was exposed to many pictures of Our Lady of La Vang wearing a blue cloak over a white tunic and trousers, her head wrapped in the traditional northern Vietnamese woman's headdress, glowing gold like a halo. She holds the Christ child in her arms, and her features and those of the Christ child are Vietnamese, so she is identified as "the Vietnamese Holy Mother." La Vang is a community in Quảng Trị, central Vietnam, where Catholics took refuge in the jungle, trying to escape the persecutions of 1798. A divine apparition of the Virgin Mary appeared, surrounded by light, and came to console them. She told them to use the golden leaves of a local fern (*lá vàng*) as a medicine and said all those who prayed to her at that site would be helped. While her sacred presence did not save their lives, it did allow them to meet their deaths as martyrs with courage and conviction. A church was later built on that site, and in 1961 it was consecrated as a basilica (Ninh 2014).

Pilgrims travel to the site of her apparition each year, and the 1988 consecration of 117 Vietnamese martyrs by Pope John Paul II has reinforced her importance. A Catholic church in Santa Ana is dedicated to Our Lady of La Vang and the martyrs, who are often pictured underneath the great wing-like extensions of her cloak.

Jessica had visions that her Catholic friends told her were archangels. Caodaists consider that the "great immortals" (*Đại tiên*) of East Asian tradition can also be considered archangels. After she left Vietnam, she did not try to make contact with Caodaists for many decades. She interpreted her experience of visions in other frameworks made available to her by mass media. At the Caodai Center in Anaheim, people said she could have been seeing the Mother Goddess (Phật Mẫu), who is also known as the Taoist Queen of the Heavens (Diệu Trì Kim Mẫu). In Tây Ninh, Phật Mẫu has her own temple, where she is represented in a painted frieze, riding on a phoenix bird and surrounded by nine female immortals. Light radiates out from behind her head, framed by a golden headdress above long robes of blue, white, and gold. I showed Jessica an image of the Mother Goddess that I had on my computer, and she described the features of the woman she saw as similar, but with some differences (a broader forehead, lips that were fuller and slightly upturned). Significantly, the image of the Mother Goddess in Tây Ninh was said to look "more Chinese" (and was in fact copied from Chinese images of the goddess), while Jessica's visions showed a goddess who looked "more Vietnamese."

Jessica also has visions of texts she cannot understand—"letters glowing like neon, some of them a bit like Chinese characters, others forming poems full of archaic language." These visions are very close to what an earlier generation of Caodaists reported when the beak of the phoenix basket traced out the letters of spirit messages as it was held by spirit mediums. When she is sitting very calmly, meditating, she says: "I can hear them in my head, as if they were dictating to me, like shorthand."

Some of the messages she had written down were thrown away, since she could not make sense of them. Later, she regretted discarding these early spirit messages, since she was told that they often come in older forms of Sino-Vietnamese, which are hard to understand. She keeps a dream diary now, and has also sketched her visions. She showed some of these sketches to us in the Caodai Center. She also told us that one of the women in white she saw in a dream told her to cleanse herself, to become a full vegetarian, and to pour holy water on her head. These instructions suggested that she was being told to prepare to be a Caodai spirit medium, since mediums must be both vegetarian and celibate. She thought she might experiment with trying to receive messages in a Caodai séance, but wanted to be able to observe some séances first.

Mediated Visions and Virtual Realities

Jessica's efforts to navigate through a stream of circulating representations, often perceived in a cinematic language, illustrates the ways in which virtual realities have come to drown us all in a surfeit of religious imagery. The inner, spiritual gaze that is supposed to be the source of visions is now mirrored and overwritten by competing simulations of divine apparitions we encounter on television, in films, or in video games. Caodaists at the temple asked Jessica if she had seen the Left Eye of God (*Thiên Nhân*)—a visionary experience cultivated in intensive sessions of meditation. The duplication of this image throughout Caodai temples prepares disciples to visualize God in this way, since it is used to focus their attention and intention. She had seen images of eyes floating in the sky, and blinking at her, but did not know if they were the

Left Eye of God. Technologies of mass reproduction have unsettled the relationship between the visible and the invisible, making almost any image available at the click of a mouse.

Although Jessica had "not yet" seen the Left Eye, she had seen many things that could be interpreted through a Caodai pantheon and séance practice. The three "Holy Mothers"—the Buddhist Quan Âm, the Taoist Diêu Trì Kim Mẫu, and the Catholic Đức Mẹ Maria (the Virgin Mary)—could all conceivably have contacted her to call her to become a Caodai medium. In *The Internet and the Madonna: Religious Visionary Experience on the Web,* Paolo Apolito (2005) suggests that modern media is bringing about a radical transformation of Catholic visionary traditions and perhaps even the nature of religion itself. Glimpses of the divine that were previously only available to a few dedicated mystics are now readily available through a Google search. Apolito speculates that the more democractic nature of access to digital technologies could lead to a return to a more archaic and mystical form of Catholicism, which existed before the reforms of Vatican II.

The existence of new media like the Internet has led to changes in communication among religious adherents and new forms of religious promotion. Jessica found the Anaheim Caodai Center on the Internet, and this discovery started her on a path that could eventually lead back to her grandfather in Tây Ninh. The Internet has made it possible for Caodaists scattered across the globe to remain in contact with each other. New media production techniques have allowed various Caodai groups to produce television shows discussing Caodai doctrine, to sponsor many rival websites (each with their own take on religious questions), to take part in international LISTSERVs, and to send images of visions as attachments to e-mail. Caodaists have been brought under what Aihwa Ong calls "the electronic umbrella of diaspora" (2008, 181). Technology has enabled the formation of new cyberpublics, who can customize global ethnic and religious identities without ever meeting.

Has the new flood of information overstimulated our minds and blocked our abilities to perceive invisible presences, which are now upstaged by technical special effects? Pessimistic thinkers associated with the Frankfurt School believed that "as their telescopes and microscopes become more sensitive, individuals become blinder, more hard of hearing, less responsive."[2] Others have countered these theories of disenchantment with arguments that religious imagination has been newly empowered in the Information Age. The widened public sphere has allowed once-marginalized minority religions to reach a broader audience. It has also reconfigured "the real," and the idea of visual evidence, in an age of virtual realities.

New Media and New Mediums: Gender Shifts

Among Caodaists, reflections on the relation between new media and new mediums have sometimes focused on the gender transformation of spirit mediums from the early twentieth century to the twenty-first century. In the formative years, "the age of revelations" from 1925–1934, all of the prominent literary mediums were male. When Phạm Công Tắc formed the College of Spirit Mediums (Hiệp Thiên Đài) with twelve Zodiacal dignitaries, each born in a different year of the Chinese zodiac, they were all men. All of the basic Caodai "scriptures" or collections of spirit messages from the twentieth century were revealed to male mediums. More recently, however, both in Vietnam and in California, most mediums have been women, and in fact several people told me that they now believed that women were "better suited" to be spirit mediums than men.

Why has this changed? I asked this question several times with different results. In 2013, at a meeting with various important officers of the Saigon Teaching Agency, I was told that this might be a result of the fact that "God wanted to restore the balance of yin and yang," so in recent years he chose to select female mediums to receive his messages rather than male ones. Later, one of the women who had been present at that meeting but had not spoken up offered another interpretation in confidence:

> In the first years of our religion, it was very important to be "yang" (*dương*). to be aggressive, forceful, and positive. These are male virtues, and the leaders at that time had to be dynamic personalities who could inspire many followers. Caodaism grew very fast then, and they all had to have these "yang" characteristics.
>
> Since 1975, the religion has been in a "yin" (*âm*) phase, where we have had to be quieter, more secretive, less assertive on the public scene. Women are more likely to be spirit mediums now because they are more willing to lead celibate lives, to be separated from the world of distractions, and to remain pure and tranquil. It is true that some of the young women who were trained as mediums later left to get married, but that was rare. Now we are nourishing our community more gently, so women are better spirit intermediaries than men.

The founders of Caodaism took pride in modernizing their faith by opening up high religious offices to women. The first female Cardinal, Lâm Ngọc Thanh, is represented on the front of the Great Temple in Tây Ninh. No female dignitary, however, participated directly in the early conversations with divinities (since Hương Hiếu only witnessed and recorded them). The more conventional response to the question of why female mediums have emerged as more common in the twenty-first century, of course, is simply that women have become more educated: "In the past, women would never have been able to study spirit messages, memorizing them and copying them, since they were not literate. But now many women do this kind of religious service, and it can help to train them to become mediums," I was told. Given that the human medium is "the instrument" on which the spirits play their music, this "instrument" must be nuanced and finely tuned in order to produce the most beautiful music.

The idea that Caodaism has entered a "yin phase" of greater female prominence is also related to ways in which spirit messages are now archived and exchanged electronically. Men dominated literary circles in the early twentieth century, and intimate spirit writing séances were usually all male. Female mediums were common in the trance dancing tradition of Đạo Mẫu, but they were often illiterate (Endres 2002, 2011). Cyberspace has allowed private homes to become platforms for the publication and distribution of new messages, and women's willingness to remain in the shadows has come to be seen as better adapted to the discrete, low-key forms of séance that happen behind closed doors and circulate anonymously on the Internet.

The relationship between the gender of spirit mediums and various forms of technology has been the subject of several fascinating studies of European spirit mediums by scholars like Alex Owen and Jill Galvan. Owen (2004) explores how beliefs that Victorian women were uniquely qualified to commune with the spirits of the dead may also have helped undermine conventional class and gender relations. Galvan follows the same story into the early twentieth century, which saw not only the emergence of the telegraph, the telephone, and the typewriter, but also a fascination with séances and occult practices like automatic writing as a means for contacting the dead. Like the new technologies, early twentieth-century spiritualism promised to link people separated by space or circumstance; and like them as well, it depended on the presence of a human medium to convey these conversations. Whether electrical or otherworldly, these communications were remarkably often conducted in offices, at telegraph stations, and telephone switchboards, and in séance parlors by women. Galvan (2010) focuses on how two allegedly feminine traits, sympathy and a susceptibility to automatism, enabled women to "disappear into their role as message carriers."

As we have seen in Chapter 1, the first Caodai spirit mediums were clerks and secretaries in offices, but in the colonial society of the early twentieth century, these jobs were exclusively held by men. They did see spirit séances as a new technology, which emerged at the same time as many other modern forms of communication. In the twenty-first century, after female literacy and employment has increased dramatically in Vietnam, the idea of female "literary" spirit mediums has also to some extent come of age.

The particular "susceptibility" of women to become the more or less empty vessels for communication with the spirits has been noted in a great many other cultural contexts where women predominate in spirit possession groups (see Lewis 1971; Boddy 1994; Morris 2000). While Ioan Lewis' idea that spirit mediumship offers compensation or consolation to women who have been disempowered has been criticized as too simplistic (Boddy 1994), there does seem to be a connection between shifts in gender roles and shifts in the ritual roles most often occupied by women and men.

Jessica Dung Nguyễn fit well into the new expected background for a Caodai medium, and so expectations were high that she might be willing to undertake the stages of preparation. In the late 1970s, when Bạch Diệu Hoa started receiving spirit messages in San Jose, her behavior seemed radical and totally unconventional, as did her assumption of colorful costumes once worn only by men. But thirty years later this is no longer the case. In fact, a few years later, two other female spirit mediums connected to the Chiếu Minh branch contacted the Caodai Center by e-mail. As Bùi Đắc Hùm wrote to me on July 3, 2013:

> Hoàng Anh, the granddaughter of Ngô Văn Chiêu, lives in California. She said that his spirit is using her body to contact Caodaists overseas, and that my wife, Khâm, and I have the mission to work for this new direction. Ngô Văn Chiêu received a new meditation method before he died and taught it to his last disciple, Minh Chơn. Four years ago, Minh Chơn was ordered by spiritual messages to leave Vietnam for the U.S. four years ago to spread Caodaism. Another female medium in Vietnam has established a new group, Sacred Communication Palace (Thông Linh Điện), which is also based on new spirit communications. Their new facility was visited by Khâm and will be completed in 2014. Teaching esoteric practice in this new way should be a better fit for Western people, because it is more open, simpler, and has fewer requirements than traditional Chiếu Minh.

Leaders of the Anaheim Caodai Center want to expand their teaching of meditation, and they were encouraged by these new contacts and possibilities. The emphasis on esoteric techniques like meditation does seem to overcome differences of language and the material trappings of ritual, since all of these are more or less dematerialized by the deep concentration required in stilling the mind to meditate.

"Internet Converts": Non-Vietnamese Caodaists in America

Jessica's vision was certainly "mediated" by her exposure to a variety of religious images, as was the 1993 vision of Ngasha Beck, an American woman married to a Cambodian husband, who converted to Caodaism in the 1990s and coauthored *Caodai Faith of Unity*. Ngasha Beck described her vision to me in an e-mail in 2004 in these terms:

> I was reclined in meditation when a shining image of the Divine Eye came shooting from infinity toward me, and at the time that it collided or encompassed me there was a very loud sound like a gun going off beside each ear, which jolted me upright. It was instantaneous; there was no thought, no sentiment other than wonder possible in the time frame of the vision. But unlike a dream, it did not fade as moments passed; instead, there was like an urgency to understand. And unlike most meditations, I did not emerge contented but rather searching my mind, seeking for answers. I paced (I never pace). I remembered that I had read or heard somewhere about a Vietnamese religion who worshipped an Eye and had Victor Hugo as a Saint. I hadn't been to school (properly) and didn't know who Victor Hugo was, other than he was famous for something. Even so, I felt right about asking Victor Hugo if he would guide me, to do so. Suddenly, everywhere I looked, the newspaper, TV, there was mention of Victor Hugo. On a weekly trip to the library I was attracted to a book about Sarah Bernhardt, the actress; opening the book I saw reference to Victor Hugo having practically worshipped her in his lifetime. There were just too many coincidences. I now believe that Victor Hugo is the one who named me.[3]

Ngasha Beck felt that her calling to Caodaism was reinforced and reaffirmed when she looked for images of Victor Hugo in mass media, and his name kept coming up in a number of different contexts. It helped her to make sense of an earlier vision in which she was given a ritual name (Ngasha) that initially made no sense to her. She found confirmation of this calling when she read about Caodaism on the Internet, and so she initiated contact with Dr. Bùi Đắc Hùm in California. He suggested that Ngasha might be a shortened form of Nguyệt-Tâm (moon pure heart), which is also a component of Victor Hugo's Vietnamese name. She can perhaps be counted as the first of the "Internet converts," who began their spiritual search in cyberspace but later became intensely involved with Caodai congregations. She went on to spend many years translating Caodai spirit messages into English verse, so that their poetic character in the original language would not be lost to a new English-reading public.

In a fascinating account of Muslim traditions of dream interpretation, Mittermaier speculates that: "Media technologies can raise questions about the trustworthiness of the senses, potentially calling for a new valuation of the imaginary" (2011, 230). A plethora of images enriches our fields of perception and imagination. Cinema and other technologies provide a wealth of metaphors for describing, imagining, and sharing visionary experiences. The scope of "reality" has to be remapped, using the new coordinates of the virtual canvas on which these techno-pictures are painted. Religious scholars in Tây Ninh and at the Saigon Teaching Agency in Hồ Chí Minh City have selected "official" spirit messages and designated others as "unofficial." But dreams and visions are more effective in bypassing the authority of religious scholars (as well as the watchful "eye of Hanoi" government surveillance). No official institution in Vietnam or California can decide whether a vision was real or fake, divinely inspired or the work of the devil.

Jessica tried to come to an understanding of her own experiences by approaching Caodaists who had been an important part of her family legacy. Should she choose to pursue these connections and train as a spirit medium, her heritage would play a role in legitimating her—but many other factors would also be involved. The nebulous, fleeting images of dreams and visions become concretized in images that play across the various websites devoted to such experiences, so increasingly people seek to "recognize" the goddess that they have seen through digital images, which may both bring into focus and orient their interpretations of what their inner gaze had revealed.

History of Outreach to Non-Vietnamese Members

Ngasha Beck's experiences reveal both the connections to media depictions and the theme of "uncommon attractions" found in many non-Vietnamese Caodaists. From the earliest period, Caodaists have seen their faith as universal, and so have made efforts to include people of all backgrounds. When Trần Quang Vinh traveled to Paris in 1931, he made contact with French Spiritists there and "converted" a French novelist and philosopher named Gabriel Gobron, who founded a "Spiritist circle," or Cénacle, in Paris (as we saw in Chapter 3). The thirteen members of this circle—almost all of them French—practiced their own idiosyncratic form of Caodaism, which has left its traces in various editions of Gobron's books on the *History and Philosophy of Caodaism,* as well as the collected photographs of *Le Caodaisme en Images* (G. Gobron 1948, M. Gobron 1949). In the 1950s and 1960s, Gustave Meillon, a professor of Oriental languages at the Sorbonne, was a "fellow traveler" who wrote sympathetically about Caodai theology and has also been counted as a follower by many Caodaists (Meillon 1984).[4] During the years of the American war, most Caodai leaders, like Đỗ Vạn Lý, avoided discussions of their religion with American friends, preferring to see it as a way of preserving Vietnamese values from deleterious American influence (see Chapter 4).

But once they arrived on American shores, a number of American "converts" remained faithful members of the New World congregations. These included Đỗ Vạn Lý's own son-in-law, a research biologist married to his daughter Merdeka, and several American Vietnam War veterans, journalists, and others who established ties to Vietnam that sometimes included marriage to Vietnamese women. Stephen Stratford, a veteran who was traumatized by his war experiences, had one of the most dramatic conversion stories:

> I was part of the secret war on Laos, identifying bomb targets by the pattern of crops planted. I realized that I was signing the death warrants for lots of innocent women and children, and ended up numbing my mind with drugs. I came back to the U.S. as a heroin addict, spent years in prison for credit card fraud, then became active in the Vietnam Veteran's Restoration Project. They sent me back to Vietnam to build medical clinics and help the people we had once tried to kill. I was sent to a Caodai orphanage in Tây Ninh. When I arrived there, they told me that they were waiting for me. A spirit message had told them that the first American G.I. to convert to Caodaism was on his way. I was astonished by this prophecy, but did not know what to do about it. The government would not let us proceed in that area, so the orphanage did not become part of the Restoration Project. But four years later, I received my own set of spirit messages, calling me to convert. Through the Internet, I made contact with Dr. Bui in California, and he agreed to teach me about Caodai doctrine. I performed the gateway ceremony (*nhập môn*) and they made me a member of the Thanh Hương generation of converts. I have been a member of the Caodai community for over fifteen years now, even living with Dr. Bui and his family for several months. My own family is Mormon, but I excommunicated myself from them thirty years ago. Caodaists are like Mormons in some ways, in their discipline and their devotion, but they are not racist or patriarchal. I feel that—although I am not Vietnamese—I have finally found my spiritual home. I have roots with them, which I feel good about. It is the only organized religion I can relate to and feel comfortable in.

Stephen's conversion was paralleled by similar moves by a number of American war veterans who became Buddhists after the war, since they described it as a way of "recovering their souls" and dealing with a bad conscience. In his case, the pathway leading Stephen to accepting Spiritism was laid by his reading of the *Course in Miracles* (Schucman and Thetford 1976) during a period when he was imprisoned for drug-related credit card fraud. The *Course in Miracles* is a New Age "classic" that is also embraced by a number of Caodaists, and its enormous popularity in prisons seems to stem from the fact that it teaches that everything can be forgiven, and a new spiritual home can be found.

Another Caodai convert in southern California, Michael Nally, was a journalist stationed in Hanoi who had a vision that he was being called "to follow the great way." He had grown up in Quebec, in a city where the statue of Jeanne d'Arc dominated the landscape, so he felt that she, as a Caodai saint, had reached out to him during his travels in Asia and eventually led him to a faith that combined his childhood search for a French mother with his fascination for Oriental mysticism. He returned many times to Vietnam and eventually married a Vietnamese woman, but in his case the marriage came only after this mystical calling. Michael Nally prays in a particular posture—with his arms outstretched and his gaze raised to the altar of the Left Eye of God—which appears in French Catholic missionary images. He sees his destiny now as that of a "reverse missionary"—a Westerner called to witness the power of Asian wisdom and promote it to other Americans. He is affiliated with the Westminster temple in California, which is part of a generally more conservative Tây Ninh tradition, but its leadership agreed to instruct him in Caodai doctrine and grant him full membership.

There have also been non-American converts, including several French people, who made contact with Caodaists in Paris and in Vietnam. The only one I was able to interview was a French psychotherapist whom I will call Laurent, who had traveled to Vietnam to study Oriental medicine and stayed at a small hotel managed by Đinh Thị Thanh Tùng, the daughter of the Caodai dignitary Đinh Văn Đệ and an active member of the Saigon Teaching Agency. He was committed to "direct experience and participation" in the religious traditions that he studied and decided to do the gateway ceremony to show his commitment to what he describes as a "modern version of Taoist philosophy." He was able to read fairly extensively in the Caodai scriptures that have been published in French (which, of course, include many messages originally revealed in French) and he repeated the oath of allegiance in Vietnamese, with some coaching from Francophone Caodaists. When he returned to France, he was not able to affiliate with any Caodai congregations there (and described them as practicing "ethnic exclusion"), but he has remained in electronic contact with his spiritual teachers in Vietnam.

A Non-Vietnamese Caodai Minister

In 2006, the southern California Caodai community headed by Lê Quang Sách decided to ordain its first non-Vietnamese minister, or Lễ Sanh. They had been contacted by Linda Blackeney Holverstott, an African American woman from New York City, who discovered Caodaism when she visited Vietnam in 2004 with her husband as part of a medical mission to treat AIDs patients. She was very impressed by the Tây Ninh temple and by the warmth of the people there. At her ceremony she said:

> I have traveled to many places as a medical missionary, but never was I received as warmly as I was in Vietnam. At the temple in Tây Ninh, people were very welcoming. As a person of color, I do not always feel comfortable visiting religious sanctuaries, but at the Great Temple I felt that I had finally come home. Some people have told me that I must be an Oriental inside, or perhaps I followed Asian traditions in a previous life. In any case, I was very happy to visit the Tây Ninh temple and I felt that it was a spiritual homecoming. It began the process of learning about Caodaism, which is finishing at this ceremony.

Figure 6.2. Linda Blackeney Holverstott being ordained as a Lễ Sanh, or "deacon," of the overseas Caodai community in 2006 at the Pomona temple in California

When she returned to the United States, Linda wrote to the forum at Caodai.org with a series of questions about Caodai beliefs and practices. She had been trained as a nurse in Western medicine and had also completed full training as an acupuncturist and doctor of Oriental medicine (1994–1998), which included extensive study of the Taoist principles so important in Caodaism. Caodai leaders were impressed that she had been a vegetarian for over three decades, since vegetarianism is often seen as a discipline that Westerners have trouble following. While she did not know Vietnamese, she did read the English translations prepared by Bùi Đắc Hùm and Ngasha Beck, and the oath that she took at her ceremony was recited in both English and Vietnamese.

Linda had been affiliated with One Spirit Interfaith Seminary in New York City since 2004 and was encouraged by them to reach out to other congregations that might want to participate in her ordination. The ceremony that I attended on May 14, 2006, at the Pomona temple was followed a month later by a group ceremony in New York City, where Lê Quang Sách, Bùi Đắc Hùm, and his wife, Bùi Đặng Hồng, marched with leaders of a variety of different interfaith organizations to celebrate her ordination as an official Caodai representative in New York City. Her small chapel in Harlem was planned as a place to "celebrate the unity of God" and bring young people from that community into contact with Asian traditions as well as European ones. Pomona Caodaists welcomed the fact that she would introduce racial and cultural diversity into their membership. As one of them said at her gateway ceremony: "Our body is not our self. We have different skin color, hair color, eyes, everything. Our true self is deeper than that. We should look deeply to find the real, true essence of Cao Dai." She has remained a participant in Caodai Internet forums, but defines her participation in a distinctive and idiosyncratic fashion.

The stories of Westerners who have been "called to Caodaism" through the Internet have encouraged some California groups to emphasize education in English and a more broad-based theology, which can connect not only with a new generation of American-born Vietnamese, but also with a wider public. This is particularly true of the new Caodai center where I met Jessica Dung Nguyễn.

A New Caodai Center in the Shadow of Disneyland

The new Caodai Center is affiliated with Bùi Văn Khâm and Bùi Đắc Hùm (familiar to us from Chapters 1 and 2), as senior members, but it is directed by David Tùng Chế, a younger Caodaist, who was part of the Caodai Youth Group at the Pomona temple when I first visited there in 2002. David is the older brother of Trang Chế, one of the young girls trained as a spirit medium by

Đỗ Vạn Lý in the 1980s, and his father, Nghiệp Chế, was one of the founding members of the first Caodai congregation in Los Angeles.[5] Trained as both an engineer and a dentist, he hopes to attract a new generation of American-educated Vietnamese (and non-Vietnamese), many of them professionals like himself, who can lead diasporic Caodaism in a new direction.

Like the Saigon Teaching Agency in Vietnam, the Anaheim Caodai Center is very focused on teaching, but its emphasis is overwhelmingly on teaching the next generation, rather than running meditation and divination workshops to move sophisticated adult practitioners to a higher level. On the ground floor, one can find three different classrooms devoted to children: one for preschool children, decorated with colorful banners and a large green paper tree; a second for younger school-age children, which includes pictures and calendars with images of Vietnam and traditional Vietnamese culture; and a third for schoolchildren who are trying to become literate in the Vietnamese language, in order to ultimately be able to read Caodai scripture in the original language. The children are also taught beginning meditation techniques. Many of the children come from Caodai families, or families with at least one Caodai parent, but the classes are open to anyone in the Vietnamese community and include a number of students from other religious traditions. The instructors are volunteers from the Caodai community, most of them immigrants who have spent at least ten years in the United States.

Other activities include an alternative medical clinic where patients are treated with herbal preparations, reiki healing, massage, and qi gong exercises. Martial arts is a new and popular activity for younger Vietnamese, building on the Vovinam tradition (Việt Võ Đạo) that developed in southern Vietnam during the colonial period and has been taught in the United States since 1976. Youth groups and children's groups have a wide range of activities, including holiday parties, volunteering to help feed the homeless, and visiting senior centers. In one of the back rooms, I saw an elaborate *kỳ lân* or "lion dance" costume, including the colorful head of the "lion" (actually a mythical combination of a dragon's head with a horse's body) with a long back held up by many dancers, and the ceramic masks worn by the attendants of this magical creature, which performs at Tết New Year ceremonies and also at the Mother Goddess Festival held during the autumn harvest moon season.

A higher-level course on Caodai teachings, philosophy, and meditation is taught by a senior Caodaist who is a spirit medium himself. This course has a curriculum that resembles some of the courses taught at the Saigon Teaching Agency or Tam Tông Miếu more closely. Some of its readings are drawn from the *I Ching* (*Kinh Dịch*) LISTSERV, which includes online discussions of

Caodai theology and various comparative questions. The program of study for 2011–2012 included three units: (1) the significance of the Divine Eye (*Thiên Nhãn*), (2) séance spiritual communication (*cơ bút*), and (3) Caodai thought or philosophy. The final unit addresses new ideas and how Caodai theology must evolve as it faces a new century. The new century as it is reckoned by Caodaists will start in 2026, which will be the one-hundred-year anniversary of the inauguration ceremony held in Tây Ninh in 1926.

Oral tradition in the neighborhood says that the building where the Caodai Center now stands was owned by Walt Disney several decades ago, when he was first building Disneyland. He supposedly lived there himself, using the modest kitchen on the second floor and cooking his meals as he looked out at construction of his first theme park. A special vault room in the center of the building has thick, reinforced walls and a heavy, locked door, and it was where he kept "all the money he made from Disneyland." Now the view from the window is primarily of the Interstate 5 freeway, since the walls of the theme park rise up too high to see past them into the fantasy world of animated characters and fairy-tale castles. The building was owned by a Korean Christian Church before, and they had used the detached garage as a worship space.

In 2013, a new Caodai worship space opened in the area that was once a detached garage with an innovative, modern design, reinterpreting the architecture of the early twentieth century in a sleeker, more streamlined and abstract twenty-first-century design. A curved roof with red terracotta tiles is both Asian and Spanish looking, and the spare lines and muted colors have none of the "Oriental fantasy" elements of the original Tây Ninh blueprint.

One of the goals of the organizers of the Caodai Center is to make use of new media to hold courses and teleconferences with participants in several countries, including the United States, Vietnam, and probably also France, Canada, and Australia. There is a certain tension, however, between its "international" orientation and its "heritage" mission. Bùi Văn Khâm told me:

> We cannot completely shut out the cultural influence, so we offer classes on Vietnamese language and history. But at the same time Caodaism is not simply a Vietnamese or an Oriental religion. It is more than that. Caodai is not really a religion at all, but a way of initiating the world into a new era. Caodai is like a spaceship landing on earth. In order for it to land on earth, it had to land somewhere. But the fact that it landed on Vietnam does not mean that it should be limited to Vietnamese.

Bùi Văn Khâm wants to present Caodaism to American residents in a universal form, not tied to specifically Asian features. He says "We need to peel

Figure 6.3. The modernist architecture of the new Caodai Center in Anaheim, California

away the outside cultural layers in order to reveal the real content." But he is also very interested in recent research that speculates that documents like the *I Ching* date back to the "southern lands" of Vietnam rather than China. He is also uncertain how to interpret Caodaism's millenarian message. "We have been told that Caodaism will last for 700,000 years," he told me. "But we do not know what will happen after that. Will the world end? Will we all be re-born into the Dragon Flower Assembly? How do we teach our younger genera-tions about the future in relation to this idea of 700,000 years?"

New Forms of Cyber-Spirituality on the Internet

The Internet has made it possible for a decentralized community of the devoted to remain in contact with each other. Caodaists who came as a population of refugees scattered all over the world first made contact with each other through websites. By absorbing their theology into the shifts and complexities of electronic circuitry, the intimacy of a private conversation or vision of the divine has be-come structured by technical networks and tools. Perhaps these new potentiali-ties will lead to an increasing focus on the "cosmopolitan" aspects of Caodaism.

Internet activism has played a particularly important role in the globaliza-tion of Caodai, since this globalization is to some extent based in the Silicon

Valley of California, which is also a center for information technology.[6] The importance of cyberspace as a "meeting place" for Caodaists relates to their dispersion in 1975. The U.S. government hoped that Vietnamese refugees could be spread evenly throughout the country, to prevent any one region from bearing an unusually heavy burden. So efforts were made to find sponsoring families and churches throughout America's "heartland." The largest group to sponsor Vietnamese refugees was the Catholic Rescue Mission, which tended to favor Catholic families, but also helped a number of other families to resettle. It seems most likely to me that a number of Caodai families were misidentified as "Catholic" when they came into the country simply because the name of their own religion was seen as an effort to pronounce the words "Catholic" (Hoskins 2006).

From 1980 onward, Vietnamese refugees made efforts to regroup themselves into enclave communities and to move closer to families and friends. This is when the first physical meeting places were set up, almost always starting with meetings in people's homes and then gradually moving toward the sanctification of separate physical structures. In California's endless suburbs, this separate physical structure was most often a detached garage in the back yard, but gradually evolved into former churches, synagogues, and storefronts.

With the emergence of the World Wide Web in the late 1980s, and the increasing importance of information technology jobs in California, the idea that Caodaists might be able to sacralize a "virtual home" for their religion began to emerge. The first Caodai temple outside of Vietnam, Thiên Lý Bửu Tòa, launched its website on August 15, 2000, run by Ngọc Quang Minh, a young refugee who worked as a software programmer. He compiled spirit messages and published them on the Web for the overseas community, beginning to open up the "electronic umbrella" that would eventually gather together a diasporic religion. For the great many Vietnamese Caodaists who at that point believed that they would never be able to return to their homeland, this created a new religious landscape. Its topography was represented by a variety of graphic interfaces of sites, nodes, systems, and channels between systems. It resurrected the lost visual memory of temple designs and was soon also including recordings of sermons, liturgical music, and videos.

It is perhaps significant that the most elaborate foray into cyberreligion for Caodaists was led by a non-Tây Ninh group. Tây Ninh, by identifying itself as the "Vatican of Vietnam," has taken on a role as a center for a panoply of ritual elements—elaborate iconography, vestments, music, incense, and ceremony—identified with the hierarchical structure of a religion where the magical efficacy of language is buttressed by the material spectacle of ceremony. When white-robed disciples file into Caodaist temples, the institutional authority of the dignitaries is made manifest, and the chants recited as the disciples bow their foreheads down to the floor directly evoke all the divinities called down in the verses. The physical presence of the temple plays a very important role in enabling ritual actors to be immersed in the belief system.

The smaller denominations, like the Chiếu Minh group, which was the "root" of Thiên Lý Bửu Toà, emphasize congregationalism less than meditation, individual spiritual discipline, and the more "Protestant" virtues of studying spirit messages as scripture. Aesthetic and formal elements of the liturgy are kept to a minimum, and a personal practice of self-perfection is stressed. So the publishing of spirit messages that stress this spiritual practice and orient it around textual teachings seems more appropriate to these traditions.

A different approach to international expansion was taken by the Tây Ninh "Vatican." The Tây Ninh Caodai Overseas Mission was officially founded in 1973, two years before the fall of Saigon. It was created to resurrect the idea of the overseas mission founded by Phạm Công Tắc in Phnom Penh, Cambodia, in 1927 (see Chapter 4). The head of the College of Spirit Mediums (Hiệp Thiên Đài) received a "divine decree" to extend Caodaism overseas. At that time, the acting head spirit medium, or Bảo Đạo (Protector of the Way),[7] Hồ Tấn Khoa, was appointed as the Head of the Mission. With his long white beard and peaked white hat, Hồ Tấn Khoa looked very much like the kindly wizard Gandalf of the *Lord of the Rings* saga, and he evoked a sense of the Taoist past in his demeanor. It became more or less impossible for him to do much after April 1975, however, so the mission was "dormant and inactive," as the caodai.net website says.

Diasporic Caodaists took the lead, since the center in Tây Ninh was seen as "paralyzed." Annual conferences were organized to bring Caodaists together in California in the 1980s and international meetings started in 1995. In September 1998, at the third annual conference held in Montreal, the Cao Dai Overseas Mission was formed, with fifteen delegations from around the world. It had two goals at the time: to spread Caodaism in overseas communities, and to work for greater religious freedom in Vietnam—especially reestablishing the Sacerdotal Council according to the original religious constitution.

By 1998, the Tây Ninh overseas congregations had assembled their own impressive websites, anchored in the United States, in the Washington, D.C., area where Trần Quang Cảnh was then living, and in Sydney, Australia. These websites were virtual libraries of religious texts, including the two volumes of official spirit messages and the most famous sermons of the Hộ Pháp Phạm Công Tắc. They also quickly began to archive journalism and scholarly articles about Caodaism, reissuing excerpts from the research of Ralph Smith, Jayne Werner, and Victor Oliver. The Caodai Overseas Mission united nineteen temples in the United States, Canada, France, and Australia. In 2006, political differences concerning ties to the "Communist-dominated" Tây Ninh administrative hierachy caused that organization to disband. Today, Khảm Phạm, the highest ranking Tây Ninh dignitary in California, reports that there are forty-four Tây Ninh temples and two Caodai Mother Goddess shrines in an independent alliance of overseas Caodaists.

Religious Activism and the Internet

The creation of online forums also transformed the potential for interaction among religious followers. As Stephen O'Leary has argued: "In computer networks, the global village has found its public square (the analogy to London's Hyde Park may be apt), whereby media users are transformed from negative 'couch potatoes' to active participants in dialogues performed before potentially vast publics, linked not by geography but by technology and interests alone" (1996, 786). Instead of simply being the audience for "broadcasts" of religious materials, Caodaists became able to participate in discussions, even when isolated in communities with no temples within hundreds of miles.

These online encounters were coupled with an invitation from the Pope in Rome in 1992, which helped to galvanize Caodaists in America to organize themselves more fully. The Catholic Church invited diasporic representatives of all important religions in Vietnam (Buddhists, Caodaists, Hòa Hảo) to participate in ceremonies to "pray for peace in Vietnam." One motivation seems to have been a need for solidarity among religious groups to "wait out" a period of religious suppression and to agree on a shared strategy to preserve themselves in the public eye. As the largest international religious organization in the world, the Vatican in Rome took the lead in organizing this meeting and paid the expenses of the religious leaders who attended. Two different delegations were organized (one from Tây Ninh and one from the other denominations), and this pattern of separate but parallel regroupings continued, to a certain extent, after that precedent was set. Both Caodaists and Catholics had lost a lot of property (churches, hospitals, schools, and training centers) after 1975 when the Vietnamese state had "nationalized" religious buildings, so they shared a common agenda of seeking to have that property restored at some time in the future. They hoped to be able to spread information about religious doctrine more freely and to appoint their own priests, bishops, and archbishops without submitting the nominations to government agencies first.

The Great Bamboo Firewall: Censorship of Publishing and the Internet

Restrictions on posting information on the Internet about religion in general and Caodaism in particular from within Vietnam have varied over the years. The potential expansion of "virtual religious communities" in cyberspace was evidently seen as dangerous by the Vietnamese government. A new State Ordinance on Beliefs and Religions issued in July 2004 and enacted on November 15 "clarified" what it called the "socialist understanding of religious freedom," forbidding any discussion of religion on the Internet, forbidding religious Internet postings from anyone in Vietnam, and requiring all religious officials to get government permission before speaking publicly in person, in print, or on the World Wide Web. A 2006 report on the use of firewalls in Vietnam noted that although government policies supposedly targeted pornography, in fact most of the sites that were blocked were concerned with religious freedom or human rights (Open Net Initiative 2006, 27). Among those listed as blocked were the two largest Caodai online organizations (Caodai.net and Caodai .org), as well as the Sydney Centre for Studies in Caodaism and the San Jose, California, temple website of Thiên Lý Bửu Tòa (thienlybuutoa.org) (Open Net Initiative 2006, 38–40, 46).

The most sophisticated and careful Caodai historian inside Vietnam, Lê Anh Dũng (who publishes under the penname Huệ Khải), is an English teacher and writer I have met several times since 2004. He posted a series of interesting articles about the history of Caodaism and corresponded with international scholars in English and French. With detailed knowledge of the ancient Nôm characters, as well as Chinese, he is able to read older materials, which are otherwise almost completely inaccessible to today's Vietnamese.

As government policies have liberalized, Lê Anh Dũng has managed to find a way to write a series of serious studies of the history of Caodaism, all published by the Hanoi Religion Department. These include three studies of the "preconditions" for the emergence of Caodaism, from cultural, legal, and religious perspectives, published in 2008 and 2010, and a short book titled *Caodaism under Persecution in Central Vietnam 1928–1950,* which appeared in 2012 (Huệ Khải 2008a–d, 2010, 2012). This last book seemed daring because the title suggested it would include a description of the killing of almost three thousand people in Quảng Ngãi in 1945 (detailed in Chapter 3). The sixtieth anniversary of this was commemorated in Đà Nẵng and in San Bernardino, California, in 2005. I attended both commemorations and noted that, while these killings were attributed to "Communists" in San Bernardino, where boxes of doves were released to represent their souls, in Đà Nẵng they were said to be "martyrs to their religion" who died during a "period of internecine violence" (with no more details provided).

The burying of the victims of the 1945 Quảng Ngãi killings in massive shallow graves (some of them, according to eyewitnesses, alive) did not allow for them to be ritually processed as ancestors and required their descendants to perform a series of rituals to compensate them for this "grievous death." Their ghostly spirits are believed to continue to cause trouble for as long as the processes of commemoration and consolation have not been completed. Kwon (2006, 2008) and Viet Thanh Nguyen (2006, 2009) have documented the importance of dealing with the "ghosts of war," whether at famous sites like the 1986 Mỹ Lai massacre (also in Quảng Ngãi Province) or at less-well-known ones. The sixty-year anniversary commemorations of the deaths at Quảng Ngãi were intended to bring a sense of closure to this tragic history, but also to preserve it in the memories of those still alive.

Lê Anh Dũng's book, however, does not mention any killings in 1945, although it contains a picture of the Holy See of the Central Vietnam Mission where the commemoration was carried out in 2005. It focuses on a series of French circulars issued from 1928 to 1950, including the ban on all religious flags and banners bearing the Buddhist swastika, because of its resemblance to the main icon of Nazism during World War II. In a phone conversation in 2013, Lê Anh Dũng told me that the 1945 Quảng Ngãi killings were not included "for editorial reasons": The book could not have been published if they had been included. And yet, its title may be a way of quietly drawing attention to the history that cannot be told and affirming that Caodaists of all denominations should honor those who suffered persecution, and even death, at that time.

Vietnamese government officials worry about the organizing power of the Web. They have sporadically blocked social-networking sites such as Facebook (which includes several Caodai sites, such as the new Caodai Center in Anaheim) and tried to popularize their own, state-controlled alternatives instead. More than a third of Vietnamese are now online, a higher percentage than in Indonesia or Thailand, so dissidents increasingly are going online to discuss what they view as the country's failings in its rush to become a modern, industrialized economy.

In 2012, several prominent blogs emerged to criticize the lavish spending habits and lifestyles of top Communist Party officials, embarrassing the government and prompting Prime Minister Nguyễn Tấn Dung to try to muzzle online criticism. So far, Vietnamese authorities have focused on legal threats to quash dissent. Technology analysts say that Vietnam lacks the sophisticated

Internet monitoring and blocking technology employed by China, so Hanoi instead resorts to making an example of dissident bloggers. New laws may be introduced soon that would force Vietnamese to use their real names online—a move that Internet-driven businesses worry will stifle the growth of online commerce and would greatly reduce the number of people in Vietnam willing to contribute to religious websites.

Global Travel and Pan-Asian Collaborations

Religious leaders in Vietnam have been prevented from attending international conferences or meetings by being denied visas. In July 2004, several Caodai and Minh Lý religious leaders were invited to participate in the Parliament of World Religions in Barcelona, and none of those based in Vietnam were allowed to attend. Diasporic leaders, including Bùi Đắc Hùm and Lâm Lý Hùng, did choose to attend and found it an inspiring experience that galvanized their determination to globalize their faith.

In May 2013, Cardinal Tám, the head of the Tây Ninh Holy See, requested permission to visit Japan, invited by representatives of Oomoto, a "new Japanese religion" that has long had a formal visiting relationship with Caodaism. First established in 1934, the relationship was revived in the 1950s, but then lay dormant for sixty years. Approval was granted for a delegation of fourteen dignitaries (three women and eleven men). All but two had never left the country or traveled by plane before. An "invited guest" from the government, the Chairman of the Tây Ninh Religious Affairs department, also came along. After a brief stopover for sightseeing in Hong Kong, they flew to Kyoto and traveled from there to the Oomoto Center.

For the first time since the death of Phạm Công Tắc, a group of Caodai religious leaders visited another country. While the Hộ Pháp had traveled as a diplomat and advisor to Bảo Đại, this group traveled to explain their religious doctrines, not to promote a political position. In Japan, they met representatives of the Taiwan-based new religion Tao Yuan, which shares with Caodaism and Oomoto a set of scriptures derived from spirit writing. In July 2013, an eight-member delegation from Tây Ninh's Sacerdotal Council traveled to Taiwan and participated in a séance on July 22 at the Tao Yuan headquarters in Taipei. The séance was conducted by two mediums, who held "a big pen, with two hands like a scissor" used to write Chinese characters on a rectangular surface covered with sand.[8] Trần Quang Cảnh told me, "It was the spirit of Lao Tzu (Thái Thượng Lão Quân) who called on the Tao Yuan association to make contact with Caodaists. Spiritism is what brings us together, forging the spiritual links that we reinforce through physical visits and exchanges." Leaders of both Oomoto and Tao Yuan have been invited to attend the Mother Goddess Festival (Lễ Phật Mẫu) in Tây Ninh in 2015, beginning a move to restore the foundations for Pan-Asian religious collaboration.

A Religion in Exile vs. a Global Faith of Unity

The Caodai Center in Anaheim presents a view of Caodaism as a "global faith of unity," and promotes this vision through its website (www.caodai.org) and publications. Ethnically based congregations in California cities like Garden Grove, Westminster, and San Jose emphasize an idea of a "religion in exile," which must circle the wagons and defend itself against the encroachment not only of Communist censure but also of American materialism and consumerism. Posts to the Sacerdotal Council to Restore Religious Rights (www .hoithanhphucquyen.org) indicate that many see its mission as restoring religious freedom to Tây Ninh and opposing the policies of the Vietnamese government. The Tây Ninh Caodai Overseas Mission, in its 1998 incarnation (CDOM, www.caodai.net) also followed this pathway to a certain extent, mobilizing its membership to protest violations of the Caodai Religious Constitution in the homeland. Since 2005, however, Trần Quang Cảnh has followed a new road, dialoguing with government officials and finally joining the embattled official Tây Ninh hierarchy. He also moved his once oppositional website to Vietnam, so that it is now based in the very country many of its members once fled—www.caodai.net.vn. This reconfiguration of the Internet has also reconfigured the shape of the cyberspace confrontation between diasporic refugees and homeland defenders of their religious heritage.[9]

The different websites reflect different interpretations of the role of diasporic Caodaism. For Bùi Đắc Hùm, one of the key "lessons of exile" was that Caodaists should overcome their denominational differences and work together. In 2001, he proposed a new name for Caodai overseas organizations—Hội Thánh Duy Nhất Minh Triết—the Sacerdotal Council of Unity and Enlightened Philosophy. This new organization was envisioned as one that would be open to Caodaists of all backgrounds, and would be free of the "Communist influence" that tainted organizations like the official Tây Ninh hierarchy or the Saigon Teaching Agency. Discussions began about founding an independent American organization, the Overseas Sacerdotal Council (Giáo Hội Cao Đài Hải Ngoại), based in California, which could train and appoint its own clergy. The 2004 ordination ceremony (discussed in Chapter 5) and later promotion of Lê Quang Sách to the rank of Bishop (Giáo Sư) have continued this process. When I visited the Đà

Năng temple of the Central Vietnam Mission (Truyền Giáo) in 2010 to ask them about the formation of a separate organization in California, they were cautiously supportive: They did not want to interfere with Lê Quang Sách's efforts to build diasporic Caodaism, but also realized that there was no way that they could provide official sanction for his promotion. It seems that if a separate organization were formed, it might become simply another denomination (*chi phái*), and that of course is not seen as desirable by those who keep hoping to bring Caodaists together, instead of dividing them even more.

Related issues have been resolved differently for the larger Tây Ninh organization, since Trần Quang Cảnh was determined to forge an official link to the administrative hierarchy where his father had such influence in the 1940s and 1950s. The Caodai Overseas Mission that he founded in 1998, and served as president of until 2006, was dissolved because of internecine conflict on this issue. For some Tây Ninh Caodaists, it was unthinkable to forge an official link, because any dignitaries ordained in Vietnam would become only "tools of the Communist government." So far, only three Caodai temples in the United States (in Richmond, Virginia; Camden, New Jersey; and Washington, D.C.) have joined Trần Quang Cảnh in affiliating with the official Tây Ninh hierarchy. A new organization, Cơ Chế Chung, was established in San Jose, California, to criticize Trần Quang Cảnh's efforts and maintain the "purity of Caodaism in exile."

Trần Quang Cảnh was involved in an altercation at the "California temple" in Garden Grove, California, on August 5, 2012, when he tried to talk to a number of other Caodaists about the possibility of formally affiliating with the Tây Ninh Holy See in Vietnam. He approached one of the temple directors and put his arm around his shoulder, urging him to come outside to speak privately. The director began shouting that he did not want to be handled by Cảnh, adding "Don't strangle me!" Eventually, the police were called to resolve the dispute, and Cảnh was advised not to return to the California temple. A week later, on August 12, the temple administration from the Chestnut Street temple, Westminster (Orange County) gathered and produced a document with three specific guidelines that were adopted by the Tây Ninh overseas organization, and posted on their website "News from Caodai Overseas" (bantin.caodaihaingoai.org):

1. Do not follow the orders of the current Holy See under the management of the Sacerdotal Council and recognized by the communist government of Vietnam.
2. Refuse to welcome anyone who belongs to the communist Holy See and the Ministry of Religion (of Vietnam).

3. Do not collaborate with the Ministry of Religion, which conceals the activities of the communist government of Vietnam in plundering, deceiving, and hindering the progress of the Caodai religion overseas.

Their position was presented as nonnegotiable.

Different perspectives about the relationship of Caodaists to the government have been characteristic of the religion since it was born as a largely oppositional force in French Indochina. Phạm Công Tắc had an ambivalent relationship to the French, the Japanese, and the Ngô Đình Diệm state, and since 1975 many overseas Caodaists have emphasized anti-Communism more than religious tolerance. Bùi Đắc Hùm has expanded his outreach to non-Vietnamese in part because he does not want to try to work with the Hanoi government, while Trần Quang Cảnh says there is no other way, and so Caodaists must move forward with a liberalizing state.

"People asked me how can we have a dialogue with the government?" Cảnh told me rhetorically in a conversation at his home. "We are not at the same level as the Communist authorities. And people like Cardinal Tám will not participate in this. But a few years later I did establish a dialogue with the head of religious affairs in Hanoi and Saigon. And they did change their religious policy." Cảnh feels that incremental reforms of religious laws have vindicated his choice.

In January 2013, the Vietnamese government issued Decree 92, which modifies the 2004 Ordinance on Beliefs and Religion. From 2005 onward, religious groups were to be controlled through a registration process. Any group that carried out religious activities without state recognition could be considered to be "infringing on national security." Local officials in the People's Committee had to approve requests to hold a religious festival, ordain new religious dignitaries, or even to pray in a new space. The 2013 Decree streamlines that process but does not seem to have decreased state management of religious affairs.[10] It remains to be seen whether the decree will advance the cause of religious freedom—as it claims to do—or simply organize surveillance in a new way.

The Communist government has propagated a cult of national heroes, especially Hồ Chí Minh, which has become widely popular, but is already reeling out of state control (Malarney 1996; Ngô and Hồ Tài 2014). While Caodaists have had to accept—usually with great reluctance—the bust of Hồ Chí Minh in their temple offices, in many parts of northern Vietnam, the first president speaks through spirit mediums, heals the sick, and is worshipped as a god. At the Tết New Year festivities in 2005, a message from three anonymous spirit mediums was posted on the website of the Vietnamese American Student Association in Utah. The spirit spelled out his name as Hồ Chí Minh through the first word in each of the first lines of verse and provided a message of over three thousand words. Like Pasquier and Doumer, the French governors who expressed posthumous regret for having persecuted Caodaists (Chapter 3), Hồ Chí Minh announces that since he has arrived on the astral plane, he has come to regret killing so many Caodaists and wishes that he could cultivate himself in the afterworld although he has no body to do so. He hopes that his son (Nông Đức Mạnh, long rumored to be Hồ Chí Minh's illegitimate son) will become a Caodaist and in his capacity as general secretary of the Communist Party will lead the country in a new direction. He also advises him to resist China's efforts to control the Hoàng Sa Islands and to form new alliances with the United States. He notes "I followed Karl Marx's theory with my delirium when I lived. But right now in the astral plane I have known the truth."[11]

I heard rumors of other messages from Hồ Chí Minh while doing field work in Hồ Chí Minh City in 2010 but was not able to obtain any texts or other details. But the idea that Hồ Chí Minh might once have been sympathetic to the goals of Caodaism is not totally far-fetched. A letter he wrote to a pastor in 1921 (using his earlier name Nguyễn Ái Quốc) expresses a syncretic and tolerant religious orientation not far from that of the founders of Caodaism. The young Hồ Chí Minh wrote:

> Like all things ideal, religion does not and should not have any borders, and those who take on the task of propagating it should be above all nationalism and any political interest.... I believe that only one philosophy, one principle, one religion, exists for everyone, because only one Truth exists. We are only permitted to see this Truth from whatever side we find ourselves on, and we name it according to what we see and how we are able to see it: Confucianism or Buddha for Orientals, and Christ for Occidentals. Buddhism + Confucianism + Christianity = Goodness. Since we have the good fortune to contemplate these three lights at the same time, would it not be better for you to love all of them and try to harmonize them with our nature in order to make that nature better, rather than placing these three in opposition to one another? (Hồ Chí Minh, Bourdeaux, and Abu-Zeid 2012, 2–3)[12]

The young Hồ Chí Minh, like many Caodai leaders, was initiated as a Free Mason during his Paris years and moved in many of the same nationalist circles in Paris, Hong Kong, and Shanghai as Đỗ Vạn Lý (Quinn-Judge 2003). When I visited the Đô Thành [Capital City] Caodai Temple in Hanoi (affiliated with the Ban Chỉnh Đạo branch), they said that Hồ Chí Minh himself had visited their temple and prayed there in 1946, as he was gathering support for the Fatherland Front to oppose the French. In 2005, I was told that some Caodaists in Hồ Chí Minh City wanted to elevate Hồ Chí Minh's spirit to become a great immortal (Đại Tiên) within the Caodai pantheon.

Conclusion

Most Caodaists did not appreciate Graham Greene's description of their sacred temple as a "Walt Disney fantasia of the Orient." "It makes us sound like a Mickey Mouse religion," as one Caodai leader told me. But they have embraced aspects of Disney's influence in other ways: in trying to spread their religious message through popular media, through cyberspace and even through animation. The eerie spectacle of a single, blinking animated left eye can still be found at one of the German Internet sites. Their choice of Anaheim, the home of Disneyland, as the site of a new Teaching Center speaks volumes to their confidence in transcending a once-sarcastic assault and creating a new package of sophisticated media technology and modern communication strategies.

While Caodaists were eager to move from being a "virtual community on the Internet" to having physical meeting spaces and building temples with their distinctive architecture overseas, their pathway to doing so was marked by its initial configuration in cyberspace. None of the architecturally distinct Caodai temples that now stand in Garden Grove; New Orleans; Dallas; Houston; or Wichita, Kansas, were built before the Internet sites that served as fundraising centers. Spirit messages came to be primarily transmitted through websites rather than through publications, firewalls became the primary mode of censuring religious publication rather than book burning, and the active websites of places like Thiên Lý Bửu Tòa in San Jose have magnified their impact way beyond the relatively modest congregations that have gathered there. The "Divine Eye on the Internet" managed to achieve an illusion of omniscience and omnipresence, even for a small and embattled religious community, because it was able to gaze out from computer portals to a newly networked world.

CHAPTER 7

A RELIGION IN DIASPORA,
A RELIGION OF DIASPORA

The diaspora experience as I intend it here is defined, not by essence and purity, but by the recognition of a necessary heterogeneity and diversity; by a conception of "identity" which lives with and through, not despite, difference; by hybridity. Diaspora identities are those which are constantly producing and reproducing themselves anew, through transformation and difference.

Stuart Hall, *"Cultural identity and Diaspora" (1990, 235)*

Vietnam and California are spatially configured to face each other across the ocean, their long coasts tempting people on each side to gaze out across to the other. Histories of dangerous escapes, migratory yearnings, and promised returns tease the imaginations of both those who remain in the home country and those who ventured out. The sublime oceanic horizon is a screen of possibilities onto which people project their dreams, desires, and delusions. This chapter traces the conceptual trajectory shared, to some extent, by all of the California religious leaders we have followed, who have journeyed at least once (and often many times) across the Pacific. The "outrageous syncretism" of colonial revelations opened up new conceptual possibilities, preparing Caodaists for the experience of exile and giving them tools that they would eventually use in the diaspora. The reflexive self-consciousness and comparative analysis of other traditions that were part of that early explicit syncretizing moment anticipated many of the later changes that came as Caodaism became a "new immigrant religion" in the United States and began to serve a more widely dispersed diasporic population.

Figure 7.1. Entrance to the California Cao Dai temple in Garden Grove, California, which flies both the U.S. flag and the flag of the Republic of South Vietnam

I argued in the Introduction that the founding generation of Caodaists developed a critical awareness of religious similarities and differences between East and West and ordered all religious experience into five levels of spiritual attainment. Building on a complex mixture of Buddhist, Taoist, and Confucian figures, as well as indigenous mother goddesses and local heroes, Caodaists proposed a modernist hierarchy and a centralized administrative system. Caodaism has, in a sense, its own "indigenous" theory of comparative religion, social evolution, and even anthropology. It represented an early effort by colonized intellectuals to "provincialize Europe," in Dipesh Chakrabarty's (2000) sense of refusing to see Europe as the origin of history and modernity, in relation to which all others are derivative. Since it extends this theory to Jesus and includes him in its pantheon, it also may cause us to reconsider not only the anthropology of Christianity but also what Fenella Cannell has called the "Christianity of anthropology" (2006)—the possibly unconscious theological underpinnings of our own thinking about religious boundaries.

The study of syncretism is the study of how religious difference has been managed: by separation, by opposition, by the erection of strict boundaries and territories (as has been the tendency of the Abrahamic religions, under the banner of an exclusivist monotheism), or by incorporation, by fusion, by emphasizing common elements and finding certain overarching themes (as has been the tendency of more fluid Asian traditions). Fluidity should not, however, be equated with incoherence, and in Asian tradition it is articulated in relation to hierarchical principles, so a syncretistic religion is not a religion where "anything goes," but it is one in which different traditions are ranked and absorbed into an all-encompassing unity.

While Caodaism is in many respects a highly structured and institutionalized religion, it is also one whose theology has been flexible enough to allow a number of different perspectives. Each of the earlier chapters reflects on a particular perspective, articulated by one of the founders of the religion, and carried into the present by followers in the diaspora. The "global syncretism" that emerges from these different perspectives has moved from the particularities of Vietnamese historical experience to a transnational conception of the fusion of Asian and Western religious heritage.

In this final chapter, I explore the tension between colonial syncretism and postcolonial diaspora in relation to the concept of the religious field of practice, postcolonial studies, the concept of diaspora, and theories in the anthropology of religion that have tried to grasp how religions are formed and reformed on a global scale.

Competition in Bourdieu's Religious Field of Practice

Bourdieu's key modification of Weber's *Sociology of Religion* was to emphasize the interaction of priests, prophets, and magicians in a competitive religious field.[1] He argued that we need to pay attention to the objective structure of relations between these agents, not just to their "ideal type" characteristics. His interest in exposing the sources of social inequality would seem well suited to explore the relationship between religon, race, and colonial conquest.

Applying this framework to twentieth-century French Indochina, the Catholic Church had a structure of (largely French) priests who were religious specialists trying to monopolize access to the "goods of salvation" in Vietnam. The people of southern Vietnam were reluctant to convert to Catholicism, feeling that they were "dispossessed" (in Bourdieu's term), not only by colonial conquest but also by the lack of respect for their own traditions. Younger colonial intellectuals wanted to be modern and to steal the script of the powerful. Caodaism created a new group of religious specialists: Vietnamese "priests"—who were generally described as "dignitaries" or "notables" (terms used for local officials under the older Confucian administrative system). These new religious specialists were then organized under an administration as complexly structured as that of the Vatican.

Phạm Công Tắc became the charismatic prophet of Caodaism, proclaiming that the spirit messages he received were the "voice of God" (*vox Dei,* as Weber puts it). Bourdieu argues that we need to focus more on the field of relations than on the personal attributes of the prophet: The prophet needs to arrive at the right time to respond to a preexisting sense of unease and diffused discontent. He has to speak with the "voice of the people" (*vox populi*), since he "gives discursive expression to representations, feelings and aspirations that existed before his arrival" (Bourdieu 1987, 130). Caodaism came into being as the result of a committee of founders who signed a declaration and declared that they wanted to be unified. Its elaborate institutionalization defies usual expectations of a prophetic movement, since its prophet later took on some attributes of a "Pope." The political turmoil of twentieth-century Vietnam meant that the transfer from personal charisma to the "charisma of office" was incomplete: It now seems unlikely that there will ever be another "Pope" (after the death of Lê Vân Trung) or another Hộ Pháp (after the death of Phạm Công Tắc). But Caodaism itself has reemerged as an important religion in Vietnam and is also expanding globally. In Chapters 2 and 3 I described the techniques Phạm Công Tắc used to gain control over Tây Ninh, and I also described the formation of alternative Caodai organizations in Chapters 1, 4, 5, and 6.

Caodaism fulfilled the two social functions Bourdieu identified for a religious field with political ramifications: First, the founders of the religion consecrated the existing Vietnamese blending of Confucianism, Buddhism, and Taoism as coherent and as "a religion." Then, in the confusing upheavals of colonial conquest, the new structure of religious leadership provided people with a means to make sense of their positions in the social order. After 1975, this structure also served the function of providing positions of leadership for many men (and some women) who had held important appointments under the earlier regime, but experienced a huge fall in status (and years of incarceration) after the Communist victory.

Surprisingly, while Bourdieu's scheme stresses the importance of competition within the religious field, it says relatively little about the competition *between* religions. In choosing his examples from the history of the Catholic Church, he focused on the struggle between religious authorities and those they considered heretics, but says little about situations of religious plurality. At the time of its emergence, Caodaism was in direct competition with both the Catholic Church (which condemned it as "blasphemous") and with a somewhat less institutionalized Buddhism (Hoskins 2010a). Caodaism claimed more followers within a few years of its founding (two million) than Catholicism had gained in over three centuries of missionary activity in the southern colony of Cochinchina (Werner 1981, 4). A Buddhist revival focusing on a socially engaged "Buddhism for this world" appeared in Vietnam in the 1930s, in partial response to this new religious diversity (Devido 2007; McHale 2004, 2009). Clashes between Buddhist and Catholics brought an end to Ngô Đình Diệm's regime in 1963 and inspired Caodaists to try to act as mediators to forge a more unified Republic.

After 1975, however, the radical change to an officially atheistic Communist regime meant that all religious organizations reduced their presence in the public arena dramatically, if they were not completely closed down. Catholics and Caodaists formed alliances to seek a way through the long and drawn-out process of normalization, which is still ongoing. Both groups have tried to get back buildings, schools, churches, and temples that were "nationalized." They joined forces with Buddhists, who were also forced to unite under a politically appointed "governance committee," which was not necessarily popular among lay members. Now there are many interfaith activities where members of all three of Vietnam's largest religions meet in an atmosphere of cooperation and collaboration. In January 2013, I visited a free medical clinic, which rotates from Caodai and Minh Lý temples to Catholic churches on various days of the week. "Religious solidarity" has become the rule, since at this point the leaders of all organized religions in Vietnam are hoping to navigate their way through a delicate and fragile process of resurfacing on the national scene.

Syncretism can be explored by using the idea of the religious field, as Rey (2007) and Goossaert and Palmer (2011) have shown, but Bourdieu's framework has to be nuanced a bit to do so.[2] The relational concept of charisma needs to be paired with a recognition of the diverse package of "spiritual capital" the Vietnamese context provided. Caodaism built on notions of "tradition" as a religious habitus—both an embodied practice and literary transmission of chants, prayers, and séance messages. This habitus became the "matrix of perception" through which all religious experience and stimuli were filtered (Rey 2007, 117–118). Even the most "licentious improvisations" needed to resonate with earlier notions of religious mixtures. The separation of Confucian tradition from the French colonial state led not only to its partial "rebirth" in Caodai ritual, but also to the simultaneous production of religion, secularism, and modernity.

The interaction of multiple religious fields opens up the possibilities for popular movements (like Caodaism) to create new elites who present an alternative to the orthodoxy of the "monopolistic" Catholic Church or Buddhist sangha. These prophets of a new orthodoxy restrict access to forms of esoteric knowledge (séance messages) and produce new forms of spiritual capital through an exegetical tradition, turning many lay members into consumers. In opposing the colonial order, however, Caodaism was also an emancipatory movement, which subverted European domination and reconceptualized millenarianism.

Caodaism and Colonial Studies: A Religion for the Postcolonial Era

Caodaism emerged in a colonial context because it was the age of empire that first created the conditions for a new global faith. Empires built transnational networks of communication and made it possible for Asians and Europeans to engage in the (hierarchically structured) "long conversation" of the colonial encounter (to adopt a phrase Malinowski developed to describe anthropological fieldwork).[3] While empires could whet one's taste for world unity, their very nature—the violence of conquest and the surveillance of indigenous organizations—made it impossible for them to create a real unity based on ethical consensus. So a truly global religion could only be realized—according to Caodai teachings and prophecies—in a postcolonial world.

This is why I feel it is appropriate to describe Caodaism as first a religion of decolonization (for the generation of the founders) and second as an emerging diasporic formation, a vision of a postcolonial global faith. Formulated amid the vicissitudes of the colonial period, it developed over many decades of American military intervention and then had to reconstitute itself in exodus and exile. While its practice in the United States today retains some aspects of what Benedict Anderson (1998, 58–76) has called "long distance nationalism," it is now absorbing a more international orientation and also a more culturally diverse congregation of disciples. Caodaism once placed itself along the axis between colony and metropole, seeking to heal the wounds of colonialism. It has now reoriented itself along a Transpacific axis and addressed issues of religious freedom and social inequality in the new global context.

One of canonical texts of postcolonial studies, Homi Bhabha's "Signs Taken for Wonders," begins with an extended description by an Indian native missionary of the effects of distributing copies of the Christian Bible in Hindi in 1817 under a tree outside Delhi. Excited by finally being able to read the words of God directly, in their own language, virtually everyone wanted a copy of the book, and soon they had formed their own party, all dressed in white, to implement its teachings. But they refused to take the sacrament, since they had read that it was eating the blood and body of Christ, and they knew that Christians ate cow flesh. They explained to the frustrated missionary that they could never become so unclean. In the same year, another missionary lamented that although everyone wanted a Christian Bible, some saw it as a curiosity, others as a source of income, and some even used it for waste paper. As soon as the Holy Book was made accessible to them in their own language, Bhabha argues, it became "ready for a specific colonial appropriation" (1994, 159).

Religious movements—identified with transcendent ideas of unity, infused with moral authority and a search for justice, offering access to divine knowledge—have often been the focus of ideological battles, and even bloody military ones, in the colonial context. Yet postcolonial theory has paid little attention to religion, as noted in a recent history of postcolonialism: "The field is distinguished by an unmediated secularism, opposed to and consistently excluding the religions that have taken on the political identity of providing alternative value-systems to those of the west" (Young 2001, 338).

Postcolonial historians like Partha Chatterjee (1993) and Dipesh Chakrabarty (2000) have, however, provided more sensitive discussions of religion. Their work provides the theoretical basis for my argument that the Caodaist vision of 1926 was an early attempt to rethink nationalism, not as a derivative discourse borrowed from the West, but as a new spiritual discipline to restore a sense of dignity and self-worth to a country torn by war and colonial persecutions. Asian nationalism has been misunderstood by Westerners, according to Chatterjee, because they focus only on its political expressions, direct challenges to European rule, and neglect the important fact that nationalism as a cultural construct must first create "its own domain of sovereignty within colonial society." It does so by dividing the world into an outside sphere of material phenomena— the economy, statecraft, science, and technology—and opposing this to an inner spiritual domain of religion, customs, and the family:

> In fact, here nationalism launches its most powerful, creative and historically significant project: to fashion a "modern" national culture that is nonetheless not western. If the nation is an imagined community, then this is where it is brought into being. In this, its time and essential domain, the nation is already sovereign, even when the state is in the hands of the colonial power. The dynamics of this historical project is implicitly missed in conventional histories in which the story of nationalism begins with the contest for political power. (1993, 6–7)

This was the project addressed by Caodaism in the 1920s and 1930s, when it was born amid widespread strikes and demonstrations against the French, and a new form of the same project was made necessary during the period of American military intervention, in the 1960s and 1970s. The final set of challenges involved in rebuilding the religion in exile in California is what led to the formation of Caodaism as a religion of diaspora.

Chatterjee writes that the nation was imagined first as a spiritual entity. While he limits his examples to India, it is clear that this argument also applies to Vietnam. Since Vietnam is the only country in the East Asian cultural world to have been completely under European colonial domination, it applies perhaps more strongly to Vietnam than to many other Asian examples. Caodaism, which explicitly called itself a "religion of the nation" (*quốc đạo*), assembled a modern group of disciples educated in French but anchored in the East Asian traditions of Buddhism, Taoism, and Confucianism. Caodaists argued that their dialogues with the Great Master Teacher created a faith that was born in dialogue with the West, but not subservient to Western ideas. Caodaism was universalist, but also distinctively Vietnamese, and, rather than being isolated and vulnerable, its openness to the outside world made it strong and flexible, able to absorb modern statecraft, science, and technology without losing its own cultural identity.

Caodaism was formed, in part, to resist the loss of agency and dignity that has been called the "colonization of consicousness." Chatterjee formulates this clearly in responding to Benedict Anderson's *Imagined Communities* (1991): "History, it would seem, has decreed that we in the postcolonial world shall be only the perpetual consciousness of modernity, Europe and the Americas, the only true subjects of history have thought out on our behalf not only the script of colonial enlightenment and exploitation, but also that of our anti-colonial resistance and postcolonial misery. Even our imaginations must remain forever colonized" (1993, 5). History is both re-created and reconceptualized in Caodai theology. The Foucauldian question of the relationship of the subject to power is rearticulated in an extraordinary project to create an alternative apparatus of power within a French colony. The descendants of the former mandarins energetically and comprehensively re-created the hierarchical structure of the old Confucian order but invested it with a new revolutionary message. They sought not a return to the imperial past, but an Asian modernism in which Asians themselves would be in control.

Dipesh Chakrabarty's argument about "deprovincializing Europe" is focused on the Bengali middle class, which he calls "the first Asian social group of any size whose mental world was transformed through its interactions with the West" (Tapan Raychaurdhuri quoted in Chakrabarty [2000, 4]). While it seems pointless to quibble about the exact chronology, it is notable that Vietnamese intellectuals made more or less the same claim in the early twentieth century, seeing themselves as the only outpost of East Asian civilization subject to direct colonization.[4] Saigon, in particular, as the capital of the colony of Cochinchina, was placed under French administration and more thoroughly transformed than the protectorates of Annam and Tonkin (Smith 1972; Peycam 2012).

European scholars work within a secular framework of disenchanted time and space, while for Indians, "practices which called upon gods, spirits and other spectral and divine beings were part of the network of power and prestige within which both the subaltern and the elite operated in South Asia" (Chakrabarty 2000, 14). Chakrabarty calls history "a knowledge system that is firmly embedded in institutional practices that invoke the nation-state at every step" (2000, 41), and urges us to contest the idea of the European modern and move toward seeing "the modern as inevitably contested" (2000, 46), just as Prasenjit Duara calls on us to "rescue history from the nation" and break away from the orthodoxies of both nationalist and imperialist historians (1995, 2014).

Early Caodaism was deeply infused with the "aspirational nationalism" of the struggle for independence from the French, but it has been alienated from the "official nationalism" (Anderson 1998) of the current socialist state. In its emerging diasporic formation, it has had to forge a new transnational identity grounded in a more cosmopolitan understanding of Vietnamese national culture. With Caodaists now scattered in dozens of countries, the "global faith of unity" has taken on the attributes of a religion in diaspora.

Rethinking Diaspora and Religion

Several recent scholars have developed a new vocabulary for studying the relationship of religion and diaspora using concepts like "diasporic religion," "diasporic horizons," and even "diasporic theology." The rethinking began with Paul Gilroy's notion of the "Black Atlantic" (1993) and J. Lorand Matory's criticism of the "arborescent metaphor," which describes the relationship that overseas communities have to their homelands as one of "returning to the roots" of a great ancestral tree (2005). The roots metaphor implies that there is one source or trunk, rather than a number of heterogeneous historical interactions, for each community, and that the trajectory of "return" is a single, one-way journey. The concept of diaspora has been used to suggest "that homelands are to their diasporas as past is to present," but more recent work has emerged to challenge that assertion (Matory 2005, 280). Speaking of a "tree and its roots" assumes a single departure and obscures the ongoing dialogue between the homeland and the diasporic community, which can and does influence both sides, and is part of many other cosmopolitan conversations in a globalized world.

Notions like diaspora require us to imagine ourselves beyond the boundaries of race and national territory. Since Matory notes that "traveling colonial subjects and postcolonial immigrants often have a stake in the mythology of citizenship," they have been especially visible in forging new syncretistic religions and in connecting these religions to diasporic communities (2005, 292). Grasses have networklike roots, which unite multiple roots with multiple shoots, and this idea of a "rhizome" of connections has recently emerged as a new metaphor for transnational linkages.[5] Matory's work showed the important role that well-traveled writers and merchants had in developing African-inspired religion in Brazil, the United States, and even Africa. In a similar way, this book has hoped to show intersections between the roles played by the founders of Caodaism in 1926 and their diasporic successors in the period after 1975, when an Asian-inspired religion began to put down roots in American soil.

Thomas Tweed's *Our Lady of the Exile* (1997) was the first study to focus on the components of "diasporic religion" among Cuban Catholic refugees in Miami. Practices of "crossing and dwelling" were later developed into a theory of religion on the move (Tweed 2006), focusing on how certain practices were made mobile and portable, extended into new spaces, and were used to sanctify and inspire new senses of belonging, ethnic identity, and institutional form. Tweed focuses on emotional ties to the symbol of Mary and the metaphor of exile that inspired a piety to name and overcome the sadness prompted by dislocation from the home country. For him, as for Engseng Ho (2006) in his study of diasporic Hadarmi Arabs, diaspora is about absence:

> While globalization denies absence by rushing around to cover it up, diasporas do the opposite. They acknowledge absence and chronically explore its meanings and its markings, such as at the grave. Is the absence of the dead forever? Will they come back, or will we join them? Is the absence of emigrants permanent? Will they come back, or will we join them? In old diasporas, questions of absence never go away; they continue to provoke responses each generation. Indeed, the sharing of such questions, and arguments over them, create and demarcate a society that one might call a diaspora. In this sense, a diaspora is not unlike a religion. For diasporas, as for religions, absence can be highly productive. (Ho 2006, 4)

Since diasporas tend to sacralize and idealize the homeland, they are "not unlike a religion," and they produce ritualizations of longing.

Paul Christopher Johnson describes how "African diasporic religion" emerged out of a number of related local practices drawn together into a community that was both "indigenous" and "cosmopolitan." "Diasporic horizons" are the imagined screens of another territory and time, against which people may project present events and their present selves. They connote both "a spatial edge of longing and a temporal edge of, on the one hand, nostalgia, and on the other, futility and desire" (2007, 7). The ancestral homeland becomes the source of identity, and often the standard of authentic religious practice, but other destinations may also be sacralized as part of a religious trajectory. The Garifuna people Johnson studied in New York, for instance, activated imagined ties to Africa as well as to Central America, their homeland of birth and recent residence.

Temporally, the diasporic horizon evokes not only the practices of the past but also projections into the future: "To announce a diaspora is not simply to express authentic origins but to actually press them into existence" (Johnson 2007, 9). Diaspora is an ideological project, evoking a voluntary commitment to a distant location, whose place in myth and memory is valorized by a series of actions—"an expansive idea of territorial invocations made not just through residence or nostalgia, but also through imagination, ritual practice, narratives, and the plotting of futures, as well as the summoning of ancestral pasts" (Johnson 2012, 108). Johnson argues that diasporic membership is not determined simply by descent, but that it designates "a subject position an individual moves in and out of, or a way of seeing adopted to various degrees" (2007, 3). Discourses about identity and its significance have to be activated by those who "join" a diaspora.

Diaspora before Diaspora: The Colonial "Loss of the Country"

The question of what constitutes a diaspora and whether all or just some overseas Vietnamese can be considered members of a diaspora is controversial. In a careful comparison of Vietnamese communities in Quebec with those in California, Louis-Jacques Dorais argues that the "diasporic moment" is tied to anti-Communism and the strategy I have referred to as "purity and exile" (following Malkki 1992, 1995): An eclave community of refugees "centered on collective memories of uprooting and dispossession" constitutes itself as an alternative to the impurity of the present regime in Vietnam (Dorais 2010, 123). Younger scholars, many of them Vietnamese American, have contested this limitiation of the term and choose to define it in a more fluid and open-ended fashion (Anh Thắng Đào 2012; Cannon 2012a; Duong 2012; Small 2012; Quang Tuệ

Trần 2012; Valverde 2012). They stress the diverse ways in which individuals engage with the past outside of institutions and political organizations.

I agree with these younger scholars that diaspora can be built on positive impulses for reconciliation as well as negative ones for conserving a wounded community after a traumatic upheaval (Espiritu 2014; Quang Tuệ Trần 2012). I find elements of both strategies among Caodaists, but the movement seems to be toward more openness. Even someone like Đỗ Vạn Lý wanted to move beyond the divisiveness of the war years as he moved toward a new notion of nationalism:

> For me, nationalism is first and foremost about learning to respect yourself, to respect your ancestors, to be proud of your own traditions. Vietnam is like India in many ways because we were both so damaged by our colonial past. We felt humiliated, discriminated against, so we had a real thirst for freedom, for independence. . . . There was an overpowering sense that escaping foreign domination was all that mattered. . . . But now we can see that spiritual nationalism has to come from within. It transcends the differences between communists and anti-communists, since we all loved our country and struggled to be free.

Religion has played an important role in constituting the Vietnamese diaspora and policing its borders. Buddhist and Catholic Vietnamese have struggled to form their own ethnic parishes, resisting incorporation into multiethnic congregations of these "world religions" (Ninh 2013a, 2013b). Spirit mediums "serving the Mother Goddess" through the trance dances and possessions of Đạo Mẫu have established dozens of temples in southern and central California (Fjelstad and Nguyễn 2011). Johnson might well consider Vietnamese pagodas and churches in California as diasporic religions for this reason: "Diasporic religions are the collected practices of dislocated social groups whose affiliation is not primarily or essentially based on religion, but whose acts, locutions, and sentiments toward a distant homeland are mediated by, and articulated through, a religious culture" (2012, 104). The formation of new ethnic congregations is a consequence of diasporic dispersion, not its cause.

But Caodaism has, I have argued in Chapter 4, had a "diasporic doctrine" from its earliest revelations, since it was a new religion given to colonized intellectuals who felt that they had "lost their country" even though they were still living in it. The "outrageous syncretism" that French observers decried was a call for parity and respect, putting Vietnamese traditions on the same level as those of the Catholic mission. Early prophecies that Caodaists would be sent all over the globe to form new communities and spread a global faith provided a "diasporic narrative" that is not found among Vietnamese Buddhists or Catholics. Stuart Hall identified diaspora as a cultural survival strategy that required somewhat porous boundaries (1990, 235), the same sort of porous boundaries that we have characterized as part of syncretism. The founders of Caodaism, raised in between Vietnamese tradition and French literary culture, realized this sense of hybridity in a universalist religious vision that tolerated difference. They willingly and enthusiastically incorporated elements of Christianity, Spiritism, and Theosophy, but restructured them to provide a basis for a Vietnamese-led religious movement.

Hall articulated the connection between syncretism and a "diasporic aesthetic" for the cultural identity of African Americans in the New World. The sense of loss stirs up the need to imagine the self in new ways and to sanctify the idea of the free subject:

> It is because this New World is constituted for us as place, a narrative of displacement, that it gives rise so profoundly to a certain imaginary plenitude, recreating the endless desire to return to "lost origins", to be one again with the mother, to go back to the beginning. . . . Who has not known, at this moment, the surge of an overwhelming nostalgia for lost origins, for "times past"? And yet, this "return to the beginning" . . . can neither be fulfilled nor requited, and hence is the beginning of the symbolic, of representation, the infinitely renewable source of desire, memory, myth, search, discovery. (Hall 1990, 236)

For Vietnamese refugees in America, the twenty-year period (1975–1995) during which there was very little contact with their homeland intensified a sense that a new community would have to be built in the imagination, replacing a country that was lost. The imagery of diasporic longing requires us to examine how space is being *re*territorialized by people located in multiple fields of power, who valorize their interconnections at times more than their "roots" (Gupta and Ferguson 1992). The debt that refugees may feel for the "gift of freedom" they received in escaping religious persecution in Vietnam has relocated them in a new landscape of possibilities and potential pitfalls (Mimi Thi Nguyen 2012).

Séance and Its Challenges to "the Christianity of Anthropology"

The central importance of Caodai séance and its spirit messages has long been a source of discomfort to foreign observers, and it has emerged as the most contentious issue that Vietnamese Caodaists are now negotiating with their government. Séance is part of the "living theology" that Caodaists aspire to revive, in the New World and in the Old. It is premised on the possibility of an ongoing conversation between the living and the dead, which is at odds with Christian ideas of a sharp separation between heaven and earth, and a great distance between the human and the divine. The spirit messages that had such influence on the Caodaists whose lives I have outlined here defy the Christian idea of a religion revealed once and for all during the lifetime of Jesus Christ. Caodai notions of transcendence are relative, not absolute, and they do not correspond to the ascetic, somewhat "Protestant" notions of religious belief and practice used by many anthropologists (Asad 1993; Cannell 2005). The mechanisms for linking disparate religious traditions in Caodai theology draw on séance messages and reincarnation, so that Caodaism's "discursive tradition" stretches back through the centuries.

Anthropologists of religion have become increasingly aware of how much of their supposedly "objective" toolkit of comparative concepts comes from Christian traditions and Christian ideas of what a "religion" is supposed to be. The impetus for Caodaists to modernize East Asian traditions and unite them into an organization that could "claim a seat for Vietnam" at the Parliament of World Religions reflects a fusion of theological "modernity" with Christian-like doctrine. Caodaism is "a bit Christian" but not "Christocentric," and it produces "latter-day saints" who will be become divine in the afterlife, in some ways like Mormonism (Cannell 2005, 349). Caodism includes Jesus, but places him at a lower level in the divine hierarchy than many Asian sages, so in the past Caodaists were more likely to be accused of blasphemy than praised for their tolerance (Hoskins 2010a). In a critical examination of the anthropology of secularism, Fenella Cannell notes that "implicit claims for the hierarchical ordering of reality in modernity, in which the political is seen as more real than the religious, continue to create disjunctures in the range of debate that new ethnography has the opportunity to address" (2010, 85).

Caodaists see their religion as the culmination of an historical evolution toward a universalistic spirit, but at the same time they also see this evolutionary trajectory as predestined, because all religious diversity originally came from a single source. Syncretism is therefore both the starting point and the ending point of history. Through diaspora, syncretism is projected out across space, and the uniquely Vietnamese characteristics of early Caodaism are inscribed onto a much wider geographical expanse. These religious ideas have produced changes in the relationship between religion and diaspora that I outline here in my conclusion.

Religions in Diaspora versus Religions of Diaspora

In the early years, California Caodaists were a "religion in diaspora," in the sense that they were displaced refugees, scattered across the country as the "victims" of a war in which the United States did not emerge as the victor. But as they have reorganized, begun to translate their scriptures, and rethought their connections to other religions, they have become a "religion of diaspora," creatively using their multiple global locations to create a virtual community of believers, posting spirit messages on the Internet and opening up lines of communication with Caodaists in Vietnam.

Today, Vietnam—as the birthplace of their religion, and the location for the intersection of Chinese, Vietnamese, and French elements—is the primary diasporic horizon activated by Caodaists. Tây Ninh itself, as a sacred city and "the Vatican" for more than half of all temples, is also a significant diasporic horizon—"like Rome for the Catholics." Pilgrimages to Tây Ninh and participation in religious festivals there are an important part of trips planned to visit relatives. And even other Caodai denominations include a picture of the Great Temple at Tây Ninh in their religious offices, showing respect for its role as the mother church and materializing this diasporic horizon as an emblem of the faith as whole.

"Little Saigon" has become a new "diasporic horizon" for overseas Vietnamese, sanctified by the construction of cemeteries to honor South Vietnamese veterans and animated by performances like the elaborate Tết festivities to celebrate the New Year (Aguilar-San Juan 2009; Padgett 2007). Virtually all Vietnamese American religious buildings—Buddhist pagodas, Catholic churches, and Caodai temples—fly the yellow-striped flag of the Saigon Republic, and it is often reverently placed on the family ancestral altar at home. As the ghost of a now-dead country, the flag's presence revives and commemorates a lost homeland, which may (for some people) have little relation to the current nation of Vietnam. For some Caodaists, the goal of the California temples is to retain the "purity of the past," uncontaminated by Communism. But for others, the new goal has become to use their diasporic dispersal as a strategic resource for outreach and the more cosmopolitan perspective of religious universalism.

Johnson (2012, 107–108) argues that diasporas "make religions" firstly by dislodging religious practices from their embedded, unspoken status and making them a discrete object of contemplation. Which rituals can be revived in another land and which must be discarded? This needs to be renegotiated in a new context. Secondly, making religions requires their public recognition and usually the translation and publication of religious texts. Thirdly, these religions require new spatial coordinates—from ceremonies held in apartment living rooms to the construction of new temples and cultural centers. And lastly, these diasporic religions catalyze new forms, sources, sites, and brokers of the sacred. A female spirit medium emerges as the founder of the first Caodai temple in California, and she receives messages from Joseph Smith, tying Caodaism to America's own "indigenous religion," Mormonism (Hoskins 2006, 206).

Johnson also argues that when a religious group "becomes diasporic," it starts to view itself "against new historical and territorial horizons that change the configuration and meaning of its religious, ethnic and even racial identification in the present" (2007, 3). Caodaists of the founding generation in French Indochina defined their new religion in contrast to the "colonial horizon" of French Catholicism and secular Freemasons. Fifty years later, refugees and immigrants in California had to redefine their religious activities to fit a system of Sunday services (instead of the twice monthly celebrations of the new moon and full moon ordered by the lunar calendar). They also had a "Christian majority horizon" within a religiously plural society with an even greater diversity of competing groups. New encounters with Protestants and evangelicals, Hindus, Muslims, Baháʼís, and Mormons changed the religious landscape in significant ways. As the practitioners of an overtly and proudly syncretic religion, Caodaists were challenged to articulate the connections their scriptures had to these other traditions. The temple in Pomona where I first encountered Caodaism, for example, now has wall plaques with quotes from the scriptures of Islam, Baháʼí, and the Church of Latter-day Saints, as well as Buddhism, Taoism, Confucianism, and Christianity.

The memory of the past is transformed even as it is rebuilt in the new spaces of emigration. Despite the passionate desire of Tây Ninh Caodaists to "follow the divine blueprint" of their Great Temple overseas, when the Garden Grove temple was constructed in California in 2007, there had to be many changes—in the materials used, the placement of glass in the windows, limitations due to zoning laws of the number of colors that could be used on the outside. These physical changes of substance and shade mirror conceptual changes in how this vividly eclectic temple would be perceived in a conservative neighborhood in Orange County.

Maurice Halbwachs has argued that the "materiality" of religion—its rites, costumes, architecture, and offerings—provides the most stable component, since there can be multiple interpretations of ritual actions, and there is more splintering over doctrine than imagery (1992, 116; Johnson 2007, 46). While there are minor differences in Caodai iconography between Tây Ninh (which uses ancestral tablets before the great globe) and other denominations, like Bến Tre (which uses statues), all Caodai temples share a common visual vocabulary. Re-creating that distinctive religious architecture in California was tremendously important to emerging Caodai congregations, since it restored the "materiality" of Vietnamese ritual life, attaching symbols from the homeland to new sites in the hostland.

Diasporas have been defined as "social identifications based on shared memory bridges linking a lived space and a left-behind place" (Johnson 2007, 48). The "double consciousness" that Gilroy described for the Black Atlantic (1991) requires residing in two different places (at least in the imagination), and engaging with gaps in both space and time or memory. These gaps become a source of meaning in diasporic religion, through the ritualization of the idea of return. Distance from the homeland is seen as displacement and disempowering, and the function of ritual is to seek a momentary reconnection. For some strongly anti-Communist Caodaists, any talk of returning to today's Vietnam is seen as blasphemous, since it implicitly recognizes the legitimacy of the present government. But the impossibility of return to a real country intensifies the longing for the lost one, and the discourse of "purity in exile."

I see a new direction in the more globally oriented Caodaists, who are moving from being a religion "in diaspora" to being a religion "of diaspora." They are turning some of these gaps into strategic resources, which become positive and empowering. The multiple global sites of Caodai temples can become a transnational network of great value not only to immigrants, helping them to settle in a new land, but also to returning pilgrims and religious leaders. They provide the basis for new creative exchanges and interactions, many of them carried out on the Internet, and they create a new cosmopolitan ideal. For a younger generation of educated Vietnamese, the idea of studying and traveling overseas has become so alluring that diasporic communities are envied intensely. While many Vietnamese in California may dream of returning to visit their "roots," others in Hồ Chí Minh City want desperately to be part of an international community. The two sides of the Pacific are now linked by dense networks of remittances, some of them channeled through temples and religious networks, but most of them circulating between family members (Small 2012; Thai 2014). Vietnamese remittance recipients depend on funding sent from "over there" (ở bên kia) to build new houses, educate the younger generation, and nourish international aspirations. The syncretistic, totalizing theology of Caodaism provides a basis for linkages and travel in both directions.

Jonathan and Daniel Boyarin make a related argument about reconceptualizing diaspora as a "positive resource in the necessary rethinking of models of polity" (2002, 5), a way for people to regenerate themselves through statelessness.

In arguing *for* diaspora, they say it "offers an alternative 'ground' to that of the terrtorial state for the intricate and always contentious linkage between cultural identity and political organization" (2002, 10). Rather than seeing the scattering of a people as condition of helplessness and a pathology to be overcome, they argue that it can be unique source of power and strength. Diasporic peoples establish fluid but effective communities with distinctive ways of life that cross national boundaries and may form increasingly useful networks in the modern world system.

Many Caodaists use the example of Jewish history, and in particular the Holocaust, as a comparison that explains their commitment to regenerating their religion after the "great tragedy" of April 30, 1975. They seek to reestablish professional and religious ties to earlier colleagues in Saigon and dream of an eventual return to a transformed Vietnam—but one that will not mean the end of the global outreach established over the past forty years by generations of refugees and immigrants. They argue that the Vietnamese, like the Jews, cannot return to being a "one country" people, but will remain scattered, cosmopolitan, and creatively engaged with multiple global contexts.

Migration itself may destabilize some geographical connections and open up others. "In the migration to New York, the Garifuna found Africa," Johnson argues (2007, 48), in the sense that that they came to identify with Africa as an ancestral homeland, and they joined the religious African diaspora. In the migration to California, did Caodaists "find Asia"? Not in the same sense, for several reasons: The opposition between "Asia" and "Europe" had been important in the colonial era, and Caodaism's attempts to reconcile the two had featured importantly in the syncretistic impulse discussed in the Introduction.

But what Caodaists did find in California was a new possible identity as Asian Americans. They saw how other Asian religions had adapted to the American setting, and they became conscious of the fact that they were a racialized community linked to stereotypes of a "model minority," obsessed with education and Confucian ideals. Sharing a similar history of displacement due to war and "Communist aggression" with Taiwanese and Korean immigrants, they found a place within a religiously and ethnically plural society that had already absorbed generations of Asian newcomers.

Diaspora and Hierarchy

Several prominent theorists of diaspora identify diasporic communities with an egalitarian impulse. Daniel Colucciello Barber tells us "diaspora is able to conceive, stand against, and move beyond the mode of domination because it is just as differential as such domination" (2011, 113). Johnson argues that "religious bases for identity are enchanced through exile," and "shared exile status and a sense of equality take primacy over homeland hierarchies, opening spaces for the reworking of gender, class, ethnicity and religious authority" (2007, 41). For this reason, "horizontal" dimensions are stressed more than "vertical" ones, since simple membership in the religion becomes more significant than status within it.

The history we have just outlined of the Caodai diaspora offers some support for this statement in the first quarter century of exile, when ties to Vietnam were cut off and new temples led by female spirit mediums emerged. The "nondenominational" Caodaists like Bùi Đắc Hùm, Đỗ Vạn Lý, and Bùi Văn Khâm hoped that the diaspora would provide a context for a unifying vision, which could transcend the hierarchical competition and factionalism that characterized the homeland. At the beginning of the twenty-first century, however, these hierarchical and denominational divisions resurfaced, and conflicts about renewing contact with the religious leadership and its "communist" administration in Vietnam were amplified.

Diasporic religion is transformed in response to constraints and opportunities posed by the host society, but this confrontation with differences may not necessarily dissolve hierarchies as much as rearticulate them in a new context. The "boundary work" that diasporic groups need to do to stabilize a sense of their "authentic tradition" is—like the struggles of the founding generation in French Indochina—a series of defensive maneuvers, creative innovations, and sometimes inventions. Some enclave communities decide to "circle their wagons" and appeal only to members of the Vietnamese community who are already familiar with Caodaism. Others, like the San Jose temple Thiên Lý Bửu Tòa, innovate by publishing "new books of the Bible" with messages from American spirits like Joseph Smith. And others invent a new kind of teaching center, focused mainly on the younger generation, which identifies Caodaism as the carrier of Vietnamese cultural heritage and is open to followers of any religion.

The various indigenous religions of Garifuna, Santeria, Vodou, and Candomble have established new networks based on a shared ancestral tie to Africa. Caodaism's efforts to unite Asian religious traditions of Buddhism, Taoism, and Confucianism build on many centuries of a "three teachings" framework in China, Korea, and Japan, but at least so far this has not produced new "pan-Asian" religious networks.

Syncretism and Diaspora: Contrasting Concepts

Syncretism brings together disparate religious traditions in one place, creating a particular "package" in which elements are reordered in a specific way, related to the needs of religious actors in a particular historical context. Vietnamese colonized intellectuals hoped to fuse Chinese, French, and Vietnamese elements into a coherent belief system that would systematize all of the religious teachings found in twentieth-century Saigon. Syncretism therefore seeks intellectual unity and cohesion by fusing teachings from different times and places that come to coexist in a single locality.

When followers of a particular religion are spread out in a diaspora, this "package" is exported to new places. The spatial dispersion of believers motivates each smaller community to reexamine its faith and practices in a new context. "Diaspora" is a new term that has emerged in the globalized world of compressed time and space, where modern social media have made it possible for diasporic religious followers to remain part of a "shared conversation" even across great geographic distances. The syncretistic impetus of the founders of Caodaism was to create spiritual unity in one place. Diasporic dispersal links a diversity of places to a single spiritual "home."

The processes would seem to be opposites—one compresses conceptual differences into unity, while the other unifies different locations through a common "origin." But what they both share is the fact that they provide models for managing and overcoming religious differences and geographical challenges. Facing the colonial "crisis of meaning" in French Indochina, early Caodaists found ways of enlisting both Asian sages and prominent French figures in the defense of their own right to self-determination. Facing the tragic displacement of exile, refugees bound together and forged new ties to an idealized homeland in order to regenerate a sense of community and mission in the New World.

It would be accurate to describe members of the founding generation of 1925—Ngô Văn Chiêu, Phạm Công Tắc, Trần Quang Vinh, Đỗ Thuần Hậu, and Âu Kiệt Lâm—as "syncretizers," since each of them developed an idiosyncratic "package" within the larger framework of Caodai theology. And it would also be accurate to describe their successors among those who emigrated in 1975—Bùi Văn Khâm, Bùi Đắc Hùm, Trần Quang Cảnh, Đỗ Vạn Lý, and Lâm Lý Hùng—as "diasporic," since each of them formulated a particular way of reconnecting to a spiritual homeland through activism in Caodai networks overseas. But I am also convinced by the strong sense that each one of these people—following a teacher, a father, or a grandfather—was also engaged in a parallel process of reassessment, self-questioning, and self-cultivation. While separated by half a century of history and the world's widest ocean, these paired figures were following similar pathways and showed a strong loyalty to a sense of ancestral heritage. Syncretism and diaspora are not so different after all.

Diasporas rework the idea of a national culture from a distance, through the lens of exile. In today's world they interact and influence the home country, not only through remittances, but also through cultural exchanges. They evoke a remembered past, but rework it in order to move it into the future. The diasporic project is an imaginative rehearsal of what isn't yet but could be.

For immigrants and exiles, diaspora can be constructed as a narrative of "crossing and dwelling" (Tweed 2006), in which movement through space is given meaning by ideas of a transcendent connection to "home," making the longed-for land of origin into a "holy land" (*thánh địa*) of universal importance. Diasporas themselves "make new religions" by creating the conditions for more syncretism through dialogues between followers of different religious traditions. In fact, Caodaism could realistically be called a syncretic religious machine for producing and reaffirming diasporic sentiments, a religion that includes diaspora as one of its most significant doctrines, and—to some extent—a belief system that draws on religious notions of diaspora and updates them to the twenty-first century to create a global syncretism. In this sense, it is itself a fascinating and innovative diasporic formation.

NOTES

Introduction

1. The original passage is from Graham Greene "Indochina: France's Crown of Thorns," *Paris Match,* July 12, 1952, reprinted in Greene (1996, 218–219). Greene's phrase, "a Walt Disney fantasia of the East," is quoted in the *Footprint Handbook to Vietnam* (Colet 2002, 289), the *Moon Handbook to Vietnam Laos and Cambodia* (Buckley 2000, 433), *The Rough Guide to Vietnam* (Emmons 2012, 112), and *Berlitz Handbook* (Bray 2013, 221).

2. Jack David Eller (2009, 188) lists Caodaism as tied with Shintoism for tenth place among "world religions" at 4 million. On May 23, 2013, the website adherents .com listed estimates of Caodaists ranging from 2 to 8 million. The Vietnamese Department of Religion estimated 3.2 million in 2007 (Phạm Bích Hợp). I cite their figures of 2.2 million "official" Tây Ninh Caodaists and 1 million in other denominations, although I agree with religious leaders that there may be at least a million more "unofficial" followers. The number of official followers has grown since 2007, since dozens of temples have been restored and reopened, and it has become less of a liability for Vietnamese citizens to profess a religion on government ID cards.

3. With my colleague Viet Thanh Nguyen, I have developed the new interdisciplinary field of Transpacific Studies, which describes a more dynamic relationship between homelands on one side of the Pacific and diasporic communities on the other side (see Hoskins and Nguyen 2014).

4. Geertz's classic, but now controversial, *The Religion of Java* (1960) inaugurated an ethnographic study of religious encounters, continued in *Islam Observed* (1968) and many other places (Brook 1993; Peel 1968). Recent studies of syncretism range from those who are most dismissive (Lincoln 2001), to others who propose new directions (Berner 2001; Leopold and Jensen 2004; Stewart 1999; Stewart and Shaw 2004) to comparative studies of syncretism and spirituality in different parts of Asia (DeBernardi 2009; Van Der Veer 1996, 2009, 2014). Stephan Palmié has argued that syncretism is a conceit that "has gone sour for everyone involved" (2014, 145): "To qualify a religion as 'syncretic' also presupposes the assumption that 'religions'—much like cultures, languages or societies—can be represented, enumerated, and taxonomized as

discretely speciating entities, instead of as products of human maneuver, including the kind of boundary work engaged in by religious orthodoxies, compilers of ethnographic surveys, educational authorities intent on policing proper language use, and national immigration services" (Palmié 2014, 268–269). This criticism is valid for the pejorative use of the term, but not for cases where syncretism is a deliberate and explicit strategy of bringing together different traditions—as in Caodaism, or many other Asian "new religions." Caodaists would agree that today's organized religions are "products of human maneuver," and it is their project to maneuver to reconcile them to return to a divine plan of unity.

5. Charles Stewart provided me with this clarification (e-mail, April 17, 2013): "The correct (accepted) etymology is from the verb *syn-kerannumi*, 'mixed together.' *Kerannumi*, meaning 'to mix,' and *syn*, being the prefix 'with.' Deriving from *kerannumi* is the noun 'mixture,' *krasis*, or *crasis*, as it is transliterated into English in the rhetorical term, which means joining two words together, e.g., 'y'all' instead of 'you all.' Idiosyncrasies in medieval—probably already in antiquity—medicine and psychology meant 'temperament.' Why? Because each of us has his/her own mixture of humors that gives us our particular temperament—our idiosyncrasy. We are each a special brew." See also discussions in Stewart (1999) and Stewart and Shaw (2004).

6. Melville Herskovits (1958) developed a syncretic paradigm for studying the "African origins" of New World black identities, which has been much debated (Apter 2004; Johnson 2007, 2012; Matory 2005; Palmié 2014) but helped to found what became diaspora studies. Clifford Geertz (1960) described the different strains of Javanese religion as syncretist combinations, and while this view has been criticized and updated (Hefner 2000; Picard and Madinier 2011; Varisco 2007; Woodward 1989; 2010), it has also established a grounding for studies of syncretism in Southeast Asia (DeBernardi 2009; Kitiarsa 2005).

7. Lewis (1951, 44). *The Footprint Handbook to Vietnam* (Colet 2002, 1) repeats this quote as a caption to a photo of the Tây Ninh temple facing its table of contents.

8. The ferociousness of Norman Lewis' attacks on Caodaism might stem from his childhood trauma of being abandoned by his parents when his father became a spirit medium and his mother a healer after the sudden deaths of his three older brothers. In his memoir, *Jackdaw Cake,* he writes: "My father, a lonely, rather retiring man, had been thrust into prominence as a speaking medium for a Spiritualist church of over 200 people who congregated in the garden shed" (1985, 36–37). The description is eerily similar to what he says about Phạm Công Tắc—"a tiny, insignificant figure of a man, with an air of irredeemable melancholy," dwarfed by the grandiloquence of the temple he designed (Lewis 1951, 42).

9. Spirit Message received on Vietnamese New Year Tết (*Thánh Ngôn Hiệp Tuyển,* 1972).

10. The Chinese "New Religion to Save the World," formed in Beijing in 1919, combined the worship of six historical sages—Confucius, Buddha, Lao Tzu, the Jade Emperor, Jesus, and Mohammed—and spread rapidly throughout China by 1925. The

"Fellowship of Goodness," founded in 1915, had mediums who were possessed by Confucius, Buddha, Lao Tzu, Christ, Mohammed, Buddha, George Washington, and Tolstoy, and was found throughout northern China by the 1920s. Woodside describes both of these as an "attempt by less Westernized sections of Chinese society to bring under control the stormy mental phantasmagoria of China's cultural revolution," but notes that they seem to have been thoroughly destroyed by the later Marxist cultural revolution (Woodside 1976, 184).

11. See Bourdieu (1991) and Tambiah (1970). Tambiah's "religious field of practice" includes other religions but also secular institutions, "the exigencies of history," and memory in local communities.

12. Similar distinctions have been made by other scholars of Southeast Asia, such as Jean DeBernardi's discussion of symbolic "amity" vs. fusion or encompassment (in which a hierarchical ranking is introduced): "Where awareness of the multiple sources remains active I regard these as symbolic expression of syncretic amity, and distinguish them from symbolic encompassment, which is the practice of incorporating elements of another religious tradition in a subordinate symbolic role" (2009, 141).

13. Spirit message received February 24, 1934, in Tây Ninh. Later in the same message, Jeanne d'Arc notes "Communism is only a bluff. It is a great exploitation of the credulity of oppressed peoples, an ointment that calms their pain but does not cure it" (Trần Quang Vinh 1962, 90–91). For more of Jeanne d'Arc's spirit messages and her relation to other Caodai mother goddesses, see Hoskins 2008.

14. Speaking to a French woman attending the séance, Mme. Perreux, as well as other dignitaries, Jeanne d'Arc stressed the gender parity of Caodaism: "This is the only religion which grants to women a spiritual power virtually equal to that of men. This is a kind of justice that Christianity has long denied women." Spirit message received on September 22, 1934, in Tây Ninh (Trần Quang Vinh 1962, 103). French spiritist Léon Denis highlighted the feminist potential of Jeanne d'Arc's messages in "recuperating" her legacy as a spirit medium in the years immediately before the emergence of Caodaism (Denis 1923, 145–169).

15. Madame Lâm Ngọc Thánh (1874–1937) was a wealthy woman, the former wife of a Swiss jeweler, who gave a large amount of money to buy the land on which the Holy See was constructed. Known to the French as "Madame Mounnier," she became the unmarried companion of another wealthy landowner Nguyễn Ngọc Thơ (1873–1950) and the founder of the Caodai women's division (Jammes 2006a, 149).

16. Đức Nguyên is the pen name of Nguyễn Văn Hồng, and Lê Anh Dũng uses the pen name Huệ Khải. I have listed their published works under the name that they used in the publication. Chí Tín published several works circulated on the Internet, which have been translated into French by Quách Hiệp Long. I have met both of these French-based Caodaists, as well as all of the California-based authors I cite, and all of the living Vietnam-based authors, but I have never met the Australia-based Đồng Tân or Đào Công Tâm (the translator of Phạm Công Tắc's sermons, in collaboration with Christopher Hartney).

Chapter 1.   Conversations with Divinities

1. Caodai spirit messages usually include a poem in the six-eight format of traditional verse, in which the first letter of each line also spells out the name of the spirit concerned.

2. This poem was translated by Bùi Văn Khâm, with minor adjustments to the English by myself.

3. See Jordan and Overmyer (1986), Brook (1993), Clart (2003), and Smith (1970a).

4. See Taussig (1993), Viswanathan (2000), and Weiner (2007).

5. Allan Kardec (1804–1869) was the pen name of Hippolyte-Léon-Denizard Rival, a French writer and teacher who coined the word "Spiritism" for his experiments with séances and table tipping, eventually transitioning to the use of a "beaked basket" similar to the Chinese phoenix basket later used by Caodaists. His best-known works are *Le Livre des Esprits* (1860), *Le Livre des Mediums* (1861), and *L'Evangile selon Le Spiritisme* (1880). They are all now available online in English translation at http:// www.geae.inf.br/en/books/codification/gospel.pdf

6. *Chez Victor Hugo: Les Tables Tournantes de Jersey* was published in Paris in 1923. It contained only two-fifths of the original transcripts, some of which now seem to have been lost. Many sections were translated into English by John Chambers in *Conversations with Eternity: The Forgotten Masterpiece of Victor Hugo* (1998), and in a later edition as *Victor Hugo's Conversations with the Spirit World* (2008).

7. Huệ Khải identifies this as the *Mingsheng jing,* a set of moral lessons passed on from the Qing dynasty in China (Huệ Khải 2008a, 74).

8. When I visited the temple in 2005, I was asked to translate this séance message into English. It had been published in French and Vietnamese in 1925, and the temple leadership wanted to publish it in English as well. The English title was "The True Path to Eternal Life," but the message was mainly that good moral conduct was more important than occult practices. The temple is now primarily a Buddhist pagoda, but they were proud of their association with Ngô Văn Chiêu and the history of Caodaism.

9. These events are also described in Đỗ Thiên (2003, 78–79), and more briefly in Oliver (1976).

10. The Vietnamese Caodai historian Lê Anh Dũng notes that the term Cao Đài was already in use in Cochinchina, since it appeared in a text published in 1912 in Shanghai, where it was used to refer to the Supreme Being (Huệ Khải 2008c, 82). Ralph Smith (1970b) reports that the Chinese terms Cao Đài were used to refer to Jehovah in translations of the Bible by the British Bible Society.

11. There are several other religious figures in Vietnam who had similar revelation experiences. The Buddhist monk Thiên Quảng had a similar vision by the seaside in 1898, roughly two decades before Ngô Văn Chiêu, and this vision is cited as the beginning of the Buddhist reform movement (Jammes 2006a, 67; Trần Tri Khách 2002).

12. Hương Hiếu (religious name of Nguyễn Thị Hiếu, wife of Cao Quỳnh Cư) (1968). This journal was reprinted in 1997 by Thánh Thất Đốc Đai in Westminster,

California, from the mimeographed text by the author, a female Cardinal who participated in the first séances with Cao Đài. This text was used by Đỗ Vạn Lý (1989) in his book *Tìm Hiểu Đạo Cao Đài* [Understanding Caodaism], and translated by Bùi Đắc Hùm in his article "Spirit Séances," posted on caodai.net.

13. The twelve names were the following:

> *Chiêu, Kỳ, Trung, Hoài* (line 1);
>
> *Bản, Sang, Quý, Giảng* (line 2);
>
> *Hậu, Đức, Tắc, Cư* (line 3).

However, since there were in fact two disciples named Sang (Cao Hoài Sang and Võ Văn Sang), this message is usually interpreted as designating Chiêu as the head of a group made up of twelve followers.

14. The story of a great hero who "rides a golden dragon" is one that is found throughout the Mekong Delta, related to myths of kingship documented by Liang Yongjia (2011) in "Stranger-Kingship and Cosmocracy; or, Sahlins in Southwest China." This mythological model presents Ngô Văn Chiêu as a hero whose power extends out through the Mekong Delta and radiates in many directions.

15. Đồng Tân (1967, 133). Aristide Le Fol was the resident governor of Cochinchina under Alexandre Varenne (1925–1928), a reform minded Socialist who advocated a more "humane" colonial policy.

16. All of the translations of séance texts here come from Hương Hiếu 1997, vol. 1, and were initially translated by Bùi Đắc Hùm and his wife Hồng. I have made some minor changes in vocabulary and grammar to make the English more accessible, but depend on them for theological interpretations.

17. How should we interpret these verses? For Vietnamese speakers the mention of "spiciness" and "saltiness" refers to feelings of skepticism. When a Vietnamese speaker calls something "spicy" (*cay*), he may mean close to what an English speaker means by saying that something "smells fishy": it is impure, contaminated, strange tasting, and perhaps spoiled. It seems that A Ă Â, in one interpretation, was challenging these young Spiritists for remaining skeptical and asked them to suspend their feelings of disbelief long enough to start to learn from him.

18. In using this terminology, I am following the example of Jérémy Jammes (2006a) in his thesis "Le Caodaisme: Rituels médiumiques."

19. Bùi and Beck (2000) render this worship of locally consecrated spirits as "Shintoism" (16), and Phạm Công Tắc also makes this connection in translations into French. There are fascinating parallels between Japanese folk religion and Vietnamese folk religion, but I find this label more confusing than helpful.

20. The fact that the Jade Emperor chose to come down in a séance was not totally without precedent in the rituals of Chinese redemptive societies. Robert Fox Young describes the Daoyuan ("Sanctuary of the Tao"), a redemptive society founded in Shandung Province in 1921, which received messages from a Venerable Patriarch who

bears a strong resemblance to Cao Đài (but is not identified as the father of Jesus), and Philip Clart describes the Yiguandao, which eventually became a large redemptive society in Taiwan, and also emerged in Shandung in the early 1920s, in which messages came from the Mother of the Heavens, and also from Jesus (Young 1989; Clart 2007).

21. Among the many studies on new Christian-influenced forms of monotheism in China are Spence (1996), and Munro (1989).

22. Caodaists recognize what the Sinologist Daniel Overmyer has called the "convergence" of the traditions of Vietnamese or Chinese deified historical figures and the Catholic saints (Overmyer 1997, 1–4). Catholic theologians who chose the Vietnamese term *thánh* to translate the word "saint" facilitated this association, as did their choice of the term *tiên* (immortal) to translate "angel," and the term *đại tiên* (great immortal) to translate "archangel." At the end of his article, Overmyer says that these similarities developed in popular practice but were not recognized by Chinese intellectuals. Early Caodaists recognized these similarities, but displaced the agency of this "discovery" onto the Jade Emperor, saying that God told them that he sent both Asian saints and Christian ones.

23. See Goossaert and Palmer (2011, 121). I follow them in adopting the term "redemptive society," coined by Prasenjit Duara (2003) to refer to societies with a common project of saving individuals and the world as whole.

Chapter 2.   A Spirit Medium as Nationalist Leader

1. One group of Dallas-based Caodaists apparently hoped to bring Phạm Công Tắc's remains to Texas, where a new Caodai temple was planned, using the three-million-dollar jackpot that a Caodai follower near Dallas had won in the lottery. To persuade the King of Cambodia to oppose moving the remains back to Vietnam, they presented a large "gift" to charity at the royal court. Rumors of bribes to other ministers also circulated. But ultimately, Vietnamese government pressure proved more powerful than dollars sent from overseas congregations.

2. Studies of Caodaism from a political perspective include Blagov (2001a), Fall (1955), and Werner (1976, 1980, 1981). Religious histories written by Caodaists include Đỗ Vạn Lý 1989, Đồng Tân 2006, Huệ Khải 2008a–c, Huệ Nhãn 2005, Huỳnh Tâm 1990, and Trần Văn Rạng 1971 (in Vietnamese). The Australian scholar Trần Mỹ-Vân (1996, 1999, 2000) and the French anthropologist Jérémy Jammes (2006b, 2014) have made important recent contributions.

3. This insight comes from conversations with Caodaists in California, France, and Vietnam, and also from conversations with Jérémy Jammes in France in 2005, and the reading of his 2006 dissertation (Jammes 2006a), a work that straddles Vietnamese and diasporic communities and contributed greatly to my understanding of Caodaism.

4. Phạm Công Tắc's critics within Caodaism do not deny his charismatic powers, but instead argue that his own spirit became too strong to be a vessel for God's messages. Reports of Phạm Công Tắc successfully healing patients with his hands and exorcizing

evil spirits were not considered consistent with the modern form of Caodaist teachings (Đồng Tân 2006, 44–46) and criticized as following a mystical formula established by older religious traditions (*huyễn thoại cựu giáo*) (Đồng Tân 2006, 49).

5. Đỗ Vạn Lý 2005, personal communication, interviews in Chatsworth, California.

6. References to the sermons are all from the Sydney Centre for Studies in Caodaism website (Phạm Công Tắc 1947–1949), translated by Đào Công Tâm and Christopher Hartney.

7. The Caodai historian Huệ Khải has published an analysis of the legal strategies involved in presenting this declaration (Huệ Khải 2008b).

8. This concern is expressed in *Rapports mensuels du résident de Tây Ninh,* 1929–1933. Virginia Thompson compared the Caodai leader to Gandhi in *French Indochina* (1937), Ralph B. Smith speculated about Gandhi's influence in *Viet-Nam and the West* (1968, 75), in his article "An Introduction to Caodaism: Origins and Early History" (1970a), and posthumously collected papers *Pre-Communist Indochina* (2009, 117). He also noted that another Indian self-sufficient community, Tagore's Santinekatan, might have been an inspiration (1968, 75).

9. On May 30, 1948, during the period that the Hộ Pháp was delivering his sermons in Tây Ninh, a séance was held in which the Invisible Pope Lý Thái Bạch clarified his position further by designating him as "Hộ Pháp Chưởng Quản Nhị Hữu Hình Đài"—"the Defender of the Faith who has supreme powers over both visible palaces," meaning the Hiệp Thiên Đài (Palace to Unite with Heaven, or Legislative/Spirit Medium Section) and the Cửu Trùng Đài (Palace of the Nine Spheres or the Executive Section). This message also contains the line "Nhị kiếp Tây Âu cầm máy tạo," which can be translated "in a previous life, he spread this message in Europe." Some interpret this as evidence that Phạm Công Tắc was a reincarnation of Jesus Christ, but it is in fact rather vague about which "European" person Phạm Công Tắc has reincarnated (*Thánh Ngôn Sưu Tập* 1972, 3–4, 72).

10. The Buddha Sakya Muni did appear in a séance on April 8, 1926, at Vĩnh Nguyên Tự and on June 26, 1926, at Cần Giuộc and Lao Tzu (Thái Thượng Đạo Tổ) appeared on the sixteenth day of the seventh lunar month in 1934.

11. When Phạm Công Tắc was imprisoned in Madagascar, Trần Quang Vinh received a short message from Victor Hugo at an unofficial séance in Căn Cứ on October 19, 1944, telling him to be careful but persist in his efforts (Trần Quang Vinh 1972, 164). After the Hộ Pháp returned, the divine sanction for the creation of the Caodai Army was confirmed in an official séance in the Cung Đạo Tòa Thánh on April 9, 1948, by messages from the Invisible Pope, Lý Thái Bạch, and Lê Văn Trung, with the Hộ Pháp as chief medium (Trần Quang Vinh 1972, 187–189).

12. In Chinese spirit medium practices, the medium is called the *tang-ki* (equivalent to the Vietnamese *Đồng tử*), literally meaning "young medium," but his intimate connection to the god that possesses him is expressed by calling him the "ritually adopted child of the deity" (Seaman 1980, 67). His birth parents give up their child to the service of the gods, and the medium must learn to behave as "someone who has the high reputation of his divine father to consider" (Seaman 1980, 68).

13. *The Journey to the West* is a very famous Chinese religious novel (which influenced the later American Wizard of Oz story) that follows the adventures of a monkey saint who accompanies a Buddhist monk on his travels to India to get Buddhist scriptures. It is extremely well known in China and Vietnam, and films based on this classic text are still very popular in both countries. Intriguingly, several recent scholars (Seaman 1986, 488; Yu 1983) have speculated that popular Chinese religious accounts of supernatural voyages (*The Journey to the West, The Journey to the North*, in Vietnamese *Tây Du Ký, Bắc Du Ký*) may themselves have developed out of spirit writing séances in which the medium was—as we see in this passage—"playing all the parts," or at least narrating them for his audience.

14. In the spirit message from Lý Thái Bạch received by the Hộ Pháp on April 9, 1948, Phạm Công Tắc is asked "not to feel hurt that the army was established in his absence," but instead to accept it as part of a Divine mechanism. He is however cautioned that his main trials lie ahead, since "this divisiveness does not help to save the world" (*mà lại đố kỵ chẳng dám cứu đời*), and if the Vietnamese people do not respond to the call to religion, they cannot be saved (Trần Quang Vinh 1972, 188–189).

15. This 2006 interview with Bùi Đắc Hùm appears in the 2008 documentary that I wrote and produced (with Susan Hoskins), *The Left Eye of God: Caodaism Travels from Vietnam to California* (distributed by Documentary Educational Resources).

Chapter 3.   The Spiritual Sons of Victor Hugo

1. See séance transcripts in *Chez Victor Hugo: Les Tables Tournantes de Jersey,* 1923 (original edition), 323; English translations can be found in Stephens 1983; Hugo 1998, 178–179; and Josephson 1942, 413–414.

2. Hugo's paintings and drawings are catalogued in *Soleil d'Encre: Manuscrits et Dessins de Victor Hugo* (Hugo 1985).

3. The second medium was Cao Đức Trọng, who later became one of the twelve "Zodiacal" dignitaries in Tây Ninh, one born in each year of the Chinese Zodiacal calendar.

4. At this séance, Vinh was also given his religious name, Hiến Trung, which is combined with his given name in this message calling him to the religion.

5. Adèle Hugo here takes on many of the attributes of the Taoist queen of the heavens, as described by Philip Clart in the phoenix halls of Taiwan: "As we saw, cultivation in a traditional phoenix hall setting is basically the spiritual version of the examination candidate's struggle for office in Imperial China, leading to salvation only in a gradual process of merit accumulation conducted under the supervision of stern, schoolmasterly male deities. Cultivation in a maternist context, by contrast, is clothed in the touching imagery of homecoming, of long-lost children returning to their home and to their compassionate and loving mother" (1997, 26).

6. Séance night of April 21–22, 1930, 11 p.m. (Trần Thu Dung 1996, 275).

7. Séance at midnight, December 30, 1931, at the home of Thái Thơ Thanh, in the presence of Pope Lê Văn Trung and Trần Quang Vinh (Trần Quang Vinh 1962, 58–59).

8. Captain Paul Monet (1884–1934) was a soldier who served in Indochina during World War I, then returned to Hanoi and established a dormitory for Vietnamese students, publishing a bilingual journal and joining "Confucius," the first Freemason lodge to admit Vietnamese members. He wrote books critiquing racial exclusion in the colony: *Francais et Annamites* (1926), *Entre Deux Feux* (1928), and *Les Jauniers* (1930), which argued that the exploitation of peasant labor was a "yellow slave trade" in which uneducated workers were duped into signing lifelong contracts. While Monet was known as an "Annamitophile," he wanted to reform colonialism rather than end it all together. In a séance on December 15, 1926, the Spiritual Pope of Caodai, Lý Thái Bạch, spoke directly to Monet, who attended the séance in Tây Ninh. He said, "You have tried to create a moral relationship in this country between the two races of the French and the Vietnamese, so that they can live together in a community of shared lives and interests. Your wishes will be realized. . . . You will later be one of my most fervent disciples, preaching peace and harmony to the world" (Trần Quang Vinh, 1962, 39). It is unclear how Monet responded to these instructions.

9. Pasquier himself wrote a *Circulaire aux familles au sujet de l'envoi des étudiants indochinois en France,* published in 1930, which explains why he found European studies ill advised for Indochinese students (Norindr 1996, 136).

10. This incident is reported in Đỗ Vạn Lý 1989, 181–182, and the message from Pasquier is found in *Thánh Ngôn Sưu Tập* (Unofficial Selection of Spirit Messages) 1972, 2: 107. Pasquier's message, in Vietnamese, includes this poem:

The title and the throne of a king are like a prison,

So are the high positions in officialdom.

I have aspired to hold the country in my hands.

All these honors are just like a death sentence.

11. *Thánh Ngôn Sưu Tập* (Unofficial Selection of Spirit Messages) 1972, 1: 333.

12. Victor Hugo's sons by birth all died well before he did. The first, Léopold, born in 1823, died as an infant. Charles (1826–1870, reincarnated as Đặng Trung Chữ), who served as the chief medium at the séances in Jersey, died at the age of forty-four of a heart attack followed by a massive hemorrhage caused by long winter nights spent manning the guns on the ramparts of Paris during political uprisings (Robb 1997, 462). He and his brother François had been imprisoned in the Conciergerie, when the prison had become "an informal socialist University" where Victor Hugo prophesied a revolution that would lead to the "United States of Europe" (Robb 1997, 290). François, the younger son (1828–1873, reincarnated as Trần Quang Vinh), translated Shakespeare into French and defended the 1871 uprising, finally dying of tuberculosis two years later (Robb 1997, 490). While both had relatively short lives, they were filled with political turmoil, literary aspirations, and spiritual longings.

13. The speech is quoted in Bernardini (1974, 84–85) and also in Gobron (1949, 91).

14. French archives (Inspection Generale de Service de Police, SCR de SG, Secret document #6093-SSCO, dated September 30, 1940) contain a brochure circulated by Lê Văn Bảy, a critic of Phạm Công Tắc, with these accusations. A spirit message received after Tắc was exiled also revealed that Lê Văn Bảy had denounced him (*Thánh Ngôn Sưu Tập* [Unofficial Spirit Messages], 1972, 211).

15. Arthur Dommen explains the reasons for the French actions:

> The adherents of the Cao Dai, on the other hand, although they foreswore violence, constituted the closest thing to a mass movement outside the government's own organizations, and thus were in a position to act autonomously. In a vast police operation on August 24, 1940, supported by the Garde Indochinoise and army units, 328 Cao Dai temples were entered and searched and 284 of them were closed. Cao Dai private schools and charity clinics were likewise closed. In all, using the tons of documents seized by the police to incriminate ever more of their membership, a total of more than 5,000 members of various Cao Dai sects were arrested, of which 1,983 members of the clergy, notables, and simple faithful were kept in prison until their liberation by the Japanese on March 9, 1945. (2002, 53)

16. After 1975, the local government removed the commemorative monument with a list of the names of all those who "died for their religion," since it identified the killings as initiated by "Communists." In 2006, the sixtieth anniversary of the founding of the Truyền Giáo Việt Nam Trung Kỳ (Missionary Society of Central Vietnam), memorial ceremonies for these martyrs (which I attended) were held in San Bernardino, California, and in Đà Nẵng, but at the ceremonies in Vietnam there was no specific reference to the circumstances of their deaths. Doves were released to "free the souls" of those who had died violent deaths and allow them to be reincarnated in order to fulfill their spiritual destinies of progression to a higher state (Nguyễn Trung Hậu, 1956; Đồng Tân, 1970).

17. His acceptance of the militarization of Caodaism is, for other Caodaists as well as for many outsiders, the most controversial aspect of the Hộ Pháp's career. He called the Caodai militia "the fire inside the heart which may burn and destroy it" (*Tâm muội hỏa;* Bui and Beck 2000, 85) and immediately moved its military headquarters out of the Holy See, but did see its benefits in preventing more killings of Caodaists and allowing him political leverage. American advisor Edward Lansdale paid Caodai generals to betray the religious leadership in 1955, assimilating them along with militias formed to defend Hòa Hảo Buddhists and Catholic congregations (Blagov 2001a, 102)

18. Jérémy Jammes notes that since Hugo lived from 1802–1885, his life in fact overlapped with that of Nguyễn Du (1766–1820), which would seem to challenge the idea of "reincarnation," since it is difficult for one soul to be split between two bodies. He notes, however, as I have also seen, that this detail does not seem to bother Tây Ninh followers at all (2006a, 199).

19. The prime ministers of these governments were Trần Văn Hữu, Nguyễn Văn Tâm, and Bửu Lộc, and he was joined by two other prominent Caodaists: Trần Văn Quế—who was later to found the Caodai Teaching Center in Saigon—and Lê Văn Hoạch (Werner 1976, 388).

20. Several Greene biographers have agreed on this evidence, including W. J. West (1998, 155–166) and Norman Sherry (1989, 423–434). The incident is also reviewed in Fredrik Logevall's *Embers of War* (2012, 293–310). Most of these authors agree that Greene himself was also engaged in espionage for the British Secret Service, although he denied this charge.

21. This clip also appears at the beginning of the documentary film *The Left Eye of God: Caodaism Travels from Vietnam to California,* produced/written by Janet Hoskins and edited/directed by Susan Hoskins (2008). The story of the demonstration at the time of the 1957 filming in Tây Ninh opens Jessica Chapman's *Cauldron of Resistance* (2013, 1–2). Her account, based on a *Time* magazine article dated February 25, 1957, however, repeats a serious mistake made in the article: She claims that only after the demonstration "did twenty thousand disillusioned Cao Dai followers sit down to elect a new pope, finally accepting that the old pope was gone for good" (Chapman 2013, 2). Aside from the fact that Phạm Công Tắc never was actually the "Pope," the election of another Pope in Bến Tre Province happened in 1934, not 1957. Erroneous reports in *Time* magazine from 1956–1957 are also responsible for the extensively reported stories that both Winston Churchill and Charlie Chaplin became Caodai "saints" in the 1950s, several decades before they died (*Time* 1956, 1957). There are no records of either of them having this role in Caodai scripture, and of course only deceased persons can become "saints" or communicate with the living through séances.

22. Sergei Blagov has published an extensive review of all of the evidence about General Thế's activities in his book *Honest Mistakes* (2001b). He also published a review of the 2001 film that notes the impossibility of the claim that General Thế could have been involved in the Việt Minh killings of Catholic villagers in Phát Diệm. There was a lively exchange about the distortions of the 2001 film in the Vietnam Studies Group LISTSERV in 2011, which involved the production advisor for the film, Carl Robinson, who was a Former AP Correspondent in Saigon from 1968 to 1975, and American Mike High, who notes that "General Thế's 'force' was "strictly regional, based in Tây Ninh, worlds away from the Red River delta," online at www.lib.washington.edu/SouthEastAsia/vsg/.

23. The style of Caodai séances that produces texts is completely illegal in today's Vietnam, but since 1995, spirit mediums who dress as various historical spirits and perform in a trance dance format have been allowed to resurface, as followers of the new "indigenous" religion of Đạo Mẫu, the way of the mother goddess. See Hoskins (2011b, 2013, 2014a, 2014b) for discussions of the differences between Caodaism and Đạo Mẫu.

24. During his exile from 1852–1870, he wrote not only the mystical poems of *Les contemplations* (1856), but also the satirical *Les chatiments* (1853), the epic *La Légende*

des siècles (1859), and worked on the manuscript of *Les Misérables* (began in 1845, finished in 1862). See Robb (1997) and Josephson (1942).

25. In 1984, at the time of Halley's comet, Vietnamese police discovered that weapons had been stockpiled near Tây Ninh, as part of a plan to organize an armed resistance. Among those arrested and later executed for participating in that plan were Hồ Thái Bạch, the son of Hồ Tấn Khoa (the Bảo Đạo, or head of the Hiệp Thiên Đài, in Tây Ninh), and Lê Văn Túy, said to be a grandson of Trần Quang Vinh. Trần Quang Cảnh says, however, that his family members do not acknowledge any relation to Lê Văn Túy.

26. Details of this ceremony and a number of photographs can be found on the new caodai.vn website that Cảnh maintains: http://www.caodai.vn/vn/news-detail /le-minh-the-cho-cac-vi-le-sanh-tan-phong-hai-ngoai.html.

27. Details of the Caodai delegation's visit to the Allan Kardec Center can be found online in Vietnamese at http://www.caodai.vn/vn/news-detail/ky-su-truyen-giao-au -chau-nam-2012-ao-va-phap.html, as well as in French in the print journal *Le Spiritisme: Bulletin de L'Association du Centre Spirite Lyonnais Allan Kardec,* and online at http://spirite.free.fr.

Chapter 4. The Fall of Saigon and the Rise of the Diaspora

1. I met with Đỗ Vạn Lý at his home in Chatsworth, a suburb half an hour north of Los Angeles, for a period that stretched over three years (2004–2007), sometimes weekly, sometimes twice a week. Many of our sessions focused on his own life, but he also advised me on translations of scripture, the interpretation of his volume on Caodai history, and many other things. I was deeply saddened when he died on August 11, 2008 (Rourke 2008).

2. Louis-Jacques Dorais has described similar experiences for Vietnamese refugees of all religious backgrounds in his article "Faith, Hope and Identity: Religion and the Vietnamese Refugees" (2007).

3. The Indonesian name Merdeka means "independence" or "freedom," and his daughter was given this name because she was born in the newly independent Indonesia when Đỗ Vạn Lý was stationed in Jakarta as the head of the Saigon government's diplomatic mission there.

4. Đỗ Vạn Lý's belief in Ngô Đình Diệm was not shared by many English-language historians, but more recent research using Vietnamese sources (Miller 2004, 2013) has tried to rehabilitate Ngô Đình Diệm to a certain degree, arguing that he had his own vision of democracy, but it was simply not the same as the U.S. vision. I asked Đỗ Vạn Lý about rumors that Diệm's younger brother and advisor Ngô Đình Nhu had been secretly negotiating with Communist forces, and he said "Diệm realized how serious the situation was, and in such a situation you do what you can."

5. This temple had been founded as part of the Minh Tân ("New Enlightenment") Minh group (discussed in Chapter 5) that had become part of Caodaism in the late 1920s.

6. Hoàng Mai is the maternal granddaughter of Lê Văn Lịch, one of the first Cardinals (*Đầu Sư*) at the Holy See, who was also a *Pháp Sư* (altar master) of the Minh Sư Taoist tradition (Huệ Nhãn 2005, 388). She is still at the Saigon Teaching Agency and I met her several times in Hồ Chí Minh City.

7. Đỗ Vạn Lý's American friends included journalist Sol Saunders (whom he first met at Columbia), novelist and journalist Robert Sampson Elegant (who knew him at Columbia and in New Delhi, and asked me for Lý's current address), and U.S. Ambassador Ellsworth Bunker (who served from 1967–1975), who knew him in India and in Saigon.

8. Đỗ Vạn Lý, following to some extent the example set by Ngô Văn Chiêu, declined a whole series of positions he says were offered to him, including leading the Bảo Đại government as Prime Minister in 1950 (a position briefly occupied by another Caodai follower, Nguyễn Phan Long), and heading a Vietnamese government-in-exile in California (which still exists, although without his participation).

9. Đỗ Thuần Hậu's school is still active and, under the entrepreneurial leadership of his former "disciple" Lương Sĩ Hằng (a Chinese-Vietnamese now in the United States), maintains a website (www.vovi.org) and has recently published works in California in both Vietnamese and English (Đỗ Thuần Hậu 1994; Lương Sĩ Hằng 2002). Đỗ Vạn Lý is critical of these publications, which he says "make a business" of his father's teachings and are not true to their original intentions. He met Lương Sĩ Hằng once in California but felt he was not sufficiently deferential or respectful.

10. For followers of Chiêu Minh meditation, these "unclean" foods are all those that disturb tranquility, including onions, garlic, spices, carbonated beverages, coffee, dairy products, refrigerated water, and so on (Lê Minh Sơn 2004).

11. Đỗ Vạn Lý met Prince Cường Để four years before his death in 1950 and found him rather rigid and authoritarian. His refusal to collaborate with the French had made him a hero to many Vietnamese in an earlier generation, as is documented in Trần Mỹ-Vân's *A Vietnamese Royal Exile in Japan: Prince Cường Để 1882–1950* (2006).

12. Hương Hiếu (1968, 1: 242), also in the unofficial collection of messages received at Tây Ninh (*Thánh Ngôn Sưu Tập* 1972, 82).

13. This prophecy has been reprinted and translated in many different ways. It appears in a book by an English Caodaist, Khánh Phan (2000, 135); in the newsletter of the Caodai temple in Alfortville, a suburb of Paris, in 2004; in Christopher Hartney's dissertation on Australian Caodaism (2004, 154) and on the first page of a privately printed and internally circulated assessment of Caodaism since 1975 (Ngô Bái Thiên 2003) by Caodaists in Hồ Chí Minh City. Both Hartney and Phan translate *nòi giống* as "country." Đỗ Vạn Lý said that today the division into three can also be interpreted as referring to Vietnamese from the North, South, and the diaspora, or the division of world religions into the three great Eastern traditions, Christianity, and Islam.

14. The French sentence "La race française et la race annamite sont mes deux bénites" is translated into Vietnamese in Caodai scriptures as *"Dân tộc Pháp-Việt là hai giống dân được nhiều huệ phúc nhất"* (*Thánh Ngôn Hiệp Tuyển* 1972, 1: 40). Since two

separate words are used for "race," the Vietnamese text could be paraphrased as "The French and Vietnamese people are the two descent lines that have been most favored."

15. Quotes from conversations with Đỗ Vạn Lý at his home on Chatsworth in 2006. Some of the interviews were videotaped and selections from them appear in the documentary I produced and wrote (with Susan Hoskins) called *The Left Eye of God: Caodaism Travels from Vietnam to California* (2008).

Chapter 5. A "Caodaist in Black" Returns to Live in Vietnam

1. The figure of about a million people comes from a report on a conference held on August 7, 2012, in Cầu Kho, titled *Văn Kiện Hội Nghị Giao Lưu Các Hội Thánh và Các Tổ Chức Cao Đài Lần V,* which provides figures of 986,003 people registered in twenty different participating organizations in 2010, plus 3,876 new members who were initiated (*nhập môn*) in 2011 and 2012 (18).

2. Studies of redemptive societies in China include De Groot (1972), Duara (2003), Goossaert and Palmer (2011), and Ownby (2008).

3. There are a number of verse formats used in spirit poems, all of them with challenging formal restrictions. Some use six-syllable lines followed by eight-syllable lines (*lục bát*), while others start with two lines of seven syllables, then one of six, and one of eight (*song thất lục bát*). The most complex one—used in a great many messages—has four lines of seven syllables (*thất ngôn tứ tuyệt*) followed by eight lines of seven syllables (*thất ngôn bát cú*) in which the name of the divinity is spelled out in the first syllable of each line, so it is a kind of anagram. I was told that ordinary mortals are not capable of writing such complex verses, so the high standard of literary quality is a sign of divine inspiration.

4. Several scholars see these messages as very much within the Taoist tradition, sharing the perspective of the redemptive societies that were active in China in the 1930s. David Palmer, in particular, says these texts are "Chinese religion in vernacular Vietnamese" (Jammes and Palmer 2013). The Caodai historian Huệ Khải agrees, writing that it is "possible to regard Cadoaism to some extent as the Vietnamization as well as the modernization of old-age Taoism" (Huệ Khải 2010, 140). The "modern" elements include an endorsement of the principles of Darwinian evolution, which are supplemented by spiritual evolution through reincarnation.

5. See the brief history of this group in Nguyễn Trung Hậu's account (1956), especially p. 137.

6. An interview with one of the girls trained as a spirit medium, Trang Chế, is included in the documentary *The Left Eye of God: Caodaism Travels from Vietnam to California* (Hoskins and Hoskins 2008).

7. Joseph Smith is appreciated because his revelations from the Angel Moroni can be seen as part of a tradition of Spiritism including Caodaism. His background as a Freemason has also meant that many "Caodai symbols" ("the all-seeing eye, the moon and the stars") appear on the outside of Mormon temples. As we will see in the next

chapter, several non-Vietnamese converts to Caodaism, including Ngasha Beck and Stephen Stratford, were former Mormons, who renounced Mormonism as patriarchal or racist, but came to find a more welcoming (and perhaps somewhat familiar) spiritual home in Caodaism. The message received from Joseph Smith urges people to practice vegetarianism and to sublimate the flow of *khí* (breath) in their bodies in practices of bodily purification that seem more Asian than Mormon (archived at the Thiên Lý Bửu Tòa website www.thienlybuutoa.org).

8. Video footage from the ceremonies held at Thiên Lý Bửu Tòa in 1997 and 2003 is included in the documentary *The Left Eye of God: Caodaism Travels from Vietnam to California* (Hoskins and Hoskins 2008).

9. Spirit message accessed on September 15, 2004, at thienlybuutoa.org.

10. In "My Stay at Poulo Condor until March 9, 1945" (*Côn-Lôn Quần-Đảo Trước Ngày 9-3-1945*), published in Saigon in 1961, Quế argued that prison teaches self-reliance, since in order to survive it is necessary to develop individual resources and personal endurance, rather than depending on family support (Trần Văn Quế 1961, 124, cited in Zinoman 2001b, 132). Quế's memoir contains many candid accounts of the collective emotional experiences of prisoners and their loss of freedom and family ties:

> Prisoners serving 20- or 30-year sentences have many reasons to be sad. Twenty or thirty years is a long time to survive in these conditions. Even if your health holds up, release may be as devastating as incarceration. Families and villages will have changed drastically. Parents will be dead; wives and children will have moved away. Surviving relatives will be old and feeble. What hope will be left? Most likely, you will be on the verge of death yourself. (Trần Văn Quế 1961, 120)

One of his friends and companions in Poulo Condor was the famous nationalist and secret society leader Nguyễn An Ninh, who quoted Chamfort's epigram: "*En prison, le coeur se brise ou se bronze*" ("In prison, the heart either breaks or becomes as hard as bronze") to explain his own reaction to incarceration (Hồ Tài 1992, 153). Quế told Caodaist historian Đồng Tân that Communist prisoners, led by future Communist Party head Lê Duẩn, poisoned Nguyễn An Ninh to death, alienating other nationalists (Đồng Tân 2006, 166).

11. The renaming of Paul Bert Street in Hanoi as Trần Hưng Đạo Street during the "independent" administration headed by Trần Trọng Kim was the work of Trần Văn Quế. The Tây Ninh Temple in today's Hồ Chí Minh City is also found on Trần Hưng Đạo Street. Liam Kelley (2012) suggests that Trần Hưng Đạo was "finally taking a place of prominence" by the mid twentieth century, when he became generally recognized as a national hero in both Hanoi and Saigon.

12. Trương Như Tảng (1985, 75–77). The author of this memoir, the former Minister of Justice of the National Liberation Front, was himself descended from two prominent

Caodaists: His maternal grandfather was Nguyễn Văn Thơ, who donated three hundred hectars of land to the Holy See, and his stepmother, Madame Lâm Ngọc Thanh, was the first female Cardinal. His mother was also a high-ranking dignitary (4).

13. The title Bảo Đạo is considered one rank lower than that of Hộ Pháp, since no one felt that Phạm Công Tắc could be replaced. Until 1975, the deceased Hộ Pháp continued to send spirit messages through séances to "administer the religion from above." As séances were banned after reunification, the Tây Ninh hierarchy has had to function without direct spiritual guidance from its founders.

14. This is the Vietnamese original: *Hiệp Thiên Đài là cơ quan bảo pháp, nơi thông công cùng Thượng Đế và các Đấng Thiêng Liêng.*

15. Huệ-Tâm Hồ Tài has published a detailed history of Bửu Sơn Kỳ Hương and Hòa Hảo Buddhism movements in her 1983 book *Millenarianism and Peasant Politics*.

16. Early Caodaists did not want to be associated with this tradition. In 1926, in the midst of the great excitement generated by the "Opening up of the Way," two people had spontaneously fallen into trance, possessed by the spirits of the Buddhist goddess of mercy, Quan Âm, and the Monkey King. This was seen as inappropriate to the solemn ceremonial character of the occasion, and the two were quickly controlled and led away. In conversations in California, Đỗ Vạn Lý speculated to me: "I think the French were behind all this monkey business. They wanted to be able to dismiss Caodaism as some form of shamanism or popular superstition. They did not want to take our movement seriously, so they probably got their own agents to misbehave in that way." While I do not necessarily share his proclivity for conspiracy theories in understanding this outbreak of uncontrolled religious inspiration, I find the logic of this argument fascinating. It goes to the heart of division between a literary, elite tradition of spirit writing and a more popular, theatrical one of trance and dancing while possessed by spirits.

17. See Norton (2009), Endres (2011), Fjelstad and Nguyễn Thị Hiền (2006, 2011), and Phạm Quỳnh Phượng (2009).

Chapter 6. The Divine Eye on the Internet

1. The Graham Greene quote is from a 1952 *Paris Match* article: "Indochina: France's Crown of Thorns," reprinted in Greene (1996); Baudrillard (1995).

2. Mittermaier (2011, 204). Mittermaier is quoting from Horkemeier (1978).

3. From an e-mail received from Ngasha Beck in July 2004. Beck was raised a Mormon, and left the church because she found it patriarchal and racist. The name Ngasha she now interprets as Bà Nguyệt, or "moon lady," and related to the Vietnamese name for the spirit of Victor Hugo, which is Nguyệt Tâm Chơn Nhơn. Nguyệt means "moon," Tâm "heart," and Chơn Nhơn is a title given to archangels or immortals in the Taoist tradition who have attained the fifth rank of sanctity.

4. Gustave Meillon's essay, "Le Caodaisme," was republished as a preface to *Les Messages Spirites,* edited by Trần Quang Vinh (1962).

5. David Tùng Chế, his sister Trang Chế, and his father Nghiệp Chế all appear in *The Left Eye of God: Caodaism Travels from Vietnam to California* (Hoskins and Hoskins 2008) in a section focusing on the period during which Trang Chế was trained as a spirit medium.

6. In 1997, Silicon Valley had the second largest concentration of Vietnamese in the United States, with 1,645 Vietnamese engineers, 478 computer scientists, 289 managers, 2,272 secretaries and administrative support people, 2,472 engineering and science technicians, 1,299 other technicians, and 1,422 assemblers (Freeman and Huu 2005, 26).

7. As noted in Chapter 5 (footnote 13), no dignitary in the Tây Ninh hierarchy has taken on the title of Hộ Pháp after the death of Phạm Công Tắc. Instead, the head of the College of Spirit Mediums or Hiệp Thiên Đài has held the rank of Bảo Đạo (Protector of the Way), considered just below that of Hộ Pháp (Defender of the Dharma). In the period since his death in 1959 up to the Communist victory in 1975, the spirit of Phạm Công Tắc sent more spirit messages than any other spirit, and so the deceased Hộ Pháp was able to "guide the religion from above." Some people have suggested that the return of his body in 2006 (and the hoped-for resumption of séances) should allow him to do so in the future as well. There has also never been another Interim Pope after the death of Lê Văn Trung in 1934.

8. A full account of this visit and many photographs are archived at the caodai.com .vn website http://caodai.com.vn/en/news-detail/journey-to-taiwan-by-the-sacerdotal -council-of-cao-dai-tay-ninh-holy-see-part-3.html, including a description of the séance.

9. Other Caodai websites include http://www.caodaigiaoly.freefr, a collection of religious teachings founded in Germany by Hà Phước Thảo (who is now in Vietnam), which is now run from France; http://www.daotam.info/, also known as the Sydney Centre for Studies of Caodaism, founded in Australia by Đào Công Tâm, with extensive archives and translations; http://www.thienlybuutoa.org, founded in San Jose, discussed in Chapter 5; http://nhipcaugiaoly.com, the website of the Saigon Teaching Agency (CQPTGL); http://ddtnhhn.caodaiyouth.org/, the youth group of Tây Ninh Caodaists; and http://www.caodaism.org, founded by by Nguyễn Chánh Giáo of Australia, to archive materials related to Tây Ninh Caodaism.

10. Buddhist and Christian reactions to Decree 92 can be found at the following sites: www.queme.net/eng/news_detail.php?numb=1955 and http://www.asianews .it/news-en/Decree-92:-Hanoi-chooses-Chinese-model-and-clamps-down-on-reli gious-freedom-26521.html. Caodaists did not make a public comment on this new law.

11. The spirit message was posted to http://web.utah.edu/vasa on February 10, 2005, and forwarded to me by various California Caodaists. None of them said that it was authentic or that they believed it, but they did find it "interesting," and said we should wait to see if anything that it contained later came to pass.

12. The letter was dated September 8, 1921, and authenticated and published by Pascal Bourdeaux (Bourdeaux and Abu-Zeid 2012). Intriguingly, Hồ Chí Minh also

refers three times to Captain Monet, a French Protestant who was designated in a spirit séance on December 15, 1926, to represent Caodaism at the Parliament of World Religions and told to spread its message to the world. (Trần Quang Vinh 1962, 39). See more discussion of Captain Paul Monet in Chapter 3, footnote 8.

Chapter 7.   A Religion in Diaspora, a Religion of Diaspora

1. Bourdieu defined the stakes in a competitive religious field as "the monopoly of the legitimate exercise of the power to modify, in a deep and lasting fashion, the practice and world view of lay people, by imposing on and inculcating them in a particular religious habitus." The "habitus," in turn, was defined as a "lasting, generalized and transposable disposition to act and think in conformity with the principles of a (quasi-) systematic view of the world and human existence" (1987, 126).

2. Verter develops a "Bourdieuian model" of religion, but notes that Bourdieu's own writing "employs categories that are too rigid to account for the fluidities of today's spiritual marketplace" (2003, 151). He focuses on "spiritual capital" as a more widely diffused commodity, not completely controlled by religious specialists, and governed by more complex patterns of production, distribution, exchange, and consumption.

3. Malinowski argued in *Argonauts of the Western Pacific* that the goal of this "long conversation" was "to grasp the native's point of view, his relation to life, to realize *his* visition of *his* world" (1922, 25). Clifford Geertz has updated this idea in several essays reexamining the issue of ethnographic subjectivity and fieldwork (Geertz 1983, 1988) and applying them to "natives" engaged in complex cosmopolitan interactions (like Caodaists).

4. I have argued (in Chapter 4) that the Caodai vision of the particular destiny of the Vietnamese people could be seen as a sort of "Vietnamese exceptionalism" (at least as it was articulated by Đỗ Vạn Lý), but it seems equally true that a fair amount of postcolonial theory could be charged with "Bengali exceptionalism" for many of the same reasons.

5. The rhizome metaphor is used by Deleuze and Guattari (1987) and Paul Gilroy (1991).

REFERENCES

Aguilar-San Juan, Karin. 2009. *Little Saigons: Staying Vietnamese in America.* Minneapolis: University of Minnesota Press.

Anderson, Benedict. 1991. *Imagined Communities: Reflections on the Origin and Spread of Nationalism.* London: Verso.

———. 1998. *The Spectre of Comparisons: Nationalism, Southeast Asia and the World.* London: Verso.

Apolito, Paolo. 2005. *The Internet and the Madonna: Religious Visionary Experience on the Web.* Translated by Anthony Shuggar. Chicago: University of Chicago Press.

Apter, Andrew. 2004. "Herskovits's Heritage: Rethinking Syncretism in the African Diaspora." In *Syncretism in Religion: A Reader. Critical Categories in the Study of Religion,* edited by Anita M. Leopold and Jebbe S. Jensen, 160–184. New York: Routledge.

Asad, Talal. 1993. *Genealogies of Religion: Discipline and Reasons of Power in Christianity and Islam.* Baltimore: Johns Hopkins University Press.

———. 2009. "The Idea of an Anthropology of Islam." *Qui Parle* 17 (2): 1–30.

Barber, Daniel Colucciello. 2011. *On Diaspora: Christianity, Religion and Secularity.* Eugene, Ore.: Cascade Books.

Baudrillard, Jean. 1995. *Simulacra and Simulation: Selected Writings.* Translated by Sheila Glaser. Ann Arbor: University of Michigan Press.

Bayly, Susan. 2004. "Conceptualizing from Within: Divergent Religious Modes from Asian Modernist Perspectives." In *Ritual and Memory: Toward a Comparative Anthropology of Religion,* edited by Harvey Whitehouse and James Laidlaw. Lanham, Md.: Altamira.

Bernardini, Pierre. 1974. "Le Caodaïsme au Cambodge." Thèse pour le Doctorat, Université de Paris VII.

Berner, Ulrich. 2001. "The Notion of Syncretism in Historical and/or Empirical Research." *Historical Reflections / Réflexions Historiques* 27 (3): 499–509.

Bhabha, Homi K. 1994. "Signs Taken for Wonders: Questions of Ambivalence and Authority under a Tree outside Delhi, May 1817." In *The Location of Culture,* 102–122. New York: Routledge.

Blagov, Sergei. 2001a. *Caodaism: Vietnamese Traditionalism and Its Leap into Modernity.* New York: Nova Science Publishers.

———. 2001b. *Honest Mistakes: The Life and Death of Trịnh Minh Thế (1922–1955): South Vietnam's Alternative Leader.* Huntington, N.Y.: Nova Science Publishers, Inc.

Boddy, Janice. 1994. "Spirit Possession Revisited: Beyond Instrumentality." *Annual Reviews in Anthropology* 21: 407–434.

Bourdeaux, Pascal, and Kareem James Abu-Zeid. 2012. "Notes on an Unpublished Letter by Hồ Chí Minh to a French Pastor (September 8, 1921) or the Art of Dissenting Evangelization." *Journal of Vietnamese Studies* 7 (2): 8–28.

Bourdieu, Pierre. 1987. "Legitimation and Structured Interests in Weber's *Sociology of Religion*." Translated by Chris Turner. In *Max Weber: Rationality and Modernity,* edited by Sam Whimster and Scott Lash, 119–136. London: Allen and Unwin.

———. 1991. "Genesis and Structure of the Religious Field." *Comparative Social Research* 13: 1–43. (Orig. pub. 1971, in French as "Genèse et structure du champs religieux." *Revue française de sociologie* 12: 295–334.)

Boyarin, Jonathan, and Daniel Boyarin. 2002. *Powers of Diaspora: Two Essays on the Relevance of Jewish Culture.* Minneapolis: University of Minnesota Press.

Bray, Adam, ed. 2013. *Berlitz Handbook to Vietnam.* Berlitz Travel: Berlitz Publishing.

Brocheux, Pierre. 2003. Le Mouvement Indépendantiste Vietnamien pendant la Seconde Guerre mondiale (1939–1945). In *L'empire coloniale sous Vichy,* edited by Jacques Cantier and Eric Jennings, 265–290. Paris: Odile Jacob.

Brocheux, Pierre, and Daniel Hemery. 2009. *Indochina: An Ambiguous Colonization, 1858–1954.* Translated by Ly Lyan Dill-Klein. Berkeley: University of California Press.

Brook, Timothy. 1993. "Rethinking Syncretism: The Unity of the Three Teachings and their Joint Worship in Late Imperial China." *Journal of Chinese Religions* 21: 13–44.

Buckley, Michael. 2000. *Moon Handbook to Vietnam Laos and Cambodia.* Chico, Calif.: Avalon Travel Publishing.

Bùi Hùm, Bùi Hồng, and Ngasha Beck. 2003. *Guide to Caodai Spiritual Celebration: Cẩm Nang Hành Lễ Cao Đài.* Pomona, Calif.: Booklet published for use at services.

Bùi Đắc Hùm, and Ngasha Beck. 2000. *Cao Đài, Faith of Unity.* Fayetteville, Ark.: Emerald Wave.

Cadière, Léopold. 1949. *Croyances et pratiques religieuses des Annamites.* Hanoi: École Française d'Études Orientales. (Reprinted in 1958 in Saigon by the Imprimerie Nouvelle d'Extrême Orient with the title *Croyances et pratiques religieuses des Vietnamiens.*)

———. 1989 [1959]. *Religious Beliefs and Practices of the Vietnamese.* Translation of only the first introductory chapter by I. W. Mabbett. Melbourne, Australia: Monash University.

Campany, Robert. 2003. "On the Very Idea of Religions (in the Modern West and in Early Medieval China)." *History of Religions* 42 (4): 287–319.

———. 2006. "Secrecy and Display in the Quest for Transcendence in China, ca. 220 BCE–350 CE." *History of Religions* 45 (4): 291–336.

Cannell, Fenella. 2005. "The Christianity of Anthropology." *Journal of the Royal Anthropological Institute* N.S. 11: 335–356.

———, ed. 2006. *The Anthropology of Christianity.* Durham, N.C.: Duke University Press.

———. 2010. "The Anthropology of Secularism." *Annual Review of Anthropology* 39: 85–100.

Cannon, Alexander M. 2012a. "Introduction: Epic Directions for the Study of the Vietnamese Diaspora." *Journal of Vietnamese Studies* 7 (3): 1–6.

———. 2012b. "Virtually Audible in Diaspora: The Transnational Negotiation of Vietnamese Traditional Music." *Journal of Vietnamese Studies* 7 (3): 122–156.

Capra, Fritjof. 1975. *The Tao of Physics: An Exploration of the Parallels Between Modern Physics and Eastern Mysticism.* Berkeley, Calif.: Shambala Publications.

Carruthers, Ashley. 2002. "The Accumulation of National Belonging in Transnational Fields: Ways of Being at Home in Vietnam." *Identities: Global Studies in Culture and Power* 9 (4): 423–444.

———. 2008. "The Trauma of Synchronization: The Temporal Location of the Homeland in the Vietnamese Diaspora." *Crossroads: An Interdisciplinary Journal of Southeast Asian Studies* 19 (2): 63–91.

Cầu Kho temple. 2012. *Văn Kiện Hội Nghị Giao Lưu Các Hội Thánh và Các tổ Chức Cao Đài Lần V.* [Report on the 5th Conference of Caodai Sacerdotal Councils and Leaders]. Hồ Chí Minh City: Privately circulated report.

Chakrabarty, Dipesh. 2000. *Provincializing Europe: Postcolonial Thought and Historical Difference.* Princeton, N.J.: Princeton University Press.

Chapman, Jessica M. 2013. *Cauldron of Resistance: Ngo Dinh Diem, the United States and 1950s Southern Vietnam.* Ithaca, N.Y.: Cornell University Press.

Chatterjee, Partha. 1993. *The Nation and Its Fragments: Colonial and Postcolonial Histories.* Princeton, N.J.: Princeton University Press.

Chen, Kuan-Hsing. 2010. *Asia as Method: Toward De-imperialization.* Durham, N.C.: Duke University Press.

Chiếu Minh Đàn. 1950. *Đại Thừa Chơn Giáo* [Great pathway of esoterism]. Edited by Nguyễn Văn Huấn. Saigon: Chiếu Minh Đàn [Cenacle of Transcendance].

Chí Tín (religious name of Lê Văn Bá). 1995. *Notions fondamentales du Caodaïsme.* Translated from Vietnamese into French by Quách Hiệp Long. Munich: Bureau de Diffusion du Caodaïsme en Allemagne.

Chong, Denise. 2000. *The Girl in the Picture: The Story of Kim Phúc, Whose Image Altered the Course of the Vietnam War.* Toronto: Viking.

Clart, Philip. 1997. "The Phoenix and the Mother: The Interaction of Spirit Writing Cults and Popular Sects in Taiwan." *Journal of Chinese Religions* 25: 1–32.

———. 2003. "Moral Mediums: Spirit-Writing and the Colonial Construction of Chinese Spirit-Mediumship." *Ethnologies* 25 (1): 153–190.

———. 2007. "Jesus in Chinese Popular Sects." In *The Chinese Face of Jesus Christ,* edited by Roman Malek, 1315–1333. Sankt Augustin, Germany: Monumenta Serica Monograph Series L/3b.

Clifford, James. 1988. *The Predicament of Culture.* Cambridge, Mass.: Harvard University Press.

———. 1992. "Traveling Cultures." In *Cultural Studies,* edited by Lawrence Grossberg, Cary Nelson, and Paula Treichler, 96–116. New York: Routledge.

———. 1994. "Diasporas." *Cultural Anthropology* 9 (3): 302–338.

Colet, John. 2002. *The Footprint Handbook to Vietnam.* Bath, England: Footprint Handooks Ltd.

Coulet, Georges. 1926. *Les sociétés secrètes en Terre d'Annam.* Saigon: Imprimerie Ardin.

Đặng, Kim Phượng. 2013. "Drifting Lotus: The Spirit of Survival." Unpublished manuscript.

Đào, Anh Thắng. 2012. "Living without Quê: The Ethnic Minority and Freedom in Thuận's Chinatown." *Journal of Vietnamese Studies* 7 (3): 55–79.

Đào Công Tâm, and Christopher Hartney. 2007. "The Sydney Centre for Caodaist Studies: Translations (with Christopher Hartney) of Phạm Công Tắc's Sermons from 1947–1949: *Con Đường Thiêng Liêng Hằng Sống* [The divine path to eternal life]." http://www.daotam.info/tam.htm

DeBernardi, Jean. 2009. "Wudang Mountain and Mount Zion in Taiwan: Syncretic Processes in Space, Ritual Performance, and Imagination." *Asian Journal of Social Science* 37: 138–162.

De Groot, J. J. M. 1972 [1910]. *The Religious System of China.* Vol. 4, bk. 2. Taipei: Ch'eng-wen Publishing.

Deleuze, Gilles, and Félix Guattari. 1987. *A Thousand Plateaus.* Minneapolis: University of Minnesota Press.

Denis, Léon. 1923. *Jeanne d'Arc: Médium.* Reprinted in 2001 by Editions Transatlantiques, Aubenas D'Ardèche. France: Imprimerie Lienhardt.

Desbarats, Jacqueline. 1990. "Repression in the Socialist Republic of Vietnam: Executions and Population Relocation." In *The Vietnam Debate,* edited by John Morton Moore, 192–202. Lanham, Md.: University Press of America.

Devido, Elise Anne. 2007. "'Buddhism for This World': The Buddhist Revival in Vietnam, 1920 to 1951, and Its Legacy." In *Modernity and Re-enchantment,* edited by Phillip Taylor, 250–296. Singapore: Utopia Press.

Đỗ Merdeka Thiên-Lý Hưng. 1994. *Cao Daism: An Introduction.* Perris, Calif.: Centre for Đại Đạo Studies.

Dommen, Arthur. 2002. *Indochinese Experience of the French and the Americans: Nationalism and Communism in Cambodia, Laos and Vietnam.* Bloomington: Indiana University Press.

Đồng Tân. 1967. *Lịch-Sử Cao Đài Đại-Đạo Tam-Kỳ Phổ-Độ: Phần Vô-Vi* [The history of Caodaism: Esoteric pathway]. Sài Gòn: Hòa Chánh.

———. 1970. *Lịch-Sử Cao Đài Đại-Đạo Tam-Kỳ Phổ-Độ: Phần Phổ-Độ* [The history of Caodaism: Exoteric pathway]. Sài Gòn: Hòa Chánh.

———. 2006. *Nhân Vật Cao Đài Giáo* [Caodai personnages: Biographies of prominent Caodaists]. Carlton, Victoria: The Caodai Cultural Association.

Dorais, Louis-Jacques. 2005. "Mémoires migrantes, mémoires vivantes. Identité culturelle et récits de vie d'aînés vietnamiens au Québec." *Ethnologies* 27 (1): 165–193.

———. 2007. "Faith, Hope and Identity: Religion and the Vietnamese Refugees." *Refugee Survey Quarterly* 26 (2): 57–68.

———. 2010. "Politics, Kinship and Ancestors: Some Diasporic Dimensions of the Vietnamese Experience in North America." *Journal of Vietnamese Studies* 5 (2): 91–132.

Dorais, Louis-Jacques, and Nguyễn Huy. 1990. *Fleur de Lotus et Feuille d'Érable: La vie religieuse des Vietnamiens du Québec.* Quebec: Département d'Anthropologie, Faculté des Sciences Sociales, Université Laval.

Đỗ Thiên. 2003. *Vietnamese Supernaturalism: Views from the Southern Region.* London: Routledge Curzon.

———. 2004. "Charity and Charisma: The Dual Path of the Tinh Do Cu Si, a Popular Buddhist Group in Contemporary Vietnam." In *Vietnamese Society in Transition,* edited by John Kleinen. Amsterdam: IIAS/Her Spinhuis.

Đỗ Thuận Hậu. 1994. *Phép Xuất Hồn* [The method of soul travel]. Santa Ana, Calif.: Đại Nam.

Đỗ Vạn Lý. 1959. *The Stork and the Shrimp: 34 Folk Stories from Vietnam.* New Delhi: Vietnam House.

———. 1960. *Aggressions by China: A Peep into the History of Vietnam.* 2nd ed. New Delhi: Vietnam House.

———. 1989. *Tìm Hiểu Đạo Cao Đài* [Understanding Caodaism]. Perris, Calif.: Cao Đài Giáo Việt Nam Hải Ngoại.

Dror, Olga. 2005. *Cult, Culture and Authority: Princess Lieu Hanh in Vietnamese History.* Honolulu: University of Hawai'i Press.

Duara, Prasenjit. 1995. *Rescuing History From the Nation: Questioning Narratives of Modern China.* Chicago: University of Chicago Press.

———. 2003. *Sovereignty and Authenticity: Manchukuo and the East Asian Modern.* Lanham, Md.: Rowman & Littlefield.

———. 2010. "Asia Redux: Conceptualising a Region for Our Times." *Journal of Asian Studies* 69 (4): 963–983.

———. 2014. *The Crisis of Global Modernity: Asian Traditions and a Sustainable Future.* Cambridge: Cambridge University Press.

Đức Nguyên (religious name of Nguyễn Văn Hồng). 2000. *Cao Đài Tự Điển.* [The Caodai dictionary]. Vols. 1–3. http://caodaism.org/CaoDaiTuDien/cdtd.htm.

———. 2001. *Đức Phật Vị Hộ Pháp, Danh Nhân Đại Đạo* [The life of the Hộ Pháp, great men of the great way of Cadaism]. Vol. 1: 1507. http://caodaism.org/CaoDaiTuDien /cdtd.htm.

Duong, Lan P. 2012. *Treacherous Subjects: Gender, Culture and Trans-Vietnamese Feminism.* Philadelphia: Temple University Press.

Edwards, Penny. 2007. *Cambodge: The Cultivation of a Nation 1860–1945.* Honolulu: University of Hawai'i Press.

Eller, Jack David. 2009. *Introducing the Anthropology of Religion.* London: Routledge.

Emmons, Ron, ed. 2012. *Rough Guide to Vietnam.* 7th ed. New York: Rough Guides.

Endres, Kristin. 2002. "Beautiful Customs, Worthy Traditions: Changing State Discourse on the Role of Vietnamese Culture." *Internationales Asienforum* 33 (3–4): 303–322.

———. 2008. "Fate, Memory and the Postcolonial Construction of the Self: The Life Narrative of a Vietnamese Spirit Medium." *Journal of Vietnamese Studies* 3 (2): 34–65.

———. 2011. *Performing the Divine: Mediums, Markets and Modernity in Urban Vietnam.* Copenhagen: Nordic Institute of Asian Studies.

Espiritu, Yến Lê. 2014. "Militarized Refuge: A Critical Rereading of Vietnamese Flight to the U.S." In *Transpacific Studies: Framing an Emerging Field,* edited by Janet Hoskins and Viet Thanh Nguyen, 201–224. Honolulu: University of Hawai'i Press.

Fall, Bernard. 1955. "The Political-Religious Sects of Vietnam." *Pacific Affairs* 28 (3): 235–253.

Fall, Dorothy. 2006. *Bernard Fall: Memoirs of a Soldier-Scholar.* Washington, D.C.: Potomac Books.

Fitzgerald, Frances. 1972. *Fire in the Lake: The Vietnamese and the Americans in Vietnam.* Boston: Little, Brown and Company.

Fjelstad, Karen, and Nguyễn Thị Hiền. 2006. *Possessed by the Spirits: Mediumship in Contemporary Vietnamese Communities.* Ithaca, N.Y.: Cornell University Press.

———. 2011. *Spirits without Borders: Vietnamese Spirit Mediums in a Transnational Age.* New York: Palgrave Macmillan.

Freeman, James. 1989. *Hearts of Sorrow: Vietnamese-American Lives.* Stanford, Calif.: Stanford University Press.

Freeman, James, and Nguyễn Đình Hữu. 2005. *Voices From the Camps: Vietnamese Children Seeking Asylum.* Seattle: University of Washington Press.

———. 2011. *Spirits without Borders: Vietnamese Spirit Mediums in a Transnational Age.* New York: Palgrave Macmillan.

Galvan, Jill. 2010. *The Sympathetic Medium: Female Channeling, the Occult, and Communication Technologies, 1859–1919.* Ithaca, N.Y.: Cornell University Press.

Geertz, Clifford. 1960. *The Religion of Java.* Chicago: University of Chicago Press.

———. 1968. *Islam Observed: Religious Development in Morocco and Indonesia.* Chicago: University of Chicago Press.

———. 1983. "'From the Native's Point of View': On the Nature of Anthropological Understanding." In *Local Knowledge: Further Essays in Interpretive Anthropology,* 55–72. New York: Basic Books.

———. 1988. "I-Witnessing: Malinowski's Children." In *Works and Lives: The Anthropologist as Author,* 73–101. Stanford, Calif.: Stanford University Press.

Gilroy, Paul. 1993. *The Black Atlantic: Modernity and Double Consciousness.* Cambridge, Mass.: Harvard University Press.

Gobron, Gabriel. 1948. *Histoire et Philosophie du Caodaïsme: Bouddhisme rénové, spiritisme vietnamien, religion nouvelle en Eurasie.* Paris: Dervy.

Gobron, Marguerite. 1949. *Le Caodaïsme en Images.* Paris: Dervy.

Goossaert, Vincent, and David Palmer. 2011. *The Religious Question in Modern China.* Chicago: University of Chicago Press.

Goscha, Christopher E. 2009. "Widening the Colonial Encounter: Asian Connections Inside French Indochina During the Interwar Period." *Modern Asian Studies* 43 (5): 1189–1228.

Grant, Bruce. 1979. *The Boat People.* Harmondsworth, U.K.: Penguin.

Greene, Graham. 1996 [1955]. *The Quiet American.* Edited by John Clark Pratt. New York: Penguin.

Gupta, Akhil, and James Ferguson. 1992. "Beyond 'Culture': Space, Identity and the Politics of Difference." *Cultural Anthropology* 7 (1): 6–23.

Halbwachs, Maurice. 1992. *On Collective Memory.* Translated by Lewis A. Coser. Chicago: University of Chicago Press.

Hall, Stuart. 1990. "Cultural Identity and Diaspora." In *Identity,* edited by J. Rutherford, 222–237. London: Lawrence and Wishart.

————. 1996. "The Question of Cultural Identity." In *Modernity: An Introduction to Modern Societies,* edited by Stuart Hall, David Held, Don Hubert, and Kenneth Thompson, 596–634. London: Blackwell.

Hanegraaff, Wouter J. 1998. *New Age Religion and Western Culture: Esotericism in the Mirror of Secular Thought.* Albany, N.Y.: SUNY Press.

Hartney, Christopher. 2004. "A Separate Peace: Cao Dai's Manifestation in Australia." PhD diss., University of Sydney, Australia.

Hefner, Robert. 2000. *Civil Islam: Muslims and Democratization in Indonesia.* Princeton, N.J.: Princeton University Press.

Herskovits, Melville J. 1958. *The Myth of the Negro Past.* Boston: Beacon Press.

Ho, Enseng. 2006. *The Graves of Tarim: Genealogy and Mobility across the Indian Ocean.* Berkeley: University of California Press.

Holston, James. 2000. "Alternative Modernities: Statecraft and Religious Imagination in the Valley of the Dawn." *American Ethnologist* 26 (3): 605–631.

Horkemeier, Max. 1978. *Dawn and Decline.* Translated by Michael Shaw. New York: Sebury Press.

Hoskins, Janet. 1993. *The Play of Time: Kodi Perspectives on Calendars, History and Exchange.* Berkeley: University of California Press.

————. 1998. *Biographical Objects: How Things Tell the Stories of People's Lives.* New York: Routledge.

————. 2006. "Caodai Exile and Redemption: A New Vietnamese Religion's Struggle for Identity." In *Religion and Social Justice for Immigrants,* edited by Pierrette Hondagneu-Sotelo, 191–210. New Brunswick, N.J.: Rutgers University Press.

————. 2008. "From Kuan Yin to Joan of Arc: Female Divinities in the Caodai Pantheon." In *The Constant and Changing Faces of the Goddess in Asia,* edited by Deepak Shimkada, 80–99. Cambridge: Cambridge Scholars Press.

————. 2009. "Can a Hierarchical Religion Survive Without Its Center? Caodaism, Colonialism and Exile." In *Hierarchy: Persistence and Transformation of Social Formations,* edited by Knut Rio and Olaf Smedal, 113–141. London: Berghahn Books.

————. 2010a. "Seeing Syncretism as Visual Blasphemy: Critical Eyes on Caodai Religious Architecture." *Material Religion* 6 (1): 30–59.

————. 2010b. "Derrière le voile de l'oeil céleste; Le rôle des apparitions dans l'expansion du Caodaïsme." *Péninsule* 56 (2): 211–249.

————. 2011a. "Diaspora as Religious Doctrine: 'An Apostle of Vietnamese Nationalism' Comes to California." *Journal of Vietnamese Studies* 4 (1): 45–86.

————. 2011b. "What Are Vietnam's Indigenous Religions?" *Newsletter of the Center for Southeast Asian Studies* 64: 3–7.

————. 2012a. "A Posthumous Return from Exile: The Legacy of an Anti-colonial Religious Leader in Today's Vietnam." *Southeast Asian Studies* 1 (2): 213–246.

————. 2012b. "A Spirit Medium as Architect: Caodaism's Visual Theology." In *The Spirit of Things: Materiality in the Age of Religious Diversity in Southeast Asia,* edited by Julius Bautista, 43–60. Ithaca, N.Y.: Cornell University.

———. 2012c. "God's Chosen People: Race, Religion and Anti-Colonial Resistance in French Indochina." *The Asia Research Institute Working Paper Series* No. 189, September 2012, National University of Singapore.

———. 2013. "Trance Dancers or Interlocutors of the Immortals? Gender and Vietnamese Spirit Mediums in Contrasting Traditions." In *Reassessing Ritual: Conference Proceedings,* edited by Yoko Hayami, 35–51. Kyoto University Center for Southeast Asian Studies, in collaboration with the Asia Research Institute, National University of Singapore.

———. 2014a. "Folklore as a Sacred Heritage: Vietnamese Indigenous Religions in California." In *Asian American Identities and Practices: Folkloric Expressions in Everyday Life,* edited by Jonathan H. X. Lee, 185–198. New York: Lexington Books.

———. 2014b. "The Spirits You See in the Mirror: Spirit Possession in the Vietnamese American Diaspora." In *The Southeast Asian Diaspora in the United States,* edited by Jonathan Lee, 74–101. Cambridge: Cambridge Scholars Press.

———. 2014c. *From Colonial Syncretism to Transpacific Diaspora: Re-Orienting Caodaism from Vietnam to California.* DORISEA Working Paper No. 7. Goettingen, Germany: German Consortium on Religion in Southeast Asia.

———. 2015. "Symbolism in Anthropology." In *International Encyclopedia of the Social and Behavioral Sciences,* edited by Ulf Hannerz. London: Elsevier.

Hoskins, Janet, and Susan Hoskins. 2008. *The Left Eye of God: Caodaism Travels from Vietnam to California.* Documentary Educational Resources, 54 minutes, 2008, DVD.

Hoskins, Janet, and Viet Thanh Nguyen, eds. 2014. *Transpacific Studies: Framing an Emerging Field.* Honolulu: University of Hawai'i Press.

Hồ Chí Minh. 2012. "Unpublished Letter by Hồ Chí Minh to a French Pastor." Translated by Kareem James Abu-Zeid. *Journal of Vietnamese Studies* 7 (2): 1–7.

Hồ Tài, Huệ-Tâm. 1983. *Millenarianism and Peasant Politics in Vietnam.* Cambridge, Mass.: Harvard University Press.

———. 1987. "Religion in Vietnam: A World of Gods and Spirits." *Vietnam Forum* 10: 113–145.

———. 1992. *Radicalism and the Origins of the Vietnamese Revolution.* Cambridge, Mass.: Harvard University Press.

Huệ Khải (penname of Lê Anh Dũng). 2008a. *Đất Nam Kỳ Tiền Đề Văn Hóa Mở Đạo Cao Đài* [Cochinchina as a cultural precondition for the Foundation of Caodaism]. Hà Nội: Nhà Xuất Bản Tôn Giáo.

———. 2008b. *Đất Nam Kỳ Tiền Đề Pháp Lý Mở Đạo Cao Đài* [Cochinchina as a legal precondition for the Foundation of Caodaism]. Hà Nội: Nhà Xuất Bản Tôn Giáo.

———. 2008c. *The Emergence of Caodaism in Cochinchina.* Hồ Chí Minh City: Cơ Quan Phổ Thông Giáo Lý Đại Đạo, Nhà xuất Bản Tôn Giáo.

———. 2008d. *The Life of Ngo Minh Chieu.* Hồ Chí Minh City: Cơ Quan Phổ Thông Giáo Lý, Nhà xuất Bản Tôn Giáo.

———. 2010. *Tam Giáo Việt Nam Tiền Đề Tư Tưởng Mở Đạo Cao Đài* [The three teachings of Vietnam as an ideological precondition for the Foundation of Caodaism]. Hà Nội: Nhà Xuất Bản Tôn Giáo.

———. 2012. *Cấm Đạo Cao Đài ở Trung Kỳ 1928–1950* [Caodaism under persecution in central Vietnam 1928–1950]. Hà Nội: Nhà Xuất Bản Tôn Giáo.

Huệ Nhãn (pen name for Võ Thành Châu). 2005. *Khai Đạo: Từ Khởi Nguyên đến Khai Minh* [The inauguration of the faith: From its first beginnings to the official declaration]. Hồ Chí Minh City: Cơ Quan Phổ Thông Giáo Lý Đại Đạo, Nhà Xuất Bản Tôn Giáo.

Hugo, Adèle. 1984. *Le journal d'Adèle Hugo*. Vols. 1–3 (originally printed in 1853, republished in three volumes). Paris: Lettres Modernes.

Hugo, Victor. 1923. *Chez Victor Hugo: Les Tables Tournantes de Jersey. Procès Verbaux des Séances*. Edited by Gustave Simon.

———. 1985. *Soleil d'Encre: Manuscrits et Dessins de Victor Hugo*. Paris: Bibliothèque Nationale.

———. 1998. *Conversations with Eternity: The Forgotten Masterpiece of Victor Hugo*. Translated by John Chambers. Boca Raton, Fla.: New Paradigm Books.

———. 2008. *Victor Hugo's Conversations with the Spirit World: A Literary Genius' Hidden Life*. Translated by John Chambers. Rochester, Vt.: Destiny Books.

Hương Hiếu (religious name of Nguyễn Thị Hiếu, wife of Cao Quỳnh Cư). 1997 [1968]. *Đạo Sử* [History of the religion] Vols. 1–2. Repr. Thánh Thất Đốc Đao: Westminster, Calif. (Orig. pub. Vietnam: Tòa Thánh Tây Ninh).

Huỳnh Tâm. 1990. *Tiểu Sử Đức Hộ Pháp Phạm Công Tắc* [Biography of the Head Spirit Medium Pham Cong Tac]. Paris: Ban Đạo Sử Cao Đài Âu Châu.

Jammes, Jérémy. 2005. "Caodaïstes de Ben Tre (Viêt-nam) après 1975: la pratique médiumnique oraculaire en question." *Aséanie* 16: 61–88.

———. 2006a. *Le Caodaïsme: Rituels médiumiques, Oracles et exégèses, Approche ethnologique d'un mouvement religieux vietnamien et de ses réseaux*. [Caodaism: Mediumistic rituals, Oracles and exegesis. An ethnographic approach to a Vietnamese religious movement and its networks]. Thèse de Doctorat, Université Paris X Nanterre.

———. 2006b. "Le Saint-Siège Caodaïste de Tây Ninh et le Médium Phạm Công Tắc (1890–1959): Millénarisme, prosélytisme et oracles politiques en Cochinchine." *Outre-Mers Revue d'Histoire* 94 (352–353): 209–248.

———. 2009. "Caodaism and its global networks: An ethnological analysis of a Vietnamese religious movement in Vietnam and Abroad." In *Moussons: Recherche en sciences humaines sur l'Asie du Sud-Est* Nos. 13–14. Edited by Christian Culas and Jean-François Klein, 330–349.

———. 2010. "Divination and Politics in Southern Vietnam: Roots of Caodaism." *Social Compass* 57 (3): 357–371.

———. 2014. *Les Oracles du Cao Đài: Étude d'un mouvement religieux vietnamien et de ses réseaux*. Paris: Les Indes Savantes.

Jammes, Jérémy, and David Palmer. 2013. "Ethnic Identity and Transnational Religious Innovation in Modern Vietnam: Conjugating Chinese Redemptive Societies and French Occultism in the Cao Dai Religion." Paper presented January 10, at the Asia Research Institute workshop, "Invisible Connections Between Asia and the West: Syncretism and Esotericism."

Jensen, Carsten. 2000. *I Have Seen the World Begin: Travels through China, Cambodia and Vietnam*. Translated by Barbara Haveland. New York: Harcourt Books.

Johnson, Paul Christopher. 2007. *Diaspora Conversions: Black Carib Religion and the Recovery of Africa.* Berkeley: University of California Press.

———. 2012. "Religion and Diaspora." *Religion and Society* 3 (1): 95–114.

Jordan, David K., and Daniel Overmyer. 1986. *The Flying Phoenix: Aspects of Chinese Sectarianism in Taiwan.* Princeton, N.J.: Princeton University Press.

Josephson, Matthew. 1942. *Victor Hugo: A Realistic Biography of the Great Romantic.* New York: Doubleday, Doran and Co., Inc.

Kardec, Allan (pen name of Hippolyte Léon Denizard Rivail). 1860. *Le Livre des Esprits.* Paris: Union spirite française et francophone.

———. 1861. *Le Livre des Mediums.* Paris: Didier et Cie.

———. 1880. *L'Évangile selon le Spiritisme.* Paris: La Librairie Spirite. (All of these works by Kardec are available online in English translation at http://www.geae.inf.br/en /books/codification/gospel.pdf.)

Kehoe, Alice Beck. 1989. *The Ghost Dance: Ethnohistory and Revitalization.* New York: Holt, Rinehart and Winston.

Kelley, Liam. 2007. "Divine Lord Wenchang Meets Great King Tran: Spirit Writing in Late Imperial/Colonial Vietnam." Paper presented at the "Beyond Teleologies" conference on the Colonial History of Vietnam, Seattle, University of Washington.

———. 2012. "Moral Exemplar, Our General, Potent Deity, Confucian Moralizer and National Hero: The Transformations of and the Emergence of Vietnamese Nationalism." Unpublished manuscript.

Kinh Thiên Đạo và Thế Đạo (Prayers for the Celestial Path and the Secular Path). 1975. Published by Tòa Thánh Tây Ninh [The Holy See]. (English selections in Bùi, Bùi, and Beck [2003].)

Kitiarsa, Pattana. 2005. "Beyond Syncretism: Hybridization of Popular Religion in Contemporary Thailand." *Journal of Southeast Asian Studies* 36 (3): 461–487.

Kwon, Heonik. 2006. *After the Massacre: Commemoration and Consolation in Ha My and My Lai.* Berkeley: University of California Press.

———. 2007. "The Dollarization of Ghost Money in Vietnam." *Journal of the Royal Anthropological Institute* 13: 73–90.

———. 2008. *Ghosts of War in Vietnam.* Cambridge: Cambridge University Press.

Lalaurette and Vilmont. 1931. "Le Caodaisme. Rapport du services des affaires politiques et administratives de Cochinchine." Sureté report on file at the Centre des Archives d'Outre Mer (Center for Overseas Archives), Aix-en-Provence, France.

Lâm, Trương Bửu. 2000. *Colonialism Experienced: Vietnamese Writings on Colonialism 1900–1931.* Ann Arbor: University of Michigan Press.

Lang, Graeme, and Lars Ragvald. 1998. "Chinese Spirit Writing and the Development of Chinese Cults." *Sociology of Religion* 59 (4): 309–328.

Lê Minh Sơn. 2004. *Về Tổ Đình Cần Thơ* [Concerning the Main Temple in *Cần Thơ*]. Cần Thơ: Ban Tôn Giáo Thành Phố Cần Thơ.

Leopold, Anita M., and Jebbe S. Jensen, eds. 2004. *Syncretism in Religion: A Reader.* New York: Routledge.

Lê Thanh Chơn. 2002. *Huyền Thoại Đất Phương Nam* [The legend of the Southland: The life of Cao Triều Phát]. Thành Phố Hồ Chí Minh: Nhà Xuất Bản Công An Nhân Dân.

Lewis, I. M. 1971. *Ecstatic Religion: A Study of Shamanism and Spirit Possession*. Harmondsworth, U.K.: Penguin.

Lewis, Norman. 1951. *A Dragon Apparent: Travels in Cambodia, Laos and Vietnam*. London: Jonathan Cape.

———. 1985. *Jackdaw Cake: An Autobiography*. London: Eland Books.

Liang Yongjia. 2011. "Stranger-Kingship and Cosmocracy; or, Sahlins in Southwest China." *The Asia Pacific Journal of Anthropology* 12 (3): 236–254.

Lincoln, Bruce. 2001. "Retiring Syncretism." *Historical Reflections / Réflexions Historiques* 27 (3): 453–459.

Logevall, Fredrik. 2012. *Embers of War: The Fall of an Empire and the Making of America's Vietnam*. New York: Random House.

Lương Sĩ Hằng. 2002. *Tình Trong Bốn Bể* [Love under pressure]. Santa Ana, Calif.: Đại Nam.

Malarney, Shaun. 1996. "The Emerging Cult of Ho Chi Minh? A Report on Religious Innovation in Contemporary Northern Viet Nam." *Asian Cultural Studies* 22: 121–131.

Malinowski, Bronislaw. 1922. *Argonauts of the Western Pacific*. London: Routledge and Kegan Paul.

Malkki, Liisa. 1992. "National Geographic: The Rooting of Peoples and the Territorialization of Identity among Scholars and Refugees." *Cultural Anthropology* 7 (1): 24–44.

———. 1995. *Purity and Exile: Violence, Memory and National Cosmology among Hutu Refugees in Tanzania*. Chicago: University of Chicago Press.

Marr, David G. 1971. *Vietnamese Anti-Colonialism 1885–1925*. Berkeley: University of California Press.

———. 1981. *Vietnamese Tradition on Trial: 1920–1945*. Berkeley: University of California Press.

———. 2000. "Concepts of 'Individual' and 'Self' in Twentieth-Century Vietnam." *Modern Asian Studies* 34 (4): 769–796.

Masuzawa, Tomoko. 2005. *The Invention of World Religions, Or, How European Universalism Was Preserved in the Language of Pluralism*. Chicago: University of Chicago Press.

Matlock, Jann. 2000. "Ghostly Politics." *Diacritics* 30 (3): 53–71.

Matory, J. Lorand. 2005. *Black Atlantic Religion: Tradition, Transnationalism and Matriarchy in the Afro-Brazilian Candomble*. Princeton, N.J.: Princeton University Press.

McHale, Shawn Frederick. 2004. *Print and Power: Confucianism, Communism and Buddhism in the Making of Modern Vietnam*. Honolulu: University of Hawai'i Press.

———. 2009. "Understanding the Fanatic Mind? The Việt Minh and Race Hatred in the First Indochina War (1945–1954)." *Journal of Vietnamese Studies* 4 (3): 98–138.

Meillon, Gustave. 1984. "Le Caodaïsme: Annonce et Naissance du Caodaïsme." *Cahier de l'Asie du Sud-Est* 15–16: 161–200 and 17–18: 153–195.

Miller, Edward. 2004. "Vision, Power and Agency: The Ascent of Ngô Đình Diệm, 1945–54." *Journal of Southeast Asian Studies* 35 (3): 433–458.

———. 2013. *Misalliance: Ngo Dinh Diem, the United States, and the Fate of South Vietnam*. Cambridge, Mass.: Harvard University Press.

Mittermaier, Amira. 2011. *Dreams That Matter: Egyptian Landscapes of the Imagination.* Berkeley: University of California Press.

Monroe, John. 1999. "Making the Séance 'Serious': 'Tables Tournantes' and Second Empire Bourgeois Culture, 1853–1861." *History of Religions* 38 (3): 219–246.

———. 2003. "*Cartes de Visite* from the Other World: Spiritism and the Discourse of Laicisme in the Early Third Republic." *French Historical Studies* 26 (1): 119–153.

Morris, Rosalind. 2000. *In the Place of Origins: Modernity and its Mediums in Northern Thailand.* Durham, N.C.: Duke University Press.

Munro, Robin. 1989. "Syncretic Sects and Secret Societies—Revival in the 1980s." *Chinese Sociology and Anthropology* 21 (4): 1–107.

Mus, Paul. 1952. *Viêt Nam: Sociologie d'une Guerre* [Vietnam: Sociology of war]. Paris: Editions du Seuil.

Nandy, Ashis. 2005. "Final Encounter: The Politics of the Assassination of Gandhi." In *Exiled at Home,* 70–98. New Delhi: Oxford University Press.

Ngô Bái Thiên (pen name for Lê Anh Dũng). 2003. *Đạo Cao Đài trong khoảng Ba Mươi năm qua 1975–2003* [Caodaism in the thirty years since 1975]. Published for internal consumption at the Saigon Teaching Agency (Cơ Quan Phổ Thông Giáo Lý Đại Đạo).

Ngô Thị Tâm, and Huệ-Tâm Hồ Tài. 2014. "Seeing like the State but with Difference: Ho Chi Minh cult in contemporary Vietnam." Research project on the website of the Max Planck Institute, Goettingen, Germany, http://www.mmg.mpg.de/research/all-projects/ seeing-like-the-state-but-with-difference-ho-chi-minh-cult-in-contemporary-vietnam/.

Nguyễn Hồng Dương. 2009. *Minh Lý Đạo.* Hà Nội: Nhà Xuất Bản Tôn Giáo.

Nguyen, Mimi Thi. 2012. *The Gift of Freedom: War, Debt and Other Refugee Passages.* Durham, N.C.: Duke University Press.

Nguyễn Ngọc Châu. 2001. "Un Peu d'histoire . . . Peu Connu: Les Vietnamiens Francs-Maçons." *Bulletin d'information de l'amicale des anciens élèves du lycée Chasseloup-Laubat/ Jean-Jacques Rousseau* 16: 7–10.

Nguyễn Trung Hậu. 1956. *Lược Sử Đạo Cao Đài* [Summary of Caodai History]. 2nd ed. Đà Nẵng: Truyền Giáo Việt Nam Trung Kỳ, republished by Cao Đài San Bernardino Temple. (Orig. pub. 1954, Tourane [the colonial name for Đà Nẵng].)

Nguyen, Viet Thanh. 2006. "Speak of the Dead, Speak of Viet Nam: The Ethics and Aesthetics of Minority Discourse." *New Centennial Review* 6 (2): 7–37.

———. 2009. "Remembering War, Dreaming Peace: On Cosmopolitanism, Compassion and Literature." *Japanese Journal of American Studies* 20: 1–26.

Nguyen, Viet Thanh, and Janet Hoskins. 2013. "Introduction." In *Transpacific Studies,* edited by Janet Hoskins and Viet Thanh Nguyen, 1–38. Honolulu: University of Hawai'i.

Ninh, Thiên Hương. 2011. "God Needs a Passport: The Struggle of Vietnamese Caodaists in Cambodia for Religious and Ethnic Recognition across National Borders." *Encounters* 4 (Fall): 1–28.

———. 2013a. "Religion of Another Color: Vietnamese Catholic and Caodai U.S.-Cambodia Ties in Comparative Perspective." PhD diss., University of Southern California.

———. 2013b. "The Caodai Mother Goddess in a Globalizing World: Mediation Between Religious Universalism and Homeland Orientation among Vietnamese Caodaists in the U.S." *Asian Anthropology* 12 (1): 53–67.

———. 2014. "Mary, Miracles, and Martyrdom: The Vietnamization of the Virgin Mary in a Globalizing World." Paper presented at the Fourth International Conference on Visualizing Asia, Yale University (New Haven, Conn.: May 10–11).

Norindr, Panivong. 1996. *Phantasmagoric Indochina: French Colonial Ideology in Architecture, Film and Literature.* Minneapolis: University of Minnesota Press.

Norton, Barley. 2009. *Songs for the Spirits: Music and Mediums in Modern Vietnam.* Urbana: University of Illinois Press.

O'Leary, Stephen. 1996. "Cyberspace as Sacred Space." *Journal of the American Academy of Religion* 64 (4): 781–808.

Oliver, Victor L. 1976. *Caodai Spiritism: A Study of Religion in Vietnamese Society.* Leiden: E. J. Brill.

Ong, Aihwa. 2008. "Cyberpublics and Diaspora Politics among Transnational Chinese." In *The Anthropology of Globalization: A Reader,* edited by Jonathan Xavier Inda and Renato Rosaldo, 2nd ed., 167–183. Malden, Mass.: Blackwell Publishing.

Open Net Initiative. 2006. *Internet Filtering in Vietnam 2005–2006: A Country Study.* Published online by Open Net Initiative, http://www.opennet.net/vietnam.

Overmyer, Daniel. 1997. "Convergence: Chinese Gods and Christian Saints." *Qingfeng* 40 (1): 1–4.

Owen, Alex. 2004. *The Darkened Room: Women, Power and Spiritualism in Late Victorian England.* Chicago: University of Chicago Press.

Ownby, David. 2008. "Sect and Secularism in Reading the Modern Chinese Religious Experience." *Archives de sciences sociales des religions* 144: 13–29.

Padgett, Douglas. 2007. "Religion, Memory and Imagination in Vietnamese California: The Legacy of Exile among Buddhist Vietnamese." PhD diss., Indiana University.

Palmié, Stephan. 2014. *The Cooking of History: How Not To Study Afro-Cuban Religion.* Chicago: University of Chicago Press.

Peel, J. D. Y. 1968. "Syncretism and Religious Change." *Comparative Studies in Society and History* 10 (2): 121–141.

Pelley, P. M. (2002). *Postcolonial Vietnam: New Histories of the National Past.* Durham, N.C.: Duke University Press.

Pew Research Center. 2012. The Rise of Asian Americans: Social and Demographic Trends. http://www.pewsocialtrends.org/2012/06/19/the-rise-of-asian-americans/2/.

Peycam, Philippe. 2012. *The Birth of Vietnamese Political Journalism: Saigon 1916–1930.* New York: Columbia University Press.

Phạm Bích Hợp. 2007. *Người Nam Bộ và Tôn Giáo Bản Địa* [The people of the southern region and indigenous religions]. Hà Nội: Nhà Xuất Bản Tôn Giáo.

Phạm Công Tắc. 1947–1949. *Con Đường Thiêng Liêng Hằng Sống* [The divine path to eternal life]. Translated by Đào Công Tâm and Christopher Hartney. The Sydney Centre for Studies in Caodaism. http://www.daotam.info/.

Phạm, Danny. 2006. *Guide to the Holy See.* Westminister, Calif.: Tòa Thánh Tây Ninh Church.

Phạm Quỳnh Phượng. 2009. *Hero and Deity: Tran Hung Dao and the Revival of Popular Religion in Vietnam*. Singapore: Mekong Press.

Phạm Quỳnh Phượng, and Chris Eipper. 2009. "Mothering and Fathering the Vietnamese: Religion, Gender and National Identity." *Journal of Vietnamese Studies* 4 (1): 49–83.

Phan Bội Châu. 1999. *Overturned Chariot: The Autobiography of Phan Bội Châu*. Translated by Vinh Sinh and Nicholas Wickenden, Honolulu: University of Hawai'i Press.

Phan, Khánh. 2000. *Caodaism*. London: Minerva Books.

Pháp Chánh Truyền [The religious constitution]. 1972. Translated by Bùi Đắc Hùm at caodai.org. Vietnam: Tòa Thánh Tây Ninh.

Picard, Michel, and Remy Madinier. 2011. *The Politics of Religion in Indonesia: Syncretism, Orthodoxy, and Religious Contention in Java and Bali*. New York: Routledge.

Popkin, Samuel. 1979. *The Rational Peasant: The Political Economy of Rural Society in Vietnam*. Berkeley: University of California Press.

Quiet American, The. 1958 film. Directed by Joseph Mankiewicz, starring Michael Redgrave and Audie Murphy. Black and White, 120 minutes. Distributed by United Artist Corp. MGM DVD classic collection.

Quiet American, The. 2001 film. Directed by Philip Noyce, starring Michael Caine and Brendan Fraser. Color. 101 minutes. Distributed by Miramax Films.

Quinn-Judge, Sophie. 2003. *Ho Chi Minh: The Missing Years 1919–1941*. Berkeley: University of California Press.

Rapports mensuels du résident de Tây Ninh. 1929–1933. Box 65553, 7F68, Centre D'Archives d'Outre Mer, Aix-en-Provence, France.

Rey, Terry. 2007. *Bourdieu on Religion: Imposing Faith and Legitimacy*. London: Equinox Publishing.

Robb, Graham. 1997. *Victor Hugo: A Biography*. New York: W. W. Norton & Company.

Rourke, Mary. 2008. "Ex-diplomat, Cao Dai leader: Do Van Ly Obituary." *Los Angeles Times,* September 1, 2008.

Salemink, Oscar. 2008. "Embodying the Nation: Mediumship, Ritual and the National Imagination." *Journal of Vietnamese Studies* 3 (3): 261–290.

Schucman, Helen, and William Thetford. 1976. *A Course in Miracles*. New York: Foundation for Inner Peace.

Seaman, Gary. 1980. *Temple Organization in a Chinese Village*. Taipei, Taiwan: Asian Folklore and Social Life Monographs.

———. 1986. "The Divine Authorship of Pei-yu chi (Journey to the North)." *Journal of Asian Studies* 4 (3): 483–497.

———. 1987. *Journey to the North: An Ethnohistorical Analysis and Translation of the Chinese Folk Novel Pei-yu-chi*. Berkeley: University of California Press.

Shaw, Rosalind. 1994. "The Invention of 'African Traditional Religion.'" *Religion* 20: 339–353.

Sherry, Norman. 1989. *The Life of Graham Greene, vol. 2: 1939–1958*. New York: Viking.

Small, Ivan. 2012. "'Over There': Imaginative Displacement in Vietnamese Remittance Gift Economies." *Journal of Vietnamese Studies* 7 (3): 157–183.

Smith, Ralph B. 1968. *Viet-Nam and the West.* Ithaca, N.Y.: Cornell University Press.

———. 1969. "Bui Quang Chiêu and the Constitutionalist Party in French Cochinchina, 1917–30." *Modern Asian Studies* 3: 131–150.

———. 1970a. "An Introduction to Caodaism 1: Origins and Early History." *Bulletin of the School of Oriental and African Studies* 33 (2): 335–349.

———. 1970b. "An Introduction to Caodaism 2: Beliefs and Organization." *Bulletin of the School of Oriental and African Studies* 33 (3): 573–589.

———. 1970c. "The Vietnamese Elite of French Cochinchina, 1943." *Modern Asian Studies* 6 (4): 459–482.

———. 1972. "The Development of Opposition to French Rule in Southern Vietnam, 1880–1940." *Past and Present* 54 (February): 94–129.

———. 2009. "An Introduction to Caodaism: Origins and Early History [1970]." In *Pre-Communist Indochina,* edited by Beryl Williams, 115–130. London: Routledge.

Smith, Timothy. 1978. "Religion and Ethnicity in America." *The American Historical Review* 83 (5): 1155–1185.

Spence, Jonathan D. 1996. *God's Chinese Son: The Taiping Heavenly Kingdom of Hong Xiuquan.* New York: W. W. Norton.

Stephens, Philip. 1983. *Victor Hugo in Jersey.* Chichester, U.K.: Philmone and Company.

Stewart, Charles. 1999. "Syncretism and Its Synonyms: Reflections on Cultural Mixture." *Diacritics* 29 (3): 40–62.

Stewart, Charles, and Rosalind Shaw. 2004. "Introduction." In *Syncretism/Anti-Syncretism: The Politics of Religious Synthesis,* edited by Charles Stewart and Rosalind Shaw, 1–28. New York: Routledge.

Tambiah, Stanley. 1970. *Buddhism and the Spirit Cults in North-East Thailand.* Cambridge: Cambridge University Press.

Tân Luật [The new religious codes]. 1972. English translation by Bùi Đắc Hùm at caodai. org. Vietnam: Tòa Thánh Tây Ninh [The Holy See, Vietnam]. Reprint [1990] California: Xuất Bản Chân Tâm.

Taussig, Michael. 1993. *Mimesis and Alterity: A Particular History of the Senses.* New York: Routledge.

Taylor, Philip. 2001. "'Apocalpse now'? Hòa Hảo Buddhism Emerging from the Shadows of War." *Australian Journal of Anthropology* 12 (3): 339–354.

———. 2004. *Goddess on the Rise: Pilgrimage and Popular Religion in Vietnam.* Honolulu: University of Hawai'i Press.

———, ed. 2007. *Modernity and Re-enchantment: Religion in Post-revolutionary Vietnam.* Singapore: Institute of Southeast Asian Studies, Utopia Press.

———. 2014. *The Khmer Lands of Vietnam: Environment, Cosmology and Sovereignty.* Honolulu: University of Hawai'i Press.

Thai, Hung. 2014. "Special Money in the Vietnamese Diaspora." In *Transpacific Studies: Framing an Emerging Field,* edited by Janet Hoskins and Viet Thanh Nguyen. Honolulu: University of Hawai'i Press.

Thánh Ngôn Hiệp Tuyển [Official selection of spirit messages]. 1972. English translation by Bùi Đắc Hùm, www.caodai.net. Vietnam: Tòa Thánh Tây Ninh [The Holy See].

Thánh Ngôn Sưu Tập [Unofficial selection of spirit messages]. 1972. Vietnam: Tòa Thánh Tây Ninh [The Holy See].

Thiên Lý Bửu Tòa. 1984. *Đại Giác Thánh Kinh* [Revelations of sacred scripture]. San Martin: Thiên Lý Bửu Tòa Desktop Publishing.

———. 1989. *Kinh Thánh Giáo Pháp* [Scripture of sacred teachings and divine law]. San Martin: Thiên Lý Bửu Tòa Desktop Publishing.

Thompson, Virginia. 1937. *French Indochina*. London: G. Allen & Unwin, Ltd.

Time. 1956. "The Beleaguered Man." posted April 4; Pope Takes a Powder, March 5.

———. 1957. "The Disquieted Americans." February 25.

Tocqueville, Alexis de. 1835. *Democracy in America*. Translated from the French by Henry Reeve. Reissued in a modern edition in 1945. New York: Alfred A. Knopf.

Tram Thị Hương. 2004. *Đêm Trắng Của Đức Giáo Tông* [The sleepless nights of the Pope]. Hồ Chí Minh City: Nhà Xuất Bản Công An Nhân Dân.

Trần Mỹ-Vân. 1996. "Japan and Vietnam's Caodaists: A Wartime Relationship (1939–1945)." *Journal of Southeast Asian Studies* 1 (27): 179–183.

———. 1999. "Japan through Vietnamese Eyes 1905–1945." *Journal of Southeast Asian Studies* 1 (30): 126–154.

———. 2000. "Vietnam's Caodaism, Independence and Peace: The Life and Times of Phạm Công Tắc (1890–1959)." *Academia Sinica: PROSEA Research Paper* 38: 1–28.

———. 2006. *A Vietnamese Royal Exile in Japan: Prince Cường Đế 1882–1950*. London: Routledge.

Trần Mỹ-Vân, and Dean Meyers. 2006. "The Crisis of the Eighth Lunar Month: The Cao Đài, Prince Cường Đế and the Japanese in 1937–39." *International Journal of Asia-Pacific Studies* 2 (May): 1–39.

Trần Quang Cảnh. 1998. Religious Persecution of the Cao Đài Religion: Policy and Measures Aimed at the Abolition of the Cao Đài Religion by the Government of the Socialist Republic of Vietnam. Paper presented at CESNUR Conference, December 8.

Trần, Quang Tuệ. 2012. "Remembering the Boat People Exodus: A Tale of Two Memorials." *Journal of Vietnamese Studies* 7 (3): 80–121.

Trần Quang Vinh, ed. 1962. *Les Messages Spirites de la Troisième Amnistie de Dieu en Orient*. With a Preface by Gustave Meillon. Tây Ninh: Sainte-Siège du Caodaisme.

———. 1972. *Hồi Ký Trần Quang Vinh và Lịch Sử Quân Đội Cao Đài*. [Memoir of Trần Quang Vinh and the history of the Caodai army]. Vietnam: Tòa Thánh Tây Ninh. Repr., Washington, D.C.: Thánh Thất Vùng Hoa Thịnh Đốn, 1997.

Trần Thu Dung. 1996. "Le Caodaïsme et Victor Hugo" [Caodaism and Victor Hugo]. PhD diss., Université de Paris VII.

Trần Tri Khách. 2002. *Niên Biểu Phật Giáo Việt Nam* [Chronicles of Buddhism in Vietnam]. Victoria, Australia: Quảng Đức Buddhist Welfare Association. www.quangduc.com.

Trần Văn Quế (pen name Huệ Lương). 1950. "Preface." In *Đại Thừa Chơn Giáo /Le Grand Cycle d'Esoterisme* [The Great Vehicle of the Esoteric Branch], 710. Saigon: Chiếu Minh Đàn.

———. 1961. *Côn-Lôn Quần-Đảo Trước Ngày 9-3-1945* [Poulo Condor until March 9, 1945]. Saigon: Nhà Xuất Bản.

———. 1963. *Cao Đài Sơ Giải* [A perspective on Caodaism]. Saigon: Thanh Hương.

Trần Văn Rạng. 1971. *Đại Đạo Danh Nhân* [The famous adepts of the great way]. Tây Ninh: Tòa Thánh Tây Ninh.

Trương Như Tảng. 1985. *Viet Cong Memoir: An Inside Account of the Vietnam War and Its Aftermath.* Translated by David Chanoff and Doan Van Tai. New York: Vintage.

Tweed, Thomas A. 1997. *Our Lady of the Exile: Diasporic Religion at a Cuban Catholic Shrine in Miami.* New York: Oxford University Press.

———. 2006. *Crossing and Dwelling: A Theory of Religion.* Cambridge, Mass.: Harvard University Press.

Valverde, Kieu-Linh Caroline. 2012. *Transnationalizing Vietnam: Community, Culture and Politics in the Diaspora.* Philadelphia: Temple University Press.

Van Der Veer, Peter. 1996. *Conversion to Modernities: The Globalization of Christian Modernities.* London, U.K.: Psychology Press.

———. 2009. "Spirituality in Modern Society." *Social Research* 76 (4): 1097–1120.

———. 2014. *The Modern Spirit of Asia: The Spiritual and the Secular In India and China.* Princeton, N.J.: Princeton University Press.

Varisco, Daniel Martin. 2007. "Islam Obscured: The Rhetoric of Anthropological Representation." *Journal of Islamic Studies* 18 (2): 254–257.

Verellen, Franciscus. 1995. "Taoism." *The Journal of Asian Studies* 54 (2): 322–346.

Verter, Bradford. 2003. "Spiritual Capital: Theorizing Religion with Bourdieu against Bourdieu." *Sociological Theory* 21 (2): 150–174.

Viswanathan, Gauri. 1998. *Outside the Fold: Conversion, Modernity and Belief.* Princeton, N.J.: Princeton University Press.

———. 2000. "The Ordinary Business of Occultism." *Critical Inquiry* 27 (1): 1–20.

Walters, Jonathan S. 1995. "Multi-religion on the Bus: Beyond 'Influence' and 'Syncretism' in the Study of Religious Meetings." In *Unmaking the Nation: The Politics of Identity and History in Modern Sri Lanka,* edited by Pradeep Jeganathan and Qadri Ismail, 25–54. Colombo: Social Scientists' Association.

Waterson, Roxana. 2007. "Introduction." In *Southeast Asian Lives: Personal Narratives and Historical Experience,* edited by R. Waterson, 1–40. Athens: Ohio University Press.

Weber, Max. 1963. *The Sociology of Religion.* Translated by Talcott Parsons. Boston: Beacon Press.

Werner, Jayne. 1976. "The Cao Đài: The Politics of a Vietnamese Syncretic Religious Movement." PhD diss., Cornell University.

———. 1980. "Vietnamese Communism and Vietnamese Sectarianism." In *Vietnamese Communism in Comparative Perspective,* edited by William Turley, 107–137. Boulder, Colo.: Westview Press.

———. 1981. *Peasant Politics and Religious Sectarianism: Peasant and Priest in the Cao Đài in Vietnam.* New Haven, Conn.: Yale University.

West, W. J. 1998. *The Quest for Graham Greene.* New York: St. Martin's Press.

Wiener, Margaret. 1971. *Vietnam and the Chinese Model; A Comparative Study of Nguyen and Ch'ing Civil Government in the First Half of the Nineteenth Century.* Cambridge, Mass.: Harvard University Press.

———. 1976. *Community and Revolution in Modern Vietnam.* Boston: Houghton Mifflin Co.

———. 2006. *Lost Modernities: China, Vietnam, Korea and the Hazards of World History.* Cambridge, Mass.: Harvard University Press.

———. 2007. "Dangerous Liaisons and Other Tales from the Twilight Zone: Sex, Race, and Sorcery in Colonial Java." *Comparative Studies in Society and History* 49 (3): 495–526.

Wolf, Eric. 1969. *Peasant Wars of the 20th Century.* New York: Harper & Row.

Woodside, Alexander. 1971. *Vietnam and the Chinese Model: A Comparative Study of Nguyen and Ch'ing Civil Government in the First Half of the Nineteenth Century.* Cambridge, Mass.: Harvard University Press.

———. 1976. *Community and Revolution in Modern Vietnam.* Boston: Houghton Mifflin Co.

———. 2006. *Lost Modernities: China, Vietnam, Korea and the Hazards of World History.* Cambridge, Mass.: Harvard University Press.

Woodward, Mark R. 1989. *Islam in Java: Normative Piety and Mysticism in the Sultanate of Yogyakarta.* Tucson: University of Arizona Press.

———. 2010. *Java, Indonesia and Islam.* Dordrecht: Springer Science and Business Media.

Young, Robert. 2001. *Postcolonialism: An Historical Introduction.* London: Blackwell.

Young, Robert Fox. 1989. "Sanctuary of the Tao: The Place of Christianity in a Sino-Japanese Unity Sect." *Journal of Chinese Religions* 17: 1–26.

Yu, Anthony C. 1977. *The Journey to the West.* Vol. 1. Chicago: University of Chicago Press.

———. 1983. "Two Literary Examples of Religious Pilgrimage: The Commedia and the Journey to the West." *History of Religions* 22 (3): 202–230.

Zinoman, Peter. 2001a. *The Colonial Bastille.* Berkeley: University of California Press.

———. 2001b. "Reading Revolutionary Prison Memories." In *The Country of Memory: Remaking the Past in Late Socialist Vietnam,* edited by Hue-Tam Ho Tai, 21–45. Berkeley: University of California Press.

———. 2002. "Vũ Trọng Phụng's Dumb Luck and the Nature of Vietnamese Modernism." In *Dumb Luck: A Novel by Vũ Trọng Phụng,* translated by P. Zinoman and Nguyễn Nguyệt Cầm, 1–30. Ann Arbor: University of Michigan Press.

———. 2011. "Provincial Cosmopolitanism: Vũ Trọng Phụng's Foreign Literary Engagements." In *Traveling Nation-Makers: Transnational Flows and Movements in the Making of Modern Southeast Asia,* edited by Carline S. Ha and Kasian Tejapira, 126–152. Kyoto, Japan: Kyoto University.

INDEX

ABOUT THE AUTHOR

Janet Hoskins is professor of anthropology and religion at the University of Southern California, Los Angeles. She is the author of *The Play of Time: Kodi Perspectives on History, Calendars and Exchange* (1996 recipient of the Benda Prize in Southeast Asian Studies) and *Biographical Objects: How Things Tell the Stories of People's Lives* (1998), and the contributing editor of *Headhunting and the Social Imagination in Southeast Asia* (1996), *A Space Between Oneself and Oneself: Anthropology as a Search for the Subject* (1999), *Fragments from Forests and Libraries* (2001), and (with Viet Thanh Nguyen) *Transpacific Studies: Framing an Emerging Field* (2014). She has also produced and written three ethnographic documentaries, including *The Left Eye of God: Caodaism Travels from Vietnam to California* (2008, distributed by www.DER.org). She was the president of the Society for the Anthropology of Religion, a section of the American Anthropological Association, from 2011 to 2013.

Production Notes for Hoskins | *The Divine Eye and the Diaspora*

Cover design by Mardee Melton

Text design by Binbin Li with display type in Dante MT Pro and text type in Adobe Garamond Pro

Composition by Westchester Publishing Services

Printing and binding by Sheridan Books, Inc.

Printed on 60 lb. House White, 444 ppi.